Politics in Western
Europe

Politics in Western Europe

A Comparative Analysis

Fifth Edition

Gordon Smith
Professor of Government
London School of Economics and Political Science

Holmes & Meier Publishers, Inc.
New York

Fifth edition published in the United States of America
1989 by Holmes & Meier Publishers, Inc.
30 Irving Place, New York, N.Y. 10003

Library of Congress Cataloging-in-Publication Data

Smith, Gordon R.
    Politics in Western Europe : a comparative analysis / Gordon
Smith. -- 5th ed.
      p.   cm.
    Bibliography: p.
    Includes index.
    1. Europe--Politics and government--1945- 2. Comparative
government.   I. Title.
JN94.A2S63   1989
320.3'094--dc19

ISBN 0 8419 1263 7

Contents

Preface to Fifth Edition   vii

1. Introduction: The Politics of Liberal Democracy   1

2. Politics and Society   12
   The Social Bases   12
   Language and National Minorities   15
   Religion and Politics   19
   Rural and Urban Contrasts   28
   Class and Politics   32
   New Cleavages?   37
   Social Cleavages and Party Systems   41

3. Pluralist Politics: Parties and Interests   48
   The Inertia of Party Traditions   48
   Perpetuation of Left and Right   55
   The Representation of Group Interests   59
   The Age of Corporatism?   71

4. Party Systems   83
   Determining Features   83
   Imbalance, Balance and Diffusion   94
   System Trends   104
   Patterns of Opposition   106
   Breakdown of Parliamentary Systems   112
   Party Systems in Western Europe (Table)   122

5. Constitutional Balance   125
   European Constitutionalism   125
   The Distribution of Power   128
   Assembly-Executive Relations   134
   Constitutional Jurisdiction   141
   Direct Democracy   145
   Constitutional Dynamics   150

6. Non-Democratic Variants   154
   The Fascist Alternative   154
   Politics and the Military   159

Transitions from Dictatorship   165
Extremism Today   172

7. Assemblies and Governments   189
    Parliamentary Decline   189
    Elective Functions   192
    Personnel Functions   198
    Rule Functions   203
    Communications   212

8. Executive Power   217
    Political Leadership   217
    Constitutional Bureaucracy   222
    Administrative Élites   226
    Policy Styles in Western Europe   234
    Controlling Executive Power   242

9. The Territorial Axis   250
    The Resurgence of Territorial Identity   250
    Modes of Decentralisation   253
    Patterns of Local Democracy   258
    European Federalism and Regionalism   266

10. Political Integration   284
    Models of Integration   284
    European Perspectives   290
    Institutional Features of the European Community   294
    Problems of Development   298
    A European Political Culture?   304

The Nations of Western Europe   309
  1. *European Socio-Economic Comparisons (Table)*   310
  2. *European Constitutional Comparisons (Table)*   312
  3. *Political Profiles*   314
     Austria   314; *Belgium*   315; *Denmark*   319; *Finland*   322;
     France   325; *The Federal German Republic*   330; *Greece*   333;
     Iceland   337; *The Republic of Ireland*   339; *Italy*   343;
     Luxembourg   348; *Malta*   350; *The Netherlands*   352;
     Norway   355; *Portugal*   358; *Spain*   361; *Sweden*   364;
     Switzerland   367; *The United Kingdom*   370;
     Northern Ireland   374

Party Representation in West European Parliaments   378
  A Research Note by Michael Smart

Index   391

Preface to Fifth Edition

Over the years *Politics in Western Europe* has proved a useful introduction to the comparative study of European Politics, and a new edition has long been overdue. In making desirable revisions, introducing new themes, and revising some judgements, I have retained all of the original features. In particular, the emphasis is still on making across-the-board comparisons. Within each of the major themes a balance has been struck between general interpretation and the provision of sufficient background information for readers new to the subject; they should find the final section of the book, 'The Nations of Western Europe' particularly helpful in summarising the major political features and developments of all the individual countries. I should like to express my thanks to Mark Donovan, a research student at the London School of Economics, for his valuable assistance in preparing this new edition.

What perhaps has to be justified in *Politics in Western Europe* is the deliberate weight given to the historical context of present-day political concerns. Yet – thankfully – political science has moved away from its preoccupation with systemic and functional approaches, and there is a much readier appreciation that contemporary politics has to be understood as an extension of history – not its negation.

G.S.
December 1988

vii

1 Introduction – The Politics of Liberal Democracy

The major concern of this book can be simply stated: it is with how the democracies of Western Europe handle their political affairs. And we can best begin by taking a general view of the hallmarks of these states; in effect, this means examining the significant features of *liberal* democracy. There would be little disagreement about the importance of the three aspects we shall deal with here, even if the value placed upon them varies from one interpreter to another. We can say that a typical liberal democracy provides three things:

- mechanisms of political choice;
- balanced political structures;
- a stable political system.

These three characteristics are, of course, related one with another, and the general reputation of stability which liberal democracies have can be seen as a product of the other two – that choice provides the opportunity for political balance, and that choice and balance together foster stable democracy by giving satisfactory channels through which demands on the political system can be made. Such a highly-compressed account, however, misses out the context in which choice, balance, and stability operate; we should look at each term in more detail.

The premium which liberal democracies put on freedom of choice is in its *origins* an economic freedom rather than a political one, that is to say, one bound up with the free operation of the market system. A growing market economy established several requirements: the ability for individuals to accumulate capital, the mobility of both capital and labour, the basic freedom of contract, and above all the unimpeded operation of market forces to provide the most favourable situation for the exercise of rational economic choice. Historically, economic liberalism was the precondition for political liberalism, and there is certainly a tight relationship between the development of capitalism and the rise of liberal democracy – as Macpherson pointed out: 'Liberal democracy is found only in countries whose economic system is wholly or predominantly that of capitalist enterprise ... It would indeed be surprising if this close correspondence between liberal democracy and capitalism were merely coincidental.'[1] The demand for political choice acted as an important supplement to the market economy, but it was not primarily a democratic demand, rather a way of securing the foundations of the whole system. Each with its own set of institutions, economic and political choice developed in tandem.

As long as the power to exercise political choice was restricted to the few, the institutions needed only to develop a rudimentary form, but in their modern and democratic expression they are well-defined and various: fully-representative institutions, unrestricted party formation, freely-contested elections, and the operation of a competitive party system. They all hang together: if any of them is entirely eliminated then the basis for exercising democratic choice vanishes. Underlying them all is the recognition of 'legitimate opposition'; this is the cardinal principle of a liberal democracy, and in its institutional form it acts as the summation of all the others. Dahl once described the institution of 'opposition' as, 'one of the greatest and most unexpected social discoveries' that man has ever stumbled upon.[2] It is no exaggeration to say that the entire political mechanism of the liberal democratic state revolves around this one basic 'axiom'. Not only is it fundamental to the other institutions of political choice, it is also the motor of peaceful government succession. The possibility of choosing and changing governments enables minorities to establish a stable relationship with political authority and power.

If these minorities are unable to win power for themselves, their rights as a minority are nevertheless entrenched in the political system by the various balances which operate. The idea of legitimate opposition is itself an integral part of balance, but it is supplemented by a whole group of checks. There is first the belief in 'limited' as opposed to absolute government – expressed another way it is the principle of *qualified* majority rule. The sum total of these balancing arrangements is seen by Vile to amount to, '. . . a frank acknowledgement of the role of government in society, linked with the determination to bring that government under control and to place limits on the exercise of its power'.[3] This is no less than the doctrine of constitutionalism, the mainspring of all devices which seek to combine effective government by the majority with concern for individual and minority rights.

Just how much government intervention is compatible with the leading precepts of liberal democracy – justice, liberty, equality, and property rights – is problematic. The attempt to give them all a substantive content, that is, to create 'positive freedoms', must make for continuous and expanding government action, not least in ironing out the contradictions that any one of them involves with the others. Anyway, the balance provided by the strictly constitutional elements (principally those relating to the functioning of government) is only part of a wider social balance, with the political parties taking an intermediate position in linking the power of government to society.

The balance provided by a party system is said to ensure two things. Firstly, it acts as a counterpoise between the main social classes, and related to this it is a realistic expression of the plural interests in society; 'pluralism' is another way of indicating the possibilities of social balance. Essentially, the pluralist view holds that each individual is 'a universe of interests' and that no single one of them can claim his undivided loyalty. Liberal democratic society is portrayed as being composed of a host of competing and co-operating group interests, and regardless of the number of parties (as long as there is a plurality) the structuring of interests will ensure that they are adequately voiced both through the parties and at all levels of society.

At a time when the pluralist domination of political science has been superseded[4], this version will seem an uncritical account of how liberal democracy works – almost saying that 'balance' exists by definition. A critical view will question the extent to which choice is allowed to operate and deny that, except occasionally, anything like an equal expression of divergent social interests is allowed. Yet there is no doubt that the models of choice and balance do work in some such fashion. A necessary extension is that balance must be understood as relating simultaneously to the constitutional, social, and party-political spheres, so that 'balance' does not necessarily imply a condition of substantive social equality, nor preclude forms of domination and subordination which implies that a dynamically balanced system, in the short term, can more than just 'tilt' one way and another. Balance indicates the existence of a complex, relatively open structure within which social and political conflicts are essentially self-limiting. It is from this perspective that the third leading characteristic of liberal democracy, stability, should be appreciated, and in the explanations given of this term we can also see the justifications of inequality.

Democratic 'stability' is a disarmingly deceptive term. There is a natural inclination to regard *government* stability as the central measure, to view recurring government 'crises' as evidence of a deep-seated malaise. But many countries in Western Europe are quite inured to frequent changes in government without showing real signs of breakdown. At the other extreme, stability may be equated with the sheer 'survival power' of the system; in this sense, the Third French Republic, racked with crisis as it was, proved to be the most stable democratic form since the Revolution. Should one identify stability with survival and simple longevity? The time-span must be a factor, since the undisputed models of European stable democracy – the majority of Scandinavian states, Britain, and Switzerland – owe their reputation in part to the continuity of their democratic traditions; stability in depth cannot be an overnight acquisition. But the difficulty in arriving at a common criterion is well illustrated by the case of West Germany in the early post-war years. On one set of conditions Germany was described as an unstable democracy, yet others were inclined to see it as undesirably 'hyperstable'.[5] The different conclusion is related to the time factor: only since 1949 has Germany (its western part) proved to be a pillar of the liberal democratic virtues.

If it has to be conceded that general views of democratic stability are quite imprecise, then there is very little practical difficulty in assessing the situation of a particular country at a particular time. Yet the problem of accounting for stability is similarly beset by difficulties. There are numerous explanations put forward which we can group under three loose heads. There are the 'economic' explanations which show a connection between the level of economic development and democratic stability. Secondly, there are 'structural' accounts in which the emphasis is put on the compatibility of various social groupings. Thirdly, there are versions of stable democracy which concentrate on the values and beliefs of the mass of the people as well as those of key social élites.

The economic thesis is simply put by Lipset: 'The more well-to-do a nation, the greater the chances it will sustain democracy.' And in more detail, '. . . all the various aspects of economic development – industrialization, urbanization, wealth and education are so closely interrelated as to form one major factor which has the political correlate of democracy.'[6] It can easily be demonstrated that the various indices of economic well-being give the liberal democracies of Western Europe a much more favourable rating than most non-liberal systems. This is indisputable, but it may not be a real explanation. Except by invoking 'special circumstances,' the economic argument is not very helpful in explaining important lapses – such as Nazi Germany. This difficulty led Eckstein to say that it is the timing and the rate of industrialisation which helps to give the correlation between economic development and stable democracy. He points out that the high-scorers, '. . . are precisely those which developed industry most gradually, but still lead the field because of their early start . . . It becomes apparent that the level of economic development . . . matters only because the speed of economic development matters.'[7] Thus even if economic wealth is a good indicator, the reasons for stability may be found in the social effects of the *initial* changes; late or very rapid industrialisation is likely to set up tensions of a structural kind. Such a formulation goes some way in explaining the weakness of the Weimar Republic; compared at least with some other European countries, Germany had industrialised both rapidly and late.

Structural explanations of stable democracy take a number of forms. The most general of them is expressed in the idea of 'mass society'. Theorists from de Tocqueville onwards have argued that the type of social structure which is inimical to stable democracy is one which is 'unstructured', where the masses stand in a direct relationship to the state. There are no adequate secondary organisations to cushion the mutual impact of élite and mass; the result is either an unstable hyper-democracy or a totalitarian system with the masses directly available for exploitation by the élites. This is given a modern rendering by Raymond Aron: 'A classless society leaves the mass of the population without any possible means of defence against the élite, . . . (and) would superimpose a unified élite upon an undifferentiated mass.'[8] The juxtaposition of 'mass' and 'élite' is integral to structural explanations of liberal democracy and provides the clue to its functioning: the recognition that élite leadership is fundamental. This is the first strand in what we can call a 'restrictive' view of democracy.

An 'impure' element is also introduced by the theory of 'consociational democracy', originally formulated by Arend Lijphart. The consociational model attempts to account for the phenomenon of the 'stable yet fragmented' democracies, primarily the smaller ones in Western Europe such as the Netherlands and Switzerland. The important modification of the pluralist version of democracy lies in the independent role ascribed to the political and social élites. Despite the existence of social cleavages – and to an extent overriding them – the élites seek to reach a harmonious accommodation with one another. Thus the inter-elite bargains are seen as a prerequisite for continuing democratic stability.[9]

Similar reservations are made by other writers. For Bendix, who applies his argument especially to Western Europe, the critical historical factor was the development of a dual concept of representation – plebiscitarian and functional. The former gave direct representation under a national government and the latter took account of the 'differential affiliation of individuals', in other words, of their unequal power position in society. 'The two ideas', says Bendix, 'reflect the hiatus between state and society in an age of equality ... The system of representative institutions characteristic of the Western European tradition remains intact as long as this tension between the plebiscitarian idea and the idea of group representation endures, as long as the contradiction between abstract criteria of equality and the old as well as the new inequalities of the social condition is mitigated by ever new and ever partial compromises.'[10]

Bendix put forward a theory of balanced inequalities, and in rather a different form this is also true of Eckstein whose explanation combines elements of structure and values. His standpoint is that, 'A government will tend to be stable if its authority pattern is congruent with other authority patterns in society of which it is part.'[11] Since by their very nature governments must be commanding (if not authoritarian) in character, the theory of congruence requires that other parts of the political system should be so as well – especially the politically-relevant parts of society which 'impinge on government'. Thus in British stable democracy the cabinet system finds its congruent twin in the structure of the political parties: 'At no point in the segmentation of British society is there any abrupt and large change in authority patterns, and throughout one finds at least some imitation of government forms.' Eckstein contrasts the British situation with that of the Weimar Republic – in the latter, political life was democratic but social life was still authoritarian: 'Not only were society and polity to some degree incongruent; they existed in an unprecedented contradiction to one another.'[12] He concluded that the pattern of government authority should be a mixture of democratic norms and traditional-authoritarian elements, an amalgam which takes account of the undemocratic aspects of society. His finding is firmly in the restrictive vein: 'Governmental democracy will tend to be stable only if it is to a significant degree impure.'[13]

Not surprisingly, the third general version of stable democracy, based on people's values and beliefs, is equally restrictive. We can take the theory of the 'civic culture' as being representative of this type of explanation. Gabriel Almond and Sidney Verba contrasted the 'classical' ideas of how a democracy should work with the reality. In its classic rendering, one supposed the ideal-typical citizen to participate fully in political life, basing his actions and his vote on sound judgement, the model 'rationally-active' citizen.

However little that accords with what anyone really thought about the way democracy works is another matter,'[14] but it is a sharp contrast indeed if one argues that there is, in fact, a useful role for political apathy in liberal democracy – that a high voting turnout may be evidence of instability. A case in point which supports this view is the high participation at the Reichstag elections prior to the demise of the Weimar Republic, with mass support for the Nazi Party – what Kurt Schumacher, the German Social Democrat, once called 'the mobilization of human stupidity'.

The general theme advanced by Almond and Verba is unambiguous: 'There exists in Britain and the United States a pattern of political attitudes and an underlying set of social attitudes that is supportive of a stable democratic process.'[15] This particular mixture of attitudes, called the 'civic culture' does preserve the traits of the model, active citizen, but it combines them with other attitudes of passivity, uninvolvement, even a shade of deference. There is respect for government and a pride in political and other institutions together with a widespread trust in others and in public officials. There is also a high *potential* in the civic culture for the individual to become involved. But for stable democracy it is better if this remains a potentiality – the responsible citizen will normally consider 'other things' more important than politics. There is thus an active-passive balance which provides a good 'fit' with the needs of democratic government – government power tempered by a responsiveness to the needs of the people. A government has the authority to govern, but it must be ever-wary of the 'potentially-active citizen'. Typically, in such a stable democracy as Britain, there will be 'cycles of citizen involvement, élite response, and citizen withdrawal', the attitudes of the political élites neatly complementing those of the ordinary citizen, and he, '. . . must turn power over to élites and let them rule.'[16]

The original survey conducted by Almond and Verba also included West Germany and Italy, and these lacked the attributes of the civic culture. The Italian political culture was portrayed as one of 'relatively unrelieved political alienation and of social isolation and distrust'. With little in the way of national pride, citizen competence, or participation the average Italian could contribute little to stable democracy. The German citizen's view could be described as one of political detachment allied with confidence in government administration. Although the aloofness from politics was coupled with a high 'subject-competence', the individual satisfaction did not extend to a more general civic trust; the implication of the findings was that, though on some counts a stable democracy, West Germany lacked the reserves of commitment to weather a prolonged political crisis.

The general failing of the accounts we have given is that they frequently appear to idealise a given situation – the role of élites, power imbalances between one social group and another, widespread passivity. Alternatively, they may not amount to a causal explanation, but only provide an index in the way that economic wealth does. This objection applies to some cultural explanations of liberal democracy. Thus the theory of the 'civic culture' was entirely built up on contemporary survey material, and if, as is usually held to be the case, a country's political culture –the aggregate of knowledge, beliefs, values, and accepted behaviour in relation to politics – only changes very slowly over the years, then a current analysis is insufficient; it can only provide some scale of rating.

Another line of criticism against the 'snapshot' tendency of political culture approaches is, rather paradoxically, that they fail to take account of – or properly account for – the impact of basic social and political change. That criticism may be applied to the 'civic culture' version: there are sufficient indications that it is less applicable to values and attitudes in the United States and Britain than it was in the past, and yet whilst the Anglo-American prototype may be crumbling, a contrary movement may have taken place in Western Germany, a development quite unforeseen twenty or so years ago.

Brian Barry points out that it is the *performance* of the democratic institutions over a period of time which gives rise to a type of political culture, simply that people who get reasonable treatment from the authorities are much more likely to develop a civic culture than those who do not; legitimacy depends on effectiveness. Barry's argument has other important implications which can be used to counter vague allusions to democratic 'consensus' and 'legitimacy'. Belief in the legitimacy of democratic government has to be sharpened to mean 'legitimacy in the eyes of the appropriate people', and this implies alternative sets of legitimacy depending on the situation. It leads to the question: which groups by the withdrawal of their support will endanger or even topple the system? The close association of legitimacy and support, with the latter ultimately dependent on the satisfaction of demands made on the political system, brings us to the brink of saying that system performance is the real determinant of stable democracy. As a consequence structural and value-related explanations take on a subordinate role, and, as Barry concludes: 'Values are at best the last link in the chain of causation before behaviour itself.'[17] One can make this point in a rather different way via the concept of political culture. The process of political socialisation imparts the values and beliefs of the prevailing culture and in doing this it underpins the legitimacy of the political authorities and the ruling groups. Yet the socialisation process also *generates a set of expectations* concerning how the political system *should* operate, and if these expectations are continually disappointed, then the whole edifice will become suspect; political socialisation works more than one way.

The wide claims sometimes made for the liberal version of democracy go back to the optimism of the nineteenth-century liberal ideal, especially as viewed by Isaiah Berlin, with its belief, '. . . in the unlimited power of education and the power of rational morality to overcome economic misery and inequality'.[18] But this optimism was later to be tempered with the realistic requirement of a 'democratic élitism', even if there was the concession that the élites should be 'open' and 'responsive'. The open question is whether this combination of idealism and realism, the liberal democratic method, shows a sufficient appreciation of the realities of social power, whether its reliance on political techniques and parliamentary majorities is adequate to bring about basic social change. Maurice Cornforth is representative of those who have argued that the proponents of liberal democracy, '. . . deceive us about democracy . . . in their assumption that the "democratic institutional control of power" operates independently of classes, class interests and class struggles.' Furthermore: 'The causes of inequalities in property relations and class relations remain . . . only glossed over, but not alleviated, by the existence of certain "equalities" of political rights and "equality before the law".'[19]

Yet these criticisms do not gainsay the resilience of liberal democracy in Western Europe. Political choice and political balance may have worked in favour of the established class élites, but what of the social interests which were thereby deprived? European socialism in the nineteenth and early twentieth centuries rejected the values of the capitalist market economy and the terms of the new industrialism. Socialist parties first sought the legal and political rights of citizenship as the first step in transforming society, but once having chalked up these victories, they increasingly made use of the liberal political system as the means of satisfying their further economic and social demands; in so doing they also came to accept the essential tenets of the market system. Parliamentary socialism was destined to become a bulwark of the liberal democratic state and to become so without losing the support of its mass following.

From the perspective of the later 1980s, it is another question whether the style of 'parliamentary élitism' will continue to be the guiding force of liberal democracy and indefinitely be able to sustain mass confidence. The mounting claims for greater participation and for more 'open government' are joined by an increasing resort to 'direct action' and with it the underlying threat of 'ungovernability'. The new political mood in Western Europe has not as yet decisively challenged the inherited structures of liberal democracy, and it may well be the case that they are more resilient than sometimes appears. Yet the test is better seen as one of adaptability: the political stability of the Western European democracies depends in large measure on the ability to preserve the values of liberal democracy whilst at the same time being able to absorb new ideas and meet new claims. That, after all, is precisely what non-liberal regimes are unable to do.

This is a necessarily brief account of the features, assumptions and explanations of liberal democracy. Yet all the topics touched on here return in one guise or another in the course of the following chapters. Their relevance will be evident in looking at the social basis of political loyalties, the nature of the political parties, and the forms and function of opposition. This also is true of the later chapters: the implications of constitutionalism, the relationship of parliaments to governments, the challenges made to the liberal democratic order. Taken together, a study of these facets of West European politics should lead to a view of democratic stability and the terms of its future development.

Notes and References

1. C. B. Macpherson, *The Real World of Democracy*, Oxford University Press, 1966, p. 4.
2. R. A. Dahl (ed.), *Political Oppositions in Western Democracies*, New Haven: Yale University Press, 1966, p. xvii.
3. M. J. C. Vile, *Constitutionalism and the Separation of Powers*, Oxford University Press, 1967, p. 1.
4. P. Dunleavy and B. O'Leary, *Theories of the State: The Politics of Liberal Democracy*, London: Macmillan, 1987, p. 70.
5. H. Eckstein, 'A Theory of Stable Democracy', appearing as an appendix in his *Division and Cohesion in Democracy: A Study of Norway*, New Jersey: Princeton University Press, 1966, p. 271.
6. S. M. Lipset, *Political Man*, Heinemann, (rev. ed.) 1983, pp. 31 and 41.
7. Eckstein, 'A Theory of Stable Democracy,' op. cit., p. 279.
8. R. Aron, 'Social Structure and the Ruling Class', in L. Coser (ed.), *Political Sociology, Selected Essays*, New York: Harper and Row, 1966, pp. 82, 91.
9. See A. Lijphart, 'Typologies of Democratic Systems' in A. Lijphart (ed.), *Politics in Europe*, Englewood Cliffs, New Jersey: Prentice-Hall, 1969.
10. R. Bendix, *Nation-Building and Citizenship*, New York: Wiley, 1964, pp. 101–4.
11. Eckstein, op. cit., p. 234
12. ibid., pp. 247 and 248.
13. ibid., p. 262.
14 It can be argued that a 'classical' theory of liberal democracy never really existed

even in the nineteenth century. See Carole Pateman, *Participation and Democratic Theory*, Cambridge University Press, 1970.

15 G. Almond and S. Verba, *The Civic Culture: Political Attitudes and Democracy in Five Nations*, New Jersey: Princeton University Press, 1963, p. vii.

16. ibid., pp. 484 and 478.

17. B. Barry, *Sociologists, Economists and Democracy*, Collier-Macmillan, 1970, pp. 67, 96.

18. Isaiah Berlin, 'Political Ideas in the Twentieth Century', in R. C. Macridis (ed.), *Political Parties: Contemporary Trends and Ideas*, New York: Harper and Row, 1967, p. 209.

19. M. Cornforth, *The Open Philosophy and the Open Society*, Lawrence and Wishart, 1968, pp. 271 and 285.

Additional References

G. Almond and S. Verba (eds.), *The Civic Culture Revisited*, Boston: Little, Brown, 1979.

P. Bachrach, *The Theory of Democratic Elitism*, University of London Press, 1969.

B. Barry, 'The Consociational Model and its Dangers', *European Journal of Political Research*, December 1975.

B. Barry, 'Political Accommodation and Consociational Democracy', *British Journal of Political Science*, October 1975.

R. Bendix (ed.), *State and Society*, Boston: Little, Brown, 1968.

S. I. Benn and R. S. Peters, *Social Principles and the Democratic State*, Allen and Unwin, 1959.

P. Birnbaum, J. Lively, G. Parry (eds.), *Democracy, Consensus and Social Contract*, Sage Publications, 1978.

L. Bramson, *The Political Context of Sociology*, Princeton University Press, 1961.

M. Friedman, *Capitalism and Freedom*, University of Chicago Press, 1962.

M. O. Heisler (ed.), *Politics in Europe: Structures and Processes in Some Post-Industrial Societies*, New York: David McKay, 1974.

D. Held, *Models of Democracy*, Polity Press, 1987.

P. Hirst, *Law, Socialism and Democracy*, Allen and Unwin, 1986.

B. Holden, *Understanding Liberal Democracy*, Philip Allan, 1988.

W. Kornhauser, *The Politics of Mass Society*, Routledge and Kegan Paul, 1960.

A. Lijphart, *Democracy in Plural Societies: A Comparative Exploration*, Yale University Press, 1977.

J. Lively, *Democracy*, Oxford: Blackwell, 1975.

G. McLennan, D. Held and S. Hall (eds.), *The Idea of the Modern State*, Open University Press, 1984.

C. Macpherson, *The Life and Times of Liberal Democracy*, Oxford University Press, 1977.

K. McRae (ed.), *Consociational Democracy: Political Accommodation in Segmented Societies*, Toronto: McClelland and Stewart, 1974.

L. Mayer, *Politics in Industrial Societies*, New York: John Wiley, 1977.

D. Nicholls, *The Pluralist State*, Macmillan, 1975.

J. Obler (and others), *Decision-Making in Smaller Democracies: The Consociational 'Burden'*, Sage, 1977.

G. Parry, *Political Elites*, George Allen and Unwin, 1969.

A. Patience (ed.), *Democracy and the Capitalist State*, Cambridge University Press, 1981.

J. Schumpeter, *Capitalism, Socialism and Democracy*, George Allen and Unwin, (rev. ed.) 1966.

D. Spitz, *The Real World of Liberalism*, University of Chicago Press, 1982.

2　Politics and Society

The social bases

People vote, take active part, and otherwise relate to politics in a fairly predictable and consistent way. To a great extent we can, for instance, forecast likely voting behaviour given the knowledge of one or two key variables relating to a person's socio-economic circumstances. Of these, it has been usual to regard the economic influences – and the class structure to which they are related – as easily the most important. Yet even if one agrees that this is the case, there are still a number of other influences which are all to some degree independent of a strict economic interpretation: the force of nationalism, the community of language, religious commitment, contrasts in rural and urban environment.[1] Any of these can result in the formation of enclaves of loyalty which have a political significance, that is, in 'sub-cultures' which resist a uniform structuring of national politics solely on socio-economic lines. Such situations do not arise overnight; they are the product of particular types of historical development. But their 'historical' nature does not diminish their importance: often it is these non-economic alignments which provide the ingredients for head-on political conflict, rather than the muted contest of class-related politics, and even when these alignments are not paramount, they can still act to modify national politics in such a way that each country presents a different political line-up of social forces – best seen in the nature of their party system.

The countries of Western Europe are now broadly similar in the stage of their economic development, and this similarity extends to the class structure based on a common experience of the market economy of capitalist systems. All the same, there are still differences in the level of economic wealth,* and political differences are evident too. Indeed, Europe displays a variety of political culture and 'styles' – even if the liberal democratic form of government is the norm; to explain the diversity we have to take account of the basic social features of each country – historically-conditioned factors – to understand why one country,

---

* For various measures of economic development, see the table on p. 310 below.

Britain, presented a picture of a broadly homogeneous society, whilst a second, Italy was typified by political cleavage, and a third, the Netherlands, managed to contain a diversity of political allegiance within an overall consensus, for which the idea of 'consociational democracy' is one explanation.

The term 'homogeneous' in the sense we have used it here, needs some explanation; it does not mean that political loyalties are distributed randomly throughout the population regardless of socio-economic differences, but that there is only *one* major variable which has a political relevance. In a relatively homogeneous society, real differences in wealth and social class are apparent, but the other influences we have mentioned are not politically operative. This may be because there is only one language, a single, and undisputed, religion, and because the society is completely urbanised. Alternatively, it may be that the 'other influences' are distributed equally throughout society regardless of social class, and possibly for this reason they fail to result in the throwing-up of live political issues.[2]

Some European countries are anything but homogeneous in their political make-up. Blondel used the term 'sectionalism' to describe such situations where, 'the distribution of variables ... depart(s) significantly from a normal distribution',[3] to give a cluster of social and cultural traits associated with the major variable – usually to be taken as the underlying class structure.* Thus a high degree of sectionalism occurs in those countries where class differences are compounded by other, apparently independent, social and cultural distinctions. In a sectional society, the economic issues need not appear to be the critical ones; the intensity of conflict may be shown in other ways. The peculiar sharpness of non-economic questions may arise, because the disputants put forward claims which are essentially 'non-bargainable' – the Pope is either infallible or he is not; against this, economic conflict is made up of a host of issues, all open to some compromise – accommodation in terms of 'more' or 'less' or resolution by economic growth and social mobility – so that decisive confrontation is continually postponed.

The force of sectionalism is that it can harden economic conflict to give two irreconcilable camps. Thus the issue of clericalism in Italy followed the left-right axis fairly closely. Anti-clericalism reinforced anti-capitalism, and the two issues became intertwined; the Catholic Church also became an object of attack because of its

---

* For a diagrammatic rendering of various models of 'homogeneous' and 'sectional' society, see 'Social Cleavages and Party Systems', pp. 42–4 below.

vast material wealth. Geographical factors add a further dimension to sectionalism: it is not just the disparities of wealth and their association with non-economic differences, but the occurrence of these in well-defined areas which make for the most implacable cleavages. Any concentration of national minorities will help cement a sub-culture, and on an economic level, certain regions may become permanently underprivileged, with rural poverty or declining industry; these may show political tendencies contrary to more fortunate parts of a country.

However, it would be wrong to describe homogeneous society as of necessity 'conflict-free', or a sectional society as 'conflict-ridden'. In conditions of homogeneity, class differences will be the major determinant of political behaviour – the unresolved question here is whether this must mean an intensification of class conflict, and one which we shall have to consider. Likewise, a sectional society need not be one of continual conflict – especially where the sectionalism fails to generate one major line of cleavage. In the case of the Netherlands, the presence of two major Churches, Protestant and Catholic, together with a strong secular influence, combined to make economic issues less relevant: a supporter of the Catholic People's Party or of one of the Protestant parties might be rich or poor, farmer, businessman, or trade unionist. The phenomenon of the three 'pillars' of Dutch society, its *Verzuiling*, was an expression for the existence of at least three distinctive sub-cultures: Catholic, Protestant, and a 'general' latitudinarian one – the last of which itself subdivided into Liberals and Socialists on a political plane.* We may describe this as a vertical division of Dutch society; its effect was to cut across the horizontal divisions of the class structure, preventing the formation of 'armed camps' which one naturally associates with sectionalism. In a less pronounced fashion, any relatively homogeneous society will show a similar tendency: non-economic considerations act to blur the significance of the class structure without themselves coming to the forefront. And where any single commitment fails to be exclusive, people are subject to a number of cross-pressures which act against a single, major line of conflict becoming the sole preoccupation. It is the balance provided by an individual's competing loyalties that is seen as a precondition for stable democracy: 'The available evidence suggests that the chances for stable democracy are enhanced to the extent that groups and

---

* For a listing of the individual parties, see the table, 'Party Systems in Western Europe', pp. 122–3.

individuals have a number of crosscutting, politically relevant affiliations'.[4] To this extent, both the 'weak' sectional societies and a homogeneous society with a muted class polarisation are capable of containing and modifying political differences.

No two Europeans states have followed the same political pattern; yet one can argue that there is an underlying similarity, a common trend for the non-economic influences to decline in political salience, leaving the economic issues, and related aspects of social class, exposed as the main determinant of political activity. We can best examine this contention by first reviewing the main roots of party politics today. Subsequently we should take account of new factors that appear to influence voting and party loyalty and which prevent socio-economic considerations having an undisputed sway.

Language and national minorities

The rather untidy patchwork of European states has one great merit: it means that national boundaries generally run along language frontiers; the force of national aspirations in the past has resulted in a relatively large number of independent states, and removed one of the most fertile sources of political stress: the national minority. In this century, the four latecomers to national independence – Finland, Ireland, Iceland and Malta – have substantially defined the European limits of national self-determination.

For most countries, the presence of linguistic minorities is no real problem. Thus in Finland the Swedish People's Party, representing the 10 per cent of Swedish-speakers, is a gradually declining force. In Norway, the *Nynorsk* movement arose as a neo-Norwegian language form based on various dialects, an expression of 'cultural defence' against city influences and therefore a type of rural-urban conflict; but the only residual problem was how the two language variants could best be amalgamated. The German-Danish frontier gave rise to small linguistic minorities on both sides; the parties representing their interests are no longer significant, and their protection rests on an inter-state treaty. Similarly, a bitter, fifty-year dispute between Austria and Italy was resolved in 1971 by giving the German-speaking inhabitants of the South Tyrol (Alto Adige) a measure of cultural and political autonomy; a renewal of bomb-attacks in the mid-1980s did not alter the position of the South Tyrol People's Party as an integral part of the Italian party system.

There are, however, still a number of dissident minorities: the

Basques in Spain, Bretons and the Corsicans in France, Catholics in Northern Ireland, Scottish and Welsh Nationalists. The presence of a linguistic element is not a necessary feature, and the movements differ considerably in the extent of their demands and the means they are prepared to employ. Their activities may be treated as no more than pin-pricks to national unity, but their minority position makes it difficult for the minorities to work for a parliamentary majority or rely on conventional politics alone: there is the possibility of a swift progression from protest and disruption to violence and fervent terrorism. The Basque minority in Spain (only some 5 per cent of the total population) conforms exactly to the extremist model, and the transition to parliamentary democracy from dictatorship and the considerable decentralisation of political power by the creation of regional governments has not altered Basque claims nor has it led to a reliance on peaceful methods. A 'national minority' can represent the most intractable problem for any political system.

Two countries are notable exceptions to the rule of linguistic homogeneity, Switzerland and Belgium; the contrast between them is enlightening. The similarity is the presence of a very large language minority in both countries. The Flemish (Dutch-speaking) Belgians are in a majority with 55 per cent of the population, and in Switzerland German is the main language of 65 per cent. In both cases, French-speakers are in a large minority, with other very small minorities as well – German-speaking in Belgium, Italian and Romansch in Switzerland. That language differences alone do not lead to fundamental cleavage is amply demonstrated in Switzerland, where there have been no linguistic-cultural parties of any importance. Part of the answer may lie in the degree of decentralisation provided by the federal structure* – though the significance of federalism has to be appreciated in terms of historical growth rather than as a ready-made formula. What it does mean is that issues of a cultural-linguistic nature are resolved at a point below the federal level. The relation of the language frontiers to the political boundaries of the cantons is of some importance: although the linguistic divisions are clearly defined, they tend to cut *across* many of the cantonal boundaries; it is the religious boundaries which follow more closely those of the cantons. Whichever language a person speaks, the really important loyalty is to the canton, and this loyalty is reinforced by the relative religious homogeneity within the canton. In a sense, the Swiss cantons are a parallel to the vertical 'pillars' of Dutch society.

* See below, pp. 228ff.

The ingredients of the Belgian language issue are fairly simple, even if the political implications have become complex. Belgium is an overwhelmingly Catholic country, a unitary state, with a clear language frontier, little-changed since the Middle Ages, running east-west across the country with French-speaking Walloons to the south and the Flemish to the north. The position of Brussels has come to highlight the problems involved: historically it is a Flemish city, and well within the Flemish area, but the city itself is now largely French-speaking. For long, the French language was that of the dominant élite – economic, social, and governmental; in contrast the Flemings were the poor country cousins, with little to contribute to Belgian culture, and a language that was an amalgam of dialects. Above all, outside the large cities, Flanders was economically backward. Brussels became symbolic of Walloon and Francophone predominance.

What has changed in recent times is the economic fortunes of the two areas. Flemish nationalism was slow to develop; in the course of the First World War it took a 'disloyal' and separatist line, but since then most of the language demands have been met – in the fields of education, law and administration. Yet the tensions between the two communities persisted; the formal parity which was gradually achieved went along with the changing economic balance in favour of Flanders. Wallonian economic supremacy vanished as the older, heavy industries declined, and Flanders benefited from new industry and a progressive agriculture. One consequence was an economic antagonism between the two regions. Relatively prosperous Flanders objected to the economic drain of subsidies that had to be directed to ailing Wallonian industries. Thus it was the turn of the minority French-speaking population to be on the defensive, but French is still the dominant language, epitomised in the position of Brussels – now three-quarters French-speaking – a thorn in the side of Flemish aspirations.

There is a mutual suspicion: Wallonian economic weakness is accentuated by the minority position of the French speakers (40 per cent); with justification in the past, the Flemish felt the effects of cultural discrimination and now see their numerical supremacy and economic progress as means to redress the balance. In this, the Brussels-question is pivotal for both protagonists, with Flemish hopes to reassert its Flemish character and at the very least to halt the intrusion of the French language into the surrounding countryside. It took several years to brew up an acceptable compromise, the basis of which was established in the early 1970s. The terms of the proposals, involving a large measure of regional decentralisation in cultural and economic affairs, required far-reaching constitutional changes. Even though the principle of 'linguistic decentralisation' was generally accepted, giving full regional status to Wallonia and Flanders, the position of Brussels remained a bone of contention. As a third 'region', Brussels had its city limits permanently fixed and was made officially bilingual, thus meeting minimum Flemish demands, but hardly satisfying the Francophones who had come to regard Brussels as 'naturally' French-speaking and the restrictions as artificial. Thus although the regional solution worked for a large part of the country, the tensions surrounding the question of Brussels remained unresolved. Moreover, in the process of facing up to linguistic demands over the past twenty-five years, the Belgian party system has changed almost beyond recognition: the traditional parties – Social-Christians, Socialists, and Liberals – have all split to form autonomous linguistic parties; and there arose a number of specifically linguistic parties as well: the Flemish-speaking *Volksunie* and *Vlaamsche Blok*, and the French-speaking *Rassemblement Wallon* together with the Brussels *Front des Francophones*. Between them, these 'specific' parties still win around 12 per cent of the vote, sufficient to worry the larger parties and maintain a threat of destabilisation. That the linguistic issue has lost none of its potency was shown in 1987 when the national coalition collapsed and an early election had to be called following a minor local dispute over language use.

The upsurge of the language issue in Belgium, and the strains it has put upon the party system, may appear to be exceptional, but the real point may be that it is not language differences by themselves which lead to crisis, rather it is the economic and social discrimination that, wittingly or not, accompany them which lead to a fundamental cleavage. However, once the language differences become community symbols, they can take on a life of their own and lead to a peculiar intractability, and this the Belgian case well illustrates.

The 'community symbol' need not be based on language. As the disturbances and political impasse in Northern Ireland amply demonstrate, both nationalism and religious differences can achieve a similar result. The permanent Protestant majority in Northern Ireland (approximately 65 per cent of the population) had resulted in the hegemony of the ruling Ulster Unionists for some fifty years, with no possibility of democratic erosion; indeed, this was the basis of the partition of Ireland. Yet behind the reality of Protestant dominance, there was the further reality of a social and economic discrimination, with a Roman Catholic underprivileged 'class'. Although the present crisis found its origins as a civil rights movement rather than as a religious issue, the latter soon became the operative symbol and the point of cleavage – the Catholic minority was also a social minority. But behind these two factors lies the third, that of Irish nationalism, and the escalation of violence since 1971 was a reassertion that ultimately there was a *colonial* problem to be solved, 'a war of independence' – alternatively, a military action against 'lawless terrorists'. The painful search for a constitutional formula to contain the various stresses still continues; short of conceding to the Irish nationalist demands, solutions might take the direction of the Belgian reforms or even introduce elements of the Swiss collegial system of government. Despite attempts at reform, the initial difficulty of finding a basic consensual element between the two communities remains the real stumbling-block.

The Swiss situation, in contrast, is partly a result of constitutional arrangements and partly of the intermingling of the social factors, and both are the product of a long historical evolution; certainly it provides no ready-made answers. Even Switzerland has experienced its own minority problem in miniature. Beginning in 1962 there were demands for autonomy by the French-speaking minority in the Bernese Jura, and their demands eventually led to the creation in 1978 of a new canton from the existing German-dominated Canton of Bern. That case shows the ever-present potential of minority issues. Their importance may be exaggerated – apparent for both Welsh and Scottish nationalism in the 1970s – but very easily they can pose threats to the unity of the state.

Religion and politics

Apart from the rather special case of Northern Ireland, most people would probably regard the religious factor in politics as of very small importance. It may then be surprising to be informed that, 'Contrary to popular belief religion, not class, is the main social basis of parties in the west today.'[5] This finding, dating from the 1970s, does not mean, with rare exceptions, that political issues are still seen primarily in religious terms or that religious disputes are the main content of politics, rather it is that a person's religious commitment or background is an important variable in deciding the direction of his political outlook and thus his voting loyalty. One can put this connection in a slightly different way: a religious standpoint merges with and corresponds to other social variables with the result that few issues are seen as purely religious or anti-clerical arguments. But by the same token very few issues are completely divorced from them either. If religion rather than social class forms the major basis of political parties, it is to be interpreted as a passive rather than an active force in the sense that religious persuasion, or lack of it, will be a good guide to party affiliation.

We can best relate our discussion to the three patterns of religious balance found in Western Europe: the mainly Roman Catholic countries, those with approximate Catholic and Protestant parity, and countries which are largely Protestant. It is in the Roman Catholic countries that religion has the most direct political connection, and this for three reasons. The wide claims of Roman Catholicism, especially its strongly developed social doctrines, made the teachings of the Church of political relevance, so that it has frequently found itself drawn into the political arena. Secondly, its tight hierarchical structure forced it into a rigidity of attitude and thus to a ready identification with particular political lines. Thirdly, the links with Rome made it appear as an anti-national element serving ultramontane interests. These three factors often combined to give rise to strong anti-clerical sentiments, the more so when the Catholic Church in any country became firmly identified with particular socio-economic élites, and anti-clericalism became part and parcel of an attack on these élites.

In some countries, the position of the Catholic Church was so powerful that anti-clericalism scarcely arose as an issue. The dictatorial nature of the regimes in Spain and Portugal was such that the Church became part of the ruling order, and an important source of legitimacy for the authoritarian rule. Of the democratic states, the Republic of Ireland alone afforded the Catholic Church an almost unquestioned supremacy – a complete absence of anti-clericalism despite occasions when the Catholic hierarchy actively intervened in politics; the small Irish Labour Party certainly could not afford the charge of being anti-clerical. The continuing strength of religious influences in Irish society were underlined in 1983 when a constitutional change to guarantee the right to life of the unborn child was decisively approved by referendum. In 1986 a referendum, promoted by the government parties, aimed at reforming the divorce laws was rejected by a wide margin. A further indication was provided in 1988 when the new and secularly-inclined Progressive Democrats, the third largest party in the Dail, in drafting its constitution to be submitted to parliament, omitted any reference in its preamble to the Holy Trinity which is traditional for Irish parties. The furore that this omission caused led the Progressive Democrats to back-track on their decision – not wishing to be given the label of the 'Godless' party.

The more usual situation has been a sharp polarisation between the Church and secular society. When this occurred, the response of the Church was to cast its net wide into the associational groupings of society, with numerous lay organisations affiliated to the Church in evidence: trade unions, agricultural associations, women's and youth movements; these served to underpin the summit of political Catholicism – the Christian Democratic party. The inevitable accompaniment was a similar set-up on the anti-clerical side; the product was a high degree of competitive associationalism which could affect the citizen at every point in his life; his later politics were largely determined by his initial religious (or anti-clerical) contacts, and the linked associations with which he became involved tended to confirm them. The classic case of social and political bifurcation was pre-war Austria. On the one side was ranged the strongly anti-clerical Socialist Party; this was, of course, class-based and largely urban, with its stronghold in Vienna, but the party by no means had a monopoly of the working-class vote. On the other side were the Christian-Socials, an out-and-out Catholic party, strongly backed by the clerical hierarchy. The Christian-Socials were able to gain a majority in what was virtually a two-party system because they could rely on the support of practising Catholics regardless of social class and were almost completely dominant in rural Austria. The heavy involvement of the clergy in right-wing politics was balanced on the other flank by the fervour of Socialist anti-clericalism and its 'Austro-Marxist' ideology. For their part, the Socialists were remarkable in achieving '. . . a degree of political organisation unequalled in free parties, through their system of cadres . . . they controlled the workers' leisure time by providing them with a full set of avocational organisations for everyone from cyclists to anti-alcoholics.'[6] The result was two hostile camps, and a '*laager*'-mentality to match which froze political attitudes and activity around the religious and anti-clerical polarisation. The Austrian situation changed radically in the post-war era, and the nearest parallel of such acute polarisation is seen in Malta where the Labour Party, fiercely anti-clerical and in office from 1971–1987, engaged in a war of attrition with the Catholic Church and the Nationalist Party.

France provides a useful contrast, since there has never been a strong and avowedly clerical party, and the Catholic Church has been simply identified with social conservatism. But religious conflict did run deep – with the village priest and the village schoolmaster the symbols of mortal combat. The battles of the nineteenth century, culminating in the law of 1905 separating state and church have not been repeated since, but it is as well to remember that it never was a purely religious issue, since the Church was lined up with the anti-republican forces: to resist clerical power meant also to embrace the Republic and to 'accept' the Revolution. After 1905, the Catholic Church saw that it had to come to terms with history and the Republic – hence the specific rejection of right-wing Catholic extremism of the type represented by the *Action Française* between the wars; the last flicker of the old sentiments was fanned briefly into life in the support for the authoritarian Vichy regime after the defeat in 1940.

It would be wrong to conclude that religion subsequently became irrelevant for French politics. It is true that the post-war period saw the failure of the progressive Catholic MRP and the lack of impact of later successors, but that rather shows the way in which religion is identified with conservative values, and although it is rare for religion now to generate political issues, it is still an important influence on voting behaviour: 'Class dominates, but religion remains a powerful factor.'[7] That this passive attachment could be mobilised was shown dramatically in 1984 when educational reforms planned by the Socialist government which would have adversely affected the independence and financing of church-schools had to be dropped in the face of mass demonstrations and protests.

At this point, we can pause to set out the terms of a two-step process by which religion comes to be sundered from politics. The first step involves the transfer from religion as a political issue to one where it is a passive determinant of voting behaviour. This appears to be the stage reached in France, as it is too in post-war Austria – where the Catholic Church has formally withdrawn from any political involvement. The second step occurs when voting behaviour no longer shows any marked correlation with religious ties or observance. This second step has not occurred in the Catholic countries. Indeed, Ireland can be regarded as in a pre-primary stage – religious values permeated state and society; only recently has the role of religion in public and private life been questioned seriously.

Italy is just emerging from the primary phase: religion is still integral to the political scene in the inherited polarisation between the values of the dominant Christian Democrats and the various lay parties including the PC. Whilst in other Catholic countries overt intervention by the clergy is not common, in Italy pulpit-politics has been an everyday reality, supplemented by the political utterances of the Vatican – with its own radio station and newspaper. The influence of the Church on social life was sanctioned by the Concordat of 1929, and this continuing recognition remained the most controversial aspect of the 1985 Accords which brought the Concordat up to date. More than in other countries, the network of church lay organisations serves to keep the Christian Democrats in power. In particular, Catholic Action, by other European standards a right-wing association, links the demands of the Church with a socially involved and politically active élite, and Catholic Action is a major staging-post by which this élite enters parliament and government.

The case of divorce-law reform illustrates the problem of church-state relations as well as showing how Italian society is changing. Ninety-two years after it had become a live political issue, and after a five-year battle in the Italian Parliament, a bill incorporating a set of modest proposals eventually reached the statute book in 1970. On its way there, the Vatican showed unremitting hostility and used all its resources and influence to defeat the legislation, claiming that the proposals were in breach of the Concordat. Successive government crises were partly a result of this intervention, although defeat for the bill would certainly have rekindled active anti-clericalism as the issue of the Vatican tax exemption on its vast investment income had done a few years previously. Even when the divorce law was passed, the matter was not allowed to rest; it could still be challenged by popular referendum. To initiate this, a petition signed by 500,000 electors, each attested by a notary, was required. This was a formidable task, but parish priests were willing to help, using the churches as registration centres, and enjoining their parishioners to sign – for the glory of Jesus Christ and the Madonna. In the event, the petition was signed by well over a million voters but the referendum on the repeal of the divorce law (eventually held in May 1974) resulted in a clear victory for the supporters of the divorce law (59 per cent were against repeal) and was consequently a severe defeat for the Catholic Church, signalling the gradual decline of Christian Democratic hegemony.

A portrayal of religion and politics in Italy purely in these terms is certainly one-sided. Not all the bishops supported the Vatican's intransigent position, and the DC leadership was itself divided on the issue, for Christian Democracy is not simply a monolithic church party, and many inside the party would welcome a complete autonomy. Nor is the Communist Party to be equated with anti-clericalism – the party was not in the forefront of the divorce law campaign, and it has all along been anxious not to have its energies diverted into sterile anti-clericalism; indeed, its spokesmen have insisted that the party is no longer anti-clerical. One can appreciate their wisdom: as long as the party was regarded as militantly anti-church, it would be permanently cut off from any possibility of increasing voting support; additionally, with religion 'out of the way', the chances of reaching an understanding with the Christian Democrats would be enhanced. It is conceivable that the move to the second stage of passive vote determination could take place; this might still leave the Christian Democrats in a favourable position, since its vote is widely spread amongst all classes, with about one-quarter of the lowest income-groups, working class and peasantry, voting for the party.

The second pattern of religious balance, approximate Catholic and Protestant parity, occurs in West Germany, the Netherlands and Switzerland. In these countries, there is a peaceful coexistence of the two; no longer does a person's religion result in political or social discrimination; nevertheless, religion does have a salience for politics, and the two churches are still to an extent in competition with one another. In Switzerland, the relative religious homogeneity of the cantons and the cantonal competence for religious and cultural affairs serve to make religion a local affair. And although the Catholics are in a national minority, the weighting in the federal upper house, the Council of States, favours the small, and mainly Catholic, cantons; in the event, it is the language *and* religious minority which has control of the Council of States, so that the balance of interests is maintained.

The religious-political connection in the Netherlands is complex. Until the mid-1970s there were no fewer than three large confessional parties and a number of smaller ones; of them all, only the Catholic Radical Party could be described as 'on the left'. The Roman Catholics constitute a large minority of the Dutch population (around 40 per cent) and, like Switzerland, their vote went predominantly to the Catholic People's Party. But the Protestant vote was divided amongst a number of parties chiefly based on doctrinal differences; the two major ones, the Anti-Revolutionary Party and the Christian Historical Union, reflected differences which hardened in the nineteenth century: voting for one of the religious parties involved identification with a defined religious viewpoint, not just a 'Christian' commitment. Until the 1960s the total religious vote amounted to over a half of the whole – the highest proportion in any country. The most important result was that class differences were minimised. Thus, although over half of the Dutch Labour Party vote came from the lower income groups, the confessional parties were not far behind. There was also a strong tie between religious observance and voting, especially for the Catholics and the Calvinist Anti-Revolutionary Party.

We saw earlier that the pillars of Dutch Society represent a passive encapsulation of social attitudes rather than a source of active cleavage. The religious parties for long shared in coalition government, an active cooperation dating back to the last century when the Catholics and Protestants made common cause over the issue of denominational schools. Such issues became less relevant, but the passive religious connection to politics was maintained and translated into a political dominance for the religious parties. In the recent past there have been signs of a fundamental realignment of the party system in part caused by the erosion of the religious vote. One reaction was the formation in 1976 of the Christian Democratic Appeal from the CHU, ARP, and Catholics – a firm indication of weakening religious influence.

The third country with a Catholic-Protestant balance, West Germany, has shown the most rapid change in the relation of politics to religion. This transformation was aided by the division of Germany in 1945; before then the Protestants were in a substantial majority, but the loss of the eastern territories and the creation of the German Democratic Republic affected Catholic numbers very little, since they are concentrated in the south and west whilst the Protestants were weakened considerably. In the past, and with some reason, the Catholics thought of themselves as a beleaguered minority – especially at the time of Bismarck's *Kulturkampf* – and this for long hindered a wider social integration. The Catholic Centre Party, both in Imperial Germany and in the Weimar Republic, was mainly concerned to defend Catholic interests, and it retained a firm hold on the faithful, regardless of social class. The result was a so-called 'tower mentality' (after a pamphlet published in 1906, '*Wir müssen aus dem Turm heraus*', a plea to end the isolation of German Catholicism) which persisted into the Nazi era. After 1945, a successful attempt was made to end this isolation. The new spirit of cooperation with the Protestant community, until then associated with the orthodox conservative parties, was helped by the common feeling of responsibility for the Nazi success, at least by default. A unique 'double-compromise' was forged between the two confessions and, because of church following, between the classes as well. In this new-style Christian Democracy, the support of the Catholic churchgoer could be guaranteed; this was less true for the Protestants until the decline of the small right-wing parties.

On a formal count, church membership in Germany is very high, and this can be gauged accurately by the fact that about 85 per cent of the working population pay the 'church tax' – 10 per cent of a person's income tax liability collected by the state for distribution to the churches. To be set against this is the fact that only a tiny proportion of Protestants are regular churchgoers and only about one-third of all Catholics. Furthermore, the number of those 'contracting out' of the tax, deliberately leaving their church, has risen steeply in recent years. The connection between religious commitment and voting is still apparent, but there is now no barrier at all to a good Catholic voting Social Democrat. Anti-clericalism on the left is a thing of the past, although some questions do revive old feelings. That was the case over abortion law reform in the mid-1970s: the measures proposed by the SPD-led government were bitterly attacked by the Christian Democrats and the churches. Such disputes have become increasingly rare, and religious observance tends to be mainly an indicator of likely party support, but West Germany has still a way to go before entering the third stage of development – in its completed form the absence of any correlation between voting behaviour and religion.

That stage is most nearly seen in Britain and Scandinavia, countries which are largely Protestant. The Protestant churches have never been so tightly knit socially nor so corporative in spirit that they have been able to override class differences for any length of time. Unlike Roman Catholicism, the 'national' nature of Protestantism led to the ready identification of the state churches with ruling-class values; indeed, they have been the main-prop of establishment unity – to the extent that at one time the Church of England could be described as 'the Conservative Party at prayer'. By itself, Protestantism, especially with a state church, is more likely than Catholicism to expose a simple class polarisation. One can argue that Britain has entered the third stage; this accords with the observation made by Butler and Stokes in their detailed study of British voting: 'The ties of religion and party in the modern electorate are distinctly a legacy of the past'. But the attenuation of these ties observable in

Britain is of recent origin: 'It is hardly too strong to say that British politics ... were still rooted in religion in the Nineteenth Century';[8] the early years of this century saw bitter conflict over at least three religious issues (Ireland, Church Schools, Welsh Disestablishment). The erosion of the link between party and religion was greater for the young, but for the middle class, whether or not they actually went to church, the religious element was a way of identifying with the leading values of society. In *this* sense, the significance of religion in Britain, as part of a wider social order, was far from residual. But the direction of influence was reversed: religion no longer determined political loyalties, the political loyalty (of the middle class) was still supported by a religious value.

The waning of the political significance of religion – if Britain can be taken as a model – places strain on all conservative parties, as Lipset pointed out: '. . . conservative politicians know that they must find ways of securing considerable lower-class support. They cannot win without it. Conservative parties must attempt to reduce the saliency of class as the principal basis of party division by sponsoring non-class issues . . .',[9] and religion has given many of them a useful force to attract the necessary quota of the working-class or peasant vote. It need not, of course, be religion, and religion need be only one element in a wider value system which is used as an attraction.

This line of argument may go too far in stressing a relationship of religion to conservative politics. If 'Christian Democracy' is an attractive banner for conservative politicians to fly, it is also the case that these parties must be socially progressive, if they are to retain working-class support. And there is no necessary connection between religion and social conservatism. Christian Socialists were active in the West German CDU after the war, and, with their influence at work, one of the party's first post-war programmes (Ahlen 1947) was decidedly anti-capitalist in flavour. In Scandinavia, the most religious party, the Norwegian Christian People's Party, shows that the identification of religion with the right-wing does not necessarily hold in all cases, since it is in the middle of the party spectrum: 'The religiously active are least extreme in their politics and tend to shun both Socialists and Conservatives.'[10] Thus the bias of religious voting, even where it persists, is not automatically to the right. In Britain, discord between the established Church of England and the Conservative Government of the 1980s became pronounced, to the extent that one bishop described Thatcherite policies as 'verging on wickedness'.

Whether or not other countries, and particularly the Catholic ones, follow the path of the Protestant countries, it is evident that even the passive relation of religion to voting is amenable to considerable erosion in the long term, and this goes along with a general decline in religiosity, if measured in terms of formal observance, as well as in the secular influence of the church authorities.

Rural and urban contrasts

As an overwhelmingly industrial society, Britain is not typical of Western Europe in the distribution of her population, especially in its high urban concentration, with almost three-fifths living in cities of over 100,000 people; nor in the tiny proportion of the work force engaged in agriculture.* Yet in all other countries the direction of change is the same; in spite of the far higher proportion engaged in agriculture – in the southerly states, Spain, Greece, and Portugal up to 20 per cent – the trend is pointing towards a European norm of much below 10 per cent, as against around 2 per cent in Britain.

The general change can be illustrated by Denmark. In spite of her reliance on farming, the proportion employed in agriculture fell from almost 30 per cent in 1929 to below 6 per cent in the 1980s, and is still declining. At the same time, there has been a steady growth of the towns: around two-fifths of the Danes live in cities of over 100,000 people, and less than a quarter live in 'rural' districts. Before examining the political implications of these movements, we should take a further example of structural change. France, outside Paris and the larger cities, is traditionally regarded as anchored in the small town and the peasant holding. But over the past three decades there has been a virtual 'flight from the land'. As recently as the mid-1950s, farmers and agricultural workers formed over a quarter of the working population, but by the 1980s the proportion had plummeted to well below 10 per cent, more in line with the northerly states.

Even though such a basic change in occupational structure may in the end lead to greater homogeneity, to a decline in rural and urban contrasts, it is evident that the forces of social change and industrialisation do cause considerable distortion and imbalance on a *regional* level; they are factors which overlay the pre-existing rural and urban contrasts. These contrasts are not simply occupational; they are made up of cultural differences, political outlook, and economic wealth. The effect of rapid economic change and

---

* For comparisons, see the table on p. 310.

demographic movement on existing differences is considerable; and the overall effect, in the course of years, is likely to lead to a national homogeneity, in other words, that the particularities of a specifically 'rural' outlook are likely to disappear in the development of urban society. In itself, of course, there is no one rural form, as we shall see the rural vote can cover the whole political spectrum, and 'political geography' is a crystallisation of varied historical experiences. Particularly in rural areas, these can show a remarkable persistence.

Italy provides a leading example of extreme regional imbalance and with it a strikingly variegated political map. The sharpest contrast is between the high rate of economic growth of the comparatively rich and industrialised northern provinces, and until recently the persistent stagnation of the largely agricultural south. The natural process of seepage of economic benefit did not percolate southwards; instead there had to be a massive and continuing government intervention in the economy, and, with a high natural increase in population, the main safety-valve has been emigration in large numbers – roughly half to the other EEC countries and Switzerland and the other half to the urban north of Italy.

The pattern, especially in agriculture, is more diverse than this simple north-south dichotomy indicates. The nature of landholding varies greatly from one region to another and with it so do political loyalties. The north-east is typified by the small, independent farmer, the so-called direct-cultivator, who in these 'white provinces' gives strong support to the Christian Democrats. Central Italy had a widespread system of sharecropping, the *mazzadria*, and the injustices of this type of tenant farming resulted in widespread support for the Communist Party – the 'red belt' in which Communist control over local government is usual. Finally, southern agriculture is dominated by large estates, the *latifondi*, with a system of day-labouring. The high rate of emigration here hindered the emergence of a cohesive rural proletariat; political power is exercised by patronage, with the Christian Democrats naturally dominant – yet only nominally so, because there is wide scope for the influence of local notables. Thus the geographical distribution of landholding still accounts for the local variations in party supremacy; and Dogan concluded: 'In short, the political struggle in an agricultural milieu reflect(s) the conflicts between the social classes.'[11]

Although this pattern of support was partially hidden by the general advance of the Communist Party in the 1970s, it is not a transitory phenomenon – there are still similarities between the distribution of the left-wing vote now and well over fifty years ago. Sartori saw this persistence as inexplicable on purely economic grounds: 'Regions with high income have either a low or high Communist turnout. At times a rapid increase in the standard of living breaks Communist allegiance, but in other instances does not affect it in the least. Moreover, the voting behaviour of rural areas defies economic explanations.'[12] That led him to regard the critical variable as the degree of 'organisational incapsulation and cultural saturation' that the Communists (or for that matter the Christian Democrats) were able to achieve. Why this incapsulation should have arisen in the first place can be related to historical factors: much of the 'red belt' was once under papal rule, and according to Dogan, 'Where the temporal power of the Church was strong in the past, contemporary parties with a Christian orientation are weak and vice versa.'[13]

All the major parties can secure an 'incapsulation' of voting loyalties in rural areas better than they can in industrial and urban ones. The small-town and country bias of Christian Democracy is still very marked, and whilst the Communist Party was spectacularly successful in the period 1975–1985 in capturing the government of several large cities, it was also able to capitalise on the 'historical' agricultural and rural connections of the party in particular regions.

We have to read such conclusions alongside the changing rural-urban balance in Italy. By the 1980s the farm population fell to about 11 per cent, and although employment in the agricultural sector is still far higher than the average for Western Europe, the contrast should be made with the 1930s when the share was over 50 per cent. Another decade of accelerating change would even further alter the social basis of Italian politics. A greater urban concentration is also leading to an increased fluidity of party-voter relationships as industrialisation proceeds, and in consequence we should expect to see short-term fluctuations in the fortunes of the two major parties.

The phenomenon of the 'red peasant' in France was akin to that of the Communist rural vote in Italy, and there were both economic and cultural causes. Historically, the agricultural departments of the south and south-west, especially the *Massif-Central*, were very much poorer than the rest of France, a situation which persisted well into the 1960s. In contrast to Italy, the independent farmer was disposed to support the Communist Party, and in so doing his vote was quite likely to be one of general protest against the state and government – any government – rather than one of positive commitment.

One has to take account of 'cultural' factors which proved to be extraordinarily durable: 'The Revolution of 1789, by undertaking the partition of the large domains of the Church and nobility, transformed the peasants of some regions into allies of the Republic. The return of the Bourbons in 1815, with the support of the Church, renewed the question of land ownership. Thus the republicanism of many peasants was tinged with anticlericalism.'[14] The effect was to make large areas 'dechristianised' and to give a permanent left-inclination to the vote. The economic and cultural factors interlocked.

Elsewhere in Europe the Italian and French forms of agrarian Communism were not in evidence, and the normal political expression of the rural vote has been an identification with social conservatism and the established religion, and even where farming has declined in relative importance, these patterns have changed very little. To take one example, Bavaria for long had a tradition of rural backwardness – cattle-drawn ploughs were a common sight until the early 1950s. The political colouring was always deeply conservative outside the larger cities, and the Bavarian Christian-Social Union (the independent sister-party of the national CDU) is closely identified with the values of the Catholic Church. The rapid rise in the standard of living, the mechanisation of farms, and the rationalisation of previously scattered land-holdings (*Flurbereinigung*) have all altered rural political loyalties very little. The agricultural working-population has fallen from 30 to nearer 10 per cent since 1950, but the CSU has also adapted itself to the fast changing occupational structure consequent upon the growth of new industries and the tertiary sector. At the present time the party controls over half of the total Bavarian vote: traditional values have not been relinquished despite modernisation.

The conservative nature of most rural politics is well-established, but in Scandinavia another direction was taken; this was shown in the widespread occurrence of the formerly specifically 'agrarian' parties, neither sharing in the radicalism of the left nor the conservatism of the 'bourgeois' city parties; their place in the party spectrum is indicated by the general and recent change of name to 'Centre' parties. Their political importance is obvious, for they barred the way to cohesive non-socialist groupings, and frequently led to 'farmer-labour' (Red-Green) alliances. Their rise, as a Scandinavian phenomenon alone, requires explanation. Historically, the reason may be the relatively early political mobilisation of the peasantry and an independence stemming from the general lack of feudal traditions in Scandinavia.

There is no doubt that rural-urban conflict became more

embedded in the politics of this part of Europe and does much to account for the Scandinavian version of the multi-party system.* The origins of the conflict were as much cultural as they were economic; in Norway, it centred on the language-issue: the struggle to have the standard rural language accepted nationally, a form of cultural defence against the Danish-influenced language of the urban élites. Rokkan argued more generally, 'This conflict between rural claims and urban dominance goes far to explain the difference between the Scandinavian multi-party system and the English two-party system. In Scandinavia there were few and only tenuous ties between the rural and urban élites; in Norway this chasm was even deeper than in Denmark or Sweden as a result of centuries of foreign domination channelled through the cities.' He saw the basic difference in English development in the fact that the rural-urban conflict was settled *before* lower-class mobilisation got under way, whilst in Scandinavia, 'The two waves of mobilisation came close on each other's heels and one set of issues had not come anywhere near settlement before the next forced itself on the body politic.'[15] The result was a persisting double basis of cleavage, essentially a three-cornered contest – the new working class, the urban bourgeoisie, and the agrarian interests.

How far this pattern still really persists is another matter; with declining farm populations, a pure agrarian party became an anachronism, and this is conceded in the change of name to 'Centre'. The old-type rural-urban conflict is losing its basis – a substantial farm population; increasingly, issues are 'nationalised' in the context of urban society and although the outcroppings of older conflicts persist, they give way to the problems of regional imbalance. But this division is no longer a rural-urban split; it is a debate about the attraction of new industry and the rate of urbanisation, problems which appear on a regional level but which have to be settled in a national context.

Class and politics
Close to the centre of the web of influences on political loyalty are the straight economic factors. These are readily given expression in terms of social class, a common recognition of social inequality which is ultimately based on *perceived* differences in economic wealth and the consequences which stem from them. The term 'class' by itself is an abstraction – necessarily so, for it depends on a more or less arbitrary grouping of socio-economic data. Only when social groups *form* and *act cohesively* as a reaction to these

* See the diagrams, pp. 42-3 below.

differences does it become a reality. The political party is one of the main expressions of this cohesion, and class politics are an integral part of European politics. What we have said so far, however, shows that the parties and their conflicts express much more besides class interests. Indeed, nowhere in Europe can party politics be read as a straightforward translation of class issues on to the political stage.

The first comparison we can make is between the British situation and that in most of mainland Europe. Britain is a good starting-point because she is on most counts a completely urbanised society and so (arguably) a precursor of developments elsewhere. British society is also relatively homogeneous in the sense that (until the resurgence of the national issue in Wales and Scotland) there was a simple polarisation around one variable, social class. The other sources of social cleavage we have discussed have been little in evidence or have dried up. If it is accepted, that besides class explanations of politics, as Pulzer once wrote, 'all else is embellishment and detail',[16] then it does not follow that the conflict-base of the polarisation is thereby sharpened. This view was well put by Finer: 'Class is important – indeed central – in British politics only because nothing else is.'[17] This idea of the *residual* nature of class politics has to be related to a number of other changes in society – any of which, as now seems to be the case in Western Europe, can generate new lines of cleavage – and to changes in the nature of social class itself. Hence, 'residual' does not necessarily just mean 'static' or even 'attenuated', nor, if social classes are not fixed entities, will it result in a final hardening of social cleavages as suggested by the Marxist argument. Plastic as the term 'social class' is, it nevertheless conjures up ideas of cohesive blocs and the imagery of class-conflict. Yet the alternative of referring to 'socio-economic differentation', say, invites a blandness in political analysis which is just as unacceptable.

There were special features in the development of British politics, and their inter-relation gave a particular form to the political culture that resulted. Of first importance was the overriding nature of the system of social values. Evidence of that dominance was seen in the nature of the Labour Party. So strong and so pervasive were the leading values that one observer found it possible to regard even its modest challenge to the ruling order as deviant: 'Political deviance, examined from a societal level, is manifested not in working-class conservatism, but rather in electoral support for Socialism on the part of members of any social stratum. Socialist voting can be regarded as a symbolic act of deviance from the dominant values of British capitalist society.'[18] That viewpoint certainly overstated the case, but it did bring out some special features of the Labour Party, for it never broke with the leading values of the political and social establishment, was never anti-clerical, never shared in the Marxist tradition, always favoured limited reform – and yet the Labour Party, built up from the trade unions, did represent a special 'sub-culture' until, beginning in the 1960s, the 'leading values' began to crumble and the Labour Party, somewhat prematurely in view of its decline in the 1980s began to see itself as the 'natural party of government'.

The formulation of working-class conservatism as an expression of dominant class values raises the question of how these came to be enshrined in British society. The answer lies partly in the comparatively smooth way in which the evolution took place from its pre-democratic position to the filling-out of liberal democracy: it was a unified ruling class which faced the claims of mass democracy; we have just seen that in Scandinavia this was not the case. The change can be expressed alternatively by saying the critical problems of political and social development were encountered one by one, and each resolved before a new one arose. This pattern made for a high continuity of leading values and of social élites; as Norman Birnbaum pointed out: 'British history is remarkable in the continuity of its élite structure – precisely through the changes which have seen the displacement of feudal nobility by landed gentry by aristocratic magnates by new capitalists . . . A pronounced capacity to assimilate new groups with new modes of procuring wealth has frequently saved the old élites from superannuation.'[19]

The contrast with many other European states is obvious. The critical problems were often shelved or occurred simultaneously. We can see the nature of these problems and the way they can crowd in on one another in the case of Germany: 'The history of Germany in the nineteenth century might very well be written in terms of the interplay between the simultaneous problems of state and nation-building, and demands for participation and welfare. Demands for political participation, particularly on the part of the middle classes in the various German states, became assimilated into demands for national integration.'[20] And although the social élites long remained intact, the 'double-rupture' they suffered in the wake of defeat in the two world wars vanquished them and the values they represented. To a lesser extent, and with different degrees of emphasis, the same type of prolonged crisis was faced by other countries; what Otto

Kirchheimer referred to as the 'pristine beauty' of British development was largely exceptional.

Earlier we made the point that the conservative and bourgeois parties could not hope to achieve power in their own right as undiluted class parties; the necessary amount of cross-voting had to be secured by some other inducement – typically religion. The British Conservative Party did not have to induce support in this way, for it already stood as a succinct expression of social values, of which the established church was but one. The result can be shown in various forms, of which the most direct is to postulate two conditions to create a system of the British type:

- that there should be only *one* political expression of the bourgeoisie; if there is more than one major contender, then none of them can claim a monopoly of leading values;
- that given this unified political expression, then these values (especially those of a social nature) should not be challenged by the opposing class party.

In most of the European systems, only one of these conditions was met, or neither. Put briefly, working-class conservatism in Britain related very easily and in a number of ways to the dominant value system, and they almost always ran to the benefit of a single party. The ease of identification in other countries is made possible by the overt religious tie; the mainstay of many Christian Democratic parties is the lower-class Catholic worker, but the cross-cutting of loyalties works two ways: the proportion of working-class voters is only assured if the religious pull is maintained, otherwise these parties veer to becoming minority class-parties. Pre-war Austria fulfilled the first of our conditions, but not the second; the increasing strength of the post-war Austrian Socialists until the 1980s indicates that the Austrian People's Party (formerly Christian-Socials) ran into this difficulty.

The large bourgeois parties in West Germany and France may bear some resemblance to the British Conservative Party in that they fulfil the first condition in part, but neither can represent the 'unquestioned' values of society; the traumatic effect of the Nazi era prevents any party laying such a claim. In France, the RPR does extol Gaullism, yet this concept was in the past hostile to parliamentary, if not to republican values. In these two countries, the double problem the bourgeois parties face in the future is the possibility of a declining religious attraction and the certainty of the erosion of the groups (rural and small-town) for which the appeal to religion can most effectively be made. An alternative format is provided in multi-party systems where more than one bourgeois party exists and each one has a partial success in attracting working-class support; the Netherlands is the best example, and to a limited extent it is also true in Scandinavian countries. In Denmark, Norway and Sweden there have been several recent examples of 'bourgeois' coalitions ousting the once-dominant Social Democrats.

There may be a temptation to say that everyone is out of step but the British, since we have argued from the apparent 'modernity' of the British social structure – the urban society, its homogeneity leaving exposed the residual class issues. But it becomes clear that her modernity arose from special factors – resting precisely on the non-modernity of the total value system – nor are other countries likely to evolve in this way; the relationship of British conservatism to central values was the result of a long historical process. Obviously, one can go too far in explaining differences solely in 'value' terms. From other points of view, the Conservative Party in Britain is not more than a highly-successful class party. Its class skew is evident, since it always secures 90 per cent of the upper-middle class vote and three-quarters of the 'solid' middle class. To this reliable base, it has been able to add up to a third of the working-class vote, sometimes appreciably more. Yet the same order of effect is reached in other countries, singly in some, by an aggregation of the bourgeois parties in others.

The Socialist parties have to be regarded from a different perspective, for unlike the bourgeois parties they have usually relied on a specific class-appeal, and in fact this call to solidarity had to operate against all the counter-attractions of the leading value-system of society. The mass-based parties of the left were not only extraordinarily successful in mobilising the working-class vote, they also proved to be extremely resilient once they had established their position: apart from the failure of the German Communist Party after 1945 for special reasons, the electoral balance of the left has either been maintained or has been improved – one only has to refer to the contemporary situation of the left in countries with a widely different historical situation – such as France, Sweden, Greece, and Spain, all in the late 1980s with Socialist or Social Democratic governments – to appreciate the extent to which a broad 'class' designation has remained attractive, and that despite generally rising standards of living which, at least for individuals, has given the promise of upward social mobility.

This stability on the left combined with increasing working-class support has not been the result of unadulterated insistence on class issues. In the past this appeal was combined with an open anti-clericalism or a defence of parliamentary institutions, but these are no longer the rallying calls they once were. Depending on their particular support, left-wing parties anyway speak in rather different voice to farmers, smallholders, car-workers, or government employees, but these are mainly tactical ploys. The really important change has been that attempt to increase the potential of voting support, that is, by making appeals to the relatively affluent workers – not to an underprivileged class.

This drive to go beyond the traditional limits of left-wing support, beyond the working-class, is fraught with consequences. It is a basic change, and it is no longer sufficient to make a static juxtaposition of 'class' and 'party'; neither can be regarded as fixed entities. We shall take up the discussion of this theme in the following chapter, so that here a brief illustration of party change will suffice. At the turn of the century, the German Social Democrats formed the largest and the most orthodox of European Socialist parties. Its strict class emphasis gained it only a minority of votes – the 'one-third' barrier. This restriction, and the superficially Marxist programme that went with it, persisted after 1945. Faced by defeats at successive elections and the undeniable affluence, dubbed the 'economic miracle', the pressure for fundamental party reform proved irrestibile. The turning-point came with the 1959 Godesberg Conference of the party. A new party programme was penned; almost overnight, the SPD became a 'People's Party' – calling to all, irrespective of class, indeed specifically denying that it was a class party. In place of Marxist doctrine, it put a broad humanitarian idealism, and turned its back firmly on any anti-clerical sentiment. The 1959 reforms paid off: at the three elections prior to the new programme, the party averaged 30 per cent of the vote; but subsequently support rose sharply – the SPD became the largest party with 45 per cent in 1972. This sketch is open to other interpretations – one can argue that the party would have gained increased support *whatever* it did. It is probably more convincing to see the change resulting from a changing class awareness, and, appreciating, this alteration, the Social Democratic Party, particularly its leaders, attempted to redefine the content of Socialism.

New cleavages?

Our review of the social bases of politics thus far has concentrated on the 'historical' pillars of West European politics, and – in varying degrees – they can still be regarded as providing the essence of party conflict and tradition. Yet it would be wrong to suppose that these primary influences should always enjoy undisputed sway and that, given the radical changes that have taken place in the social structure of advanced industrialised societies, no new ingredients for social cleavage should be present. It is true that in the post-1945 era up to the 1960s, it seemed that the old sources of political loyalty were withering away without others taking their place, to leave behind a bland plateau of 'non-ideological' politics, but from the perspective of the later 1980s it is apparent that neither supposition was true: old loyalties are capable of rejuvenation, and they have been joined by new values and political movements.

The most influential theory of contemporary political change has been the idea of 'post-industrial' society – and is thus of particular relevance to the politics of the advanced societies of Western Europe.[21] The basis of the theory lies in the changing structure of the economy, its ability to produce a high level of affluence, and the related effect on the value structure for a significant and growing section of the population – with the emergence of so-called post-materialist values. Those new values lead in turn to a change in political attitudes and behaviour, and they become increasingly at odds with established parties and with conventional forms of political behaviour.

The changing structure of the economy is best related to the growth in the tertiary sector of employment and the decline in the primary and secondary ones, agriculture and industry. The expansion of the service sector, more generally that of white-collar employment, is accompanied by a high level of technical innovation, and both are indicative of growing productive capacity and economic growth. The social effects of these changes are seen in the decline of poverty and increased leisure, but the really vital effect is evident in the rising levels of education – which results partly from the demands of the economy but is also a reflection of the material well-being of society. The expansion of college and university education in particular greatly increases the size of the educated élite, so much so that it becomes an important social stratum in its own right. At the same time, the consequences for the value system of this expanded stratum become apparent: it is no longer tightly geared to furthering prosperity and industrial progress, no longer wedded to the 'work ethic', but more concerned with non-material values and the quality of life.

The process of change, it is argued, is necessarily fairly gradual, for only a relatively small section of the population is directly affected, and it is primarily the younger age groups which are first likely to question the established lines of political conflict – those reflecting the cleavages in industrial society and enshrined in the major parties. However, the changes are progressive, and the educated élite is also well positioned to influence wider opinion. At the outset, the fact that post-materialist values are relevant to only a small minority means that reliance on conventional political activity is likely to have little effect, so that resort to direct action and 'protest' is likely to be more efficacious. But it is not only a question of means: the fact is that post-materialist values place a strong emphasis on the value of participation in its own right and are directly opposed to the popular passivity fostered by the 'old politics' of parliamentary élitism.[22] Moreover, the harbingers of the 'new politics' – relatively leisured, articulate, not bound by the constraints and traditions of the 'work society' – are ideally placed to engage in forms of confrontation with orthodox authority.

The concept of the 'new politics' is partly represented by the value set on participation, but its major strength lies perhaps in providing an ideological counter-thrust to the values of industrial society. Since the latter is posited on a belief in continuing economic growth as the way of securing social progress, post-materialism questions that belief. Its most persuasive argument is not that economic growth is necessarily in itself undesirable but the impossibility of maintaining it without irretrievably damaging people's environment. It is no accident that environmentalists and ecologists have become the spearhead of post-material politics.

The arrival of the 'Greens' in Western Germany can be taken as symptomatic of a more general development throughout Western Europe. Their 'direct methods' in protesting against the siting of nuclear power stations, their close association with the peace movement in opposition to nuclear weapons, their marked reliance on support from the young and better educated sections of society, their uneasy relationship with the conventional parties and the entire parliamentary process – all these characteristics support the picture of a new cleavage in German society which cannot be accommodated in the spectrum of 'left' and 'right'.

No one would doubt that there has been a substantial change wrought in West European politics since the late 1960s, whether or not the rubric of the 'new politics' is employed and whatever form of measurement is taken – changes in values and attitudes, the incidence of protest behaviour, the entry of ecological and related movements into mainstream politics. However, that does not automatically mean that the new politics will supersede the old politics or that post-materialist values will become the predominant ones for Western society.

Firstly, it can be argued that post-materialism is best related to a particular phase of European development rather than representing a general trend. Economic security cannot be taken for granted, and permanently high levels of unemployment affect the outlook of even those who do not have immediate worries. To the extent that social values and priorities are changing, we should not expect to witness a wholesale decline of established parties, that is, those which in their origins represented quite different aspirations and values: they are quite capable of absorbing selected aspects of the new politics and its claims without jeopardising their own electoral position or completely subordinating their traditional appeals. Seen in that light, green and related new politics parties could have a catalytic effect rather than ever becoming important in their own right. Their function could well be that of agenda-setting, raising new issues while remaining on the side-lines of political power. The West German Greens accord with this kind of role, both generally with regard to the political system and more specifically for their effect on the German left. Indeed, many of the demands of the Greens can be identified as 'new left': an injection of fresh ideas into a largely moribund form of democratic socialism. However, there are important variations from one country to another and the equivalent green parties in, say, Austria, Belgium and Switzerland certainly could not be identified with the radical left.

A second reason for treating the idea of the new politics as a significant new cleavage line in European societies with caution involves the question of political commitment. Unlike the historical bases of European cleavages which had a secure structural rooting in society, the new politics lacks such foundation – it is at most a kind of value-sharing community which is not attached to any permanently identifiable social group or stratum.

If it is the case that the appearance of a new cleavage in West European societies is a matter of doubt – at least as far as the impact of the new politics is concerned – then we are still left with the problem of interpreting current trends in the social bases of politics. Throughout Western Europe there is evidence of a loosening attachment to political parties. This process can be seen in declining figures for electoral turn-out, in the lower levels of partisan commitment and party identification, and in the rising scale of electoral volatility. These several indications do not necessarily imply that 'politics' has somehow become less important, but rather that it is becoming more difficult for parties to mobilise and harness voters. Socio-economic issues have retained their salience, but political choice depends more on issue-voting than on a blanket endorsement of a party's programme and tradition.

The argument for a growing electoral dealignment in Western Europe is persuasive, but it has to be read in conjunction with other developments in order to gain an overall picture. There is no doubt, for instance, that there have been substantial changes in the political culture of West European societies and that the old models of the 'civic culture' and 'democratic élitism' are no longer properly applicable in an era associated with protest politics, minority dissent, the questioning of authority and claims for greater participation.

In all these respects, the changing social bases of politics has made political parties increasingly vulnerable, and West European politics is in a peculiar state of flux. Quite contrary elements are present: the traditional parties of left and right still maintain dominant positions at the same time as they have sought to make a wide 'catch-all' appeal; the impetus of active commitment associated with the new politics paradoxically coexists with a widespread disengagement from party politics. It would be hazardous to predict whether this diffusion will remain permanent or whether European society is in the throes of a realignment which could result in clear lines of social division once more becoming apparent.

Social cleavages and party systems
Some of the relevant issues regarding social cleavage and consensus which we have discussed in this chapter can usefully be summarised in diagram form. This can also be related to the prevalent types of party system, though the models set out below are not intended exactly to correspond with particular systems. The most useful distinction to be made is between 'homogeneous' and 'sectional' societies in the sense used by Blondel and defined on p. 13 above. However, it is apparent that there are both different types as well as degrees of homogeneity and sectionality; the diagrams show the main variations. The main direction of party formation is along the major source(s) of social cleavage, indicated by a continuous line. The discontinuous lines represent weak, alternative lines of polarisation, and may or may not lead to party formation along them. If they do not, the discontinuous line may represent strong consensual elements which unite the whole society or sections of it. The lettering, A–E, has been used so that the diagrams are left with general application; illustrative party formations are in brackets.

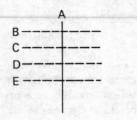

[Labour]   [Conservative]

homogeneous society

One major source of social cleavage (A). The discontinuous lines, B–E, represent cross-cutting affiliations which modify the effect of the prime division (e.g. A = socio-economic class). Party formation takes place either side of the 'A' line to give a stable two-party system with limited polarisation. The degree of polarisation depends on the number of society-wide unifying factors.

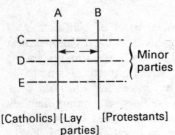

[Catholics] [Lay [Protestants]
parties]

mixed homogeneous – sectional society

'A' and 'B' are two major sources of cleavage. They do not reinforce one another (hence the diverging arrows) and there are three major sources of party formation. The potential fragmentation of the system is prevented by numerous cross-cutting affiliations (C–E) which may act as minor sources of party formation. The result may be a stable multi-party system. The vertical 'pillarisation' of Dutch Society is directly applicable here.

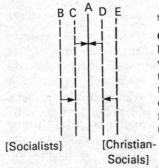

[Socialists]   [Christian-
Socials]

sectional society (1)

Only one major source of social cleavage, but the other politically-significant variables are not randomly distributed throughout the population. They therefore tend to confirm and reinforce the prime division (hence converging arrows). The result is an unstable two-party situation (e.g. pre-war Austria).

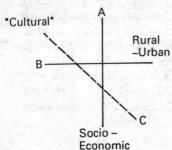

sectional society (2a)

Two major lines of cleavage running athwart one another. A limited multi-party system results: this will be stable if minor cleavages cut across two or more quadrants. This type is applicable to Scandinavian systems with the rural-urban cultural cleavage persisting alongside the socio-economic one.

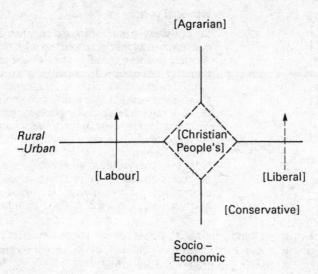

sectional society (2b)

The Norwegian party system illustrates the practical application of the general 'Scandinavian' type. The five parties shown share 75 per cent of the vote; four of these make an appeal across at least one line of cleavage – e.g. Labour to small farmers and fishing communities. The Agrarians are now the Centre Party.

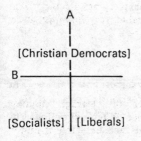

sectional society (2c)

The four quadrants of type (2a) may not be of equal significance, i.e. the effect of one of the prime divisions is nullified or overridden for certain sections of society. The T-shaped variation is of practical significance: socio-economic class only partially operative ('A' partly discontinuous, whilst a clerical/anti-clerical division, 'B', persists throughout).

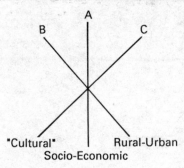

sectional society (3)

Several cleavages are apparent and they do not stand in a close relationship with one another. If these are all very strong, then the party-situation will be one of numerous 'armed camps' and likely to fragment. If they are weak, the result will be a moderately unstable multi-party system. This third major type of sectional society corresponds to Duverger's portrayal of the Fourth Republic in his *Political Parties*; however, the various 'segments' in the diagram do not show the full range of party possibilities. *Three* major cleavages, in permutation, give *eight* party directions.

Thus Lipset* shows the overlapping of cleavages in French politics giving a party configuration related to three competing traditions, and applying to the Fourth Republic:

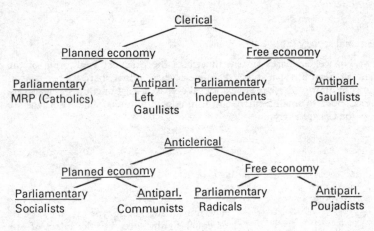

All except the Left Gaullists represent independent parties. The planned economy/free economy axis corresponds to a left/right division. The parliamentary/anti-parliamentary division is an amalgam of historical factors and social class influences.

* S. M. Lipset, *The First New Nation*, Heinemann, 1964, p. 297.

Notes and references

1. These four categories are indicated by S. M. Lipset and S. Rokkan (eds.), *Party Systems and Voter Alignments: Cross-national Perspectives*, Collier-Macmillan,

1967, p. 14. They give four critical lines of cleavage: workers – employers and owners; churches – government; primary – secondary economy; subject – dominant culture.

2. There is difficulty in determining which variables are independent and which are related to other structural conditions. For the 'age' factor: 'We must not ask how old an elector is but when it was that he was young.' D. Butler and D. Stokes, *Political Change in Britain*, Macmillan, 1969, p. 59. Of course, the *effects* of age-sex differences can be momentous. See M. Dogan in *Party Systems and Voter Alignments*, pp. 159–67. The excess of women over men voters, notably in West Germany and Italy, ran to the benefit of Christian Democracy. A German Social Democrat once complained, 'The woman's vote has ruined the party.'

3. J. Blondel, *An Introduction to Comparative Government*, Weidenfeld and Nicolson, 1969, p. 53. He illustrates the term 'sectionalism': 'A country will therefore be sectional if Roman Catholics, for instance, are not spread evenly ("normally") among the various classes, but clustered mainly among workers or in some areas. The same would be true of races or any other social variable.' The way in which the word 'homogeneous' is used in the text also follows Blondel's formulation.

4. S. M. Lipset, *Political Man*, Heinemann, rev. ed. 1983, p. 77.

5. R. Rose and D. Urwin, 'Social Cohesion, Political Parties and Strains in Regimes' in M. Dogan and R. Rose (eds.), *European Politics: A Reader*, Macmillan, 1971, p. 220.

6. F. C. Engelmann, 'Austria: The Pooling of Opposition'., in R. A. Dahl (ed.), *Political Oppositions in Western Democracies*, New Haven: Yale University Press, 1966, pp. 263–4.

7. V. Wright, 'The French General Election of March 1978: *La Divine Surprise*', in *Conflict and Consensus in France*, Frank Cass, 1979, p. 39.

8. Butler and Stokes, op. cit., p. 129 and p. 124.

9. S. M. Lipset, *Revolution and Counterrevolution: Change and Persistence in Social Structures*, Heinemann, 1969, p. 164.

10. S. Rokkan, 'Norway: Geography, Religion and Social Class', in *Party Systems and Voter Alignments*, p. 422.

11. M. Dogan, 'Political Cleavage and Social Stratification in France and Italy' in *Party Systems and Voter Alignments* op. cit., p. 149.

12. G. Sartori, 'European Political Parties: The Case of Polarised Pluralism', in R. A. Dahl and D. E. Neubauer (eds.), *Readings in Modern Political Analysis*, Prentice-Hall, 1968, p. 122.

13. M. Dogan in *Party Systems and Voter Alignments*, p. 18.

14. M. Dogan in *Party Systems and Voter Alignments*, p. 183. For a study of 'historical persistence', see L. Wylie, *Village in Vaucluse*, New York, Harvard University Press, 1964.

15. S. Rokkan, 'Norway: Numerical Democracy and Corporate Pluralism', in *Political Oppositions in Western Democracies*, p. 79.

16. P. G. J. Pulzer, *Political Representation and Elections in Britain*, George Allen and Unwin, 1967, p. 98.

17. S. E. Finer, *Comparative Government*, Allen Lane, 1970, p. 142.

18. F. Parkin, 'Working Class Conservatives: A Theory of Political Deviance', *British Journal of Sociology*, (18), 1967, pp. 278–90.

19. N. Birnbaum, *The Crisis of Industrial Society*, Oxford University Press, 1970, p. 17.

20. G. A. Almond and G. B. Powell, *Comparative Politics: A Developmental Approach*, Boston: Little, Brown, 1966, p. 138.

21. In particular, see D. Bell, *The Coming of Post-Industrial Society*, New York: Basic Books, 1973; M. Hancock (ed.), *Politics in the Post-Welfare State*, Columbia University Press, 1972.

22. S. Barnes, M. Kaase and others, *Political Action in Five Western Democracies*, Sage Publications, 1979, analyses the attitudinal basis of protest and unconventional political behaviour.

Additional references

E. Allardt and Y. Littunen (eds.), *Cleavages, Ideologies and Party Systems*, Helsinki: The Westermarck Society, 1964.

M. Anderson, 'The Renaissance of Territorial Minorities in Western Europe', *West European Politics*, vol. 1/2, May 1978.

M. S. Archer and S. Giner (eds.), *Contemporary Europe: Class, Status and Power*, Weidenfeld and Nicolson, 1971.

S. Berger, (ed.), *Religion in West European Politics*, Frank Cass, 1982.

S. Berger, *Peasants against Politics*, Harvard University Press, 1972.

J. Blondel, *Voters, Parties and Leaders: The Social Fabric of British Politics*. Penguin Books, rev. ed. 1979.

I. Crewe (ed.), *Elites in Western Democracy*, Croom Helm, 1974.

C. Crouch and A. Pizzorno, *The Resurgence of Class Conflicts in Western Europe since 1968*, (2 volumes), Macmillan, 1978.

H. Daalder, 'Parties, Elites and Political Developments in Western Europe', in J. LaPalombara and M. Weiner (eds.), *Political Parties and Political Development*, Princeton University Press, 1966.

R. A. Dahl and E. R. Tufte, *Size and Democracy*, Oxford University Press, 1974.

R. Dahrendorf, *Class and Class Conflict in Industrial Society*, Routledge and Kegan Paul, rev. ed. 1972.

R. Dalton, *Citizen Politics in Western Democracies*, Chatham, N. J.: Chatham House, 1988.

S. Flanagan and R. Dalton, 'Parties under Stress: Realignment and Dealignment in Advanced Industrial Societies', *West European Politics*, January 1984.

A. Giddens, *The Class Structure of Advanced Societies*, Hutchinson, 1973.

S. Giner and M. S. Archer, *Contemporary Europe: Social Structures and Cultural Patterns*, Routledge and Kegan Paul, 1978.

J. Hayward and R. Berki (eds.) *State and Society in Contemporary Europe*, Oxford: Martin Robertson, 1979.

R. Inglehart, *The Silent Revolution: Changing Values and Political Styles Among Western Publics*, Princeton University Press, 1977.

R. Irving, *Christian Democracy in France*, Allen and Unwin, 1973.

J. E. Lane and S. Ersson, *Politics and Society in Western Europe*, Sage, 1987.

A. Lijphart, 'Language, Religion, Class and Party Choice', in R. Rose (ed.), *Electoral Participation: A Comparative Analysis*, Sage Publications, 1980.

K. D. McRae (ed.), *Consociational Democracy: Political Accommodation in Segmented Societies*, Toronto: McClelland and Stewart, 1974.

D. Martin, *A General Theory of Secularization*, Oxford: Blackwell, 1978.

E. Nordlinger, *The Working Class Tories*, MacGibbon and Kee, 1967.

F. Parkin, *Class Inequality and Political Order*, MacGibbon and Kee, 1971.

F. Parkin, *Marxism and Class Theory: A Bourgeois Critique*, Tavistock Publications, 1979.

T. Pogantke, 'New Political Party Systems: The Emergence of a New Type of Party'. *West European Politics*, January 1987.

N. Poulantzas, *Political Power and Social Classes*, New Left Books, 1973.

D. Robertson, *Class and the British Electorate*, Oxford: Martin Robertson, 1983.

S. Rokkan and D. Unwin, *Economy, Territory, Identity: Politics of West European Peripheries*, Sage, 1983.

S. Rokkan, 'The Growth and Structuring of Mass Politics in Western Europe', *Scandinavian Political Studies*, Yearbook 5, Oslo: University Bookstore.

R. Rose (ed.), *Electoral Behavior: A Comparative Handbook*, Collier-Macmillan, 1974.

S. Rothman, *European Society and Politics*, Indianapolis: Bobbs Merrill, 1970.

M. van Schendelen (ed.), *Consociationalism, Pillarisation and Conflict Management in the Low Countries*, Rotterdam: Erasmus University, 1986.

S. Tarrow, *Peasant Communism in Southern Italy*, Yale University Press, 1967.

P. Thorburn, 'Political Generations: The Case of Class and Party in Britain', *European Journal of Political Research*, June 1977.

D. Urwin, *From Ploughshare to Ballotbox: The Politics of Agrarian Defence in Europe*, Oslo: Universitetsforlaget, 1980.

J. Whyte, *Catholics in Western Democracies: A Study in Political Behaviour*. Dublin: Gill and MacMillan, 1981.

A. Zuckerman, 'New Approaches to Political Cleavages: A Theoretical Introduction', *Comparative Political Studies*, 1982.

See also the references on pp. 80–2 below.

3 Pluralist Politics: Parties and Interests

The inertia of party traditions

Of all the expressions of liberal democracy, it is the political party which is the summation of pluralist traditions. It is not only that the parties enshrine the competitive spirit; they also show a remarkable continuity and resilience. And the fact that they arose when they did, and how they did, has had consequences for the remote future. To this extent, the parties are factors in their own right, a part of social reality, to which other social forces have to adjust.

Once established, parties develop their own traditions. These may become permanent symbols of what a party 'stands for' in its own eyes or those of the electorate. Parties also build up a permanent organisation and within it a means of leadership selection, which from the viewpoint of party officials and the leadership groups is too valuable an investment to be readily jettisoned. Alongside its symbols and organisation, the party fosters a voter-tradition; party support is hardly ever ephemeral, its core element is firmly rooted in certain sectors of the population, and voting patterns are transferred intact from one generation to another. The sum total of these traditions and vested interests imparts an inertia to the established parties which is difficult to break.

European parties encompass a variety of historical traditions, and these traditions can be represented as a number of characteristic 'streams'. The table (pp. 122–3) shows how the European traditions can be related to the parties currently represented in the various parliaments. Most are readily identifiable in the wide spread of a multi-party system, but in others they are contained within a few major parties. It is also instructive to compare this pattern with Michael Smart's analysis of party representation in Western Europe which traces the developments back to 1946.* He isolates a number of the prominent streams and shows – by aggregating the experience of all the countries – how the fortunes of the major 'political families' have ebbed and flowed over a long period. The pattern is strongly influenced by the more populous

* See below, pp. 378-89.

states, but the features of the general European trend are usually applicable to the smaller countries as well. Although certain years show a shifting 'centre of gravity', it is hard to adduce any decisive watershed, after which a new and permanent trend becomes apparent – although it may now be the case that the 'communist tradition' has entered into an irreversible decline and that the 'new politics' is now to be regarded as a permanent acquisition.

This constancy of the political streams, and in turn the tenacity of the individual parties is a hallmark of the European party systems, and it is an integral part of the balance maintained in Western democracies. This stability accords with the conclusion reached in 1970 by Rose and Urwin from the study of a number of party systems. 'The electoral strength of most parties in Western nations since the war had changed very little from election to election ... or within the lifespan of a generation ... A first priority of social scientists is to explain the *absence* of change in a far from static period in political history.'[1] Although a decade later the emphasis had shifted to the study of change, with analyses stressing the growth of electoral volatility since the 1960s, together with the possible emergence of new cleavages, as well as the rise of new parties and 'social movements', terms such as 'electoral earthquake' used to describe the Danish elections of 1973, proved to be an exaggerated reaction to the changes. Thus, towards the end of the 1980s both the realignment of voters *within* broad ideological 'blocs', and the ability of the established parties to adapt to the changed environment were just as evident as the tendency to fragmentation of the blocs themselves, so that the evidence of continuity was at least as significant as change.[2]

On occasion the hold of party inertia can suddenly be broken. Severe discontinuities in the political system can destroy long-established parties or weaken them past recovery. Thus 1945 marked a definite new era for some countries, particularly Germany and Italy; yet it is also true that for most other West European countries the former party patterns quickly reasserted themselves – the party system towards the *end* of the Fourth French Republic was essentially similar to that of the Third, and this was true for the smaller European states whether they had escaped German occupation or not. The rise of new social forces is also a factor making for long-term change, but these may be slow-moving and for long contained within the existing party system. This was not so in the late nineteenth and early twentieth centuries since existing systems were then in a state of initial flux. Brand-new parties frequently jump into the limelight but their ability to make a lasting impact depends on the ability of the older ones to meet their challenge; these have to adapt to changing social conditions by making gradual changes in their appeal, but even if they fail to respond, a loyal section of the electorate will keep them going for many years.

Patterns of the present-day can usually be traced back to the nineteenth century, and particularly to the initial growth of party systems on a restricted franchise; the original basis of party cleavage could be summed up as conservative-traditional versus liberal-progressive, with little attention paid to the non-enfranchised majority of the population. Yet within this restricted fold various polarities existed: bourgeois-nobility, rural-urban, clerical-anticlerical. The precise pattern for any country depended on the extent and social distribution of these cleavages and remained at least until the mass of the people gained the vote. Even afterwards, the grip of the older parties was sufficient to ensure that the advent of peasant and working-class politics was only an amendment to the party system, not its total restructuring.

The rapid extension of the franchise in the late nineteenth and early twentieth centuries and the equally rapid rise of Social Democracy at the same time posed several problems for the established parties. Part of the challenge was organisational, a move from the old-type 'parties of notables' and 'individual representation' towards new, mass parties. Inevitably, the Social Democratic parties led the field. Their aim of achieving Socialism by means of the democratic parliamentary institutions required a mass organisation to deliver the working-class vote and the creation of manifold links between party and member: the party acted as the focus of working-class loyalty and aspiration. The speed with which they advanced put great pressure on the other parties. One of the first expressions of Social Democracy, and for long the most powerful, was the German movement, originating in 1863 with Ferdinand Lassalle's *Allgemeiner Deutscher Arbeiterverein*, and by the turn of the century almost all West European countries had a well-organised working-class party. Thus the Finnish Social Democrats, one of the youngest of the Scandinavian parties, quickly built up a mass membership – a ratio of one member to every three voters by 1907 – and in 1916 it actually held an absolute majority in parliament with 47 per cent of the popular vote.

So quickly and naturally did Social Democracy become an integral part of the political scene, that the question originally posed by Werner Sombart in 1906, 'Why is there no Socialism in the United States?', may seem to be a purely American problem rather than a European one; yet it can be argued that it is the particular European circumstances which have to be explained. A necessary condition for Social Democracy was the rapid industrial and urban growth in the nineteenth century; a contributory one may well have been what Leon Epstein terms a 'residual feudal sense of class identification' which made the working class in Europe especially responsive to a class appeal. But were these two factors sufficient in themselves? Epstein argued that the critical condition lay in the *timing* of the working-class entry into politics, and for strong Socialist parties to develop it was necessary that, 'The suffrage on which parties are based came when large numbers of urban industrial workers were already present.'[3] In this way, the class-situation, and the sense of identity which went with it, quickly determined the nature of working-class politics once the vote was won.

All of these conditions contrasted with the situation in the United States – most importantly, the sequence of timing was reversed. Even if one allows for the great carry-over of older class values in Europe, or points to the greater social mobility in the United States, as Sombart did, it is clear that these have long since ceased to be differentiating factors. Class-*related* politics are important in the United States as they are in Europe, but the continued absence of class-*based* parties in the one and their presence in the other, underlines the particular way in which European politics has developed and the inertia of political traditions which the parties crystallise.

Faced with this challenge from the organised working class – and largely a unified one until Communism offered a more militant alternative from 1919 onwards – the bourgeois parties had a number of choices, as well as a number of restrictions. Their earlier establishment had already given a permanent expression to some cleavages in society; these could not simply be eradicated in the face of the Social Democratic threat, and the problem of securing a mass vote could not easily be overcome. Britain was largely exceptional in both respects: the party system had avoided fragmentation before the arrival of the mass vote, and the two parties, Conservatives and Liberals, continued their ruling position for some time by attracting a large part of the newly enfranchised electorate. The more normal picture was of four or even more parties (orthodox conservative, one or two varieties of liberals, agrarian and religious parties) ante-dating Social Democracy and often by their nature unsuited to make a wider appeal. They either waned rapidly, as did the Liberals in Belgium and Italy once the franchise was extended, or they carved out a fairly modest place for themselves with a sure, if restricted, clientele.

However, some were well-suited to make an appeal to the

working class. We saw earlier that religion offers a means of securing a class-compromise, protecting the existing social order and securing a proportion of the mass vote. Such a development came fairly early in the Low Countries. The Social-Christians in preponderantly Roman Catholic Belgium have been the leading government party since 1884. Their victory over the anti-clerical Liberals in the long drawn-out battle over church-state relations from the 1840s onwards (centering on the schools issue) led them in the end to become defenders of the constitutional order, with the approval and advice from Pope Leo XII at the end of the century: 'In the present state of modern society, the system of freedom is favourable to the Church. Belgian Catholics must not only refrain from attacking, they must also defend the Constitution.'[4] Belgian Catholicism thus avoided becoming identified with conservative reaction. The mass-based party, underpinned by Church lay organisations, conservative yet fully constitutional and socially enlightened, gave a strong alternative to Belgian Socialism. It was a powerful formula which others later were to emulate.

It was not immediately applicable to other countries. In Germany, the Catholics were just a strong minority, most concerned to defend Catholic interests in a hostile environment. Indeed, the success of the Catholic Centre Party in permanently harnessing a fifth of the vote meant that there was little chance of creating a large, moderate conservative party unless religious differences were settled first. In Italy, the force of anticlericalism and the dominance of the Liberals until the First World War worked fatefully in another direction. Because of the struggles of the Vatican with the Italian state, a papal edict prevented Italian Catholics from taking any part in politics. These restrictions were only lifted gradually, and it was not until 1919 that Don Luigi Sturzo received permission to form a Catholic People's Party; this had a radical programme of social and land reform. With the collapse of the Liberal Party, whose hold on Italian politics was made possible by Catholic 'self-denial' and the limited franchise (even after the 1913 reform less than 25 per cent of males had the vote), the Catholic People's Party stood a chance of taking the place of the Liberal Party. However, its appearance was belated and gave insufficient time to remould Italian politics before Mussolini's successful bid for power.

The weakness of the Liberal parties in Germany and Italy was evident elsewhere, and always became drastic when the vote widened. The Swiss Radicals together with the Old Liberals still share a quarter of the total vote, the last stronghold of European liberalism, but the Radicals experienced a rapid decline after 1919. Even without the mass vote, Liberalism suffered notoriously from a lack of cohesion, as it did in Britain. In the Netherlands after 1885 there were always two, sometimes three, Liberal parties. The same was the case in Germany: the Liberals first split in 1861, and (with new party labels) this dualism continued afresh in the Weimar Republic, and in Germany, as elsewhere, quite disparate social forces were behind the liberal banner, ranging from constitutional-radicals to power-hungry nationalists, the front-runners for heavy industry. It was rarely a united class-interest, and not one which for long could attract a large part of the working-class vote.

The fact that Liberalism tended to have a narrow class appeal, and that the religious parties were often handicapped by religious differences or their association with reactionary forces, meant that the challenge of Social Democracy was usually met on a piecemeal basis: a bourgeois coalition, failing that, even the conditional acceptance of a minority position. The working-alliance of the non-Socialist parties in the Netherlands proved quite equal to the task; the various religious parties were able to make an inter-class appeal, and these with the help of the Liberals made the Dutch Socialists an isolated and minority party. In Scandinavia, the bourgeois parties were put in a minority position, but the Social Democrats, in falling short of an absolute majority, had to rely on some other party to maintain it in power. Here we have the Scandinavian phenomenon of the 'Red-Green' alliance, and with variations this was the pivot of Scandinavian politics dating from the 1930s which only comparatively recently broke apart. The 'Green' or Agrarian parties had an important bridging function in these countries, containing Social Democracy and at the same time preventing the formation of a homogeneous non-socialist bloc. The fragmentation of the bourgeois parties did not have dire effects, for not only were the Social Democrats contained by the need for coalition, or at least voting support, they were also amongst the first of the European Socialist parties to move from a radical to a moderate reformist programme.

We can draw together the threads of this discussion of party development by examining the later consequences for three countries which initially failed to create a mass and unified party of the moderate right – Italy, West Germany, and France. The intermediate consequence was a right-wing political radicalisation, but the later development has been a consolidation of the moderate right. After 1945, the Belgian prototype of Christian Democracy was a model for the class-compromise reached in Italy and West

Germany. As the pre-war situation in Austria showed, however, the mere existence of a 'Christian' party could just as easily exacerbate class conflict unless the churches were prepared to play a passive role in political affairs. This orientation is implied in Fogarty's definition of Christian Democracy as, '. . . a movement of those who aim to solve – with the aid of Christian principles and "democratic" techniques – that range of temporal problems which the Church has repeatedly and solemnly declared to lie within the "supreme" competence of lay society, and outside direct ecclesiastical control.'[5] If the clerical hierarchies were prepared to accept this self-denying ordinance, then the Church could provide a loose framework of commitment, and within it a wide scope for political compromise. This formula worked successfully in the case of Germany, and with more hesitation in Italy – the clergy and the Vatican somewhat regretfully allowed the Christian Democratic politicians to make the running. In Austria, the refurbished People's Party (previously the Christian-Socials) cuts its clerical connections and was declared not to be a 'successor party', and though 'linked to a great and proud tradition' became 'young', even 'revolutionary' after 1945.

The success of Christian Democracy did not extend to France, and some of the instability of the post-war years can be ascribed to the failure of the MRP (*Mouvement Républicain Populaire*). Born in the spirit of the Resistance in 1944, the MRP was the political expression of radical Catholicism. The new party shouldered the full responsibility of government throughout the Fourth Republic, but the party, with its radical outlook, failed to win the confidence of the Catholic voter. After the first flush of post-war success, it rapidly dwindled to become another small party of the centre. Its support sank from over five and a half million in 1946 to two million by the end of the Fourth Republic. Its failure was due in part to the essentially conservative nature of French Catholicism; moreover, it never seemed to fit properly into the French party system. Efforts in the Fifth Republic to create a widely-based Democratic Centre were not successful either. The evolution of a moderate and mass right-wing party in France came from Gaullism, without an overt religious appeal but still relying on the support of the faithful – and in the first place that was a conservative vote. A delayed effect of de Gaulle's personal appeal was the creation of a party independent of its founder, although still embodying his values. Although de Gaulle treated his Rally of the French People and its successors, the UNR and UDR, as a supporters' club – since parties were for him a necessary evil as they always tended to play the parliamentary game – the following that grew up round him during the first decade of the Fifth Republic was not dissipated when he left the stage, and until the Gaullists lost the presidential leadership to Giscard d'Estaing in 1974, they were a self-confident governing force, and after the Socialist landslide in 1981 Gaullism still represents the mainstay of bourgeois opposition.

Whatever the precise path that was taken – the creation of a single unified party or a combination of two or more – the moderate right managed to find a tolerably unified expression and thus balance the success of class mobilisation on the left. The formula adopted had to secure the bulk of the middle-class vote along with a good slice of the lower income groups, peasant, manual or white-collar worker. With the parties of the left anchored in their apparently favourable class position, Christian Democratic parties in particular still managed to operate a successful flanking movement. The boot was thus on the other foot: the powerful momentum of the class-based parties on the left lost ground to the inter-class alternative – mass parties, weak in ideology, but with an even greater voting potential.

The new formula, embodied in the idea of a 'catch-all' party, may have had its prototype in Christian Democracy, but it was of general application. Moreover, if it were to prove successful, then it would make the old bases of European politics – especially its class foundations – increasingly redundant. Did it mean that we should no longer think in terms of 'left' and 'right'?

Perpetuation of Left and Right

The basic argument behind the catch-all party was that the socio-economic changes experienced in Western Europe in the era after 1945 had radically altered the class structure of society, that the prolonged experience of increasing affluence and occupational change had created a 'new middle class', and the new class – in time also the most numerous one – would no longer fit with the old model of class conflict. Otto Kirchheimer was a major proponent of that viewpoint: 'One may justifiably say that diminished social polarisation and diminished political polarisation are going hand in hand.'[6] In consequence of the diminishing social and political cleavages, the old 'class' ideologies would prove steadily less attractive – as would the old-type parties which propagated them. Above all, the catch-all party was a competitive phenomenon: once firmly established, its rivals would have to follow suit or go to the wall.

The post-1945 transformation of the West German party system provides a copy-book illustration of the catch-all process at work.

We have already seen how the SPD jettisoned its Marxist image to become 'a party of the whole people', but it is important to realise that the party's conversion was due in no small measure to the outstanding performance of the German Christian Democrats in the 1950s. The CDU was precisely in the new mould and against the pattern of all previous German parties. Faced with its success in attracting voters on a mass basis from all social classes, the SPD could no longer rely on its working-class and left-wing credentials unless it was prepared to languish in permanent opposition. What happened in Germany was symptomatic of change elsewhere in Western Europe, and even if the parties hung on to their old labels, they did so whilst carefully cultivating the aspirations of the new social groups just as much as those of the old social classes.

Correct as the rendering of the transformation of the West German party system may appear to be, and accurate as the evaluation of the changes in post-1945 Europe undoubtedly was in many respects, it is also apparent that the conceptions of left and right have proved remarkably durable; nor do they seem to be just pale attenuations from a past age. Even though the sharpness of the left-right confrontation has receded and the purity of traditional ideologies has been watered down – as for instance the experience of 'Eurocommunism' in the early 1970s indicated – class politics can scarcely be said to have become redundant. What we earlier termed the 'residual' aspect of class politics has to be taken into account, and that particularly applies to voting patterns. The paradox which Erik Allardt noted in the case of Scandinavia is of wider import: 'All evidence indicates that social class explains more of the variation in voting behaviour and particularly more of the working class voting than some decades ago. This has occurred simultaneously with the disappearance of traditional class barriers. As equality has increased, the working class voters have been more apt to vote for the workers' parties than before.' That finding was echoed by Butler and Stokes for Britain: 'The intensity of the class tie may have declined at the same time as its extent became more universal.'[7] Both formulations capture the idea of the *residual* quality of class politics, although neither could take into account the considerable increase in electoral volatility which became evident in several countries during the 1970s. Such volatility was not unexpected, since political–cultural ties and loyalties are subject to decline, especially in periods of consensus, so that at least in the medium term 'party dealignment', that is, the weakening of voter attachment to specific parties, is likely.

There can, however, be no similar certainty with regard to the process of 'class dealignment'. According to this thesis, catch-all parties will lose even their residual socio-economic 'skew', and this trend, in association with the fragmentation of party systems along regional/ethnic and/or, other issue-cleavages, would result in parties being defined and differentiated purely in policy terms, with no significant differences in socio-economic categories or status discernible within their electorates. A fundamental problem with this thesis is that evidence in its support derives from indices designed to measure 'class voting' in a specific historic period, but, taking into account contemporary social and socio-political changes, the defining characteristics of the relevant categories are themselves undergoing transformation. What is thus being measured, it is argued, is the increasing irrelevance of *particular* definitions of class when, in fact, the more fundamental process is precisely the redefinition of the meaning *and* content of 'class'. The political parties play a major role in promoting this process of class 'realignment', and the perpetuation of left and right could point to a resurgence of polarisation in new forms.

The final factor – and many would argue the decisive one – relates to the changing economic climate affecting Western Europe in the 1980s. The political trends of the 1960s and early 1970s were at the time extrapolated on the supposition that economic growth would continue almost indefinitely, and it was reasonable to argue that the steady march to affluence would act as a kind of universal political solvent. That optimism was shattered by successive economic setbacks from the onset of the 1973 oil crisis onwards. Whilst the prolonged period of expansion effectively glossed over the built-in inequalities of wealth and life-chances inherent in market-based economies, an era of stagnation, accompanied by mass unemployment, revealed them once more.

It is the question of 'equality' which gives the most substantial basis for differentiating between left and right, even though it is only one component of party ideology. One reason for the acceptance of the 'end of ideology' argument in the 1960s was that material progress both weakened the drive to secure equality by parties on the left as well as making it easier for those on the right to make concessions. The outcome can be expressed in the idea of a 'social democratic consensus', a general acceptance by the parties of the welfare state, a network of social provisions and obligations to be met in the context of the market system, itself geared to continuing economic growth and full employment.

In retrospect it can be seen that the *leitmotif* of equality was only temporarily obscured by the operation of the social democratic consensus. Accommodation becomes progressively more difficult in conditions of prolonged economic recession. It is not that the parties of the right necessarily reject egalitarian values, but rather that they object to the costs involved – on their argument: in the loss of individual freedom, the control of social life, the sacrifice of the dynamic features of the market economy. In particular, the right-wing viewpoint questions the feasibility of maintaining the level of social expenditure for the welfare state since its cost represents a drain on the productive employment of capital. More generally, the ideology of the right favours a curtailment of state intervention, whereas the left sees its role as being of vital importance to redress inequalities, and in a period of deepening economic crisis its sphere of action should be increased.

The crisis experienced in Western Europe could, in the future, conceivably be of such an order that the dormant ideologies of left and right would be reawakened. However, there is little indication as yet of a really sharp polarisation. Partly that may be because the welfare state has had a cushioning effect, so that social disaffection has not become widespread. Partly, it may be because the parties themselves see the benefits of maintaining the consensus, rather than risk the damaging effects of extreme political strife. It may also be because the electorates in various countries have shown little interest in radical change or inclination to revert to old-style 'class politics'. Such a reversion has anyway become less feasible with the arrival of entirely new occupational groups, the vast increase in the white-collar sector, and the enormous expansion of state activity and employment in the public sector. This heterogeneous collection of social groups – a new working class or alternatively a new middle class – makes the traditional class divisions of secondary importance, and it also renders 'class conflict' on the left-right scale less appropriate. That is confirmed by the experience during the 1980s of left-wing parties in Britain, France and Greece. Thus the British Labour Party, after veering sharply to the left in the 1970s and with the experience of two devastating defeats in the 1980s, sought to present an entirely new and moderate image. The French Socialists after their sweeping victory in 1981 implemented a series of radical policies, but their defeat in 1986 led to a remarkable shift towards moderation. In Greece, from the mid-1980s onwards, the ruling socialist party, Pasok, switched entirely from its radical course, realising that it was the only way it could maintain its hold on the government. Of course, we have to bear in mind that the political context and constraints in all three countries were different, but the point is that the new social and occupational categories are unlikely to act cohesively or collectively in a way that decisively favours the left or the right. The renewal of ideology might then find no real electoral echo – a vain attempt to resurrect class politics without the classes.

That conclusion may be premature, since there is no way of foreseeing how, say, apparently permanent and very high levels of unemployment might affect the appeal of ideology. The most that can be established at the present time is that governments in Western Europe do generally accord with a left/right dichotomy in their political complexion – at the expense of centre or straddling coalitions. Thus, in 1988, France, Greece, Spain, Norway and Sweden were all ruled by the left, whilst those with a definite bourgeois/conservative government included Britain, Denmark, the Netherlands, Portugal and West Germany. Obviously such a categorisation can give no guide to the extent of polarisation that is involved in the countries concerned, nor is the absence or presence of extreme or anti-system parties a reliable test: polarisation between left and right may become acute in a system historically noted for its moderation. Thus the British Conservative government, commencing its long period in office in 1979, was described by the Labour opposition as 'the most reactionary in the present century', and for its part the Labour Party moved sharply to the left in the 1970s before its new leader, Neil Kinnock, chose a more moderate course for the 1987 election. What is evident from the various examples is that despite fluctuations in intensity the ideas of left and right are firmly entrenched in the politics of Western Europe. It means that those political traditions have the strength to absorb and reinterpret new viewpoints and to survive changing social conditions. It does not mean, however, that the polarisation between left and right must involve some kind of deadly conflict.

The representation of group interests

Alongside the political parties, the power of organised interests is a second pronounced feature of liberal democracies. They are seen to be an essential complement to the decision-making process, providing a kind of balance to the system, working on the parties, the public, and at the governmental level. But the balance is never guaranteed; organised interests are in direct competition with the parties for the ear of government, and their influence over the parties may be so great that the latter may be reduced to a subordinate role. At various times, either a complementary or a competitive role has been taken by the main pillars of social interest: a vocal farm population, the trade unions, the Churches, the commercial and industrial interests, the small shopkeeper, and the professional organisations. Yet these are only the heavyweight members of the interest world; around them cluster a host of special interests, some defending the socio-economic position of their members, others advancing a particular cause.

This pluralist view of organised interests stresses their autonomous position and their *associational* character. An immediate contrast is apparent with traditional societies and totalitarian states; in both of these, for widely different reasons, interests are almost entirely furthered in an *institutional* setting, that is, their expression is entirely dependent on the official structure of authority; in the first, they will be a natural extension of the traditional hierarchy of power, and in the totalitarian society, in so far as they are recognised as legitimate expressions at all, the leading interests will be incorporated as a part of state activity. It would be incorrect, however, to make too sharp a distinction between pluralist and other types of society; particularly within the state-machine of all liberal democracies, it is obvious that the interests of the armed forces and of the bureaucracy are expressed in an institutional rather than an associative manner. One can also show a similarity of another kind: to the extent that democratic governments rely on direct consultation with leading interests and even make this a *formal* aspect of the deliberative process, then a reversion to an institutional type is possible. The direct links forged between the government bureaucracy and organised interests is one obvious result of increasing state involvement in economic and social regulation, and this development raises the question as to how much the boundary lines of pluralist society have in practice been redrawn, at least as far as the economic sector is concerned. The preoccupation with the idea of 'neo-corporatism', particularly in the 1970s, suggested that there might be a general trend in liberal democracies towards a more institutionalised form of politics, although the 'neo-liberal' surge of the 1980s subsequently forced a realisation that the trend could be reversed and that in competitive pluralist democracies such 'insider' politics, in the bureaucratic corporatist arena would eventually have to win support in the electoral and party arenas or risk being over-thrown. We shall take up the meaning and implications of neo-corporatism subsequently.

Alongside this general view of a trend which could be applicable to Western Europe, we can distinguish several national variations, individual styles, which both confirm and modify the broad tendency. There are three main variables which, according to Eckstein, can account for national differences: the content of government policy, the structure of government decision-making, and the prevailing norms and attitudes within a society. The first of these, government policy, viewed as a wide commitment to social and economic development, does not differ that much from one country or one major party to another in Western Europe. Though the means and the emphasis vary, policies are directed to economic growth, regional development, social security, educational and social advance; the same *type* of government intervention is required, irrespective of differences, say, about the distribution of wealth and income. To this extent we should expect common interest group patterns to emerge.

It is otherwise with the second and third variables. The way in which government decisions are reached involves both the formal rule-making apparatus and the actual distribution of power. How interests will operate will depend on such factors as the decentralisation of power and on the precise form taken by legislative-executive relations. Within these provisions, the party system will at least provide some indication of the distribution of power. Where one party is dominant for long periods, the structuring of interests will differ significantly from situations of multi-party government or where there is a fairly regular alternation. The power position of the bureaucracy is also important; partly this will depend on the formal power arrangements and the operation of the party system, but it will also be a consequence of the social composition of the state service – in what sense it is a 'representative' bureaucracy.*

The third variable, what may be termed the relevant features of a political culture, will help to establish the feasible, and acceptable, ways of promoting sectional interests, and even what kind of interest is to be allowed as 'legitimate'. Variations here may follow the lines suggested in the particular balance of 'participant', 'subject', and 'parochial' behaviour which is established in a society. Also relevant is the degree of consensus and cleavage on basic issues – a degree of mutual trust will allow organised interests considerable leeway in their dealings with parties and governments. Finally, the presence of strong subcultures will result in a fragmentation of interests which in a homogeneous society are given a unified expression.

We can illustrate the outcome of these influences by showing the marked differences in the style of interest representation which results and take some representative examples from Western Europe. One could put forward the Anglo-American system as a reference point, except that no single model emerges: in spite of the fact that they are both 'associational societies' and rank as 'civic

---

* See below, 'Administrative Élites', pp. 226–34.

cultures', with the ready articulation of specialised group interests, there are distinctive aspects in both. For instance, Almond noted a 'great substitutability of function' in the American system generally, in contrast with Britain, which showed 'a more centralised, predictable role structure'.[8] The British constitutional system is also more centralised than the American. The operation of the separation of powers at a national level in the United States spreads decision-making and allows interest groups alternative points of leverage, enabling them to 'play off' one point of power against another; the idea of the 'veto group' which emerges in this situation underlines the negative effect which strong interests can exert on public policy. The federal structure enhances the decentralisation, and the overall result is to give multiple lines of access and alternative strategies to which the loose nature of the party system gives maximum scope.

Almost all of this picture contrasts with Britain; the decision-making process is highly centralised, in the government and in the parties. There is a natural gravitation of interests towards the central government – the ministers and the permanent executive. The parliamentary parties are often of marginal importance, especially in the making of *detailed* decisions, and the sheer amount of this activity is a responsibility which the parties and public are happy enough in practice to leave to the minister and his officials. This evidence of civic 'trust' results in decisions, and often key ones, being made by relatively few people, and the whole process tends to be little publicised, less openly contentious, with the leading interests mostly identifiable as part of the political establishment. There is, of course, evidence in recent years that the picture has changed: there is a growing tendency to question élite authority, to engage in direct 'protest' action, and – as far as the political authorities are concerned – the spectre of 'ungovernability' is conjured up. Nonetheless, the central modes of decision making remain unaffected.

Of all European states, Sweden (along with Austria) appears to have carried furthest the integration of interest representation with public life. Organised interests exercise a power almost equal to that of parliament and parties. Yet this position is not based on pressure group domination; it is rather that the interest-permeation is spread in such a way that political leadership is not sacrificed in the cross-fire of competing interests. It is a balanced political system, based on a homogeneous political culture, and there is a consensus about the roles of the state, party and interest organisation. In this situation, no segment of the population feels that it is less-well represented than the others, and in spite of the ubiquity of group interests, the primacy of political leadership is not questioned. To explain this balance, one has to appreciate the highly public nature of interest representation which enables it to be accepted as a full complement of political representation by supplying a functional dimension. The important consequence is that interest groups operate as an integral part of the political scene; their activities are widely reported, their leaders in the public eye, and their members are well informed about the aims and tactics of their organisation. This openness extends to the relationship of interests to the Riksdag and the government – as we shall see later; the process of legislation is itself geared to a wide consultation with affected interests rather than to the fulfilment of party programmes.

The upshot is that organised groups can be said to be an essential part of the constitutional structure, spanning the 'input' and 'conversion' aspects of the political system to a greater extent than, say, in Britain. One can go even further and postulate a group dominance of political and social life to the extent that access to the public decision-makers is almost entirely controlled by this exclusive system of groups. These established groups which largely pre-empt the field are naturally strongest in economic affairs, with the two most powerful, the Swedish Trade Union Confederation (LO) and the Employers' Confederation (SAF) head and shoulders above the others. On the trade union side, there are separate organisations for white-collar workers, professional, and government employees. Though relatively small in comparison with the total labour force, these latter bodies are militant and well organised, quite on a par with the manual workers. Since 1966, all government employees have had the right to strike, and this led to an unprecedented situation in the early 1970s when widespread strikes dislocated government services and the government countered by threatening a lock-out of public employees – which would have led to the farcical spectacle of locking out a large proportion of Sweden's army officers! Although Swedish political life has fittingly been described as 'the politics of compromise', this is by no means an easy-going relationship, rather a hard-fought battle – according to accepted rules. The tendency to a 'nationalisation' of group interests, a 'Scandinavian corporatism', in which certain interests enjoy a paramountcy in public life and a special relationship with the government, is evident in Sweden as elsewhere; the real core of the compromise is to preserve political institutions which are not overwhelmed by group pressures.

The Swedish system has evolved over a long period, and we can take the rather rapid changes that have occurred in Germany as a contrast, starting from a quite different basis and yet giving an equal impression of cohesion. The situation now ruling is quite unlike the circumstances prevailing in the Weimar Republic, of which Merkl wrote, 'The major and minor interest groups from the trade unions to the farm, business and professional organisations of all kinds were divided along numerous lines according to class prejudices, ideological convictions and political preferences which added up to "an infinitely differentiated labyrinth" and contributed considerably to political chaos.'[9] The reshaping of these interests along simplified lines, to which the Nazi policy of *Gleichschaltung* doubtless contributed, was a feature of the period after 1945. Instrumental to the simplification were the political parties and the stable voting attachments they secured; in particular, the conglomerate nature of the CDU served to unite a diversity of interests under one roof, and under Adenauer's leadership the party developed a system of some ingenuity in channelling various economic and social demands. Outside of this largely governmental framework, and to some extent acting as a balance, came the formation of a powerful, unified trade union movement. Its unification depended on the severance of all political ties; this political neutrality probably helped organised labour to achieve a greater integration with the political system than would have been the case had it developed as a form of industrial opposition in the era of CDU dominance.

One should not be completely carried away by the new look of group activity in the post-war era; there are important aspects of historical continuity as well. Associations of economic interest in Germany have always occupied a privileged position in public life at all levels, and have had a public regulative function. Lewis Edinger has pointed out that the local trade associations, '. . . have their roots in the corporate guilds of the Middle Ages. . . . These are non-autonomous institutions of public law which exercise compulsory jurisdiction over their members and are supposed to link all major sectors of the economy to the political system.'[10] These various trade and occupational associations operate from a local level upwards and are in a strategic position to act as mediators between the public authorities and their specialised membership – at the local municipal level, within the Länder, and in negotiation with the federal government. A further dimension to the official and public nature of interest group activity lies in the structure of government itself: the individual Länder can be regarded as public-interest pressure groups as well as government structures. Each state government represents the particular socio-economic interests of its area in relation to the dispensations of the federal government, especially regarding the relative financial commitments of the two. We shall look later at the working of German federalism, but we can note that the articulation of regional and *Länder* interests is an important function and that these reach a focal point in the federal upper house, the Bundesrat, where all the state governments are *directly* represented.

Edinger once rather forbiddingly described the West German situation as reflecting 'the highly formalised patterns of polyarchic élitism and mass passivity.'[11] One can see evidence of formalisation in the special position which interest groups have in many sectors of public life; the term 'mass passivity' has to be treated with some caution: it does correspond to the idea of 'detachment' as a feature of the German political culture, with group leadership showing a high level of professional competence, independent of the membership they represent – but there are sufficient indications of changes in political culture, in particular the new emphasis on participation, to show that old stereotypes have to be abandoned.[12]

In the economic sphere, these representative élites tend to balance one another's power, and in this sense they are 'polyarchic'. Their most complete expression can be seen in a number of important national organisations, the large and inclusive 'summit' organisations or *Spitzenverbände*. These harden into half a dozen or so key groups which are all-important for the economic life of the nation. On the employers' side there are various 'roof' organisations: the Federation of German Employers' Associations (BDA) contains several hundred individual employers' associations; the Federation of German Industry (BDI) unites about forty national industrial organisations, themselves structured on a federal basis; a third 'roof' organisation brings into one fold the local and district chambers of industry and commerce – and membership of these is compulsory for all enterprises. Obviously there is a considerable overlap in membership, a criss-crossing at various levels of regional and particular industrial and commercial interests. A parallel summit is reached by the trade union movement. Most of the trade unions are members of the German Trade Union Federation (DGB), with small, but powerful, separate organisations for civil servants and for the majority of white collar workers. The placid appearance of German industrial relations since the founding of the republic is partly attributable to the highly rationalised union structure – the DGB has only seventeen constituent unions, organised on broad industrial lines and on a federal basis as well. Of equal significance has been the integration of the trade union movement and the general industrial set-up. Imperfectly as the principle of 'co-determination'

(*Mitbestimmungsrecht*) is generally admitted to have been applied in practice and only of partial application anyway, it does give expression to the corporate sentiments which have persisted for a very long time and which have made easier the handling of disputes – typically in the 'labour courts' for resolving them. The absence of industrial conflict is only imperfectly explained by the continuing prosperity; the other relevant factors are the élitist, and unquestioned, authority of the professional leadership of the unions – a 'passivity' on the shopfloor – and the incorporation of the unions into a nation-wide, 'public' network of interests.

To the economic groupings have to be added the Protestant and Catholic Churches. These, together with the economic interest groups (including those of the farmers), find it profitable to work at all levels of public life. It is in Bonn, however, that they find it most important to be represented. The corporate leanings of German industrial society are such that there is an orderly gravitation of organised interests towards the decision-making centres. The official voice of the interests harmonises quite naturally with the main 'arenas' of legislation – the federal government departments, the Bundesrat, and the Bundestag.

Now whether or not we wish to conclude that the pattern of West German interest representation signifies a form of neo-corporatism, it is quite clear that its basis is different from that existing in Sweden; in Germany, one might argue, it is their 'institutional' status which is all-important, whilst in Sweden it is their sheer power which has carved out for them a secure 'political' position. Turning to France, we can examine how far either of these standpoints could be held to be true of the Fifth Republic. It is evident that in both the Third and Fourth Republics, the power of group interests was largely political. Whilst in Sweden this power did not erode the parliamentary system, but rather dovetailed with it, in France the cross-pressures of group interests did undermine political leadership. Williams and Harrison portrayed the situation: 'Under the Fourth Republic the summit of party ambition was to win a share of power rather than to exercise it outright. One way to achieve this was to outbid one's rivals for the support of a clientele – Gaullists against Conservatives against MRP over the Catholic schools, Communists against Socialists against Radicals on behalf of secular education – and each against all for the favours of home-distillers, ex-servicemen, peasants or small shopkeepers.'[13] And for a while these last were to show, in Poujadism, that they could find their own political expression if the established parties failed to deliver the goods. Group interests were by no means victorious, but their effect was to defeat government policies and make stable government impossible. In this sense, they were politically predominant.

Powerful as many of the lobbies were in the past – for instance, the colonial and arms lobbies in the Third Republic – those relying on a degree of mass membership have usually lacked stable support and are prone to doctrinal and other feuds. Nor, in a country of individualists, is it possible to rely on a high membership. This kind of associational weakness contrasts with West Germany and Sweden. Trade union membership, at around 15 per cent of the employed population in the Fifth Republic, is far lower than for comparable countries, and it is split amongst four affiliations; the largest is the *Confédération Générale du Travail*, still mainly under Communist influence but with less than a third of the membership it had shortly after 1945. The same kind of organisational weakness besets other groups which rely on a mass membership. That applies to the farmers, most of whom do not belong to one or other of the numerous agricultural interest groups, often divided in their approach and frequently in direct competition with one another. And even with the plethora of organised channels available, this does not prevent the sporadic outbursts of violence, direct action, on the part of discontented farmers. More cohesive, and for that matter more effective, are the industrial and employers' associations, and the very largest firms, successors to the former industrial dynasties, can take up their cause direct with the government. Even within the industrial associations there are wide differences of viewpoint – the politics of national and regional economic development, the contrasting outlook of small and large firms. It is a babel of interests – labour, agricultural, and industrial – which competes for the ear of government, never a united voice.

Whilst it can be agreed that the total effect of interest representation on the Fourth Republic was destructive, seen another way the parliamentary system had a value in that the Assembly 'absorbed' interest group pressures as well as transmitting claims to the government. Both these functions dried up in the aridity of Fifth Republic parliaments. Instead, there was a natural, explicit switch of attention on the part of the interest groups from the Assembly to government – to where the decisions were made, within the executive. But the transfer of effort did not give the interest groups a greater leverage than before, although judging by the numbers they could at least expect to be consulted; there is a vast array of 'Councils', 'Committees' and 'Commissions' at various levels all bringing together interest group representatives and the government bureaucracy.

This proliferation of consultation does not at all mean that the interests hold sway; neither the government nor its bureaucracy is subject to an adverse vote, and given the fundamental disunity of the individual interests, it is not difficult to rule through division. Furthermore, the guiding principle of the Fifth Republic has all along been to tame the power of the political intermediaries – the interest groups as well as the parties. And it can be argued that the power given to the executive in the Fifth Republic rationalised and made explicit a process of decision-making that was well under way in the Fourth – especially in the field of economic planning. The French 'Plan' was never a parliamentary exercise, but a series of 'technical steps' requiring intensive preparation and co-ordination on the part of the bureaucracy in consultation with a variety of national and regional interests.[14] The Plan became symptomatic of the downgrading of parliamentary institutions, alongside the shackles imposed by the constitution. To convert it to 'democratic planning' by allowing for a wide functional consultation stumbles on the power position of the higher bureaucracy; and the evocative term 'technocracy' endows the state-machine with a political purpose. As long as this apparatus retains its cohesion and is looked upon favourably by the government of the day, then the 'political' and even the 'official' status of group interests is kept in a subordinate position.

The whole drift of modern French politics was towards a 'non-political' form of representation rather than a parliamentary one. But it would probably be wrong to treat that as an irrevocable development. As long as the parties were kept in a subordinate position in the Fifth Republic, the parliamentary system of representation suffered. But the position was considerably altered by the Socialist victory in 1981 which first established the principle of 'alternation', and which, following the uneasy balance from 1986–88, was confirmed in 1988.

Though the term neo-corporatism might still be applied, the French way of accommodating interests accords neither with the German nor the Swedish. We can introduce the fourth national style, the Italian, to show yet another variation. Indeed, this form contrasts with the other three in that it shows traits of a much older kind of politics in which 'pluralism' has not yet eroded traditional relationships. The ingredients of the Italian system are various, but related: the dominant position of the Christian Democrats, the place of the Roman Catholic Church as the strongest of all group interests, the weakness of the Italian bureaucracy; the conjunction of these three elements imposed a special pattern. Alternatively, one can portray the divisive effect of the subcultures: the deep cleavage between the Church and the anti-clerical forces, with the summits of political confrontation in Christian Democracy and Communism; the other split, just as dramatic, between north and south – industrially, economically, and socially.

Least of all did Italy develop as an associational society. The segmentation of Italian society is one aspect, the other was the hegemony of Christian Democracy over government since the war – if one adds to this the equally long period of authoritarian rule previously, then most interest groups have grown up in the context of a government that was regarded as permanently in power. This permanence makes the relationship of party and bureaucracy of special importance. Joseph LaPalombara advanced two concepts, the *'parentela'* and the *'clientela'*, which help considerably in appreciating the articulation of interest groups to the political structure. What is more, both are terms which express the persistence of older traditions in Italian society. The *parentela* relationship is almost in the way of being a kinship tie: 'In the traditional South, whence most of Italy's bureaucrats are recruited, ties of *parentela* are particularly strong, implying the kinds of rights and obligations that are generally associated with pre-industrial societies.' It was natural that these rights and obligations were accorded to the hegemonic Christian Democracy and to the interests which it represents: 'The bureaucrats and functionaries tend to obey the minister and the party in power, and ... ignore those parties and those associations that are not instruments of or representatives of the parties in power.' This pervasive outlook is supplemented by the *clientela* relationship, which involves regarding certain interest groups as, '... the natural expression and representative of a given social sector which, in turn, constitutes the natural target or reference point for the activity of the administrative agency.' And this 'naturalness' is a survival from an earlier form of society whose influence persisted long into the post-1945 era: 'The contemporary feudal power in Italy is represented by the industrialist class, and particularly by monopoly capitalism ... contemporary dominant groups have succeeded in having medieval corporative values widely accepted by vast sectors of Italian society.'[15]

What developed was a triple alliance of party, interests, and bureaucracy. Christian Democracy itself is a conglomerate of interests, and on them it depends for its voting power. Ranged behind the party are the Catholic Church, large sections of the farming community, and industrial interests. Chief of the flanking organisations in each field are Catholic Action, the Association of

Direct Cultivators, and the Confederation of Italian Industry (*Confindustria*). The first two of these are an integral part of Christian Democracy, whilst *Confindustria*, no longer the important financial backer it was in the early post-war years, preserves a more independent stance – particularly objecting to any 'opening to the left' undertaken by the Christian Democrats. It differs as well in that unlike the mass membership of the farming associations and the lay organisations of the Church, it is not in a position to 'deliver the vote'. Both Catholic Action, with its related bodies, and the agricultural interests provide a voting loyalty, and they also manage to place a large number of their members in the Italian Parliament; the parliamentary party of the Christian Democrats is composed of an alliance of interests, and the party must act as broker to various factions, all of which claim a privileged position in Italian society.

The power of Italian industry is primarily exercised through the large firms acting individually, rather than by means of the interest associations. *Confindustria* as well as the various trade associations are of importance, but the real power lies with the large firms and combines. Alongside the dozen or so very large concerns, there are two giant state combines, the IRI (Industrial Reconstruction Institute) and the ENI (National Hydrocarbons Trust). These are not nationalised concerns in the strict sense, but mixed enterprises, subject only to overall political control. The IRI is an amazing conglomerate of around a thousand interrelated companies especially strong in shipbuilding and banking, and inheriting many of its interests from the fascist period. The ENI is concentrated in the energy-producing industry, particularly oil, chemicals, mining, and natural gas – with control too of a leading Milan newspaper. How is one to sum up the total effect of this massive state intervention in almost every field of the economy? It has not led to any substantial weakening of the private sector; rather it has served to blur the division between state and private interest, placing public employees in close relation to a variety of commercial pressures. These state concerns also give a power of influence and appointment to the ruling party; a colonisation of government-controlled organisations.

Yet the parliamentary party of the Christian Democrats was not simply a strange alliance of interests which together confronted an opposing bloc, for party factions also competed among themselves, with some favouring specific 'working class' interests, and even certain interests within the main opposition parties. Thus, whilst the trade union movement was unable to present a united front opposing this peculiar corporate power because of its split into three distinct confederations – the Communist and Socialist CGIL, the Social Democratic UIL and the Catholic CISL – working-class interests were not entirely neglected, thanks to the power of the parties and the party system which represented such interests directly, through a form of parliamentary joint rule. Nevertheless, this complex system of inter-penetrating party and interest-group representation faced a major challenge in the 1970s when collaboration between the union confederations resulted in explicitly anti-party and anti-parliamentary leverage becoming effective in wringing concessions from government. This development appeared to accord with a slow shift towards a more competitive party system in which the Communist Party no longer collaborated as a subordinate member of a static Christian Democrat/Communist Party system, but came to be seen as the accepted core of an alternative government-in-waiting.

The age of corporatism?

The examples of interest group organisation we have taken make it evident that no one rendering will adequately take account of national differences and the nuances involved in the complex of party, government, interest relations. But the general drift is interpreted as the same in most countries: an elevation of interest representation to the detriment of the political parties and the parliamentary system, and an increasingly close connection between powerful interests and the government bureaucracy, in various ways and guises an institutionalisation of pressure group activity. Beyond the formal or informal institutions built up around organised interests, there are other, more basic tendencies apparent, especially those associated with the idea of 'corporatism'. This term has been used to describe a new relationship of the state with the economic sector which some feel not only threatens to by-pass the established forms of representative democracy but also to weaken the basic pluralist model of West European society. Free from any association with the fascist 'corporate state', the corporate model points to an increasingly close 'partnership' between the leading economic interests and the state. Economic and organisational imperatives, it is argued, have drawn the modern state into a whole range of commitments and responsibilities, and whilst the framework of the public/private distinction is retained, in fact the process of decision-making depends on the cooperation, even interlocking, of the state's administrative apparatus with the private sector to produce increasingly administered markets. This picture can be overdrawn, but it is apparent that the label of 'neo-corporatism' does highlight a significant shift from conventional accounts of liberal democratic politics and pluralist society.

Neo-corporatist arguments and illustrations are largely based on the economic and related policies which emanate from the triangular structuring of the state, organised business interests, and the trade unions. Although there are many variations on the neo-corporatist theme, Gerhard Lehmbruch's specification for what he describes as a 'fully corporatised polity' summarises the challenge neo-corporatism presents to the values of pluralism and party government:

– Interest organisations are strongly co-opted into governmental decision making.
– Large interest organisations are strongly linked to political parties and take part in policy formation in a sort of functional division of labour.
– Most interest organisations are hierarchically structured, and membership tends to be compulsory.
– Occupational categories are represented by non-competitive organisations enjoying a monopoly.
– Industrial relations are characterised by strong 'concertation' of labour unions and employers' organisations with government.[16]

Lehmbruch maintains that the corporatised polity is compatible with the liberal democratic institutions, and took the view that, 'Neo-corporatism in general is not considered as an alternative to parliamentary democracy but instead . . . [as] a sort of symbiosis with the party system which may take varying forms.'[17] Yet that optimism some would find misplaced. Whilst it is true that corporatist arrangements if restricted to the economic sphere need not directly conflict with the authority of the parties and with the parliamentary system, there is the probability of extension to the wider socio-economic sphere. Ultimately, too, neo-corporatist values and practices – hierarchy, monopoly, non-competitiveness, compulsory membership, concertation – are opposed to pluralist ones and thus implicitly to some of the assumptions of liberal democracy itself. This debate is likely to be open-ended, and discussion can only sensibly proceed on the basis of seeing how neo-corporatism can be applied to the experience of a number of countries.

Austria is often cited as a country with pronounced neo-corporatist traits, largely because of the highly institutionalised form of interest representation which has evolved over a long period. Separate and *statutory* representation is provided in five 'chambers' each reflecting a particular aspect of economic activity. These bodies articulate particular interests and are the basis of the 'social partnership' between the government, organised labour and business interests. The central institution of the partnership is the Joint Commission for Prices and Wages composed of government representatives, delegates from the Chambers of Trade, Agriculture and Labour as well as from the federation of trade unions. The Joint Commission, besides having the major responsibility for price and wage regulation, is also active in the formulation of social and economic policies as a natural extension of its regulative function. The consequence is that all important decisions in those fields are subject to the consensus-building mechanism of the neo-corporatist structures. In Austria the size of the public sector is considerable, accounting for almost 30 per cent of the labour force, and the state controls two-thirds of the 50 largest companies. In this situation, the government is bound to become closely involved with leading organised interests – and it is one of them itself. This entanglement gives rise to particular difficulties, as has been shown by recent Austrian developments.[18]

In other countries, such a formalisation is not in evidence, and forms of functional representation – appearing as advisory 'economic and social councils' – are usually rather weak, with the notable exception of the Dutch tripartite council. This council has, however, unlike the Austrian one, declined in significance over the past decade. Elsewhere such formal structures are not, in any case, taken as necessary for neo-corporatist practices to be present, and it has been argued, particularly in Scandinavia, that the essential socio-economic content of such bargaining is best carried out bilaterally, that is, directly between labour and business representatives, since the formal powers of the government make it a poor bargaining party, with the state actor being too easily identified as a coercive, rather than cooperative agent. The role of 'the state', it is argued, should be more passive, providing only the backcloth of a common interest, whereas active involvement should be avoided, because any perceived bias will further undermine attempts to establish a consensus. Thus, in Sweden, the formal involvement of the state in labour/business negotiations is limited, and when it occurs is indicative of a political polarisation which challenges the preferred consensual basis of policy-making.

In Britain, the overt identification of the main parties with different sides of the bargaining process led, as we shall see, to the breakdown of neo-corporatist practices or tendencies. Moreover, the desire of participants in successful neo-corporatist polities to avoid state, or government involvement has led to the rejection of corporatism as 'tripartism'. Other, more pluralistic, interpretations also reject a restricted view of neo-corporatism. In particular, they point to the participation of a peak agricultural associations, and various consumer-oriented bodies, along with the industrial, financial and commercial associations, so   that neo-corporatism is seen to promote the common good by developing a sense of responsibility for a societal-wide concertation, rather than pursuing narrow self-interest, with the hope that the outcome will be for the best. This broader conception of neo-corporatism is often associated with social-democratic versions of its utility; thus, it is no coincidence that corporatism is strong where there is, or has been, a powerful social-democratic party. Clearly, this view is far removed from more doctrinaire liberal or marxist interpretations which see neo-corporatism as either inhibiting growth and adaptation to the world market on the one hand, or else subordinating working-class interests to those of the capitalist class on the other.

That these considerations are not only of theoretical interest can be shown by reference to developments in Germany and Britain. As a broad generalisation, neo-corporatism has been stronger in the smaller West European democracies. But the apparent trend towards neo-corporatism did not leave the larger states untouched, so that from the 1960s, and more so in the 1970s, Germany and Britain were thought to be moving in this direction. In Germany the ideological basis for economic consensus was emphasised in the early 1950s by the concept of the 'social market economy' which favoured growth based on a capitalist market economy, yet qualified by the principle of social responsibility, with an active role for the state. More generally, the laissez-faire state proved to be a relic, perhaps even a myth, but the economic boom of the 1950s and 1960s allowed such fine distinctions to be ignored. The entry of the German SPD to government in the 1960s was accompanied by an increase in governmental intervention, and the strongly centralised institutional framework of the unions, industrial and financial bodies enabled the idea of 'social partnership' to be imported from Austria, and for a while was institutionalised in the tripartite committee meetings of 'concerted action' (*Konzertierte Aktion*). Neo-corporatist practices seemed at one time to have been formally institutionalised in Germany, and the 1976 law on codetermination (*Mitbestimmung*) confirmed this view. This legislation extended the existing practice of trade union representation in the coal and steel industries to the supervisory boards of all firms with over two thousand employees.

In fact, this latter development proved to be far from consensual, since the German Employers' Federation challenged (unsuccessfully) its constitutionality, and the unions withdrew from the concerted action committee in 1977 in retaliation. Industrial relations grew increasingly bitter as lock-outs followed strikes from 1978–80, whilst from 1982 the major political parties differed over how to cope with the economic crisis. The return to government of the Christian Democrats in 1982 raised expectations of industrial confrontation, but initially the new government, led by Helmut Kohl and the Industry Minister, Norbert Blüm – an ex-Opel worker from the party's labour wing – sought to conciliate the unions by introducing a state-assisted scheme for early retirement. The unions, seeking a 35-hour week as a way of reducing unemployment, rejected this approach, and in 1984 the major parties ended the post-war tradition of observing neutrality during industrial disputes and sided with the opposing forces. In this acrimonious atmosphere, already sour industrial relations were made worse by the most extensive dispute since the end of the war.

Yet this apparent breakdown should not obscure the fact that corporatist traditions have a strong historical rooting: the concept of 'social partnership' is not just a handy formula, since it has to be seen as having an important place in popular thinking. Moreover, the commitment to the 'social market economy' – shared by all the established parties – is the centrepiece of the dominant ideology.

In Britain, corporatist tendencies are shallowly rooted, and even though there, as elsewhere, tendencies can be identified that date back to the First World War, its full acceptance was prevented by several factors: the strength of liberal traditions, the doctrine of parliamentary sovereignty, the weakness of the political arm of the labour movement. In the firm attachment to 'free collective bargaining' we can see a complete antithesis to the corporatist mode. In the post-1945 era, against the background of relative economic decline, and especially in the 1970s a trend towards corporatism was evident. Yet – at least in retrospect – it appears as just an expedient favoured by one party to remedy the economic malaise. In the 1980s, any 'corporatist trend' was just as decisively reversed by the neo-liberalism of Mrs Thatcher's governments. A minimum condition for corporatism is some form of bi-partisan agreement – even if covert – between the major parties.

The strategy of confrontation between government and trade unions which ended Edward Heath's 1970–74 Conservative administration was a political failure, since Heath's appeal to the country on the basis of 'Who rules Britain?' resulted in the election of a Labour government. Confrontation was followed by Labour's determined attempt at collaboration with the unions under the Wilson and Callaghan governments. However, the intense politicisation of industrial relations made neo-corporatist experimentation vulnerable at the same time as the institutional and cultural bases for it were absent. Government attempts to create class solidarity by means of a 'Social Contract' between the unions and the government broke down because of the organisational fragmentation of the unions. Union leaders who were favourable to this development proved unable to control individual unions or the rank and file. The combination of 'workerist' ideas about the industrial basis of 'working class' power and hostility to class compromise combined with powerful sectional interests to revert to aggressively free-collective bargaining.

Any incipient West European trend towards neo-corporatism was, thus, already in doubt by 1979, and since then the neo-liberal message has been applied elsewhere, if less combatively, so that to conceive of neo-corporatism as a permanent and stable alternative to pluralism appears mistaken. Phillipe Schmitter has pointed out that neo-corporatism may be a 'fair-weather' phenomenon, flourishing in conditions of economic growth when a large number of interests can most easily be reconciled. But in periods of stagnation or long-term economic decline severe tensions will arise. Schmitter takes the view that in such circumstances neo-corporatism will, in fact, prove more resilient than a pluralist system,[19] but the situation is probably more differentiated; neo-corporatism can be reinforced in some countries, readjusted elsewhere, but become less relevant in others.

As a type of convergence theory, neo-corporatism overlooks different national histories. If we look elsewhere in Western Europe we find that a decided neo-liberal reversal has not taken place. Sweden provides a clear example of this stability, whilst Italy shows how attempts to establish neo-corporatist relations have been reinforced in the 1980s, at the same time as neo-liberal practices have actually increased.

In Sweden 44 years of Social democratic hegemony were apparently ended in 1976 when a 'bourgeois' government was formed by the Conservative, Liberal and Centre parties, and re-elected in 1979. The core social-democratic policies were, however, broadly continued, although increasing difficulties in industrial relations and the labour market, signalled by a series of strikes including a general strike in 1980, indicated problems for Swedish neo-corporatism too. In fact, labour unrest proved to be a feature of the Social Democratic government since 1982, so that rather than being an indication of the failure of neo-corporatist bargaining under 'bourgeois' governments they reflect a period of general conflict, especially as a consequence of the second steep oil-price rise in 1980 after the first shock in 1973.

The major threat to Swedish neo-corporatism was not the policies of the bourgeois government so much as the struggle over the so-called 'wage-earner funds', a series of regional investment funds with dominant union representation on the boards. These funds first became an electoral issue in 1976, a year after a plan for their adoption was approved by the LO, the Swedish blue-collar trade union. The Social Democrats lost that election, but not over the funds, rather over the nuclear-power issue, and when they fought the 1982 election on the basis of a programme centred on the funds they were returned to office. This did not end opposition, which was bitter, as the funds seemed to threaten to undermine the entrepreneurial basis of capitalism itself. Opposition reached a peak with the passage of implementing legislation in December 1983, which signalled the breakdown, for the first time, of coordinated wage negotiations between the LO and the Swedish Employers' Federation (SAF) in 1983–84 and the election of 1985, when the opposition campaigned on the basis of repealing the 'fund socialism' legislation. The confirmation of the Social Democrats in government in 1985 meant, however, that the SAF has had to recognise social democratic hegemony, and in 1986 LO/SAF wage negotiations were concluded successfully.

Far from neo-corporatism challenging the party and parliamentary basis of liberal democracy, as it has been alleged to do, Sweden shows how political developments were decisive both in maintaining and relegitimising neo-corporatism. Alternation, in 1976 and then in 1982, allowed political differences to be expressed at the highest institutional level. The confirmation of social democratic government in 1985 along with the resurgence of the centre parties, reduced the tendency to bipolarisation, and reconfirmed the powerful position that social democracy has in Swedish society. Neo-corporatism survived a period of adversity. Although the party-political reversal of neo-corporatist trends in Britain may show the dependency of neo-corporatism on pluralist party democracy, the Swedish case indicates that there can be a symbiosis between them.

In Italy, the formal exclusion of the unions, especially the socialist and communist CGIL, from influence on government did not prevent the unions playing a significant role in the 1950s and 1960s, even though it was subordinate to the strategy of the employers. In the late 1960s, however, the three major union confederations formed a coordinating federal body to further their interests. New-found union strength co-existed with weak government and that enabled the unions to win significant concessions, principally the 1970 Workers' Statute, and by gaining government support for union claims against the employers. The unions also pressed for wide-ranging social reforms to strengthen and rationalise the welfare services, housing-rights and so on – a legislative programme that the government was quite unable to fulfil.

This situation forced an awareness of the importance of the unions to the management of the economy, and in 1975, following the turbulence caused by the 1973 oil shock, the unions and the employers' federation, Confindustria, made an agreement on wage-indexing. Allegedly a pact between the producing classes against both the 'parasitic classes' and the corrupt and incapable party élites, the agreement not only excluded the state, but acted against its interests by making government management of the economy even more difficult and adding sharply to the inflationary spiral.

Both unions and government soon realised the need for a more coordinated and nationally-minded bargaining process. Partly because of the Communist Party's closeness to government, an ambitious plan was developed involving wage moderation and flexibility for industrial reconstruction, job creation and union control over the labour market. This plan was the outcome of the so-called EUR line, established in 1978. The failure of the Communist-supported governments of national solidarity and a sharpening of industrial conflict, often to management's advantage, soon halted these developments, and by the early 1980s the unions were in a much weaker position.

The restructuring of the Italian economy in this period led to a greater role for the small and micro-industries, thus weakening the grip of the unions and reconfirming the tendency towards 'dualism' – the simultaneous presence of different regimes in the economy: whereas one part increasingly escaped union influence and government regulation, so that a laissez-faire system operated, the benefits of mutual cooperation in the large-scale industries were recognised, since intense conflict was seen as being mutually self-destructive. This led to the development of centralised tripartite pacts in 1983–84, when the unions recognised that the 'social good' now meant combating inflation above all, but also that there should be no free-riders – the self-employed, notorious for their tax-evasion. The inability of the unions to force their priorities on to society as a whole was shown by the failure of the Communist-inspired referendum on wage-indexation in 1985 which sought to repeal a government decree reducing the significance of wage-indexing. Although union unity broke up over this issue, it was subsequently re-established; and in 1986 and 1987 the principle of national-level collective bargaining between the unions and Confindustria was once more recognised, and the relative industrial calm, compared with the conflict of the early 1980s, was a considerable advance. Thus, whilst one part of the Italian economy mirrors a neo-liberal paradigm, avoiding both union and government regulation, another reflected increased concertative cooperation, and by 1988 employers and government even sought to bolster the main union confederations against the threat of the increasingly anarchic 'autonomous' unions which began to appear outside the confederation structures.

What is clear from these examples is that both the theory and the practice of neo-corporatism have ambiguous features. Theoretical interpretations, based on class-related analyses, range from the 'anti-worker' state-monopoly capitalism thesis to anti-capitalist variations of a softer social-democratic 'third way' whereas structural analyses at a statist extreme stress the hollowing-out of representative democracy and at the anarchic extreme for the development of a mass and participatory 'organised democracy'. The reality – as we have seen – matches this divergent pattern of interpretation. Neo-corporatism has to be judged in relation to the variety of national contexts.

Everywhere the party arena still provides basic choices for society, and the perpetuation of left and right in Western Europe means that there can be sharp polarisation in matters affecting the economy – both in the production and distribution of wealth. The British case is illustrative of how 'basic choices' can be made. During the period of Labour government beginning in 1974, there were several signs of moves towards corporatist arrangements with an emphasis on national planning agreements to incorporate business and the trade unions. Yet after 1979, with the advent of a strongly ideological Conservative government wedded to a free-market philosophy, the idea of a British 'state corporatism' was abandoned. Even though there are powerful tendencies in European society which favour neo-corporatism, there are equally strong currents the other way.

Notes and references

1. R. Rose and D. W. Urwin, 'Persistence and Change in Western Party Systems since 1945', in *Political Studies*, September 1970, vol. 18, pp. 287–319.
2. H. Daalder and P. Mair, (eds.), *Western European Party Systems: Continuity and Change*, Sage, 1983; S. Bartolini and P. Mair, (eds.), *Party Politics in Contemporary Western Europe*, Frank Cass, 1984.
3. L. D. Epstein, 'Political Parties in Western Democratic Systems', in R. C. Macridis (ed.), *Political Parties: Contemporary Trends and Ideas*, New York: Harper and Row, 1967, p. 144.

4. V. Lorwin, 'Belgium: Religion, Class and Language in National Politics', in R. A. Dahl (ed.), *Political Oppositions in Western Democracies*, New Haven: Yale University Press, 1966, p. 156.
5. M. P. Fogarty, *Christian Democracy in Western Europe*, Routledge and Kegan Paul, 1957, p. 6.
6. O. Kirchheimer, 'The Waning of Opposition', in R. C. Macridis and B. E. Brown (eds.). *Comparative Politics*, Homewood, Illinois: The Dorsey Press, 1964, p. 287, and, 'The Transformation of the Western European Party Systems', in J. LaPalombara and M. Weiner (eds.), *Political Parties and Political Development*, New Jersey: Princeton University Press, 1956, pp. 177–200.
7. E. Allardt quoted by S. M. Lipset in 'The Modernisation of Contemporary European Politics', *Revolution and Counterrevolution*, Heinemann, 1969, p. 222. Also, D. Butler and D. Stokes, *Political Change in Britain*, Macmillan, 1969, p. 116.
8. G. A. Almond, 'Comparative Political Systems', in Macridis and Brown (eds.), op. cit., p. 57.
9. P. Merkl, 'The Structure of Interests and Adenauer's Survival as Chancellor', in *European Politics*, p. 371.
10. L. J. Edinger, *Politics in Germany*, Boston: Little, Brown, 1969, p. 207.
11. Edinger, op. cit., p. 198.
12. See D. Conradt, 'The Changing German Political Culture', in G. Almond and S. Verba (eds.), *The Civic Culture Revisited*, Boston: Little, Brown, 1980.
13. P. M. Williams and M. Harrison, *Politics and Society in de Gaulle's Republic*, Longman, 1971, p. 144.
14. See D. M. Green, 'The Seventh Plan – The Demise of French Planning?', *West European Politics*, February 1978.
15. J. LaPalombara, *Interest Groups in Italian Politics*, Princeton University Press, 1964, pp. 306, 312–13, 260, 262.
16. G. Lehmbruch, 'Neo-Corporatism in Comparative Perspective' in G. Lehmbruch and P. Schmitter (eds.), *Patterns of Corporatist Policy Making*, Sage Publications, 1982, pp. 5–6.
17. G. Lehmbruch, 'Liberal Corporatism and Party Government' *Comparative Political Studies*, April 1977.
18. For an analysis, see P. Gerlich, E. Grande and W. Müller 'Corporatism in Crisis: Stability and Change of Social Partnership in Austria', *Political Studies*, June 1988.
19. P. Schmitter, 'Reflections on Where the Theory of Neo-Corporatism Has Gone and Where the Praxis of Neo-Corporatism May Be Going', in Lehmbruch and Schmitter, op. cit., pp. 259–79.

Additional references

PARTIES
K. von Beyme, *Political Parties in Western Democracies*, Gower, 1985.
J. Blondel, *Political Parties: A Genuine Case for Discontent?*, Wildwood House, 1978.
J. Blondel, 'Mass Parties and Industrialised Societies', in J. Blondel (ed.), *Comparative Government: A Reader*, Macmillan, 1968.
F. Castles, *The Social Democratic Image of Society*, Routledge, 1978.
I. Crewe and D. Denver (eds.), *Electoral Change in Western Democracies*, Croom Helm, 1985.
R. Dalton, S. Flanagan and P. Beck (eds.), *Electoral Change in Advanced Industrial Democracies: Realignment or Dealignment?* Princeton University Press, 1984.

M. Duverger, *Political Parties: Their Organisation and Activity in the Modern State*, Methuen, 1964.

L. Epstein, *Political Parties in Western Democracies*, New Brunswick, N.J.: Transaction Books, 1980.

B. Girvin (ed.), *The Transformation of Continental Conservatism*, Sage, 1988.

S. Henig (ed.), *Political Parties in the European Community*, Allen and Unwin, 1979.

R. Irving, *The Christian Democratic Parties of Western Europe*, Allen and Unwin, 1979.

E. Kirchner (ed.), *Liberal Parties in Western Europe*, Cambridge University Press, 1988.

M. Kolinsky and W. Paterson (eds.), *Social and Political Movements in Western Europe*, Croom Helm, 1976.

Z. Layton-Henry, *Conservative Politics in Western Europe*, Macmillan, 1982.

A. Lindemann, *A History of European Socialism since 1789*, Yale University Press, 1983.

R. Morgan and S. Silvestri (eds.), *Moderates and Conservatives in Western Europe*, Heinemann/PSI, 1982.

W. Paterson and A. Thomas, (eds.), *Social Democratic Parties in Western Europe*, Croom Helm, 1977.

W. Paterson and A. Thomas (eds.), *The Future of Social Democracy: Problems and Prospects of Social Democratic Parties in Western Europe*, Clarendon, 1986.

G. Pridham, *Christian Democracy in Western Germany*, Croom Helm, 1977.

A. Ware, *Citizens, Parties and the State*, Polity Press, 1988.

See also, additional references for Chapters 4 and 6.

INTERESTS AND CORPORATISM

G. Almond, 'A Comparative Study of Interest Groups and the Political Process', in H. Eckstein and D. Apter, *Comparative Politics*, New York: The Free Press, 1963.

S. Berger (ed.), *Organizing Interests in Western Europe*, Cambridge University Press, 1981.

K. von Beyme, *Challenge to Power: Trade Unions and Workers' Organizations in Industrialized Nations*, Sage Publications, 1980.

F. Castles, (ed.), *The Impact of Parties: Politics and Policies in the Democratic Capitalist State*, Sage, 1982.

A. Cawson (ed.), *Organized Interests and the State: Studies in Meso-Corporatism*, Sage, 1985.

T. Clarke and L. Clements (eds.), *Trade Unions under Capitalism*, Harvester Press, 1978.

S. Clegg et al. (eds.), *The State, Class and Recession*, Sage Publications, 1982.

D. Coombes, *Representative Government and Economic Power*, Heinemann/PSI, 1982.

R. Dahl, *Dilemmas of Pluralist Democracy*, Yale University Press, 1982.

Government and Opposition, 'Trade Unions and Politics in Western Europe', (whole issue), Autumn 1978.

R. Harrison, *Pluralism and Corporatism*, Allen and Unwin, 1980.

J. Hayward and R. Berki (eds.), *State and Society in Contemporary Europe*, Martin Robertson, 1979.

J. Hayward (ed.), 'Trade Union Politics in Western Europe', Frank Cass, 1980.

G. Ionescu, *Centripetal Politics: Government and the New Centres of Power*, Hart-Davies, 1975.

W. Kendall, *The Labour Movement in Europe*, Allen Lane, 1975.

G. Lehmbruch and P. Schmitter (eds.), *Patterns of Corporatist Policy Making*, Sage Publications, 1982.

D. Marsh (ed.), 'Capital and Politics in Western Europe', *West European Politics* (whole issue), April 1983.

T. C. May, *Trade Unions and Pressure Group Politics*, Saxon House, 1975.

O. Newman, *The Challenge of Corporatism*, Macmillan, 1981.

L. Panitch, *Working-Class Politics in Crisis: Essays on Labour and the State*, Verso, 1986.

J. Richardson and A. Jordan, *Governing under Pressure*, Martin Robertson, 1979.

P. C. Schmitter and G. Lehmbruch (eds.), *Trends Towards Corporatist Intermediation*, Sage, 1979.

I. Scholten (ed.), *Political Stability and Neo-Corporatism: Corporatist Integration and Societal Cleavages*, Sage, 1987.

4 Party Systems

Determining features

Our examination of the social bases of politics in Western Europe pointed to a few, key social variables which – in particular combinations – shaped the nature of party politics for individual countries. We should round out this picture by considering what other factors are relevant in accounting for a characteristic type of party system. The various explanations can be grouped under two broad headings: for convenience we can label them the 'social forces' and the 'constitutional factors'. In the main, the account we have given so far has been one concerned with the underlying social features of a society – the class structure flanked by others of a cultural and geographical nature. The alternative view, and the one we shall look at in detail here, is that the party system is also the product of a number of provisions made generally to ensure the running of the state, or more particularly aimed at the working of the political parties, summed up as a 'constitutional' view. Both types of explanation are concerned with why a party system remains as it is or gives way to another type.

The constitutional determinants are often regarded as of marginal importance by those who seek a complete 'social' explanation of politics, and in Lipset's words, who '. . . tend to see party cleavages as reflections of an underlying structure, and hence . . . frown on efforts to present the enacted rules of the game as key causal elements of a social structure.'[1] But the framework within which parties grow up and continue to operate cannot be discounted entirely: the form of government, the legal constraints on the parties, the electoral system; these will all affect the expression which parties can give to the social forces they represent.

We can illustrate the effect the form of government may have on the party system by comparing the United States with Western Europe, since the particular combination of a presidential system with federalism in the USA has no counterpart in the mainly unitary and parliamentary European systems. The American structure of government results in a uniquely ambivalent two-party system. On the one hand, it is a strict two-party situation in that third parties are always unsuccessful on a national level, and this is so despite the numerous issues which would make for a multi-party system in other countries. Against that, it is a two-party system in name only, given the almost total autonomy of the state parties and of the representatives in Congress. In this respect, it can be seen that the separation of powers and the federal structure act as powerful agents of dispersion. At the same time, the presidential system, ensuring that the 'winner takes all', enforces a minimum of cohesion at the national level – contesting parties must aim at gaining half the national vote. The European situation is different in almost all respects: the great majority are unitary states with a parliamentary system of government, and national politics predominate. In West Germany and Austria, the nature of the federal system is quite secondary to the national parties.[2] Only in Switzerland does the federal form ante-date the modern parties, but the Swiss multi-party system functions without a separation of powers and without a directly-elected president.

The parliamentary system, which is general throughout Western Europe, means that there is no effective separation of assembly and executive;* it is true that this does not have any common numerical effect on the party systems – a usual minimum of three parties to twelve currently in Switzerland and eleven in Belgium – but within the assemblies there is usually a high degree of party unity and discipline. The fragmentation, where it occurs, arises at an *earlier* stage, for cross-voting on the part of deputies is regarded as a deviant act by their parliamentary parties. Contrast this cohesion with congressional behaviour in the United States where the two-party label hardly conceals the ability of representatives to vote entirely according to the issues at stake. It is reasonable to conclude that the European parties are forced into a similar mould by the common fact of government responsibility to the assembly, with all that this entails, and that this similarity transcends variations in the number of parties.

Only France closely resembles the United States in the manner of presidential election and his subsequent governing position, so that it is possible to gauge the influence of this Fifth Republic innovation on the party system. Whilst the French variant of the presidential system has as yet had no decisive effect on the party system, popular voting at the five presidential elections – each time with a run-off – has polarised issues around two candidates. At first the Gaullists were dominant, but with the election of Giscard d'Estaing in 1974, the mantle passed more generally to the parties 'of the majority'. As a result of the 1981 election they were forced

* See below, pp. 135-42.

into opposition, but there is a premium on retaining at least a minimum cohesion to have any chance in future presidential contests. On the left, there has been a similar resistance to the melting-pot effect of presidentialism. There were several efforts made to forge left-wing unity in the 1960s and 1970s, but it was not until Mitterrand's victory in 1981 that they met with success. Yet in the end it was a Socialist victory and not a Communist one – with the result that the two parties remained in a jealously competitive position towards one another, just as the Gaullist RPR resented its displacement from the presidency. The party system has thus almost been unwillingly pressed into a two-bloc mould, each bloc itself composed of antagonistic elements. Even though the presidential system has encouraged two broad 'tendencies' in French politics, a bipolarisation, the transfer from tendency to cohesive system faces the barrier of *existing* party structures, the 'inertia' of political parties mentioned earlier: they are factors in their own right, modifying the impact of social and constitutional forces. None the less, the presidential system probably has had the effect of hastening the decline of the PCF: Mitterrand's victories in 1981 and 1988 undermined the Communist vote, so that the Socialist Party became dominant within the left-wing bloc.

The fundamental arrangements of government appear to modify the expression of social differences which the political parties voice. In a similar way, provisions aimed specifically at the parties act as a constraint on the nature of the parties and the numbers competing. Two illustrations from West Germany help to make this point. The first is the provision of the Basic Law (Article 21) that parties must be 'democratic', leaving those open to prohibition which, '. . . by reason of their aims or the behaviour of their adherents, seek to impair or destroy the free democratic order or to endanger the existence of the Federal Republic.' The use of this article on two occasions, against the Communist Party and the extreme right, was of limited effect – the parties concerned only had a minute support anyway – but the potential of such limitations is vast.

The second West German innovation has less obvious but still profound implications for the party system. This is the provision for the state-financing of the political parties which has now reached considerable proportions. The measure was aimed at reducing the dependence of parties on the traditional pay-masters of politics, especially industrial interests, and by this means increase their democratic potential. The amounts received may not be critical for the future existence of the larger parties, but it could be a factor sufficient to alter the relationship of party to supporter;

a party may become less interested in building up or retaining a large membership for active help or paying dues, instead paid officials and agencies could replace voluntary help. Thus whilst parties may become less susceptible to financial blandishments they may also show an increased bureaucratisation and state-dependence, and with such a secure financial base, they may become less competitive. On the other hand, as the size of the subsidy depends on the share of the national vote, an additional spur to success is present. Moreover, since even those parties which fail to gain Bundestag representation also receive a share from the kitty, small and new parties have a continuing incentive to fight elections.[3]

Such examples as these show clearly that the impact of 'the enacted rules of the game' can affect the nature of party competition at all points. Overriding all the others, at least as a focal point for discussion, are the 'rules' of the electoral system. There is a wide divergence of viewpoint, ranging from those who trace a direct line from the type of voting arrangements used through to the number of parties represented and thence to the stability of government, even to the stability of the political system itself, and at the opposite extreme, others who are inclined to reverse the causal sequence and argue that the nature of the ongoing party system maintains a particular type of electoral system in being.

The fundamental distinction is between those countries which adhere to the principle of proportional representation and those which operate on the majority principle. The idea of proportionality is that all shades of political opinion should be represented in a popular assembly in direct correspondence to their weighting in the political community; it is a principle of representation, not one of government. Majority systems, although conceding the claim for 'one man, one vote', in effect favour the needs of government over the exact representation of opinion; in theory at least, by sacrificing exact representation, a majority system will contain political opinion within a few political parties, and these will 'govern' as well as 'represent'. The implicit extension of the argument is that since such parties are necessarily government-orientated, the 'needs of government' – presumably stable government – are likely to be better met than where representation is the sole consideration.

These are matters to which we shall want to return after examining the various types of European electoral system. Although the *principle* of proportional representation is quite explicit, how this is arrived at in practice leads to a large number of possible systems, all having particular features or bias. Only two countries operate a majority system: Britain and France. The British system of 'first-past-the-post' in single-member constituencies can result in two kinds of bias; firstly, within each constituency, the minority – or even a majority – fails to win any party representation; secondly, if the constituencies throughout the country are similar in their social make-up, then this homogeneity will always work to the advantage of one party – indeed, at an unlikely extreme it could be the only party represented at a national level. The fact that this does not happen in British circumstances depends partly on constituency size and partly on the uneven spread of political loyalties. The relatively large size of the House of Commons (650 members) reduces one bias, and the pattern of industry, and with it the distribution of socio-economic variables lessens the other. As a result, the British method is generally representative over a period of time; had it not been so, then the strength of disaffection shown in non-parliamentary ways would probably have forced a radical change in the system.

Yet a 'swing in the pendulum' may be very long delayed: the Labour Party was kept in opposition for 13 years from 1951 until 1964, and the process was repeated again by Mrs Thatcher's string of election victories beginning in 1979. In those circumstances doubts arise about the whole parliamentary system, and references to a 'one-party dominant' party system reflected the unease. Some political parties are anyway permanently under-represented or gain no seats at all. This applies to smaller parties whose support is fairly evenly spread geographically: in 1983 the Liberal/SDP Alliance had 24.6 per cent of the vote, but received a derisory 3.6 per cent of total seats. Other parties with a pronounced local appeal may have the chance to fare better: the Scottish and Welsh National parties, and these two for a while threatened to fragment the British party system in the 1970s There is a further serious distortion in the British case in that the geographical patterning of party representation has become hopelessly lop-sided. Thus as a result of the 1987 election the Labour Party (outside of London) was almost totally eliminated from the more prospering southern part of the country, whilst the Conservative Party was grossly under-represented in the industrial north and Scotland. In other words, the *apparent* polarisation between north and south in terms of party representation serves to exacerbate the *real* differences in economic fortune.

The French variation of the majority system, second ballot in single-member constituencies, is fundamentally different in its effects. Whilst the British system operates to give a fairly representative assembly over a period of years, at least to the major parties, the second ballot may not even do this. The mechanics of the second ballot give any party, with an absolute majority of votes at the first ballot, a constituency seat as outright winner. But if no party wins an absolute majority, at the second ballot, held a week later, the first-past-the-post principle operates, and the party with the most votes gains the seat. Unless the party is very strong locally, it will have to fight the second ballot, and this implies considerable horse-trading amongst the parties at a national level in order to secure favourable electoral pacts in time for the second ballot. In this situation, a party must win allies or suffer heavy discrimination; parties near the centre may have some benefit, but the smaller parties are the chief losers: in 1958 the Communist Party was awarded less than two per cent of the assembly seats with almost 20 per cent of the votes cast. Although this arrangement meets the 'needs of government', the representative principle goes by the board (and candidates with below 12.5 per cent are excluded from the second ballot), the process of government formation may be no easier than where the proportional principle is observed; the most that can be said is that it makes for a sophisticated electorate. The ingrained tendency of French parties in power to 'make' elections is never far from the surface.

This proclivity for 'managing' the electoral system was confirmed by the action of the French Socialist government prior to the 1986 election in reverting from the second-ballot system to proportional representation. Partly, it was an exercise in damage limitation: the fortunes of the PS were at a low ebb, and its weakness would have been magnified by a majoritarian electoral system. Partly too, however, the aim was to 'help' the extreme-right National Front and thus cause maximum embarrassment to the moderate bourgeois parties, the RPR and UDF. It could hardly be a matter for surprise that, following their success in 1986, the latter lost no time in restoring the two-ballot system, although – as it turned out – the 1988 election produced a majority for the parties of the left.

Some variation of the proportional principle is used in all other West European states, often of some complexity. In general, most of the systems have been employed for a considerable time, and with the exceptions of West Germany, Italy and Ireland, there has been no strong move to adopt majority systems; in the Republic of Ireland a proposal to do so was defeated by referendum in 1968. Normally the electoral system will suit the parties in power, since presumably it helped them to get there, and changes in the system, usually on par with a constitutional amendment, will require a large measure of inter-party agreement; if changes are mooted, some parties will naturally suspect the motives of the others, thus making a fundamental revision quite unlikely.

The practical application of proportional representation varies according to two rather conflicting criteria. The first is to ensure that party representation in the assembly reflects their performance at an election; the second consideration is to provide voters with some choice as between candidates, not merely between parties. If only the first condition is met, the result is a pure 'party list' system; this means that the party will have a complete say in the order of preference for its candidates, and by placing favoured ones high on the list their subsequent election will be assured – in effect, the equivalent of the 'safe seat' in the British House of Commons. The majority system can be adapted to give a measure of choice between candidates of the same party by the institution of the 'primary' election, and in rare cases in the United States, the 'open primary' – open to all registered electors, regardless of their party affiliation. However, the use of the party-list system can be adapted to the same end, giving voters a choice between parties and candidates on the same occasion. The extent of this choice varies considerably. Thus the Belgian system allows a vote either for the party's list (and therefore its order) or for one particular candidate of that party; once the party's total allocation of seats has been calculated, it is then possible to work out who its successful candidates will be according to those who voted for the party list and those who have expressed their own preference. Variations on this theme are general in Scandinavia, the Netherlands, Italy, Luxembourg, and Switzerland. In some, a large degree of choice is provided, including the possibility of combining candidates from more than one party list. The element of personal choice, to which party-list systems have to be adapted, is the leading characteristic of the Single Transferable Vote as used in the Republic of Ireland and Malta. This system, besides ensuring that no votes are 'wasted' – that is, cast in excess of what a candidate needs to win election in a multi-member constituency – also means that voters' preference always remain 'personal': the transferred vote is never to a 'party' but to a 'candidate', whilst under party list systems this distinction cannot be maintained.

A further difference between types of proportional representation arises from the size of the constituencies. Unlike majority systems where the representation is likely to be improved as the number of constituencies is increased, the reverse applies for proportionality: only in a large multi-member constituency will it be possible to share out seats at all accurately, and only if the whole nation is treated as a single constituency for this purpose will distortions be minimised – as is the case in the Netherlands. Yet this 'remoteness' of the deputy from his electorate is perhaps also undesirable; consequently, an alternative is to have sub-national constituencies and hold back a 'remainder' of seats to secure an overall (national) proportional effect after constituency allocations have been made.

By various such devices proportional systems can provide for voter choice, constituency-effect, and accurate representation. Their strict proportionality can also be modified by simply stipulating a cut-off below which very small parties gain no representation. In Denmark, it is as low as 2 per cent, in Sweden 4 per cent and in West Germany 5 per cent. This form of doctoring of the system is easy to institute since almost all the established parties will stand to gain in seats if very small parties are excluded. In Greece, a different kind of bias is engineered through a system of 'reinforced' proportional representation: those parties obtaining at least 17 per cent of the national vote receive an additional quota of seats. West Germany's electoral system is a good example of adaptation: although the overall effect is strictly proportional, half of the Bundestag members are elected by relative majorities in single-member constituencies. The voter has two votes, one for a constituency candidate and the other for a party list. The party's total Bundestag representation is decided by the list vote; from that total is then deducted the number of constituency seats (if any) it has already won. The only tangible difference is that some of a party's Bundestag membership will have won a seat in their own right and the others will be there thanks to their high position on the party list.

From these rather straightforward considerations, we can turn to some of the wider implications of electoral systems for party systems and for government. The observation made by Duverger is central to the discussion: 'An almost complete correlation is observable between the simple-majority, single-ballot system and the two-party system.'[4] The *implication* of Duverger's finding, and one which is frequently voiced, is that there is a similar relationship between proportional voting and multi-party systems. Whilst it is admitted that two-party systems frequently go together with simple majority voting, there is no question of this effect being a necessary consequence, and Duverger's formulation breaks down where there are strong *regional* loyalties – as Colin Leys remarked for British politics in the early part of the century; 'It took more than the electoral system to get rid of the Irish.'[5]

The strong association between proportional voting and numerous parties appears justified if one takes into account the numbers represented in the assemblies of Western Europe – on average six. But many are very small indeed, and if these are excluded – say, those with less than 10 per cent – then no assembly has more than four parties which can be called substantial. It is around the nature and relative size of these that a system develops its special characteristics. Further, with the exception of the Netherlands, Belgium and Denmark, no spectacular proliferation is involved; and even those systems with several parties appear to reach a natural maximum number, beyond which new parties either fail to make an impression or they replace declining ones.

But it is also true that the number of parties represented can be very low under a proportional system. Malta has only two parties, and these two share regularly 99 per cent of the poll with over 90 per cent of the electorate voting, and Austria hovered on the brink of a two-party system for years. There was a progressive decline in West Germany, from eleven parties in 1949 to four at present, though the introduction of the 'five-per-cent clause' has helped this process. France has operated numerous electoral systems in the present century, but the number of parties has remained a quite independent factor. This is not to argue that electoral systems are without effect. It is reasonable to suppose that a majority system makes it more difficult for new parties to make an initial impact (although the regional aspect should not be forgotten) and that it also leads to a more rapid extinction of declining parties. The converse is that proportional systems enable new parties to gain a foothold and rescue others that would otherwise disappear. We can show how both of these effects have worked under proportional representation.

The classic example of proportional voting helping a new party is that of the National Socialists in the Weimar Republic. At three successive elections in the 1920s, the National Socialists had a minute, and declining, support – finally under three per cent. Only in 1930 did the Nazi appeal broaden, with a significant share of 18 per cent. The argument to be favoured here is that the Nazis had a small but vociferous representation right through the 'lean' years, a base on which they were quickly able to build once the economic storm broke. The stronger argument that proportional representation had a *direct* causal influence on the growth of the Nazi Party is rejected by Georges Lavau who found a close parallel in the rapid growth of the Labour vote in Britain between 1910 and 1929 – but in the context of a 'hostile' simple majority system. He asked, if the rise of the Labour Party was a normal evolution, why should the Nazi movement be regarded as abnormal? 'Past and present experience, alas, shows sufficiently that fascism is a development just as 'normal' as democracy . . . One can ask oneself whether a simple plurality system would not have brought about a much more rapid rise of the National Socialists.' Lavau went even further in rejecting the 'foothold' argument as well: 'It is frequently asserted, with regard to the Nazi Party, that in a majority system a party which has hardly seven per cent of the votes (as was the case in 1924) would have been swept away at the following election. The example of the Labour Party does not prove this.'[6] Against this interpretation one can say that the context of the two parties was different; in Britain the Liberal Party was falling apart, and inevitably a new party was given maximum scope, whilst the Nazi Party, in the mid-twenties, had no such benefit; to this extent, the fact that it could retain a small group in the Reichstag until the situation was favourable is directly attributable to the system of voting.

The second example demonstrates the 'rescue' effect of proportional representation. Prior to 1894, Belgium had a two-party system with simple-majority voting: a Catholic party and the anti-clerical Liberals. Thereafter, the Socialists gained representation with the extension of the franchise, and there was a catastrophic fall in the number of Liberal seats. Unwilling to be left alone with the Socialists, the Catholic majority introduced proportional voting in 1900, and this quickly helped to restore Liberal fortunes – a threefold increase in Liberal seats. As a result, a genuine three-party system was preserved throughout the inter-war period. Such rescue operations may only lead to an attenuated prolongation of a spent political force – European assemblies are dotted with these survivals: the Old Liberals in Switzerland, the Swedish People's Party in Finland, the Republicans and Liberals in Italy. However, the period of survival may allow a rejuvenation to take place. The decline of the Belgian Liberals set in once more after 1945, but shedding its anti-clericalism, the party was able to make a straight bid for the middle-class vote. The principle could apply to any other party in the doldrums; Communist parties in several countries, such as France or Spain, can seek to make a renewed appeal with more success than would be possible in Britain.

Another, and related, consequence of an electoral system is sometimes said to be the resulting stability of government. The argument is that a two-party system, with simple-majority voting, leads to greater government stability. Of course, 'stability of government' is only one of a number of criteria to judge the viability of a party system. It is probably the most favoured index of government performance, since it is the least impressionistic, and it stands in the middle of two extreme criteria: the quality and quantity of government decision-making and the ability of the political system to survive intact. The implication is that 'stable government' is both a measure of the acceptability of government decision-making and of the chances that the system will not break down.

However, the problem of using 'stability' as an index of system performance is closely akin to the general one we came across in the first chapter, that of stability as a feature of liberal democracy. One may first query whether government stability, in the sense of duration of government by the same party or parties in office, is necessarily desirable. The apparent breakdown of civilian government in Northern Ireland followed on some fifty years of unquestioned rule by the Unionist Party – in fact can be held to be a direct consequence of that hegemony. Only if at the same time government decision-making is acceptable (presumably to be judged by the absence of extra-parliamentary disaffection), can one use government duration as an adequate guide. One may say that the Fifth Republic in its first ten years showed great government durability: one president, two prime ministers, and only one party effectively in power. Yet this stability was a prelude to the rising of May 1968 which showed a significant discontent in French society.

Duration of government does vary considerably, but there is no tight connection between this and the number of parties, so that even if it is conceded, as Blondel delicately worded it, 'that countries which have the majority systems are more likely to be two-party systems and countries which experience proportional representation are more likely not to have two-party systems',[7] it still does not make the electoral system a direct causal influence on government durability.[8] In fact, there is no correlation between the shortness of government life and positive evidence of social and political instability. Governmental instability – and with it frequent elections – may occur for a variety of reasons, without necessarily indicating a high degree of social discord. Thus Ireland had to resort to three elections within eighteen months in 1981–2 simply because the outcomes were not properly decisive. Indeed, in some circumstances the threat to political stability may encourage the governing parties to maintain coalitions or at least avoid having too-frequent elections in order not to make the situation worse. This reluctance to consult the electorate is a feature of Italian parties: despite the frequency of coalition breakdown, Italy has had a remarkable record of parliaments lasting for most of their full term. There is thus no firm evidence to link majoritarian government to greater inherent stability nor to treat government duration as a test of that stability.

It is rather a different question to speculate on whether the 'quality' of government is likely to be better with a two-party system. Although this system gives a ready-made 'alternative government', the other possibility – of coalition government – is not simply a 'less eligible' alternative. It can be argued that the dualism inherent in the British 'classic' type of two-party system, with the ever-alternating ins and outs of office, is more suited to some historical periods and to some political cultures than to others. The Swiss pattern of government, though unlike all other in its arrangements, gives the essence of alternative possibilities. Much depends on how the function of opposition is evaluated, and it is one perspective of party competition we take up shortly in looking at 'patterns of opposition'.

The whole debate on the relative effects of constitutional and social forces can hardly be conclusive. Even though electoral systems may affect the number of parties and that in turn may affect the *way* in which decisions are made, there is no necessary consequence for the viability of the party system. One qualification to the power of constitutional factors is that they cannot simply be accepted as 'given'; their origins and the fact that they are retained in a certain form, have to be related to the social context in which they operate. In this sense, it is the social situation (and with it the party system) which maintains an electoral system – not the other way round. The party system is the important resultant: the means by which a reconciliation is sought, and dominance expressed.

Imbalance, balance and diffusion
A classification that goes beyond a simple numerical ordering is needed if we wish to generalise about European party systems. The significant variables are:

– the relative size of the major parties;
– the deployment of all the constituent parties in respect of socially relevant issues.

The first expresses a simple power position: What numerical combination can supply a governing majority? The second takes into account the feasibility of such combinations according to the social basis of party support and the actual relations between the parties. A combination of these two features gives three typical forms of party system: imbalance, diffusion, and balance.

It is not difficult to show the numerical aspect of imbalance, since it occurs when one party, or a closely-related group of parties, is in a commanding position for considerable periods; the gap between it and the second party is large, and this will mean that, exceptional combinations apart, the dominant party is indispensable to government formation; a feature of such dominance is that it is unlikely to be eroded from one election to another.

Apart from Britain and Ireland, it has not been normal for one party to enjoy a large majority in the assembly for long periods, although the Norwegian Labour Party had a majority in the Storting until the 1960s and the Austrian Socialists were similarly placed in the 1970s. However, there are a number of sporadic examples.[9] Indispensability for the formation of government and a leading place within it may be a better guide to a modified form of dominance. Several parties have been dominant in this sense in the period after 1945. It applied to the West German CDU until the end of the Adenauer era, to the Italian Christian Democrats for the whole of the post-war era, and to the Swedish Social Democrats from the 1930s until 1976. The Gaullists in France enjoyed a similar position from 1958 until 1974. We can add the Irish Fianna Fail as well as the Social-Christians in both Belgium and Luxembourg, since they have been in office for a large part of the post-war period. The Luxembourg case is a limiting one *numerically* because the Christian-Socials rarely had a large lead over its rivals. But until 1974 it had been the senior party in every government since 1919, and the *feasibility* of the alternative Socialist-Liberal alliance was low. The Socialists and Liberals thus neatly alternated as junior coalition partners from 1947 until 1974 when they ousted the Christian-Socials. In 1979, however, the latter won back their governing position.

A diffused party system requires a relatively large number of parties, none with a decisive superiority and several having a comparable share of the vote. Just as important: the parties show no sign of a clear or pronounced polarisation; they represent rather the different facets of an overall social cohesion. The party system in the Netherlands exemplifies this category: at the present time nine parties are represented, the two leading parties have only about a third of the vote each, and the range of coalition possibilities is fairly wide. Several countries are in this position. It was a typical feature of the French Fourth Republic, and Belgium, Denmark, Finland, and Switzerland all now fulfil the requirements for diffusion. Inevitably, there is a tendency to regard a diffused system as also having the characteristic features of an unstable multi-party system, but governmental instability is not a necessary outcome. In the Netherlands, for example, the initial formation of governments is usually difficult, but over a very long period the average life of governments has been about two years. Similarly, the increasing diffusion which has been apparent in Belgium since the 1960s (with 11 parties in 1988) has forced the traditional parties of government to cooperate with one another – if they do not hang together in face of the linguistic issue, they may hang separately!

In the conditions of a balanced system the major requirement is that there should be a single clear line of polarisation. It is natural in this situation to think that there should be only two parties, but there can equally be two 'clusters' of parties. 'Balance' requires that neither pole should be predominant, and if there is a numerical balance between the two parties or clusters, then the basis for a simple alternation of government is present. In practice that alternation may not occur for long periods, but even if it does not, both contestants must act with the eventuality in mind – typically the case for Britain, although she was affected by a temporary diffusion of the party system in the 1970s. With a fully balanced system we should expect the two major parties to obtain about 90 per cent of the vote. Austria and West Germany both had very high two-party aggregates until the 1980s. Although in Germany's case the medium of a small third party has been operative in securing a shift in government power, the essentials of a balanced system are present. The less pronounced form of the 'balanced cluster' is evident elsewhere, notably in Scandinavia and the Fifth French Republic. The distinction between diffusion and the balanced cluster is important. Both are typified by multi-party systems. But in the case of diffusion we should expect centre-type parties to be well represented, whereas the balanced cluster form points to their relative weakness.

There is no doubt that balance or the balanced cluster is a typical West European form. Two points should be made. One is that the extent of balance only incidentally refers to the degree of polarisation in a system, since it is chiefly related to the patterning of government/opposition alternation. The second point is that the widespread occurrence of balanced forms at the present time underlines the extent to which the concepts of 'left' and 'right' still pervade West European politics.

This typology of party systems – imbalance, diffusion and balance – has the merit that all Western European countries can be fitted reasonably into one category or another. But we need to bear in mind that they do not occupy static positions; most systems have shown signs of change in recent years, and it is worthwhile examining those cases where there appears to be a developmental sequence. There are certainly grounds for believing that some party systems have shown a move away from long-term dominance, although it is not possible to show that either the balanced or the diffused form is becoming the predominant one for Western Europe.

In the case of diffused systems, it can be argued that where they have been based on historically defined 'cross-cutting social cleavages', the emergence of a more 'homogeneous' society should make the old lines of party cleavage redundant. A conclusion would be that that homogeneity should leave socio-economic differences as the main *residual* factor: the decline of sectionalism has favoured the development of 'balanced' systems showing only a moderate degree of polarisation. But it is also evident that West European party systems have become more open to diffusion in recent times: *historical* sectionalism has undoubtedly declined, yet multi-party systems are still the flourishing norm. The only reasonable explanation appears to be that our more homogeneous forms of society can support various political expressions and that those 'expressions' – typically seen in 'new politics' movements – as yet neither give rise to new cleavages nor offer a determined and sustained challenge to the existing political order and the stability of government.

Rather different considerations apply to imbalanced systems and their decline. One can argue that an imbalanced system results from a relative lack of cohesion in another part of the political spectrum. Where social class has been the main motor in the development of a party system, then any imbalance will have been caused through either the bourgeois or the socialist parties having failed to attain adequate or unified expression. Thus fragmentation or inadequacy on the left or on the right makes for a pronounced 'lag' – the lag is shown by a numerical inferiority and implicitly by the weak development of a party, in its structure and ideology. There is no need to assume that some kind of social parity must obtain – party imbalance might be prolonged indefinitely if the social and political lags are entrenched.

Let us take an example of a country where the conditions of an orderly developmental sequence can be clearly discerned. Western Germany in the post-war period fits a three-stage model: from initial diffusion, through temporary imbalance, reaching a current state of balance. The first stage, seemingly a throwback to the Weimar Republic, showed the two major parties, CDU and SPD, able only to muster about 60 per cent of the vote between them. That phase passed quickly with elimination of the smaller parties and the rise of the CDU from 1953 as the dominating force. We have seen that the CDU was one of the new-type parties, bourgeois yet with a general 'Christian' appeal, and we have also noted the later response of the SPD: its large numerical lag facilitated a fundamental change in the party's orientation. The end of CDU dominance came with the formation of a 'grand coalition' with the SPD in 1966, and a balanced system has operated since 1969 – the CDU was forced into opposition and the SPD became the major governing party until 1982, when the roles were again reversed. It is as yet uncertain whether the entry of the Greens will have any decisive effect on the existing pattern of alternation which depends on the small FDP being eligible for either of the two major parties.

France – spanning the Fourth and Fifth Republics – has shown a somewhat similar evolution to balanced polarisation. The hopeless diffusion which typified the Fourth Republic was quickly replaced in the Fifth Republic from 1958 by Gaullist dominance. The emergence of a mass – and moderate – bourgeois party was a new event in France, as it had been in Germany, and for a while the spectacular rise of the Gaullist party meant that the lag in development appeared on the left. The dominance of the UNR (later UDR) waned especially after de Gaulle's departure in 1969, but the cohesion of the bourgeois alliance – the Gaullists with the Independent Republicans (later the UDF) – was maintained. In its turn the French left – chiefly the Communists and Socialists – made a sustained effort to overturn the bourgeois majority, coming near to success at the presidential election of 1974. Even though the French left was so long denied governing power, the feasibility of alternation remained high – and the switch duly took place in 1981, back again to the bourgeois parties in 1986, and once more to the left in 1988. The two-bloc system which emerged in the Fifth Republic, aided by the pressures of the presidential contest, evolved from a situation of one-party dominance to reach its present form of a balanced cluster.

The dominance of the Christian Democrats in Italy was of a different order from that in Germany or France. The sheer strength of the religious vote supporting the DC for long hindered a simple class polarisation of political life. It also had the effect of making the DC less 'bourgeois' in orientation and therefore more able to take up a 'centre' position, with straddling alliances of a centre-left nature. Over the years, however, the steady rise in the Communist vote made the dominant position of the DC appear at best residual – after the 1976 election the party had to form a minority government, relying on the tacit support of the PCI to keep it in office; in 1981 and 1983 the DC even had at last to cede government leadership to a minor party. The party system is now hovering between balance and diffusion.

The largest disparities in voting support between the first and second parties – a *prima facie* indication of imbalance – were evident in Scandinavia: Denmark, Norway and Sweden. There was a long tradition of the imbalance favouring the left and concomitantly a considerable fragmentation of the bourgeois vote. Commencing in the 1930s, the Social Democratic parties were in an overtowering position in all three countries for decades at a time, but that era has now passed. For several years the Danish Social Democrats, although still by far the largest party, more often than not had to resort to minority government. Their position was helped perhaps by the dazzling diffusion of the party system which first came about in 1973 when the number of parties in the Folketing jumped suddenly from five to ten – in 1981 the *second largest* party had only 14.4 per cent of the vote, whilst the Social Democrats won 33 per cent. In a sense, therefore, it was a case of 'dominance by default'. Subsequently, the dominance entirely disappeared in the 1980s with the formation of a centre-right coalition. But the apparently balanced form resulting was deceptive, since on some issues (such as defence and the EC) governments found it hard to muster majorities in the Folketing, so that elements of diffusion counteracted the apparently balanced party line-up.

The Norwegian situation also became more complex in the 1970s. The Norwegian Labour Party lost its overall majority in the Storting in the early 1960s and suffered seriously from internal party dissension over the question of European Community membership, especially in the wake of the 1972 referendum. As the Storting is elected for a fixed term (thus avoiding frequent elections) the stability of government was not affected by Labour's decline. The outcome, in fact, was a situation of stable minority rule by the Labour Party, until the major bourgeois parties formed a governing majority after the 1981 election. In 1986 there was a return to minority Labour government.

In Sweden there is also a large disparity between the Social Democrat vote and that of the second party and a similar fragmentation affecting opposing parties. The Swedish Social Democrats were dominant for a long period, in government from 1932 until 1976, although rarely having an absolute majority. The party was usually in alliance with the Agrarians (later Centre), the red-green alignment, but in later years the Social Democrats relied on the support of the diminutive Communist Party. In the 1970s support for the Social Democrats declined, and that led to the 'historic change' of 1976 when at long last a bourgeois coalition (Centre, Liberals and Conservatives) returned to power. Their spell in office ended in 1982 since when the Social Democrats have been in office, but the era of dominance has gone, and Sweden now exemplifies the balanced cluster system.

Generally, Scandinavian party systems have moved from dominance to balance, although Denmark combines elements of both balance and diffusion, and there are other countries where diffusion has been endemic. In the Netherlands, the presence of several religious parties made it impossible for features of balance to develop, principally because the ability of the religious parties to win support across class lines worked to the detriment of the Dutch Labour Party. However, the considerable decline in the religious vote over the past twenty or so years has altered the party system considerably. One result was to promote the fusion of the three major religious parties in 1976 to form the Christian Democratic Appeal (CDA), another was the gradual improvement in support for the Labour Party. But that simplification was offset by the rise of new parties such as the progressive Democrats '66 and the Radical Catholic Party, helped by the generous electoral system. The question of whether the Dutch party system is more diffused than balanced can be looked at in two ways. The argument for continuing diffusion is based partly on the multiplicity of parties represented, but mainly on the fact that the CDA still 'straddles' the system in such a way as to obscure polarising tendencies. Against that, there is an incipient bipolarity: on the one side a 'progressive bloc' consisting of Labour, Democrats '66, and Radical Catholics, and on the other the Liberals with the CDA – those two forming a long-lasting governing coalition as a result of the 1982 election. However, it is doubtful whether the CDA will wish to be cut off permanently from a centre-left alignment, and for its part the Labour Party sees coalition with the CDA as giving it the most realistic chance of returning to government.

We have already looked at the reasons for the growing diffusion of Belgian politics; until the late 1950s there was a fairly balanced four-party system, with the leading parties, Social-Christians and Socialists, sharing 80 per cent of the vote. The active resurgence of the language issue in the late 1950s changed the pattern completely. The renewed success of the Liberals (Party of Liberty and Progress) occurred at roughly the same time as the rise of the specifically linguistic parties: the Flemish *Volksunie*, the Wallon *Rassemblement*, and the Brussels *Front des Francophones*. By the 1970s their combined vote reached over 20 per cent, sufficient with the Liberal revival to set the two major parties in disarray. The linguistic issue was also one they had failed to contain within their own parties, so that the tensions were powerful: the party system appeared to be on the brink of fragmentation. Yet the success, admittedly long drawn-out, in reaching a linguistic compromise has resulted in some minor parties being willing to participate in government. There has been a gradual loss of support for the small linguistic parties in the 1980s, and the basic stability of the political system has been maintained; a limit may now have been reached in the process of diffusion.

Such examples of developing diffusion have to be set against others where change is less apparent. Finland's party system is very static: the four largest parties share 80 per cent of the vote, and only rarely does any one reach a quarter of the total. The parties do show a clear spread on the 'left-right' axis and there is the basis for a balanced cluster. Two factors work against a clear polarisation however. One is the strategic position occupied by the Centre Party, which has been the linch-pin for most coalitions, and the party shows a preference for centre-left groupings, reminiscent of the red-green formation. The second factor relates to Finland's international position: the country is best served by broad coalitions – not excluding the Communist SKDL. These two factors favour coalitions of four or five parties, although the resulting governments have usually been unstable. The balanced cluster evident in the *distribution* of Finnish parties does not show itself at the level of government coalition, nor perhaps would it be desirable if it did. Thus, as a result of the 1987 election, the Conservatives (long kept out of government) led a four-party coalition including the Social Democrats – but *excluding* the Centre Party, a striking exception to the usual pattern of coalition formation, as well as to the postulates of formal coalition theory.

In the case of Switzerland the position is so static that we can say a form of 'institutionalised' diffusion has taken hold. The federal structure and the collegial system of government make it almost impossible to visualise *any* change. The 'government club' of the four major parties precludes any mechanism of development – beyond increasing the size of the club. The three largest parties, Radicals, Socialists, and Christian Democrats (Catholics), each with 20 to 25 per cent of the vote, have an equal and permanent share in government – two seats each, with the remaining one going to the smaller People's Party, a ratio which has remained constant since 1959. Dissatisfaction with this hegemonic 'system' led to the formation of protest parties such as the *Landesring*, and the 'National Campaign against Foreign Domination of People and

Homeland'. The latter movement was a reaction against the high level of migrant workers in Switzerland, and much of its impetus was gained from a referendum held in 1970 to cut immigration sharply, a proposal resisted by all the established parties. Protests of that nature are not insignificant, but they are unlikely to threaten government cohesion: a new party which really did become a force to be reckoned with would simply be offered a seat on the Federal Council, and its acceptance would entail a pledge of the party's future cooperative behaviour.

Quite apart from the particular examples of diffusion which have been largely historically determined, there are also more general and mainly contemporary causes to consider. Thus we can relate the earlier discussion of 'new cleavages' in a direct way to diffusion. Precisely because new movements cut across old party lines, they muffle the existing polarity and upset the balance of party systems.

On an electoral level parties which in one way or another can be grouped under the 'new politics' label have as yet only had a limited impact, and the extent to which they can be said to destabilise existing party systems can easily be exaggerated mainly because of their unorthodox tactics. The Italian Radicals quickly won a reputation as the gadfly of Italian politics, but without seriously affecting the structure of party competition. The West German Greens have had a more fundamental influence, since – in developing as a party of the radical left – they have challenged the consensual basis of the pre-existing three-party system: the SPD as a result has to decide between sticking to its moderate centre-leaning course and facing up to its radical competitor. On another level, too, the West German Greens, with their ability to put new issues on the agenda and their promotion of direct action and popular participation, have altered the political scene in the Federal Republic quite out of proportion to their electoral strength. By no means all of the new politics parties have had this kind of success. In Austria, Belgium, Finland, Luxembourg and Switzerland the various green/alternative parties have simply served to increase the sense of diffusion and – as yet – represent an addendum to a party system and not a powerful restructuring force.

Given the widespread evidence of continuing or even deepening diffusion, there is no broad movement towards balanced systems. But in some countries there has been a move away from dominance and imbalance. The case of Ireland is illustrative: Fianna Fail enjoyed many years of undisputed supremacy throughout the 1950s and 1960s, winning absolute majorities at four successive elections. A period of balance and alternation followed when for a time Fine

Gael and Labour came closer together. Yet, as shown by the 1987 election, there are now signs of progressive diffusion with the newly-formed Progressive Democrats and the Workers' Party making appreciable inroads. This development anyway has to be read in conjunction with the difficulty of interpreting Irish politics in conventional left–right terms – diffusion of party positions is already an inherent characteristic.

A similar decline of dominance can be noted for the Independence Party in Iceland which was in power almost continuously from when Iceland gained full statehood in 1944 until the 1970s. Over the years since then the Independence Party has had spells in opposition, a development which can be partly attributed to the steady rise of the left-wing vote, gradually removing the lop-sided look of the party system. For Iceland there has been an interesting twist in the process of diffusion: a Feminist Alliance won five per cent of the vote in 1983 and reached ten per cent in 1987. There is no doubt that 'founding' parties can impart an initial imbalance to a party system which may persist for many years, as the Independence Party and Fianna Fail both show. More generally, a founding party may enjoy a favoured position following a strong discontinuity in the political system: the DC in Italy after fascism, the CDU in the Federal Republic, the Gaullists in the Fifth Republic. But the benefits may be of short duration: New Democracy in Greece soon appeared to be in an unassailable position after the downfall of the military dictatorship in 1974 – only to be resoundingly defeated by the Socialist Party, Pasok, at the 1981 election. The circumstances of the founding of the new democratic regimes in Portugal and Spain also show the extent to which fundamental changes in direction have to be allowed for: Portugal quickly moved from a radical left-wing course to one of conservative consolidation, a shift reflected in the fortunes of the respective parties, whilst the reverse was true for Spain, culminating in the sweeping victories of the Socialist Party in 1982 and 1986.

Neat patterns of development are not to be expected. The model of West German evolution, leading to a balanced system, is found in only a few countries, such as Austria and Scandinavia, and other balanced ones – with Britain as the major example – have had difficulty in maintaining their balanced characteristics. Nor on the other hand should we expect the influence of new social forces to change party systems overnight or beyond recognition. Even though one or other of the older parties may go into decline for a while, its existence need not be jeopardised and it may obstruct changes for a long time. Furthermore, the party itself may belatedly adapt to changing social circumstances in order to preserve its position.

System trends

A discussion of party systems with a typology – imbalance, balance, and diffusion – is a useful way of drawing attention to specific national features and how they may be changing. But there is a more general question of whether it is possible to discern any European-wide trends. A starting-point for any examination is inevitably based on the now-famous 'freezing hypothesis' advanced by Lipset and Rokkan:[10] that European party systems in the earlier post-1945 era were still substantially based on the social cleavage patterns that had structured the individual party systems during the period of their primary formation, that is, at the time when modern parties came into being in the late nineteenth and early twentieth centuries.

What we have seen in this and earlier chapters is that those historical cleavages in Western Europe have left an indelible mark on the parties and that they are still important factors in shaping electoral choice. At the same time, it is impossible to ignore the evidence of social and economic change over the past half century. No one would reasonably suppose that party systems could remain 'frozen' forever, and the gradually rising levels of electoral volatility over the years point to the weakening hold of the cleavage appeals on which traditionally the parties could count. As we have seen, too, the rise of new issues and the new politics is indicative of the range of factors influencing voters.

Numerous theories have been advanced to account for the changes in voters' motivations and behaviour and interpretations of the wider consequences – in terms, for instance, of a 'grand choice' between electoral dealignment and a realignment of electoral forces, the former pointing to a progressive disengagement from particular parties and the latter to the emergence of a different but possibly stable pattern. Yet what is remarkable within this considerable and increasing electoral flux has been the ability of the traditional parties to maintain their position. These parties constitute the 'core' of a party system, and although their individual fortunes fluctuate, together they still dominate the scene and provide a recognisable continuity whatever the other changes taking place – the entry of new parties, the volatile behaviour of the electorate.

How is this apparent disjunction to be explained? In the first place, it may be queried whether European party systems were ever so tightly tied to cleavage patterns as the freezing argument implied. If they were rather more independent from the start, then it follows that the changes in social structure and related social affiliations would not have such momentous consequences for the parties as might have been expected.

A second kind of explanation accepts the broad terms of the cleavage model, but questions the real extent and significance of electoral volatility. Thus Peter Mair, in using the idea of 'conflict areas', distinguishes between electoral movements that take place *within* an area and those that occur *across* the lines of division.[11] We can appreciate that 'within area' volatility – for instance, between two left-wing parties – is of a quite different character from an equally large movement across from left to right. In the case of the one, there is no basic change, whereas 'inter-area' volatility does have profound implications. One problem with this approach is that parties themselves can change their position: a 'travelling party' can itself move across the lines both with regard to its programme and the kind of coalition it is prepared to enter.

A third way of looking at the problem of 'system persistence versus electoral volatility' is to stress the nature of parties as independent actors in the political process: they are not simply the passive objects reacting to social movements and electoral forces that an undue emphasis on social cleavage structures may imply. Their behaviour and strategy establishes the agenda for political debate and the level of political awareness; they can act to reinforce or dissolve the lines of political division in society. Above all else, parties are sensitive to those changes that threaten their position, so that they can show a high level of adaptive behaviour: faced with the threat of the loosening of one basis of political attachment, they will seek out another.

It is just as important not to take this line of argument too far. What the impact of rising electoral volatility and the entry of new issues and new parties does signify is that the traditional parties have become that much more vulnerable than in the past. Their vulnerability means that few, if any, of the traditional European parties can expect to enjoy prolonged periods of dominace. Nor is survival merely a question of employing a new strategy: the communist parties of Western Europe have declined whether or not they have adopted a hard or soft line towards other parties and to parliamentary democracy.

All these considerations have to be applied to the idea of 'trends'. One conclusion is that a party system is at least a partly independent variable and that its core elements can persist despite substantial electoral change. Its 'independence', however, has definite limits: for instance, the virtual absence now of pronounced 'anti-system' parties in Western Europe ultimately has to be traced to their lack of electoral appeal. Thus, the parameters of system trends are set by this constraint – and the overriding general feature is that party systems have become steadily less polarised – to the extent that cases of 'polarised pluralism' are now purely historical examples.[12] Yet within that overall framework of moderate party competition, there is wide scope for variation – as we have seen in the illustration of balanced and diffused systems; both are heavily influenced in their functioning by the nature of parliamentary government and the twin concepts of government and opposition that it embodies.

Patterns of opposition

Just how parties and systems vary with regard to the key question of government and opposition, a critical difference in the operation of party systems, we can appreciate by sketching the different ways in which the idea of 'democratic opposition' can be handled. The common faith in the necessity of allowing organised opposition, as the means of preserving political choice in the liberal democracies, obscures important differences both in the value which parties place upon it and in the way in which opposition is expressed. Dahl's account of the dimensions involved,[13] which we shall follow here, shows how various factors interact to determine the strategies adopted in their quest for power – and this quest is the reality behind any opposition. One of the factors concerns the ultimate aims or 'goals' of the parties. But how these goals are pursued will depend on the more general characteristics of the system – the 'distinctiveness' that an opposition acquires in a particular party system. In Dahl's formulation, the three factors are:

- the nature of the site for 'decisive encounters';
- the degree of competition which a system is able to maintain;
- the cohesion of opposition.

These shape the character of a system, and together with the goals of the competing parties they will determine how the political struggle is waged.

We can illustrate these terms by the case of Britain. The site for decisive encounters is normally the general election, and the system is highly competitive – in the nature of a zero-sum game: victory for one party means the total exclusion from power for the other. The opposition is also highly cohesive, for not only is it for all practical purposes located within one party, party discipline ensures as well that for most important issues the party will speak with one voice. It need hardly be said that these three features of the British system stand very much together – if elections were not decisive, then the nature of inter-party competition would change, and in turn party cohesion could be undermined. But much would depend on *why* elections became indecisive, whether that came about because of inter-party agreement or because (as was true of the 1970s) there was an increase in the number of parties.

In a formal sense, the assemblies of parliamentary democracies are regarded as the important site – ideally, with the fate of governments and legislation depending on a strongly contested assembly vote. The real situation is much more complex, for the assembly is only one of *five* possible arenas or sites. As is the case for Britain, a decisive election result may largely reduce the importance of the decision-making powers of the assembly in practice. Yet even if the election is indecisive, this does not necessarily make the assembly stronger, for the real power may rest with the subsequent coalition which is formed. Beyond this, power may be effectively dispersed to the permanent bureaucracy and in its relations with the governing parties, and finally to the relations of government with the organised interests of society at large.

Certainly, although a country's politics may be focused on just one site, the others will never be irrelevant. No parties in a competitive system can regard the outcome of elections as only marginally important, but they may well be inconclusive. The process of coalition-building becomes a factor in its own right, and even if account is taken of how the various parties fared at the preceding elections, the eventual coalition is not just dependent on electoral success. The way in which coalitions are formed becomes an important factor, and therefore interparty negotiations can be prolonged – as in Finland, the Netherlands, and Italy; further, interelection changes in government can come about without any direct reference to the preceding election. Where one party has absolute majority, the result is a foregone conclusion once the election is over. But it is comparatively infrequent for any party to be in this position, and even when it is, the addition of one or more coalition partners is frequently preferred. Thus even though the French Socialists won an absolute majority at the 1981 legislative election, they still thought it advisable to bring the communists into the government. The usual situation is for a number of permutations to be examined, with critical issues emerging concerning coalition policy, the ratio of portfolios, and party control over particular ministries.

It may be that even the formation of a coalition is not conclusive – where, for instance, decision-making is moving out of the hands of the parties into government agencies. Sheer instability of government may be one cause; sustained direction of policy becomes impossible, and by default the bureaucracy becomes involved in policy-making at a high level. This possibility is inherent in all forms of party government, however. We have earlier seen how this may work in a position of one-party dominance, as the *clientela* relationship developed in Italy. Later, we shall look more generally at the power of administrative élites. The final arena is the totality of the relationships which a government develops with organised interests, and the various 'styles' of interest group representation which we have already considered have a definite connection with the locus of decision-making in a political system.

Sweden provides an example of how the arena for decision-making may become diffused. The long-term dominance of the Social Democrats did make elections conclusive in some respects. However, the Swedish system places an emphasis on the assembly for real deliberation. The opposition is by no means helpless; it can maintain itself indefinitely by organising, mediating, and leading the various interest groups; the parties in opposition, until 1976 the never-never alternative government, worked effectively in the Riksdag and operated on the government direct. The long years of opposition for the bourgeois parties was not the wilderness it would be in Britain. This diffusion is also maintained in Switzerland, for neither the election nor the coalition is decisive, and the Federal Assembly, though it does not exact the full 'responsibility' of government, retains a share in decision-making. The diffusion is made all the more marked by the constant potential of the referendum as a feedback device. Finally, in the twenty-year 'permanent' coalition in Austria after the war, the elections only decided the ratio of ministerial portfolios between the two parties – the decision to prolong the coalition was made by the parties prior to the elections; the elections were then of marginal importance only, and the popular vote was effective with regard only to the 'Proporz' system: the exact sharing of all government appointments according to party strength. In 1987, after a gap of 20 years, the coalition was re-formed, showing that the infrastructure of consensual policy making still remained in place.

The competitiveness of a party system can be related to this issue of determining site. Thus, where what we can call 'primary' sites (elections and assemblies) are conclusive, there is likely to be a high degree of system competitiveness, and this will decline to the extent that 'secondary' sites (coalition, bureaucracy, and interests) become important. Although without exception elections are hard-fought, this struggle is often a prelude to concentration on the secondary sites. Persistent association with either the primary or secondary sites, though these are not sharp alternatives, contributes to the distinctiveness of an opposition. The third factor, the cohesion of opposition, also imparts a particular character to a system, but it is a product of various short- and long-term influences. Cohesion in the short-run depends on party morale: the strength of an opposition is to be judged in part on how quickly short-run upsets can be absorbed without a fundamental weakening of opposition. This reflects on the morale of the individual parties; in a multi-party system, any one party bears less brunt of the reverses in electoral and other fortunes, and in this sense they are more resilient than the opposition in a two-party system. However, the cohesion of the opposition as a whole is always more difficult to maintain where several parties are involved; a single party in opposition has the problem of its inner-party tensions to resolve, hence the much more critical question of party leadership in a two-party system, but once these are settled, then the united opposition presents a formidable challenge to government.

Whilst the factors we have considered so far are general to all the parties in a particular system, the distinctiveness of an opposition and the strategies it employs will also be determined by the goals which the parties pursue, and these are defined by each party for itself. Dahl lists the types of goal in ascending order of fundamental change: the personnel of government, specific government policies, the political structure, the socio-economic structure. A party limited to changing the personnel of government will emphasise the new leadership it can supply, but once in office at least, it will minimise policy changes and will be mainly concerned with succouring special interests. Most European parties have the second type of goal: specific policy changes *in addition* to changes in personnel – each level of goal subsumes those in the preceding categories. There is a tradition of issuing detailed, and binding, policy documents; in this sense they are 'programmatic'. The emphasis in a two-party system on personnel changes is not so relevant for others because it is impossible to foresee the actual make-up of government; furthermore, the 'binding' policies turn out to be bargaining-counters in the realities of multi-party coalition.

Social democratic parties have wider goals; at least in the past these have included the making of basic changes in the socio-economic structure of society. But for them the goal-ordering is not cumulative – they miss out on the third level – a fundamental re-ordering of the political structure as well. It is precisely this goal which typifies an 'extremist' party. In the case of right-wing extremism, the scrapping of the present political order may be the summit of ambition; once a new political edifice has been erected, the socio-economic order can be left intact. Only on the extreme left are all four levels of change considered integral to a party's aims. Indeed, the communist criticism of social democracy was always that its socio-economic aims are unattainable without at the same time working for the transformation or destruction of the existing political system – since this is a bastion of social and economic inequality.

In large measure, the cohesion of the West European party systems results from the similar types of goal which the individual parties are willing to pursue, and the common commitment to maintain the political fabric of liberal democracy intact. And even if a party is quite free to define or redefine its own goals, it is continually subject to the pressures of the system, to the 'parliamentary embrace'. The more a party subscribes to the dictates of the party game, so its goals become displaced and effectively come to resemble those of its competitors – a tendency long ago noted by Sorel, and finding a contemporary echo in the reaction of an 'extra-parliamentary' opposition, or even the West German Greens' idea of themselves as an 'anti-party' party.

The difficulty of throwing up and maintaining fundamental alternatives has led to the view that there is a secular decline in the quality of opposition in parliamentary systems. Otto Kirchheimer[14] saw this 'waning of opposition' as a general development affecting the 'opposition in principle' of ideologically based parties as well as those functioning in the British sense of 'Opposition' with the total emphasis on *alternative* government (which in fact requires important continuities in policies to minimise the disruption of party alternation). As we saw in the preceding chapter, this view of the decline of opposition is connected to the change from sectional to 'catch-all' parties. With this similarity, it becomes increasingly difficult for an opposition party to 'identify' itself and provide a credible alternative. The only way for a party to survive is to become a governing party, in coalition with the others. That at least seemed to be the trend: a choice between a Swiss-type coalition and permanent, basically sterile opposition.

Such a view is essentially a rendering of the 'end of ideology' seen in party terms: a series of catch-all parties, all operating near the centre of the spectrum, equally desperate to participate in government, and their consequent strategy contingent on the behaviour of all the others, with the whole system mainly responsive to the balance of group pressures. Against this deterministic view have to be set a number of qualifications. Firstly, it is not at all the case that 'Opposition' in the sense of alternative government has become less viable – the German Social Democrats did at last come to power, the bourgeois parties in Norway and Denmark were ultimately able to form governments on their own account, the 20-year Austrian coalition did in the end break down. A second objection is that parties do manage to 'breathe' for an extraordinary length of time in opposition (the left in France from 1958 until 1981) and the strength of the European party traditions is such that, as Kirchheimer himself recognised, they are unlikely to become mere brokerage parties; the competing versions of Liberalism, Christian democracy, and social democracy should not be dismissed as simply attenuations of a past age: they still provide a standpoint from which current policies can be judged and alternatives offered.

A final objection lies in the imponderable nature of social evolution. Our analysis earlier pointed to class-related issues as the chief residual factor in politics. Even in stable conditions, this cleavage provides the basis for a limited polarisation, evident in balanced systems. Nor, of course, should the potential of 'opposition in principle' be underestimated; weakened now, these party traditions are available should the contemporary limited polarisation of class become more pronounced. Moreover, the potential of the 'new politics' should not be omitted from the reckoning: its explicit rejection of parliamentary élitism and its reliance on extraparliamentary means, both as a tactic and as a form of legitimation, could lead to serious strains in the future. All of those qualifications make forecasts based on an ineluctable 'waning' of opposition of limited value. And even an apparently stable parliamentary system may fail to reflect the force of outside challenges: a party system cannot be judged solely on its success in harnessing electoral forces. As a conclusion to this discussion, we can examine the conditions under which parliamentary systems succeed or fail.

Breakdown of parliamentary systems
Putting the question, 'Why do systems fail?', may not seem particularly relevant to most West European states, but parliamentary government does fail on occasion, and for a variety of reasons. We can express this possibility of breakdown another way by saying that a successful parliamentary democracy has to fulfil the following four functions:

1. Supply governments with an assembly majority, and provide for smooth government succession.
2. Governments must be able to make an acceptable minimum of authoritative decisions within the context of assembly participation.
3. The important parties, in government and opposition, must subscribe to certain ground-rules and develop some cohesion one with another.
4. Together, the parliamentary parties must provide a means of integration for all significant sectors of society.

A syndrome of system failure, incorporating all these elements, is one where unstable and ineffective government is chained to an assembly in which the parties are at one another's throats, while outside, hostile forces are gathering to put an end to the parliamentary morass. Rarely will all these symptoms appear at once, but none is quite independent of the others. The survival power of apparently shaky parliamentary democracies depends on at least *one* of the conditions being met. Unstable government is tolerable as long as some important decisions are being made, and even when these are not forthcoming, the cohesion, possibly the inertia, of the party system may prolong its life. And if the largest parties can function together to provide workable government, then the fact that sections of the population are quite alienated from the parliamentary regime can be ignored for some time. The stability of any European system can be judged against this check-list, and weaknesses will be seen normally to be restricted to one head.

Actual breakdown in recent years has occurred only in France (1958) and in Greece (1967), so in order to bring out all features clearly we have to refer to the pre-war position as well – notably the collapse of the Weimar and the first Austrian republics. The case of Greece we examine later;* it is important because it shows

---

* See below, pp. 170-2.

that even if the parliamentary system is functioning – supplying governments and policy output within a cohesive assembly structure – the fact that an important social group (the army) found the results unpalatable was quite sufficient to topple Greek democracy. Our concern in this section is with those cases where a significant part of the collapse took place within the parliamentary framework.

Obviously any complete examination of the Weimar Republic would have to take into account a wide range of socio-economic factors, and we shall look at the role of fascism and the military in other contexts. The economic predicament and the unresolved social situation following the collapse of the Imperial order unleashed forces which the Reichstag was hardly equipped to contain; nevertheless, the party system which resulted can be said to be an accurate reflection of the currents at work in German society. This analysis concentrates only on the *parliamentary* features of instability and collapse.

On a parliamentary level, the growing and finally insuperable problem was the inability to provide a stable government combination – and near the end *any* combination at all. Normal if fairly short-lived coalitions were the rule until 1930, relying on Reichstag majorities to put measures through. From 1930 onwards it became necessary for governments to rely on the sweeping presidential decree powers, and once this path was taken, the Reichstag had effectively abrogated its authority. Resort to elections to end the parliamentary stalemate was no help either; at successive elections from 1930 onwards, swelling numbers voted for the National Socialists who promised to end the unedifying regime of the parties. Parodoxically, by 1933 it was possible to produce a Reichstag majority, but it was a majority for the extremist combination that was to put an end to the Republic.

In all this, the root cause did not rest in an undue proliferation of the parties – though there were usually around twelve represented – but in the peculiarly diffuse expression which they gave to the party system at a critical period, and this diffusion was the prior condition to breakdown. At the outset of its short life the parliamentary system provided a number of possible government combinations. The table below shows clearly the different phases by totting up the relative strength of the various coalition possibilities as a result of each election.

The overall trend from left of centre in 1919, through centre and centre-right majorities, to a final right-extremist supremacy, is readily apparent. But the three critical elections from 1930 to

1932, show an utter dispersion of the system with no conceivable coalition grouping able to supply a governing majority. The hollowing-out of the democratic centre proceeded apace from 1932 onwards, but it was the initial indeterminateness of the position in 1930 which encouraged the ultimate polarisation.

With the parties of the extreme left and right committed to the destruction of the parliamentary system, there was little chance of supplying the cohesion which seemed possible in the middle years of the Republic; nor were the parties on the left capable of working together – they were at daggers-drawn from the very beginning, and even if they had managed a common front, numerically they were always in a subordinate position. Loyalty to the Republic was also questionable on the moderate right – only the three 'Weimar'

| | 'Left' parties | Alignments and Coalitions | | Right-Centre | National Opposition | Anti-System |
		Weimar	'Great'			
1919	45	76	81	54	10	8
1920	42	44	58	57	15	20
1924-a	34	40	49	56	26	20
1924-b	35	46	56	60	24	12
1928	41	37	55	53	17	13
1930	38	40	45	43	25	31
1932-a	36	35	36	26	43	52
1932-b	37	33	35	29	42	50
1933	31	30	32	26	52	56

Notes to table. The figures in each column refer to the percentage of votes gained at each Reichstag eection by the parties making up a particular grouping, whether the grouping was formally in existence or not. Thus the 'National Opposition' was only formed in the last years of the Republic, but the constituent parties were contesting elections much earlier.

'Left' parties were the Communist Party, the Independent Social Democrats, and the Social Democrats. They were *never* in alliance, and anyway never had a majority.

The 'Weimar coalition' parties were the Social Democrats, the German Democratic Party and the Catholic Centre.

The 'Great Coalition' included the Weimar parties above and Stresemann's German People's Party.

'Right-Centre' coalitions included various combinations from the radical German Democrats to the right-wing German National People's Party – plus some very small 'conservative' parties.

'National Opposition' includes German National People's Party and National Socialists.

'Anti-System' aggregates National Socialists and Communists (and Independent Socialists until 1920).

parties, who were responsible for the constitution, were deeply committed, and even here the Catholic Centre at times played an ambivalent role. In spite of all this, up to 1930 governments achieved a reasonable policy output, especially in the field of foreign relations under Stresemann's guidance. But of the requirements we set out for successful parliamentary democracy, in the end not one was met.

The background to the Weimar Republic was one of incessant government upheaval – twenty-one governments from 1919 to 1933. And the Fourth French Republic also became renowned for government instability – no less than twenty-five in the comparable time-span, 1949 until 1958. Yet the problems facing France after 1945 were not of the same order as those facing Germany in 1919. The essential form of government was not seriously in question, there were not the destabilising influences of wartime defeat – this shock had already been absorbed by the Vichy government – and the economic problems of postwar France, though immense, were no greater than she experienced after the First World War. It may be argued that political extremism, hence lack of cohesion of the parliamentary parties, was in a large measure responsible for the eventual failure. The 'anti-system' parties: Communists, Gaullists, and Poujadists – as far as these last are to be counted – had in common at least a suspicion of the parliamentary system. But, granted they had the power of disruption, were they powerful enough to destroy? And were their actions always negative?

Undoubtedly, the greatest Communist threat came after the party left the post-war tripartite government, which included the Catholic MRP and the Socialists. Immediately the country was plunged into a series of challenging strikes, but with gradual economic recovery this impetus was spent, and it was shown in the declining electoral fortunes of the Communists, partly as a result of the voting system. Whilst the Communist Party was at first strongly represented in the assembly, it fell drastically as a result of the 1951 electoral law. It was a greater threat to the Republic at the beginning than at the end, and although the party's vote made government formation and survival difficult, its negative role should not be exaggerated: it was often prepared to sacrifice its 'conscience' in order to pass key government measures, and at the end it was one of the parties most concerned to save the Republic. The pro-system parties certainly feared the Communists, but it is doubtful whether they were a major threat. For most of the time the party was 'excluded', on the defensive, and 'manipulated' by the deliberate effects of the electoral system.

Were the threats from the political right of greater moment? At its inception in 1947, de Gaulle's 'Rally of the French People' looked capable of taking the country by storm, and its behaviour was reminiscent of a fledgling fascist movement; but the momentum quickly slackened, and from being the largest parliamentary group it had declined in 1956 to a tattered remnant disowned by de Gaulle. Blame for republican failure can hardly be laid at the door of the Poujadists either. They positively leapt into the parliamentary arena in 1956 with two and a half million votes as the almost inarticulate howl of the small shopkeepers and anti-tax lobby, but Poujadism rapidly disintegrated once the party faced political realities. Difficult as the problems of government survival were, the aggregate share of the assembly vote controlled by the anti-system parties never rose much above a third of the whole and declined long before the critical period. Nor, except by accident, were they able to act in unison.

The weakness of the Fourth Republic lay just as much in the parties which were committed to its survival. Essentially, they came to be divided amongst themselves, and their lack of cohesion proved fatal. Socialists, Radicals, MRP, and Conservatives, were the buttress of democratic government, but by no means a unified bloc, rather 'an aggregation sundered by France's historical cleavages'.[15] The divisions ran deep: church-state relations, the economic role of the state, European unity, the future of the colonial empire. Any or all of these issues could quickly destroy the fragile consensus of a government majority. To this picture one has to add the 'deputy centred' nature of the parties: deputies saw their loyalties as much in terms of their special interests and those of their constituents as with the government in power. Instability of government, an average life of seven months, is the key index of failure; behind it lay the failure of policy output.

The failure was perhaps relative; on the credit side there lay the progress towards European unity, the rapprochement with Germany, economic recovery, and some essential steps in decolonisation. Progress was often made behind the Assembly's back; French planning went on its way unhindered. Increasingly, however, all governments became deadlocked by the cross-pressures at work in the Assembly. The inability to resolve urgent issues, the failure to make decisions in spite of the widespread demand that they should be made, is summed up in the characteristic term 'immobilism'. And the tactics of government – such as 'the majority for the occasion', a constant redeployment of voting alliance – were in the end of no avail. The 'occasion' of the festering Algerian problem was to prove greater than the resources of the system.* Faced with this episode, the Fourth Republic may have been 'unlucky' just as the Third Republic was 'lucky' to have survived so long. The immediate cause of the Republic ending its own life, preferring 'the lesser evil' of de Gaulle, was the gathering of hostile forces outside the Assembly, the threat of armed insurrection in Algeria and even in mainland France. But the final threat from without was just the last stage in a long process, preceded by the failure of the political parties and a growing public indifference to the fate of the party republic. It was perhaps ironic that the last prime minister prior to de Gaulle should have enjoyed the largest vote of confidence ever accorded to a Fourth Republic politician – just before throwing in the towel!

Once again, we see the complete 'syndrome of failure' in evidence, as it was for the Weimar Republic. The third example, the pre-war Austrian Republic, differs in two important respects: the absence of extremist parties and of any party proliferation. The electorate had a clear choice between the two major parties, the Christian-Socials and the Socialists. We have already seen that the polarisation was not based on an underlying consensus, and that the cleavages in Austrian society followed the same route: the Catholic Church, rural society, and the middle classes ranged on one side, and a largely anti-clerical urban proletariat on the other. There were two antagonistic 'armed-camps', but the gulf between them was deep rather than wide. The Socialists would have no truck with the tiny Communist Party, and for their part the majority of Christian-Socials did not favour the extremism of the Austrian Nazis or that of the local product, the Heimwehr – a cross between a political party and a para-military force. At what was to prove to be the last election, held in 1930, the Nazi Party and the Communists won no seats at all, the Heimwehr was reduced to a rump, and for the first time the Socialists emerged as the strongest party. Compared with many other states of that time and later, the results might have appeared to confirm the strength of parliamentary democracy.

The Christian-Socials remained in power with the support of the remaining Heimwehr and a small peasants' party, the Landbund. This gave the government a minuscule majority, and in any system a voting-stalemate is likely to occur in such circumstances. But a complete parliamentary impasse will only

* For the role of the military in the Algerian crisis, see below, pp. 164–5.

result if there is a total lack of cohesion between the parties. The impasse was quickly reached in Austria, and Chancellor Dollfuss used it as a pretext for dissolving the assembly in March 1933; this action marked the end of parliamentary democracy. The personal leanings of Dollfuss towards some kind of corporate state should not obscure his other preoccupations: the growing threat of German fascism as well as his virulent, yet on the whole representative, hatred for the Socialists. To a later suggestion that he should reconvene the assembly and seek a reconciliation with the leader of the Socialists, he exclaimed: 'I sit again in a Parliament with Otto Bauer? Never, never!' That was the extent of the antagonism between two comparatively moderate parties, and only when the external situation had further deteriorated was there a belated attempt at co-operation. In a sense, the Austrian case is a simplified version of the French experience – without the extremist parties in the assembly, and only two divergent forces in place of the cross-pressures of the French moderate parties. Both showed a failure of the parliamentary system before outside forces effectively intervened.

Rarely does extremism make an early and sufficient impact to destroy a system quite by its own efforts. And various warning-lights are available: government stability and the ability to make key decisions are two critical areas where indications are apparent, but countries differ in the degrees of tolerance allowable: the French Third Republic showed remarkable powers of survival, Italy has contentedly carried on for years with short-lived governments – a situation that could prove intolerable in Britain after three or four doses. Countries differ as well in the type of relationship which the parties build up one with another and with society at large. The cohesion between the parties necessarily rests on some common view of the parliamentary system: the idea that it is 'representative' works two ways: on the one side, it aims to reflect the interests of all important social groups, but the other side of 'representation' is that the parliamentary process should act as an efficient method of canalising demands made on the individual parties. Thus an assembly with a strong parliamentary tradition, as in Britain, functions both to voice social demands *and* to provide the parties with some insulation from those pressures. It is the ability to balance the two which results in a cohesive system. Fundamentally, this is an élitist view of the political process, but it may be unwise to assume that *parliamentary* democracy works in any other way.

Notes and references

1. S. M. Lipset, 'Party Systems and the Representation of Social Groups', in R. A. Dahl and D. E. Neubauer (eds.), *Readings in Modern Political Analysis*, Prentice-Hall, 1968, p. 94. Lipset adds, 'Electoral laws determine the nature of the *party system* as much as any other structure available.'
2. German federalism may have helped to produce a 'quasi-party' the Christian-Social Union in Bavaria. In the Bundestag the CDU-CSU form an *Arbeitsgemeinschaft*, a working partnership.
3. Any party winning 0.5 per cent of the national vote is entitled to a state subsidy reckoned on the basis of 5 DM for every vote a party receives; thus in 1987 the extreme right NPD qualified with 0.6 per cent of the vote. A similar arrangement also applies for parties contesting *Land* elections.
4. M. Duverger, *Political Parties*, Methuen, 1954, p. 217.
5. C. Leys, 'Electoral Systems and Party Systems: The Duverger Doctrine', in J. Blondel (ed.), *Comparative Government: A Reader*, Macmillan, 1969, p. 140.
6. G. Lavau, *Partis Politiques et Réalités Sociales*, Paris: A. Colin, 1953, pp. 33–4, 53.
7. J. Blondel, op. cit., p. 201.
8. For an examination of the factor affecting the durability of governments, see A. Lijphart, *Democracies*, Yale University Press, 1984, pp. 80–3.
9. The following are examples of absolute majorities in the 1980s elections and assemblies:
    France: In 1981, the PS with a minority vote.
    Greece: Pasok in 1981 (48%) and 1985 (45.8%) with a majority of seats.
    Malta: The Nationalists won 50.9% of vote, but a minority of seats in 1981; in 1987 the Nationalists (50.9%) had a majority of seats.
    Portugal: the PSD in 1987 with 50.2%
    Spain: PSOE in 1982 (48.2%) and 1986 (44.4%) with a majority of seats.
    UK: Conservatives in 1983 (42.4%) and 1987 (42.3) with majority of seats.
10. S. Lipset and S. Rokkan, *Party Systems and Voter Alignments, op.cit.*
11. P. Mair, 'Adaptation and Control: Towards an Understanding of Party and Party System Change', in H. Daalder and P. Mair (eds.), *West European Party Systems: Continuity and Change*, Sage, 1983.
12. Two such 'historical cases' of polarised pluralism, the Weimar Repulic and the French Fourth Republic are discussed later in this chapter. One example on which Sartori based his formulation of polarised pluralism was post-war Italy. Yet although all the major party actors are still there, it would be difficult now to find very much that is polarised in the party system. See, G. Sartori, *Parties and Party Systems: A Framework for Analysis*, Cambridge University Press, 1976, pp. 139–45.
13. The discussion following is based on Dahl's typology, 'Patterns of Opposition' in R. A. Dahl (ed.), *Political Oppositions in Western Democracies*, New Haven: Yale University Press, 1966, pp. 332–47.
14. O. Kirchheimer, 'The Waning of Opposition', in R. C. Macridis and B. E. Brown (eds.), *Comparative Politics*, Ill., The Dorsey Press, 1964, pp. 280–91.
15. S. Finer, *Comparative Government*, Allen Lane, 1970, p. 294.

Additional references

H. Berrington (ed.), 'Political Change in Britain', *West European Politics* (special issue), October 1983.
V. Bogdanor (ed.), *Coalition Government in Western Europe*, Heinemann, 1983.
V. Bogdanor and D. Butler (eds.),*Democracy and Elections: Electoral Systems and their Consequences*, Cambridge University Press, 1983
I. Budge, D. Robertson and D. Hearl (eds.), *Ideology, Strategy and Party Change*, Cambridge University Press, 1987.

F. Burin, and K. Shell (eds.), *Politics, Law and Social Change, Essays of Otto Kirchheimer*, Columbia University Press, 1969.

H. Daalder and P. Mair, *Western European Party Systems: Continuity and Change*, Sage Publications, 1983.

S. Finer (ed.), *Adversary Politics and Electoral Reform*, Anthony Wigram, 1975.

G. Hand, J. Georgel, C. Sasse (eds.), *European Electoral Systems Handbook*, Butterworth, 1979.

Hansard Society, *Commission on Electoral Reform*, June 1976.

F. A. Hermens, 'Electoral Systems and Political Systems', *Parliamentary Affairs*, Winter 1976.

F. A. Hermens, 'The Dynamics of Proportional Representation', in H. Eckstein and D. Apter, *Comparative Politics*, New York: The Fee Press, 1963.

R. Irving, *Parties and Elections in Europe: France, Germany and Italy*, Oxford: Martin Robertson, 1983.

E. Kolinsky (ed.), *Opposition in Western Europe*, Croom Helm, 1987.

E. Lakeman, *How Democracies Vote*, Faber and Faber, 1970.

E. Lakeman, *Nine Democracies: Electoral Systems in the Countries of the EEC*, Arthur MacDougall Fund, 1975.

A. Lijphart, *Democracies: Patterns of Majoritarian and Consensus Government in Twenty-One Countries*, Yale University Press, 1984.

A. Mclaren Carstairs, *A Short History of Electoral Systems in Western Europe*, Allen and Unwin, 1980.

P. Merkl (ed.), *Western European Party Systems: Trends and Prospects*. New York: The Free Press, 1980.

W. Miller, *Electoral Dynamics*, Macmillan, 1978.

A. Milnor, *Elections and Political Stability*, Boston: Little, Brown, 1969.

G. Pridham (ed.), *Coalitional Behaviour in Theory and Practice: An Inductive Model for Western Europe*, Oxford University Press, 1986.

D. Rae, *The Political Consequences of Electoral Laws*, Yale University Press, 1967.

R. Rose (ed.), *Electoral Participation: A Comparative Analysis*, Sage Publications, 1981.

R. Rose (ed.), *Electoral Behavior: A Comparative Handbook*, op. cit.

R. Rose and I. McAllister, *Voters Begin to Choose*, Sage, 1986.

R. Rose and D. Urwin, 'Persistence and Change in Party Systems', *Political Studies*, September 1970.

D. Sanders and V. Herman, 'The Stability and Survival of Governments in Western Democracies', *Acta Politica*, 1977, vol. 3.

G. Sartori, *Parties and Party Systems: A Theoretical Framework*, New York: Harper and Row, 1977.

G. Sartori, 'European Political Parties: The case of Polarized Pluralism', in R. Dahl and D. Neubauer (eds.), *Reading in Modern Political Analysis*, op. cit.

L. Sigelmann and S. Yough, 'Left-Right Polarization in National Party Systems, *Comparative Political Studies*, October 1978.

S. Wolinetz, 'The Transformation of Western European Party Systems Revisited', *West European Politics*, January 1979.

S. Wolinetz (ed.) *Parties and Party Systems in Liberal Democracies*, Routledge, 1988.

See also the references in Chapter 3.

Breakdown of parliamentary systems

F. L. Carsten, *Fascist Movements in Austria: From Schönerer to Hitler*, Sage Publications, 1977.

T. Eschenburg and others, *The Road to Dictatorship, 1918–1933*, Wolff, 1964.

F. Fellner and J. Rath, 'Austria', in P. F. Sugar (ed.), *Native Fascism in the Successor States: 1918–1945*, Oxford: The European Bibliographical Centre, 1971.

D. MacRae, *Parliament, Parties and Society in France, 1946–1958*, Macmillan, 1968.

N. Leithes, *On the Game of Politics in France*, Stanford: Oxford, 1959.

J. Linz and A. Stepan (eds.), *The Breakdown of Democratic Regimes*, Baltimore: Johns Hopkins, 1978.

S. M. Lipset, *Political Man*, Heinemann, (rev. ed.) 1983.

R. Manvell and H. Fraenkel, *The Hundred Days to Hitler*, Dent, 1974.

K. J. Newman, *European Democracy between the Wars*, Allen and Unwin, 1970.

A. J. Nicholls, *Weimar and the Rise of Hitler*, Macmillan, 1968.

A. J. Nicholls and E. Matthias (eds.), *German Democracy and the Triumph of Hitler*, Allen and Unwin, 1971.

G. B. Powell, *Social Fragmentation and Political Hostility: An Austrian Case Study*, Stanford University Press, 1970.

A. Sturmthal, *The Tragedy of European Labour*, Gollancz, 1944.

P. M. Williams, *Crisis and Compromise: Politics in the Fourth Republic*, Longmans, 1964.

See also the references in Chapter 6.

Party systems in Western Europe

	Communist	Independent Socialist	Social Democrats	Liberal-Radical	Centre
Austria			SPÖ		
Belgium			BSP/PSB		
Denmark		Socialist	Social Democrats	Radical-Liberal	Centre-Democrats
Finland	SKDL Deva		Social Democrats		Centre
France	PCF		PS	Left-Rads.	
Germany			SPD		
Greece	KKE	Comm.-Int.	Pasok		
Iceland	People's Alliance		Social Democrats		Progressive
Ireland		Workers' Party	Labour	Fine Gael	
Italy	PCI	Democratic-Proletarian	PSI	PRI PSDI	
Luxembourg	Comm.	Ind. Soc.	Socialist	Liberal-Democrats	
Netherlands		Pacifist-Socialist	PvdA	Dem. '66 Radical	
Norway		Soc.-Left	Labour		Centre
Portugal	Comm.	Democratic Renewal	Socialist		
Spain	PCE		PSOE		Soc.-Dem. Centre
Sweden	Comm.		Soc. Dem.		Centre
Switzerland	Labour		Social Democrats		Swiss People's
United Kingdom			Labour	SD/Liberal SDP	

See notes on p. 124.

Christian	Liberal-Conservative	Conservative ('National')	Right-Wing	Ethnic/Regional	'New Politics'
ÖVP			FPÖ		Greens/Alt.
CVP/PSC	PVV/PRL			RW/FDF VB/Volksunie	Ecology/Alt.
Christian	Venstre	Conservative	Progress		
Christian		Conservative	Rural	Swedish	Ecology
	UDF	RPR	FN		
CDU	FDP	CSU			Greens
		New Democracy			
		Independence Citizens'			Feminists
	Prog. Dems.	Fianna Fail			
DC	PLI		MSI	South-Tyrol	Radicals Greens
Christian-Social					Greens
CDA Calvinists (3)	VVD				
Christian		Höyre	Progress		
CDS	PSD				
			Popular Alliance	PNV/HB CCatalan	
	Liberal	Conservative			Greens
Christ.-Dem. Evangelical	Lib.-Dem. Rad.-Dem.	Independents	National Campaign		Prog./Alt. Greens
		Conservative		SNP Ulster WWales	

Notes

The table of 'Party Systems in Western Europe' shows the spread of parties represented in national parliaments in mid-1988 on a broad 'right' and 'left' axis. The eleven 'streams' used for the classification include almost all of the major European political traditions. (In most but not all cases the streams correspond to those used by Michael Smart in 'Party Representation in Western Europe', p. 385 below.) Only a few countries actually come near to being represented in all the streams – notably Denmark. Whilst the ordering of most party groups is reasonably unambiguous, there are exceptions. The positioning of a 'Liberal' party – whether it is liberal-conservative or liberal-radical is best gauged from the nature of alliances and coalitions which it enters – thus the British Liberal Party through its pact with Labour from 1977/8 is counted as 'liberal-radical'. The German FDP, because of its switch from alliance with the SPD to one with the CDU in 1982, has been moved from liberal-radical to liberal-conservative, a comment on the ambivalent nature of German liberalism, and the same is true of Austria. The 'Independent Socialist' stream may contain parties which in some ways are more radical than the 'Communist' one – as is the case for the Democratic Proletarians in Italy. There are some difficulties in allocating 'Social Democrats' – the party label may be misleading as with the PSDI in Italy and the Portuguese PSD. Both are more right-wing than their titles suggest; to count them as 'liberal' is only one of the possibilities.

Some parties are difficult to classify at all since they enshrine special national peculiarities. That is evident in the case of the Irish Fianna Fail and Fine Gael. The same is the case for France, especially for the Gaullist RPR, in some ways a conservative party yet also with a *travailliste* following. It is also difficult to disentangle the RPR from the UDF on a conventional left-right ordering. There is a general difficulty existing for most 'Christian' parties, for they have a wider appeal than implied by their insertion between 'Centre' and 'Liberal-Conservative', and there is wide individual variation. Parties classified as 'Right-wing' may be neo-fascist as with the Italian MSI, but may be more Poujadist and 'protest' in character as with the Danish Progress Party. The Ethnic and Regional stream has no fixed political direction. The Basque HB is extreme left, whilst the Belgian *Vlaamsche Blok* is well to the right – as is the case for the Ulster Unionists.

The difficulty of a left/right ordering is made more apparent by the impact of the 'new politics'. In several countries, Ecologists have won representation under various names, and in several respects the Italian Radical Party belongs in the 'new politics' stream which also includes the Icelandic Feminists.

5   Constitutional Balance

European constitutionalism

From the focus in the preceding chapters on the basic social forces and their expression in the political parties, we can turn to the more formal institutional context in which they operate. Really, this aspect all hinges on the exercise of government power, and on the control of that power; behind both stands the liberal democratic doctrine of constitutionalism. Partly the term implies 'limited' as opposed to 'absolute' government, but more than this is involved. It has also been called 'a practical limitation of democracy', [1] and this is surely the point: that it limits the *public* power, as well as that of government. The two elements of constitutionalism are well brought out in the term 'liberal democracy', and in Macpherson's formulation that such states became liberal first and democratic later.[2] Their liberal institutions at first guarding against the threat of absolutist rule were later to serve a more general purpose of 'modifying' democracy.

Constitutional government in Western Europe arose as the product of two different sets of historical forces. The first was the sustained struggle to bring absolute government under *legal* control; the second was to bring it under *popular* control. The former resulted in governments which were bound by the supremacy of law and which at the same time were subjected to numerous institutional checks to give 'balanced' systems of power – of these the pure theory of the separation of powers is an extreme example. In general, one can say that the legal and institutional controls were the contribution arising from the political struggles of the rising bourgeoisie. The later, popular impact on the development of constitutionalism was of a quite different order; it was a claim for the political representation for the whole of the people, not for institutional balance; it was a demand for a government responsible to the people, not primarily for a limited one. Yet the popular governments which emerged, representative and responsible as they became, were in fact grafted on to the prior conceptions of balanced and limited government.

One can read this development in two ways. One can portray it as a harmonious continuity. In practice this was often the case, for the demand for popular participation was satisfied by having a greater voice in the working system; there seemed to be no need to create a new one. And in this respect we should take into account the real gains which were made in securing individual and corporate freedom; all classes stood to benefit from the extension of civil rights. Why should not the same system secure equality in other directions as well?

The alternative reading shows the tensions and possible contradictions involved. Here we can best refer back to our initial discussion of liberal democracy and to the concept of a dual system of representation put forward by Bendix. The duality is expressed in the direct plebiscitarian principle existing alongside a group representation based on 'the differential affiliation of individuals'; the one corresponds to the idea of popular control and a national citizenry, the other to a balance of forces in society and in government. Bendix saw this tension as a source of continual compromise, and from that point of view providing a dynamic for political development. A rather different conclusion is that the 'differential affiliation' gives such a sharp imbalance of power in practice that there is a blatant contradiction between formal popular participation and the actual direction of government decision-making, that the power of economic wealth makes for gross inequalities in the effects of affiliation.

The disparate strands which together make up modern European constitutionalism perhaps give it a rather fragmented aspect, but it is a single, unified idea as well. This unity can best be expressed by pointing to the high *normative* quality of the individual constitutions: it is the constitution itself which is said to speak with authority, irrespective of the nature of particular powerholders. The authority of the constitution, as a higher form of law, can be traced to the special place which the legal profession came to occupy in these societies and to the central part it took in the early development of constitutional government. But the regard for abstract, legal principles is also symptomatic of the trends in Western society over a long period, portrayed by Max Weber as a move to societies based on the exercise of 'legal-rational' authority; both 'legality' and 'rationality' are fundamental to all normative constitutions.

However, if we ask what it is that gives these constitutions such a sanction in the West European states, we are finally referred back to the social context, to the political culture of a country. It is the prevailing consensus of attitudes and beliefs which sustain constitutional government, provide the necessary support, and give a sense of legitimate authority. For the narrow confines of written constitutions and constitutional law, one has to substitute whatever is to be regarded as 'acceptable' behaviour on the part of the political authorities – and those who challenge them. This question of acceptability is taken up by Sartori in what he calls the 'role theory approach': 'What is the impact, or the role, of a constitution vis-à-vis the role-taking of the power holders? That is, does it help to enforce, and if so to what extent, a desired 'role performance' upon the persons in office?'[3]

From the idea of the constitution enforcing particular roles, one can turn to its 'symbolic capability' as part of the wider capability of the political system taken as a whole. The symbolic appeal lies partly in the history which the constitution enshrines and also because it can act as 'a showcase of the norms and symbols of a given society'.[4] We can see this appeal to good effect in the constitution of the Fifth French Republic. In its preamble and first five articles, most of the national symbols are displayed. Besides defining France as an 'indivisible, secular, democratic and social Republic', attention is drawn to the Declaration of 1789, the tricolour, the Marseillaise, the Republican motto of 'Liberty, Equality and Fraternity'. In 1958, the political authorities had to draw heavily on these symbols to strengthen the claims of the new order; of itself, the constitution was just one more in a long line, and lacked the legitimacy which time alone could give it.

Because of its long duration, and perhaps just because it is unwritten and quite flexible, the British constitution is a powerful admixture of normative and purely symbolic elements. The once-powerful institutions of state which have since become 'dignified façades', and which in Bagehot's view concealed the real working of the system, have not just become of nominal importance; they have been promoted to high symbolism – the sovereignty of Parliament, the role of the monarchy. The 'efficient secret' of the British constitution lies partly in the facility with which the empty shell of political institutions can be retained as symbols whilst they are robbed of substantive power.

Not all constitutions can claim historical sanction or act as a showcase for national symbols. For instance, the founding of the German Federal Republic in 1949 came at a time of sharp discontinuity, and almost every historical tradition was unavailable. The one acceptable symbol was that of a unified German nation, and this was given due expression in the preamble to the Basic Law: 'The entire German people is called upon to achieve by free self-determination the unity and freedom of Germany,' and to that end the whole constitution was made provisional, pending reunification. Such a constitution as the West German has to be regarded, with its detailed attention to procedures and allocation of functions, in mainly instrumental terms for achieving an acceptable distribution of power. This restriction does not necessarily make it less effective; in Germany, legal norms are powerful, and the previous failures of the political system helped to make the sanction of the 'Basic Law' the major determinant.

How should we sum up the doctrine of constitutionalism so far? We have seen that it is concerned to limit the power of government and to contain the 'arbitrary' effect of popular will. We can add that, in theory at least, the doctrine does not limit the development of state or society to any particular direction – simply expressed, it is only concerned with 'how' things are done, rather than with 'what' is done, that ultimately it is a set of procedural devices. But no constitution can be ideologically neutral; indeed, its whole genesis and operation will voice prevailing beliefs even if these are not made explicit. That the liberal democratic constitutions can avoid an explicit statement of ideology is made possible because the nature of the procedural arrangements arrived at provides precisely the wide ambit demanded by a pluralist society, which may, in fact, serve to perpetuate an existing power balance. The symbolism and the formal arrangements add up to an ideology which helps to give an idealised description of the way in which the system actually works. How far this idealisation merely conceals the real adjustments of social forces, and how far it disguises the true nature of political power, is the more elusive problem. Thus a Marxist would argue that any constitutional limitation of powers is, in effect, a 'bourgeois device' for trammelling the working class, and dismiss constitutionalism as the generic term for such schemes.

At least we should be on guard against regarding constitutionalism as existing apart from the society in which it operates. Whatever interpretation is put on its basic nature, three power-related characteristics stand out: it seeks to place limits on the power of governments and of the public; it is one of the means by which power in society is legitimised; it is an expression of the integral power balance in society.

The distribution of power

The individual hallmark of a constitution lies in the specific provisions made to secure a dispersion of government power. In liberal democracies, these provisions vary considerably in their scope and stringency. In the United States, there is a strict divorce of the executive from the legislature, together with a federal system, and these are backed by an inflexible constitution and the wide sweep of judicial review. The West European pattern differs fundamentally in actually merging legislative and executive powers in important respects, although the degree of emphasis laid on any one technique of power distribution varies considerably. We shall look at these in detail in the following sections;* here, we should examine the more general question of the efficacy of constitutions in securing a power dispersion, whilst bearing in mind that the constitutionalist prescription of controlling power by ensuring its dispersion is only one of several possible approaches.

The normative quality of a constitution is an essential feature if power is to be dispersed significantly. To appreciate the full flavour of this, the predominantly normative type of constitution in Western Europe can be contrasted with situations where it does not apply. One possibility is the purely 'semantic' constitution; this kind is not simply a linguistic exercise having no connection with reality, rather it merely formalises and rationalises the actual power distribution within a state. We have to go outside Western Europe for an extant example, and the German Democratic Republic provides an illustration: Article 48 of the 1968 constitution gives the single-chamber Volkskammer full sovereign powers. Article I, however, bases the leadership of the socialist state on 'the working-class and the Marxist-Leninist Party'. Since the 'sovereign' Volkskammer almost always accepts this leadership unanimously, one can argue either that complete harmony prevails or that it is just a rubber-stamp. In fact, there is no contradiction between what the constitution states and what actually happens. We can say that the whole document is semantic, and that the only relevant condition is Article I. Given the fact of leadership by the Marxist-Leninist Party, the constitution is unnecessary, for the form of leadership is a permanent feature of the state and is sufficient to determine, except in detail, its entire functioning. Thus the nature of such a constitution is mainly semantic, but it also pays symbolic homage to the power of legal forms.

The nature of West European society has precluded this type of development, but it has not prevented the emergence of constitutional forms which can be labelled as 'nominal'. This

---

* For a broad comparison of constitutional provisions, see the table on p. 311 below.

description applies to those constitutions which, although setting definite standards, remain largely inoperative, are irrelevant to the real exercise of power, and can be altered at the whim of government. The nominality of a constitution is a question of degree, and the dividing line between what is nominal and what is normative can therefore only be decided by particular cases, and the conduct of elections is the acid-test for a liberal democracy. The experience of the Portuguese dictatorship provides a good example, for the 1933 constitution did provide for a representative National Assembly, and elections to that body took place regularly. However, the only legal political organisation was Salazar's National Union, and it always won all the seats at elections – thanks in part to the electoral system which was based on relative majorities in multi-member constituencies, the 'block vote'. Even at the last, relatively free, election held under the old regime in 1969, not a single opposition candidate was elected, a wave of arrests followed the election, and the power of the secret police was undiminished.

Examples of constitutions which for one reason or another lack a normative impulse, make it clear that the distribution of power is unlikely to spring from the constitution itself, but to result from a deeper social balance, of which the law and the constitution form a part. It implies a willingness of important groups in society, not just the government, to accept certain restrictions. A particular concern in this respect has been for the protection of individual liberties and the containment of arbitrary decisions; de Tocqueville's fear of 'democratic despotism', the tyranny of the majority, refers to both, and the two precepts can be illustrated in their European context. Many states seek to protect individual liberties by an extensive Bill of Rights in the constitution. Italy, West Germany, Switzerland, and the Irish Republic do so, whilst the Austrian constitution incorporates many of the laws of the Habsburg Empire; the current Danish constitution (1953) provides such guarantees. On the other hand, France, Belgium, and the Netherlands, together with the majority of the Nordic states, make no specific provision. A typical and extensive listing of such rights is given in the West German Basic Law, Articles 1–19.[5] Quite reasonably, such countries as Germany, with recent experience of oppression, were most concerned to build constitutional safeguards; they provide some protection against an over-zealous servant of state, if not against the rulers themselves. These rights are regarded as fundamental to the liberal democratic creed; where they are not separately listed, they have long become a part of the law of the land – the battles have been fought and won in courts and parliaments.

Constitutional provisions can become nominal in other ways as well, by going beyond the power or even the inclination of governments to enforce. Thus the Portuguese 'revolutionary' constitution of 1976 was replete with socialist ideals, and it was assumed that Portugal was firmly on the road towards a socialist society. However, it soon became evident that an era of conservative retrenchment was to follow – and many of the constitutional provisions became redundant. In consequence, several amendments were made in 1982. A further example of nominality is to be seen in the Irish constitution which has a special chapter on 'Directive Principles of Social Policy', but Article 45 goes on to declare that they 'shall not be cognisable by any court'. A typical clause says that the ownership and control of the community's resources should be distributed 'amongst private individuals and the various classes as best to serve the common good'. In a similar vein, the Italian constitution in Article 4 establishes 'the right to work', and Article 32 states that 'The Republic protects the health of the individual . . . and guarantees free medical treatment to the poor.' The most that we can be sure of is that the hearts of those who framed the constitution were in the right place.

That a constitution simply cannot give blanket guarantees is shown by Article 13 of the West German Basic Law. This says that 'The home is inviolable', but its categorical assurance is heavily modified in the next two sub-sections: besides the power of judges or 'other legally prescribed bodies' to permit entry, the home is violable 'to avert a common danger' or an 'imminent danger to public security', to counter terrorism or even to alleviate the housing shortage, to combat the danger of epidemics and to protect endangered juveniles. It is very little special protection that the German citizen obtains from this clause.

The real protection lies in the adjudication of the courts and the curtailing of executive discretionary power. This safeguard is summed up in 'the rule of law', but this effect can hardly be established by constitutional edict; it is the product of a long process of 'structural differentiation', resulting in a degree of freedom for the courts from political interference. Besides obvious regard for the verdict of the courts, their freedom is shown in matters of personnel appointment, security of tenure, and of preferment. Taken as a whole, the courts of Western Europe have gained independence in these areas – there is an effective dispersion of power.

In most European countries, the status of a judge is more that of a civil servant than in Britain, and often, as in West Germany, that means being trained as a career judge under state supervision. In practice, it makes little difference to the subsequent independence of the judiciary, and the judges are pretty well irremovable – thus in Finland when civil servants lost security of tenure by law of 1926, judges were specifically excepted. One device used to insulate the judiciary from political pressure is to have an independent judicial council, with complete supervisory and appointive powers. This innovation in the French Fourth Republic was made against strong opposition from the Ministry of Justice, and the High Council of the Judiciary that was set up – consisting of professional judges and of jurists selected by the National Assembly – quickly showed itself to be independent of the government; in spite of efforts by the Ministry of Justice to sabotage its work, the Council finally came to control the career structure of French judges. This is the type of in-fighting that has to be expected, for the habits of patronage and active intervention die hard. Italy is similar in having made constitutional provision for the autonomous organisation of the judiciary. In West Germany, on a federal level, judges are well-protected by the constitution; possibly initial appointment, since judges are civil servants, may appear to be more under the influence of the political authorities, and that could apply in the courts of the Länder. However, dismissal is only possible 'under authority of judicial decision', and the federal judges can only be dismissed by a decision of the Constitutional Court. Even though the members of the Constitutional Court are subject to initial political appointment, their election requires a two-thirds majority from the Bundestag or Bundesrat, they can only be removed on the initiative of the Court itself. Similar protection is granted in other countries. In both Italy and West Germany at least, the problem was at times having too great a security of tenure; the courts in both countries were for long peppered with judges who had over-loyally interpreted the will of the totalitarian parties.

In this way we can see that the root of the problem is perhaps not the constitutional position ascribed to the judiciary, nor the conditions of service or civil service status, but the question of whether the judiciary can develop a corporate 'professional unity' independent of the executive. In Britain, the professional ethic emanates from the legal profession itself, with High Court judges recruited from active members of the Bar. But this can hardly serve as a general model – the French Council of State is an integral part of government administration; yet it has not prevented a professional unity from emerging within this body, as part of the élitist *'grand corps'*. One simple device which helps ensure its independence and cohesion is to make promotion strictly according to seniority.

The importance of such professional independence, however it originates, shows that the real dispersion of power is likely to operate at a deeper level than the constitutional provisions. This is what Vile had in mind when he referred to the 'internal rules' which develop alongside formal rules and status, and his view of the Lord Chancellor in Britain has a much wider application: 'This man, when acting as a judge, is expected to show impartiality and that expectation is enforced by the attitudes of the members of the legal profession, who would quickly denounce any attempt to use the office for purely party ends.'[6] The idea of internal rules is evidence of the deeper cross-currents at work in a constitutional system. It provides a clue to the reality of judicial independence, and to the dispersion of power more generally. The longer such internal checks have been left to develop, the more effective they are likely to prove. But there is a price to pay, for the 'professional ethic' has élitist implications, and the independence of the judiciary may lead to the emergence of a judicial caste, and its undesirable features may be reinforced to the extent that it is based on a common *class* recruitment.

So far, we have concentrated on giving a more or less 'legal' account of constitutionalism; this is but one aspect of the doctrine. A normative constitution also gives some definition of how government power is to be exercised – the definition alone acts as a counterweight to political authority. Although lip-service may be paid to unabridged sovereignty – the ruler, people, or parliament – the plural nature of authority is never far from the surface. The usual formula is to ascribe sovereignty to the people, as expressed in representative institutions, but in a federal system this is quickly dispersed, as in Switzerland: 'The Cantons are sovereign in so far as their sovereignty is not limited by the Federal constitution' (Article 3), and later in Article 71, 'Without prejudice to the rights of the people and cantons, the supreme power in the Confederation is exercised by the Federal Assembly.' In other ways, parallel types of power dispersion are typical for all liberal democracies.

Whilst traditional accounts of, say, the separation of powers were couched in terms of institutions which, like early versions of the atomic particle, were considered as homogeneous entities, constitution framers were well aware that this was not the whole story. Nevertheless, the balancing of various *total* institutional story. Nevertheless, the balancing of various *total* institutional structures was seen as the best, practical means of securing a dispersion of power; the more subtle, internal checks could only develop within a functioning institutional framework. With that in mind, the four broad areas of power distribution can be summarised as:

1. Assembly-executive relations.
2. Constitutional jurisdiction.
3. The devices of direct democracy.
4. Federal structures.

As will become apparent, there is a considerable variation from one country to another, in the use made of each 'area' and the actual application. Switzerland, West Germany, and Austria as federal states show a wide spread, whilst the European monarchies have a narrow concentration. We can take each of the first three areas in turn as the basis of comparison, leaving the question of federalism until we examine the various aspects of the territorial dispersion of power.*

Assembly-executive relations

At the heart of the liberal democratic order is the relationship which has evolved between assemblies and their executives; historically, it has been the struggle between these two which in the end provided the essential constitutional structure, around which the other institutions are grouped in a supportive manner. The power balance that resulted gave two common qualities: a strong executive and a substantial degree of unification between executive and legislature. We can say that a 'unified system' is one in which:

– the executive is not separately elected (or if in part it does come to office by other means, then this only involves a formal exercise of power);
– the executive is responsible to the legislature.

Both of these conditions need amplification. In the case of 'election', this can literally be so in West Germany, where the members of the Bundestag vote for the chancellor, or effectively so, as in Britain, where the prime minister chosen is the leader of the majority party. The second condition, involving executive responsibility to the legislature, can be expressed the other way round – that an executive, if it is to stay in office, must have control

* See below, pp. 266–82.

over the decisions of the legislature. The executive is responsible to the assembly, but the price is to accept executive leadership – via the party system.

These conditions, whatever the variations in detail, are the essentials of parliamentary democracy. There are two other possibilities. The first is a presidential system, involving direct election of the chief executive and some form of separation of powers. In this case, neither of our two conditions is met. The other possibility is 'convention' government; in this situation both conditions are fulfilled, with the important difference from the parliamentary system that the government is never in a position to control the decisions of the assembly. Parliamentary systems can always slide towards to 'government by assembly' whenever governments are unable to control the parties for any length of time. Parliamentary and presidential systems are normally sharply distinguished; the chief exception is the hybrid type of the Fifth French Republic which we examine shortly.

Needless to say, the conditions we have outlined for a unified system require realistic amendment to take account of the overriding importance of the political parties; parliamentary democracy has long since become party democracy, and party democracy makes for some additional features in unified systems:

- that the government should be in the hands of the majority party (or with a coalition having that majority);
- that an assembly itself does not decide; it only mirrors the decisions made by the electorate on the one hand, and by the party (or coalition) in power on the other.

This is an 'ideal-type' version. As de Gaulle said of the party system of the Fourth Republic, the 'mirror' may be cracked, and if it is, then there results a virtual autonomy of the assembly parties from *all* other institutions, government and electorate. Rather than party democracy, it means a 'democracy of the parties'.

The normal European form is a unified system based on executive responsibility to the assembly. The West German system can be taken as the model: 'The Federal Chancellor is elected, without debate, by the Bundestag on the proposal of the Federal President. The person obtaining the votes of the majority of the members of the Bundestag is elected. . . .' (Article 63). The second principle, that of responsibility to the assembly, is expressed in West Germany by the formula of 'constructive no-confidence': 'The Bundestag can express its lack of confidence in the Federal Chancellor *only* by electing a successor by the majority of its members' (Article 67). It must be said that this idea of constructive no-confidence, aimed at eliminating purely negative actions on the part of assembly parties, is peculiar to West Germany – its use in 1982 led to the toppling of Helmut Schmidt and the SPD-led government – but in one way or another all the European assemblies seek to enforce responsibility with the ultimate sanction of a vote hostile to the government. Thus, even in Britain, where the two-party system usually ensures that the government controls a parliamentary majority, the Labour Government succumbed to an adverse vote in the House of Commons in 1979.[7] The sole exception to this rule of responsibility is to be found, as we shall see, in the case of Switzerland.

In Italy, although the initial appointment of the head of government is formally made by the president, both he and his ministers must subsequently obtain votes of confidence from both houses of the Italian parliament. In most other countries, as in Britain, responsibility is to one house only, and practice varies as to whether an initial positive vote is required. In theory, the first test of confidence comes for a British government on the division following the Queen's speech – which led to the fall of the Baldwin government in 1924 – but normally it is the election returns which are decisive before Parliament ever meets. Whatever the variations in detail, unified systems ultimately require the executive power to be sustained by an assembly majority.

In this context, the two important anomalies are France and Switzerland, and the unification which we have outlined is for both seriously incomplete. Before we assess the extent of their departure from the prevailing pattern, we should first deal with those countries where the exceptions are of marginal importance. Thus the European monarchies – Britain, the Netherlands, Belgium, Luxembourg, Norway, Spain, Sweden, and Denmark – all reserve only symbolic and representational functions to the monarchy. Thus in Sweden a constitutional change was made in the 1970s whereby the monarch was divested of all political functions, and the power to nominate a new prime minister in the event of a government crisis now belongs to the speaker of the Riksdag. However, there is always the possibility of political involvement in the case of a grave constitutional crisis. In Greece, the decision of King Constantine initially to accept the colonels' coup in 1967 gave the military a cloak of legitimacy – when democracy was restored in 1974, a referendum vote decided against the continuation of the monarchy. Even though monarchs have generally been reduced to taking the role of a figurehead, their ability to express the strength of national consensus should not be underestimated – an advantage which they have over a president who is necessarily elected on a partisan basis. In this respect, the part played by King Juan Carlos in Spanish politics after his accession in 1975 was of outstanding importance. The problems of moving from the Franco dictatorship to parliamentary democracy required skilful handling given the divided nature of Spanish society, and the King's position – identified with no social force or political faction – proved vital in the process of building up a democratic consensus.

Of the European republics, the presidents in West Germany, Austria, Iceland, Ireland, and Italy all have very limited powers which hardly affect the working of the parliamentary system. After the disastrous experience in the Weimar Republic, where the president was elected by popular vote and had strong appointive and reserve powers, the Bonn Republic opted for a simple figurehead, chosen by a federal assembly of the Bundestag together with representatives from the *Land* assemblies. Similarly, the Italian president is elected by parliament, frequently resulting in a huge number of ballots before one candidate is ultimately successful, a process quite out of proportion to the president's modest powers. He has some power of veto, but his chief practical importance is to act as a mediator in the difficult task of forming new coalitions. He most nearly resembles the president of the French Third and Fourth Republics, and in France before the advent of de Gaulle the president was always regarded as an assembly nominee and a quite minor figure – 'I always vote for the stupidest', Clemenceau once remarked. But even where the president is directly elected, this is no guarantee of special power; the presidents in Iceland, Ireland, and Austria have little power in spite of their popular origin.

The Finnish president is a partial exception. He is elected by a special electoral college, in turn popularly constituted, and enjoys prestige and power quite independent of the Finnish parliament. Even before the war, Finnish presidents had become national figures, a position which has both political and constitutional grounds. The congenital instability of Finnish governments – on average a new ministry every year since 1919 – gave the president an amount of power by default, for he has a free hand in selecting the numerous caretaker administrations. Presidents have usually been political figures in their own right before coming to office; once elected, a president becomes non-partisan, but the constitution gives him considerable powers, especially 'to determine the relations of Finland with foreign powers' (Article

33); the president also has a suspensory veto over legislation, and on the fifty occasions this has been used since 1919, only four times – with an intervening election – has the veto been overridden by parliament. Finland therefore represents a mixed parliamentary-presidential system; only a marked decrease in international tension or an unusual increase in government stability would diminish his political functions.

The other two countries to depart from strict unification, Switzerland and France, do so in different ways. Whilst the French system is a parliamentary-presidential hybrid, the Swiss position does not result from any presidential element, but from one important variation in parliamentary practice. Unlike any of the other states, the government, the Federal Council, is not responsible to either house of the Federal Assembly in the sense that it can be dismissed by a vote of no-confidence. Both the Federal Assembly (the Council of States and the National Council) as well as the Federal Council have the same *fixed* period of life – four years. Their conterminality has been described as 'a stroke of constitutional genius';[8] its genius, if that is the right word, guarantees government stability, without at the same time having to resort to a different channel of executive selection which a presidential system requires. In constituting the Federal Council by election from the Federal Assembly, an essential ingredient of the parliamentary system is maintained.

The resulting government stability is further enhanced by the collegial system of government. In effect, this is government by permanent coalition, without any one person or party being able to take a commanding position. As the excluded minor parties claim, it is government by a cartel, but unlike an economic cartel, it is never worth the while of any member party to leave it, since the result would be a permanent exclusion from government. There are manifest reasons for the Swiss system: the need to preserve national unity, the counter-balance provided by the cantonal structure, the belief that 'real' democracy resides more in the rights of the people, using direct methods, rather than in the idea that parliamentary opposition is the necessary corollary of parliamentary government. The conditions underlying the Swiss system are unlikely to be met elsewhere; thus the semi-permanent coalition in Austria after the war was a move towards collegial government, but the balance of the party system allowed the possibility of one party being able to rule on its own account, as was the case from 1966 until 1983.

The constitution of the Fifth French Republic was an attempt to overcome the parliamentary weaknesses which had bedevilled the Third and Fourth Republics. Both the previous editions were in the parliamentary mainstream, even at times verging on 'government by assembly', with a largely powerless president and a government unconditionally bound to parliament. The avowed aim of those who framed the constitution was to achieve a 'genuine' and 'responsible' parliamentary system, whilst taking into account the special problems of France, in particular the nature of the party system. It appeared insufficient to rely on simple devices to shore up government power and stability vis-à-vis the assembly; this method had to some extent already been tried in the Fourth Republic without success. The solution was to incorporate both parliamentary *and* presidential elements: a government still in the last resort responsible to the assembly, and a president armed with strong powers who was quite immune to parliamentary pressures.

They succeeded in creating a constitutional structure which, although in a formal sense retaining many parliamentary features, became increasingly presidential in tone – a not unexpected development since de Gaulle dominated the political scene. The change in the mode of presidential election made by referendum in 1962, from electoral college to direct popular vote, merely confirmed the developments which had taken place since 1958. It is true that the constitution speaks of the president as a kind of passive arbitrator who 'endeavours to ensure respect for the Constitution' and who provides for 'the regular functioning of the public authorities and the continuity of the state' (Article 5). But unlike other European presidents he is not very easily kept aloof from the process of government, for his powers are not just 'reserve' or 'emergency'; the truth is that the constitution gives him ample leeway to become the effective head of government as well as head of state. Thus the constitution gives him the right to appoint the prime minister – not merely to nominate him – and effectively to dismiss him as well. The constitution also gives the president the chairmanship of the Council of Ministers; this was a formality in the Fourth Republic, in the Fifth it made the prime minister a subordinate of the president in the cabinet.

He also became a powerful force against the assembly, since the right of dissolution is his, and there are no reciprocal controls; the power of the assembly, such as it is, could only be used against the government, the president remains immune. Add to this his power to use the referendum, to negotiate with foreign powers, his completely unrestricted right to declare an emergency – with a blank cheque as to what he does and for how long the emergency is to last – and the total sum of his powers appears formidable, all on a seven-year (renewable) term of office.

There is no real comparison here with the presidency in the United States, for the French president controls the life of the assembly, and the government controls its work. Nor in the absence of effective counter-controls does the system provide a responsible parliamentarianism. Yet, despite the imbalance, the French version of presidentialism has worked without signs of grave constitutional or political crisis. It is also very significant that the French left – despite all its expressed dissatisfaction when first in opposition and its commitment to make constitutional changes – now fully accepts the presidential system since its victory of 1981, and President Mitterrand seems quite happy to have inherited the powers tailor-made for de Gaulle.

Yet there were underlying problems. One concerned the possibility of the president being faced by a hostile assembly (with the power to dismiss the president's prime minister). That this situation had not arisen was for long masked by the correspondence between the parliamentary majority and the political colouring of the president. Separate election of assembly and president does not give an automatic correspondence – as the experience of the United States shows, and there the president's term of office is linked much more closely to congressional elections.

In 1981 when François Mitterrand first won the presidency for the Socialists, he promptly dissolved the National Assembly, and there was a predictable coat-tails effect which gave the Socialists a sweeping parliamentary majority. But the threat of confrontation and constitutional crisis arose as a result of the 1986 election which put the right in control of the assembly. The crisis was, however, avoided since right and left sought a form of accommodation for which the term 'cohabitation' was coined – the co-existence of a prime minister from the right, Jacques Chirac (UDR), with the Socialist president. This arrangement worked well enough if somewhat uneasily for some two years. But the functioning of cohabitation signally depended on President Mitterrand being prepared to take a much more modest view of his constitutional powers than he or his predecessors had done previously. In particular that meant not standing in the way of the new government implementing its legislative programme, especially its planned privatisation measures.

The practice of cohabitation may well have had a steadying effect on the political system, since polarisation between the major political forces was thereby contained. But it proved to be a temporary phase, since after his triumphant re-election in 1988, Mitterrand again dissolved the National Assembly, and the following election brought the Socialists back to office, albeit this time without an overall majority.

In all the systems we have looked at, the key aspect is the nature of assembly-government relations, and we shall examine these in more detail in Chapter 7. At this point, we can turn to the supportive institutions: constitutional jurisdiction and direct democracy.

Constitutional jurisdiction

This term refers to power of ordinary or special courts to give an authoritative interpretation of the constitution which is binding on all the parties concerned. To avoid a treatment which might become involved, we can summarise this power of judicial review as applying to:

1. Conflicts between the state and individuals (or groups) in relation to their basic rights under the constitution;
2. Ruling on the constitutionality of laws;
3. Deciding on inter-organ conflicts concerning areas of constitutional competence.

In the United States, the home of judicial review, the Supreme Court exercises its powers under all three heads. In Europe, the two extremes are best represented by Britain and West Germany. We can also distinguish between those states where there is no special provision for review outside of the ordinary courts, and those where a special constitutional court exists apart from the normal court system. Those countries which have a special review body are: West Germany, Italy, Austria, and France. The remainder rely on the normal courts, and as is to be expected, their jurisdiction is much more limited. Particularly in Britain, the absence of a codified constitution would make judicial review in the full sense (1–3, above) a highly political and uncertain weapon; for this reason the doctrine of the supremacy of Parliament means that the courts are limited to ascertaining the will of Parliament and to determining whether particular acts of the executive are *ultra vires*.

The really effective contribution of British courts has been under the first head only – in protecting individual liberties within the framework of common and statute law. This limited function of the judiciary is typical of the West European countries. Traditionally, there is a preference for relying on political means to settle disputes of constitutionality and competence – and the ability to do this is an index of the strength of their political systems. The experience of France and West Germany shows that the securing of individual liberties need not be left to the ordinary courts. It has often seemed odd to outside observers that the French Council of State, which stands at the apex of the administrative hierarchy, should be the final court in cases involving the citizen in dispute with the public authorities. Partly this is to be explained on a 'pure' separation of powers argument – that the ordinary courts should have no jurisdiction in cases involving the public service. Once this view is accepted, then the rational development is to have a separate body of administrative law, administrative courts, and finally 'administrative justice' – an abomination for those brought up in the tradition of Dicey. Yet the fact remains that the Council of State does act as an independent review body; in this, and in other aspects of its work, one simply has to accept the fact of its independence from government: 'As a court the Council is completely independent, in fact probably freer from pressure than the ordinary judiciary where advancement is not necessarily based on seniority.'[9]

The constitutional court in West Germany is easily the most powerful review body in Western Europe.[10] As far as the protection of individual rights is concerned, and numerically this function forms the great bulk of the court's work, there is the important innovation of granting direct access for public complaints, besides giving rulings which are incidental to cases coming through the normal courts. The court has a punitive power as well: individuals and groups can be deprived of some of their constitutional protection if they breach the constitution in specified ways – we have seen how this power can be used in relation to the political parties. The very detailed listing of basic rights in the West German constitution means that the court can be involved in a number of ways – and legislation can be quashed if these rights appear to be infringed. The protection of basic rights has a special significance in relation to the power of the executive, and we look subsequently again at this problem in the context of the control of the executive power.

The second area of judicial review, that of ruling on the constitutionality of laws, can only be fully implemented where a special court is provided – Austria, West Germany, and Italy. In France, there exists the equivalent of the Constitutional Council, the prime function of which is to watch over legislation, and it became particularly involved after the Socialists came to power in 1981, especially with regard to its rulings concerning the government's extensive measures of nationalisation. In the main, the other states are unwilling to allow the challenge to extend beyond the bounds of the national parliament, and where they do, it is to allow for some form of popular decision. There are no problems of interpreting competence in Britain, given the flexibility of the constitution and the supremacy of Parliament. For states with a written constitution the position is not so clear-cut. In Norway, there is some tradition that the courts are able to rule on the constitutionality of laws. In others, such as Sweden and Finland, formal machinery exists in the parliaments to advise governments on the constitutionality of proposed legislation. Where a clear constitutional amendment is envisaged, then special assembly majorities are needed to pass the legislation, an intervening general election, a referendum, or some combination of these. As we shall see, in Switzerland the possibility of challenging legislation by referendum is of particular importance as the Federal Tribunal has no power to rule on federal legislation, although it does have this power with regard to the cantons.

The importance of the Constitutional Council in the Fifth Republic arises from the partial separation of executive from assembly, and from the rather complex division of legislative authority between the two – analogous to the division of competence in a federal state; it rules on whether the correct legislative procedure has been adopted according to the various types of law specified in the constitution. But it has had to overcome the suspicion that it was one more control device to be used by the government against the assembly.

Inherent in any such judicial procedure there is a political element at work. The Italian constitutional court, after its inception in 1956, was much concerned in judging the validity of laws passed in the fascist era and still on the statute book. The West German court has had to concern itself with several highly-charged political matters – for instance, whether the European Defence Community commitment was constitutionally valid and later (1973) in ruling on the validity of the Basic Treaty between East and West Germany. In the United States, there is an inherent tendency to seek a judicialisation of political decision-making, and the dangers of the overt politicisation of the Supreme Court were only overcome after the 1937 crisis. In the European countries, this extreme position has not yet had to be faced.

There is a wide range of judicial activity concerned with the question of the validity of legislation: from a constitutional court whose decision on voiding legislation may make it the centre of political controversy, to the behind-the-scenes activity of, say, the French Council of State acting in its role of expert adviser to the government. It is this body (not the Constitutional Council) which at the drafting stage of both ordinary and delegated legislation vets the government proposals, and its advice becomes virtually binding on governments. Ministers will not want to see their laws or decrees voided at a later date by the Council of State acting as an administrative court of appeal. It was the Council of State which in 1962 had the temerity to rule invalid the special military tribunal set up by de Gaulle, using his emergency powers, to try the army leaders of the Algerian revolt. The verdict of the Council of State was as binding as that of the most powerful constitutional court.

The third area of judicial review, ruling on inter-organ conflicts, is best applied to the special problems of federal states. The territorial division of competence, since it cuts across almost every field of government and legislative activity, has to allow for some formal process of adjudication – otherwise there would be a rapid accretion of powers in one direction or another, probably to the centre. The constitutional courts of West Germany, Austria, Switzerland, and Italy are all concerned to achieve a central-local balance. For Italy, this function involves securing the position of the regional governments. Of the federal states, the Swiss Federal Tribunal and the West German court have helped to resist centralising pressures, with the former only having the power to rule on competence, not on actual legislation. The Austrian court does not appear to have acted as the champion of states' rights, rather the reverse, that the needs of the central government should be paramount. Inter-organ disputes in unitary states mainly involve assembly-executive relations, and any attempt to judicialise them is simply an admission that the political system is not viable. In unified systems, it will not be the case that two distinct sets of personnel become involved. As a result, disputes can be settled 'internally' in the context of the party system. Thus the *political* aspects of inter-organ control are more important than the legal ones in unified and non-federal systems.

On the general question of whether judicial review is a significant aspect of the dispersion of power, an unqualified agreement is only possible in the first area, that of individual rights. For the other two areas, organ competence and constitutionality of laws, it is apparent that there are a number of diverse approaches. As far as legislation is concerned, it is probably wiser to relate the problem of 'constitutionality' to the *whole* legislative process, rather than to the narrow basis of judicial review; this then becomes essentially a political problem in a similar fashion to that of the competence of the various organs of state. Only in a federal system, where the political authorities are explicitly divided, is a straight political resolution usually unworkable. And if the territorial dispersion of power in Europe becomes much more marked than it is at present, say by a greater emphasis on regional government, the need for a 'third party' judicial balance will become apparent.

Direct democracy

Until the spate of referenda held in Ireland, Denmark, Norway and Britain in the early 1970s on the question of their membership of the European Community,[11] it could be said that direct methods were only of marginal importance for the countries of Western Europe. Certainly, the climate of opinion is changing in favour of a greater popular share in decision-making. Yet generally the parties view direct intervention in the decisions of government as hostile to the representative system to which they are bound. Issues which appear to be tailor-made for a referendum are also capable of splitting parties down the middle and of raising the political temperature considerably. Far better to resolve the issue by inter-party agreement than to pass the hot potato to the electorate. The Norwegian experience confirmed the pessimistic view, for subsequent to the 1972 EEC referendum the party system was threatened with fundamental disruption.

Nevertheless, there is widespread provision for some form of popular voice. West Germany, exceptionally, has no use for direct methods at a national level (the issues of the recognition of the German Democratic Republic and acceptance of the Oder-Neisse line would have been relevant opportunities). Often, as in Finland, and Iceland the direct vote is mainly restricted to the election of the president. In Ireland, the president is also popularly elected, and all constitutional changes are subject to referendum approval. In 1968 a proposal to institute a relative majority system of voting was defeated, although the measure was favoured by the largest party. In Scandinavia, the consultative referendum is much preferred to the binding form, since by 'consultation' the supremacy of the legislature is retained. The Scandinavian referendum is used for issues which may or may not be of a basic constitutional nature. Thus in the inter-war years Norway had two referenda on the question of prohibition, and in Sweden the referendum has been used by the government to give the electorate a choice between alternative pensions plans. In 1955, the Swedish electorate voted overwhelmingly against changing the rule of driving on the left of the road, but it was only a consultative referendum; some years later, without further recourse to the electorate, the change was made just the same.

It is true to say that for most countries the use of direct methods in practice is quite sporadic. The first referendum held in post-war Austria, in 1978, was a setback for the government, for the vote went against its nuclear energy policy. Specifically the question involved the commissioning of Austria's first nuclear plant, already built at huge cost, and 50.5 per cent of those voting were hostile. Belgium provides an example of how the decision made by referendum can exacerbate matters. The issue before the electorate in 1950 was whether King Leopold III should return to the throne. The question split the nation in two, and although a majority voted for his return, this was a minority in two important areas, Wallonia and Brussels. Since the vote was in his favour, the king attempted to resume his reign, but this action was greeted by widespread disorder, and he was forced to abdicate.

In Spain, the referendum was used in 1978 to legitimise the new post-Franco constitution, a use broadly comparable to that made of the referendum instrument in post-war France, Belgium and Italy, and, on a fairly high turn out of 68 per cent, 87 per cent of voters supported the new constitution. Eight years later, in March 1986, the referendum was used again, reflecting the increasingly general use of the referendum by Western European governments, and in particular its use for issues which could undermine governing parties' electoral cohesion. On this occasion the Socialist Party, now in government sought popular backing to maintain the country's membership of NATO, despite the party's opposition in 1981, when the centre-right government had pushed the enabling legislation through parliament, and despite the Socialist Party's manifesto pledge of 1982 which had promised to back a referendum to end NATO membership. The referendum attracted considerable United States and European interest, and even direct campaign involvement, both for and against. The turn-out for this referendum fell to 60 per cent, but since the leader of the conservative opposition called for 'active abstention' to try to embarrass the Socialist government, without actually voting against remaining in NATO, the degree of popular mobilisation was high. In fact, popular involvement was vigorous, and was dominated by the Communist left which exploited widespread anti-American feeling, especially regarding the military bases in Spain, a result of the military pact signed with the Franco regime in 1953. The government hindered the 'no' campaign by denying the latter access to the media and by using its control over local administration. Threatened by opposition on two fronts, the

Socialist leadership used party discipline to prevent the Socialist trade union and youth organisation – both of which opposed the leadership's line – from campaigning. The government used massive party and state resources to gain support for a 'yes' vote, not stressing the NATO issue directly, but emphasising the technological and industrial implications of cutting Spain out of a major sphere of Atlantic and European cooperation. The government won the backing of 52 per cent of those who voted, with only 40 per cent against and eight per cent spoiled papers. Throughout, the Socialists benefited from the weakness of the Communist left and the unwillingness of the Socialist electorate to risk damaging the party's standing.

Italy provides the most interesting study in the contemporary use of the referendum. Although Article 75 of the 1948 constitution sanctioned popular initiative to repeal specific laws, the necessary implementing legislation was not passed until 1970, and then mainly because of pressure by Catholic lay organisations hoping to repeal liberal divorce laws which had been enacted. In the event, this initiative was defeated: it proved to be a decisive turning-point indicating the growing secularisation of Italian society, besides pointing to the increasing vulnerability of the DC.

The Radical Party then adopted the referendum as a weapon against what it saw as the corrupt rule of the established parties and their élites. Thus in 1978, although narrowly failing to win

Use of the Referendum in Italy

Issue	Date	Turn-out (%)	For Repeal (%)
Divorce	May 1974	87.7	41.7
Public Order	Jun. 1978	81.2	23.3
Party Financing	Jun. 1978	81.2	43.7
Public Order	May 1981	79.4	14.8
Abolition life sentence	May 1981	79.4	22.7
Handgun Control	May 1981	79.4	14.0
Abortion† ('pro-Life')	May 1981	79.4	32.1
Abortion† (Radical)	May 1981	79.4	11.5
Wage indexing	Jun. 1985	77.9	45.7
Judicial Responsibility	Oct. 1987	65.2	69.6
Commission Reform	Oct. 1987	65.2	74.1
Planning Control*	Oct. 1987	65.2	70.4
Local Tax*	Oct. 1987	65.1	69.1
Involvement abroad*	Oct. 1987	65.2	63.0

† The Pro-Life campaign sought to repeal the 1978 legislation; the Radical councounter-referendum to repeal most remaining restrictions.
* Nuclear energy issues

the repeal of the law providing public funding for the parties, the Radicals could none the less claim a moral victory. Later it was the turn of the PCI to employ the referendum as an explicitly party-political weapon. It sponsored an initiative to repeal a law which modified the wage-indexing system, believing that it was bound to win mass support and also embarrass the governing parties.

A series of five referenda held in 1987 represented a development in party strategy: the PSI sought to promote its populist image at the expense chiefly of its major coalition-partner – and rival – the DC. The success of these initiatives for the PSI is, however, perhaps of less value for the political system, since it could serve to erode public confidence in the operation of the parliamentary system. Moreover, the success of the initiatives was combined with a sharp fall in the level of participation – in itself scarcely a recommendation for the referendum as an alternative expression of the democratic will, besides building a greater degree of uncertainty into the process of policy decision-making.

The opposing views on the value of the referendum are summed up in the contrasting experiences of France and Switzerland, the only two countries where historically it has played a central part in the political process. Its use in France has a long and vexed history: the referendum can even be regarded as an anti-democratic technique: the power of a dictator to manipulate the popular will and always to obtain the answer he requires, as Napoleon III was able to do. In the Third and Fourth Republics, the parties made no use of the referendum, except in 1945 and 1946 to gain acceptance for a new constitution. The results were hardly satisfactory. In 1945, the draft constitution was rejected, and in the following year it was approved, but this did not build up a new consensus: the electorate was split three ways: nine million in favour, eight million against, and a further eight million abstaining.

In de Gaulle's hands, under Article 11 of the 1958 constitution, the referendum became a weapon to be used against the parties in the assembly, part of his 'dialogue with the nation.' Each successive referendum was aimed to create a strong presidential system identified with his person – they were just as much personal votes of confidence as a means of settling the issue at hand. The approval of the 1958 constitution, the Algerian issue twice, in 1961 and 1962, and the method of presidential election in 1962, all of these consultations resulted in large, favourable majorities. His one defeat, in 1969, highlights some of the objections. The issue facing the electorate was formally about proposals to reorganise the

Senate and to reform local government, but it was also an issue of confidence in de Gaulle. The terms of the referendum required one answer to at least two distinct questions; it was a complex document of 68 articles requiring the amendment of 19 articles of the constitution. The bemused voters could work up no enthusiasm, and the defeat of the referendum bill led to the departure of de Gaulle.

The referendum on the changed method of electing the president shows particular unconstitutional features. The proposal for direct election was clearly a constitutional change, and under Article 89 required the prior approval of the National Assembly. This provision de Gaulle blithely ignored, the Constitutional Council declared itself powerless to intervene, and of course the favourable result made the action retrospectively constitutional. Napoleon III had also obtained such retrospective popular sanction for his overthrow of the Second Republic.

The contrasting feature in the Swiss use of the referendum lies in its completely depersonalised nature; it is a weapon for the electorate. Swiss voters have two important powers: to challenge federal laws, and to propose and vote upon constitutional changes. There is an absence of power, at a federal level, to promote legislation; this is not such a serious restriction since the very detailed constitution is open to the type of amendment which in other countries would be the province of ordinary law-making. The constant use made by the electorate of 'challenge' and 'constitutional initiative' shows that the referendum need not be a destabilising influence, and in fact it is well-integrated with the rest of the political system. The issues raised can be handled by the political parties, and the nature of Swiss government ensures that the challenges made never become a question of 'confidence', since the federal government cannot 'fall'; this may well be the reason why direct democracy does not easily combine with normal party government – frequent resort to referendum would hinder coalition and party unity. Even in Switzerland, the Federal Council over the years has developed techniques for avoiding popular challenge to its legislation.

The only country to follow Switzerland to some extent has been Denmark where, as a result of the 1953 constitution, the upper house was abolished and a popular check introduced instead. Constitutional changes require a positive vote with at least 40 per cent of the *electorate*. Perhaps more far-reaching is the provision that one-third of the assembly can demand a referendum on a bill – and this will result in its defeat if it is rejected by a majority of voters (and 30 per cent of the electorate). Thus a government with a narrow assembly majority will find it difficult to pass controversial legislation. In addition, Denmark has made use of the advisory referendum. Thus in order to overcome the hostility expressed in the Folketing to ratification of the Single European Act, as required by the European Community, the government put the issue to the electorate in 1986 and so outflanked the opposition.

The limited British experience of the referendum shows how public opinion may differ from established party lines. The 1975 referendum (67.2 per cent in favour of European Community membership) demonstrated a substantial consensus despite party rhetoric and the deep divisions within the Labour Party. The 1979 referenda on the proposed Scottish and Welsh assemblies exposed the hollowness of 'nationalist' party claims: far from the required 40 per cent of the *electorate* in favour, in Scotland it amounted to only 32.5 per cent and in Wales a mere 11.8 per cent of those entitled to vote.

How should we assess the value of the referendum as an instrument of decision making? On the one hand, its 'moral value' has to be conceded for after all it is the 'people' who are deciding an issue for themselves, and since they are forced to give close attention to the issues involved, a referendum campaign may be a much more valuable form of political education than that provided by party elections. A referendum may also have the healthy effect of breaking the muzzle of a purely 'party consensus', although the effect may be to destabilise the political system – and that is important in considering the potentially negative effect of direct democracy. The point is that the strength of West European parliamentary institutions was built up on the basis of the *representative* principle, in effect an emphasis on parliamentary and party élitism. Many of the tensions that arise in contemporary parliamentary democracies stem from the conflict between the mutually exclusive demands and assumptions of 'participation' and 'representation'. However, it is clear that the referendum itself is a cumbersome instrument for policy decisions on a continuous basis, just as constant resort to its use can inhibit the exercise of political leadership. It is another matter when fundamental issues are at stake, especially those of a basic constitutional nature. Yet that formulation only succeeds in begging the question of what is 'fundamental'.

Constitutional dynamics

The ways of securing a distribution of power which we have just examined can only provide a partial explanation of the tensions and balances that are integral to the idea of constitutionalism. Some of these techniques are only of very partial application, and even where, as for instance with judicial review in relation to individual rights, the function is of general application, there is a passive aspect; of course, judicial power is itself politically passive. Once a constitutional order has been settled, it is the relationship between the executive and assembly which becomes the critical and active factor. The balance and tension which operates here is of a special kind in unified systems. Although the basic, and formal, order may remain unchanged, there is also a dynamic balance which results from what can be termed the sub-constitutional factors – a shorthand expression for which is the party system.

The special nature of 'party democracy' in unified systems lies in the way that the parliamentary system provides a framework for the parties to effect a synthesis of electoral will and government power. In linking the social forces with the power of state, we can see that the party system operates at the crossover point where the input and output functions of the political system merge. In this respect unified structures provide a *single* focus for this activity, whilst any system operating a separation of powers results in two, probably competing, bases of authority; a unified system apparently offers a more open-ended process of constitutional development. That does not make the European version of party democracy necessarily more successful than other forms. The onus placed on the party system to achieve a purely parliamentary integration may prove to be too great. However, to the extent that an integration is achieved, it is the party system – as the totality of interaction – which provides the dynamic just as much as the contribution of the individual parties.

The party system is not the only constitutional ingredient, and the idea that constitutionalism requires a number of internal checks and balances can be widely applied. There can never be a one-to-one correspondence between function and institution, and certainly any relationship will not remain constant over time. Within all macro political institutions there is a continuous process of hiving-off and increased specialisation – in effect a growing 'structural differentiation' to which we referred earlier, and that is a leading trait in the development of advanced societies. The combination of this process together with alterations in the party system make for a constantly changing picture, but these changes are harmonised with the more static elements of the constitutional structure to give the 'recognisable continuity' which are inherent in the idea of constitutionalism. The continuity represents a form of constraint which continually serves to modify political action, but it is not to be thought of merely as a system of 'legal' checks, for it is more the product of historical and social development. In the final analysis, we are concerned not so much with constitutions as with the political and social structures that sustain them.

Yet in turn these structures depend for their efficacy on an underlying social consensus; if this is not present, constitutional government must continually be subject to question. And the consensus is not simply one to be equated with a parliamentary working majority. The breakdown of 'constitutional' government in Northern Ireland is a relevant example. The study made of political attitudes in Northern Ireland by Richard Rose[12] revealed that no single group of attitudes towards the regime found the support of more than a quarter of the population, and this was true for the Protestant majority as it was for the Catholic minority. In that situation, the dominance of the Ulster Unionists only succeeded in masking the unresolved problems as long as the status quo could be maintained; once it was disrupted, the constitutional framework became irrelevant.

In later chapters we shall examine the structure of assemblies and governments, and their interaction, to appreciate how the parliamentary balance works in practice, but before doing so it is appropriate to take account of those states and movements which reject the constitutional order of liberal democracy.

Notes and references
1. H. V. Wiseman, *Political Systems: Some Sociological Approaches*. Routledge, 1966, p. 66. 'In Western democracies . . . constitutionalism accepts a certain ambiguity and falling-short of "ideal" standards . . .as being "mature".'
2. C. B. Macpherson, *The Real World of Democracy*, Clarendon Press, 1966, p. 10. 'It is not simply that democracy came later . . . It was something the competitive society logically needed.'
3. G. Sartori, 'Constitutionalism: A Preliminary Discussion', *American Political Science Review*. December 1962, pp. 853–64.
4. P. H. Merkl, *Modern Comparative Politics*, New York: Holt, Rinehart and Winston, 1970, p. 426.
5. The West German Basic Law in Articles 1 to 19 provides for the basic freedoms: of speech, assembly, association, religious faith, choice of trade or profession, petition, movement, and of asylum. It also gives security to the home, family, and person as well as granting equality before the law, secrecy of the mail, protection of property (or just compensation) – protection of inheritance rights, security of citizenship. In Article 21 the free formation of political parties is guaranteed – as long as they respect the democratic order. The Constitutional Court has a final jurisdiction in all these matters.
6. M. J. C. Vile, *Constitutionalism and the Separation of Powers*, Oxford University Press, 1967, p. 324. He adds, 'There is no separation of powers here, for the "internal" restraints upon the Lord Chancellor are dependent upon his position in a profession the vast majority of the members of which operate *outside* the government machine.'

7. The first election in February 1974 was indecisive, since neither Labour nor the Conservatives had an overall majority. The second (October) election gave Labour an initial majority, but subsequently, by 1976, it was in a minority position and finally succumbed to a no-confidence vote in March 1979 – the first such defeat since that of the Labour minority government in 1924.
8. C. Hughes, *The Federal Constitution of Switzerland*, Oxford University Press, 1954, p. 108.
9. C. E. Freedemann, *The Conseil d'Etat in Modern France*, New York: Columbia University Press, 1961, p. 58.
10. See N. Johnson, 'The Interdependence of Law and Politics: Judges and the Constitution in West Germany', *West European Politics*, July 1982.
11. The results of the referenda on EEC membership were as follows: Ireland (June 1972) 80.0% in favour (71.0% voting). Norway (September 1972) 53.5% against (77.6% voting). Denmark (October 1972) 63.7% in favour (90.1% voting). Britain (June 1975) 67.2% in favour (63.2% voting).
12. R. Rose, *Governing Without Consensus: An Irish Perspective*, Faber and Faber, 1971. The conclusions Rose drew are based on survey material made in 1968 immediately prior to the onset of the crisis that has persisted for the past 20 years.

Additional references

W. G. Andrews, *Constitutions and Constitutionalism*, Princeton: Van Nostrand, 1961.

P. Blair, 'Law and Politics in Germany', *Political Studies*, September 1978.

V. Bogdanor (ed.), *Constitutions in Democratic Politics*, Gower, 1988.

D. Butler and U. Kitzinger, *The 1975 Referendum*, Macmillan, 1977.

D. Butler and A. Ranney (eds.), *Referendums. A Comparative Study*, Washington: American Enterprise Institute, 1978.

T. Cole, 'Three Constitutional Courts: A Comparison', in H. Eckstein and D. E. Apter (eds.), *Comparative Politics*, New York: The Free Press, 1963.

S. A. de Smith, *Constitutional and Administrative Law*, Penguin Books, 1974.

I. D. Duchacek, *Constitutions and Politics*, Boston: Little, Brown, 1970.

European Journal of Political Research, The Referendum in Western Europe (whole issue), 4/1976.

C. J. Friedrich, *Constitutional Government and Democracy*, Ginn and Company, 1950.

P. Furlong, 'The Constitutional Court in Italian Politics', *West European Politics*, July 1988.

R. Holme, *Time for a Constitutional Change*, Macmillan, 1988.

N. Johnson, *In Search of the Constitution: Reflections on State and Society in Britain*, Oxford: Pergamon, 1977.

J. Jowell and D. Oliver (eds.), *The Changing Constitution*, Oxford: Clarendon, 1985.

D. P. Kommers, *Judicial Politics in West Germany*, Sage Publications, 1976.

K. Loewenstein, *Political Power and the Governmental Process*, University of Chicago Press, 1965.

P. Norton, *The Constitution in Flux*, Oxford: Martin Robertson, 1982.

G. Smith, 'The Referendum and Political Change', *Government and Opposition*, vol. 10/3, Summer 1975.

H. J. Spiro, *Government by Constitution*, New York: Random House, 1959.

C. F. Strong, *Modern Constitutions*, Sidgwick and Jackson, 1963.

K. C. Wheare, *Modern Constitutions*, Oxford University Press, 1966.

L. Wolf-Phillips, *Comparative Constitutions*, Macmillan, 1972.

A. J. Zürcher (ed.), *Constitutions and Constitutional Trends since World War II*, New York University Press, 1955.

6 Non-Democratic Variants

The fascist alternative
Set against the doctrine of constitutionalism, and the institutions and behaviour it implies, are the various forms of dictatorial rule. The chief of these, fascism, has been paradoxically one of Western Europe's contributions to the twentieth century. It is the sharpest contrast to liberal democracy because it goes beyond simply arbitrary or despotic rule and adds the pretensions of a unified movement and a particular philosophy of state power to what would otherwise be a straightforward dictatorship. The classic form of 'revolution from above' as Barrington Moore described fascism, is now largely a part of the history of the inter-war years, with little direct relevance to the politics of present-day Europe. Yet, apart from the fact that it is the perfect antithesis to constitutionalism, an appreciation of fascism helps to understand the problems of countries which have experienced dictatorship; it is also necessary to be able to assess the possibility of its active resurgence in Western Europe, in one form or another.

The 'pure' form of fascism has three attributes which have to be added to its principally *class* character:

1. A mass-appeal.
2. A revolutionary ideology.
3. An apparatus with which to create a *totalitarian society*: the leader, the party, techniques of social control.

It is obvious that in all three respects fascism differs markedly from conventional right-wing authoritarianism. Thus a run-of-the-mill dictatorship can get by with a minimum ballast of ideology, little popular appeal, and an economy of repression – a break-even point may actually be reached where the measures of a police-state appear to rest fairly lightly on the general population. Even so, despite the contrasts in impact and form, it can be argued that fascism and dictatorship have the same kind of effect on society, halting certain social changes, fostering others, to the benefit of particular élites and classes.

Mussolini's Italy and National Socialist Germany are usually regarded as the exemplary cases of fascism, perhaps the only authentic ones. Granted that the social conditions in the two countries were quite dissimilar (Germany already a largely industrialised state and Italy still having the bulk of its population working on the land), in both, the three attributes of fascism were present as strands of a unified movement. Most readily appreciated are the techniques of totalitarian control; the 'total' control of society which resulted in both countries has to be seen as integral to the ideological basis of a fascist movement. Fascism, as an extreme opponent of both socialism and communism, must necessarily deny their basic premise of class conflict in society. Since the existing class structure has to be regarded as fundamentally in harmony, the fascist view is to reproduce the existing social order under a new guise. The idea of a 'corporate state', alternatively of a *Volksgemeinschaft*, fulfils these requirements. Class conflict is made redundant by definition, and organisations and parties which reflect a divisive, even a pluralist version of society are abolished or absorbed into all-embracing national movement.

This view of society has to be enforced by a whole host of controls to ensure that corporative unity is maintained, ranging from police powers to social welfare measures. Put more starkly, the control involves three totalities: total terror, total regimentation, and total control of opinion. The control apparatus can be identified with the political party, and this seeks to enhance national unity as embodied in the power of the state. It is then a short step to the glorification of this power as personalised in the party leader. The leader-figure represents the polar opposite of liberal democratic values: not only is his charismatic role sharply opposed to the exercise of rational authority, the *Führerprinzip* which he incorporates is unashamedly arbitrary.[1]

There is also the mass-appeal of the fascist movement. We have said that the fascist ideology is revolutionary, and this gives it a wide following; mass support is attracted because fundamental changes are promised. There is, first, a sweeping *political* revolution: as promised, all the institutional trappings of the liberal democratic state are abolished, and they include the political parties, the standard-bearers of pluralist politics; at the very least, as with the churches, they will be kept on a short rein.[2] At the same time, fascism also promises a *socio-economic* revolution – implicit in the idea of 'National Socialism' – but this revolution either fails to take place, or else takes a direction different from that which most supporters expect.

Despite the promises of the fascist leaders, wide differences in wealth and social prestige persist, and the economic basis of society remains unaltered. There are, however, fundamental social effects;

chiefly, it is not a change in the relationship of person to person, nor of class to class, but in the relationship of the individual to the state. Shorn of the insulation given by pluralist organisation, social life is dominated by state activity. And it is the new state bureaucracy – widely conceived to include the state party as well – which adds a new dimension to social class. Thus the old social order is supplemented by a new state élite; the masses are then in a doubly subservient position: the state machine must reinforce the class division, since the official ideology cannot admit that the basis of class conflict is present. Ultimately, popular support will wane, but that is incidental to later development; it is the promise of the socio-economic transformation of society which gives fascism its initial mass base.

The appeal of fascism is greatest in periods of extreme social dislocation: to those who are uprooted, to those who see their position in society threatened. This is especially the case when a society is in the throes of modernisation. Thus Organski saw a critical precondition for fascism in the changing nature of the rural-urban balance, a measure of which is the relative importance of the industrial and agricultural sectors.[3] He found that a zone of instability lies in the area where non-agricultural employment is rising to 40 per cent and persists until it reaches 55 per cent; beyond this point, a society will have become substantially modernised. On this criterion, fascism is not a feature of advanced industrial societies, or if it is, then quite different conditions are relevant.

In the conditions of fundamental social change associated with modernisation, it is not the changing balance of occupations which is in itself important, but the consequent social upheaval. The social context of fascism involves a triple line of conflict: the rural-urban one, the contest between élites, that is, between traditional and modernising ones, and the underlying pattern of class conflict on which these other two are superimposed. From one point of view, fascism can be seen as an attempt to slow the pace of industrialisation, or at least to stem its consequences and shift the costs; from another, it is a failure to 'tame' the traditional élites associated with the predominance of agriculture.[4] A successful fascist movement secures an alliance between new and old élites – as a reaction to the growing demands and successes of the urban proletariat; the 'mass entry' into politics of this new force is in the first instance a political threat which presages economic and social threats to follow.

For a variety of reasons, this pattern of conflict was avoided or mitigated in a number of countries. Changes were often gradual, and the rural-urban tensions were handled by the new economic élites on their own terms. Just why some societies managed to avoid a critical impasse and others stumbled from one crisis to another is a question we cannot pursue here.[5] It is sufficient to point out the varieties of development that are possible in the type of social situation that leads to dictatorship or fascism. Where the old social and economic élites are still in control of the economy and of the state machine, a simple takeover is possible via the intervention of the armed forces. That was true for Portugal in the 1920s, where the old élites were still fully in command, and the dictatorship, set in train by the military, operated at an early stage of modernisation. Where political mobilisation has proceeded further – as was the case of republican Spain in the 1930s – the net result may be the same, but a political battle, involving the masses, has to be fought as well; hence one saw a pseudo-fascist movement (the Falange) being used as well as armed force, first to gain some popular sanction and later as an agent of political demobilisation, but Franco's Spain never had to go very far in the direction of a fully fascist state.

In Italy, the homeland of fascism, all the apparatus was fully employed – the mass appeal, the revolutionary ideology,[6] the totalitarian order – and, as in Spain, the fascist movement faced a well-organised working class which first had to be demobilised. But once this was accomplished, the trappings of fascism as part of a new social order began to wear thin, and the Italian dictatorship, apart from the figure of Mussolini, showed little fundamental difference from the more conventional forms. According to Woolf, the final decade, '. . . saw an accentuation of factions within the party, while the centrifugal forces of an undisciplined, municipalistic-minded society reasserted themselves. Italian fascism was increasingly a dictatorship and ruled in a void by a particularly impressionable dictator.'[7]

The quality of German fascism was essentially different from the other three cases we have mentioned: at least on an *economic* level, Germany had already become a modern, industrial state; the agricultural population had already fallen below 25 per cent in the 1920s. Further, with the complete collapse of the Imperial order, *political* control of the new Weimar Republic was firmly in the hands of the mass parties. The social dislocation was not primarily a consequence of urban-rural changes, but of the economic disruption of defeat, inflation, and the slump. That this should have led to fascism arose in part from the continuing *social* power of the old élites; the democracy of the Weimar Republic scarcely altered their power position – most notably, and strategically, in the German officer corps and in the political and social connections of the German High Command. This social élite was hardly an overpowering political force in its own right, but the values it represented were still dominant for large sections of German society, particularly the farming community and the Protestant middle class.

Hitler's political finesse was to play on the fears of the social élite, together with those who still accepted this élite leadership and value system, but at the same time to make a genuinely mass appeal, measured in millions. To achieve this wide alliance was only possible if the revolutionary ideology of fascism was given full expression. The political revolution then took the normal course: the destruction of liberal democracy and the demobilisation of the masses. What was different from other dictatorships was that there also occurred a social revolution. It was certainly not the special form of 'socialism' promised, nor was the distribution of economic power significantly altered. What it did involve was the destruction of the influence and power of the old social élites – of which the eventual 'liquidation' of the military élite was the most striking. In this respect, German fascism was quite different from other dictatorships. Following the German collapse in war, and with the destruction of the fascist élite, a temporary *social* vacuum appeared in German society; put another way, the impact of German fascism had been to complete the modernisation of German society.

In all the four states we have considered liberal democratic systems were supplanted by dictatorial regimes, and although each antidemocratic intervention took place in societies at different levels of social, economic, and political development, together their experience can be seen as part of a continuum. In one sense, the effect of the intervention was to secure the position of dominant élites and classes, if only temporarily; in another sense, the effect was to pave the way to a more modern form of society – and this is irrespective of whether the dictatorial power-holders came from the old or the new élites, or, as in the case of Germany and Italy, from neither.

This line of argument accords with Organski's conclusions. He wrote: 'Fascism is part of the process of transition from a limited participation to a mass system, and fascism is a last-ditch stand by the élites, both modern and traditional, to prevent the expansion of the system over which they exercise hegemony. The attempt always fails and in some ways the fascist system merely postpones some of the effects it seeks to prevent.'[8]

Politics and the military

The armed forces in Western Europe are almost everywhere in a quiescent condition, accepting the decisions of the political leaders with docility. It is hardly the case in other parts of the world, and two questions we have to answer here are, why this happy situation should exist, and whether it is a permanent state of affairs. We need only to bear in mind the recent history of France, the dictatorship in Greece and the military backing to the regimes in Spain and Portugal, and latterly the rule of the Portuguese Armed Forces Movement – to be aware that the feasibility of military intervention in politics, even of military rule, is nowhere quite impossible. Even if, unlike the army in developing countries, the military in Europe cannot easily don the guise of 'modernising agents', in principle there are various pretexts they can use to justify political action.

The readiness of the armed forces to take a back seat politically is not something new; in fact, active intervention, though always striking when it occurs, is very much the exception in European history. To explain this, Andreski drew attention to the early view advanced by Gaetano Mosca, who '. . . considered the subordination of the military to the civilian authority to have been one of the most distinctive and crucial features of the European civilisation. . . . It was proof of Mosca's genius that, diverging from all current opinions, he put forth the view that the relative docility of the European armies depended on the rigidity of class divisions in their midst.'[9] Thus on the one hand the military leaders were an integral part of the ruling social order, yet on the other they were always 'divided from their men by an impassable economic and cultural abyss.' These different facets of cohesion and division served to neutralise the army as a political force.

Other factors can be added to the basic orientation. For instance, Janowitz explained the subordination from an early time as arising from, '. . . the low specialisation of the military profession [which] made it possible for the political élite to supply the bulk of the necessary leadership for the armed forces'.[10] Further, the ability of the political system to avoid 'sharp discontinuities' meant that there was no prolonged period when this leadership was not in evidence. However, a precondition of stability in *all* cases is the social homogeneity of the political rulers and the military élite; without this, the tensions between the political and the military orders are likely to become acute – such was the case in Spain, Portugal, and Greece.

The particular problem in Western Europe was to secure the continued subordination of the military into the democratic era;

the close link which the armies had with conservative traditions, as part of a pre-democratic and feudal order, provided no promise at all that the military would meekly accept a new political establishment. Whilst Mosca's formulation helps to show the difficulties of an officer class in effecting a successful coup, this applies much more to the period before the onset of political democracy when the political leaders and the military ones had an identical social background. It was still true in the democratic era that the continuing rigidity of class divisions within armies meant that they were never a cohesive force; this division made intervention more risky, yet not necessarily less desirable, from a right-wing and military viewpoint.

In assessing the political role of the military and its degree of subordination to the democratic political order, there are three areas of explanation which we can usefully consider:

- the social background of the officer class;
- the leading values of the military, and their concept of what is a 'legitimate' political order;
- the degree of 'isolation' of the armed forces from wider society, both in a social and technical sense.

We should expect that the military could take on an independent political colouring in conditions where its recruitment is from the privileged classes, where it regards the democratic order with suspicion, and where, in its isolation, it becomes 'a state within a state' developing military values as the yardstick of its judgement. Each of these conditions has to be related to the actual course of development in the various countries.

As far as the social background of top military personnel is concerned, what is immediately apparent for Europe is that there was no sudden democratisation of recruitment. What happened in most European states was a relatively gradual shift from the predominance of the nobility towards one of the middle class, a shift that lasted for the best part of a century. The important point is that the change in composition was gradual, yet at the same time it was for the most part an unhindered process. C. B. Otley has shown the wide variations from one country to another.[11] Thus in the Netherlands, middle-class officers were already in a large majority in the last quarter of the nineteenth century, but this was exceptional. For Britain in the same period, the nobility and the middle class shared high-ranking military positions in about equal proportions. At the other extreme, the German army élite was almost exclusively of the nobility – well over 90 per cent in 1872. Otley's figures show that there was a gradual, but never dramatic shift in the twentieth century, and in Britain it was actually at a slower rate than for other European countries. Exceptionally again, even by 1939 the German nobility still supplied a third of the high-ranking officers. In all European countries, it has been only in the most recent past that the top positions have covered all sections of the middle class; the slow transfer was from the nobility to the upper middle class in the first place; of course, lower class recruitment to top positions is still an extreme rarity.

The significance of the changing pattern is twofold. In most states, the widening social background of the officer class meant that an increasing proportion came from the same background as the new political leaders; secondly, the gradual nature of the change did not present a challenge to leading military values – to some extent the middle-class officers were happy to accept them – and no sudden crisis in the status of the military resulted. The continuity of military traditions was also protected by the considerable inbreeding amongst the officer class; family background is very important in the decision to take up a military career, and anything from a third to a half of military leaders have some prior connection with the armed forces. A conclusion to the question of social background and the political involvement of the military is that whilst it is important that a socially representative officer hierarchy should emerge, the terms on which it does so are of equal importance.

The second determining feature is the 'legitimacy' of the civilian rulers. This authority is not something which the military has a free hand in interpreting, and which it can call into question at will. Of importance here is the historical subordination of the military élite to the political leaders, for this was largely taken over into the democratic era, and where the democratic institutions were peacefully grafted on to the older system, the transfer of legitimacy occurred without question; at no stage did the military face a sharp clash of loyalties. Just as important as the military view of the civilian order is the civilian view of its own institutions, in other words the relative maturity of the political culture. As Finer put it, 'The greater the degree of consensus in society and the width and organisation of this opinion, the less the likelihood of a military intervention and the less likely, in the event, its success.'[12] The extent to which organised opinion can be gauged is another matter; it depends on the cohesion of the party system, the ability to marshal public opinion, and on the presence of strong secondary groupings such as trade unions. All three of these will help deter the military from intervening, and should it nevertheless do so, the extent of civilian resistance may weaken the army's resolve –

especially that of the lower ranks who will be much less disposed to question the civilian norms.

The third area of explanation depends partly on the other two. We have called this the degree of 'isolation' of the military, and it is related to the social basis of recruitment and to the prevailing civilian consensus. But the isolation can lead to the armed forces defining their own role in society, not just allying themselves with an old and threatened social order. Blondel terms this independence a form of 'professionalism': 'The isolation of the military from the rest of the nation tends to increase the professional nature of the army. . . . It will tend to develop its own values and attitudes to greater extremes than it would otherwise do.'[13] A 'professional' army of this kind has its own code – foremost, it will see itself as the sole guarantee of national honour. However, the forces acting against it being able to do so are considerable. Firstly, there are the basic socialising influences to which the military leaders are subjected, and these are specifically reinforced by the strict idea of obedience which characterises any army. In Britain, this subordinating function was for long performed by the public schools, of which Otley says, '. . . although they did not lack militaristic features, they were basically *class* training centres. . . (They) provided a general training for the performance of "diffuse" leadership roles.'[14] Where this subordination was not achieved, the military role was not clearly defined, and the obedience which military leaders could command was at their disposal in defining their own role.

The other force acting against the development of an isolated and professional army may be called 'technical. Superficially, it might appear that any technically-advanced army would become more professionalised. But the nature of modern warfare has made the armed forces less rather than more self-sufficient. In order to develop its techniques the military is forced to maintain a range of contacts with non-military groups. There is no longer any *special* military mystique, only multi-disciplinary, military technicians. Increasingly, modern armies are unable to operate effectively unless they can secure co-operation from their civilian counterparts, and this involves the army at all points; it cannot retreat into a shell of its own myth-making.

It is instructive to examine those cases where the subordination of the military was *not* so much in evidence, and we can take the French and German armies to illustrate the application of the three general conditions we have already outlined. At the present time, it appears that the armed forces in both countries now fully accept the primacy of the political and democratic order, but in both cases the transfer was far from smooth. We have already drawn attention to the social composition of the German military élite in the early part of the century; the preponderance of the nobility meant that the armed forces at the disposal of the politicians of the Weimar Republic were simply unreliable; the military still believed in the values of Imperial Germany, and if a restoration of the monarchy was impossible, this only served to increase the isolative tendencies in the German Army. Before the German defeat in the First World War, this isolation was not in evidence; instead there was a 'dual legitimacy' – a civilian government linked to the assembly and a military élite directly responsible to the Emperor.

Yet the military representatives of the old ruling class did not resort to an open attack on the Weimar Republic. The Kapp Putsch of 1920 was not engineered by the German High Command, and its failure can be directly ascribed to the strength of the 'civilian consensus'. But even at that time one can see the army's own definition of its role, especially in the attitude of the German High Command towards the attempted coup. The answer to the government's request to deal with it was simply: 'The Reichswehr does not shoot at Reichswehr'. If the army leaders did not go so far as to topple the civilian government themselves, it was certain that they would do little to save it either.

The German Army came to regard itself not just as a servant of the state, but identical with it; in the eyes of the military, the political game was played out on a lower level entirely. This is not to say that the military leaders remained aloof from politics; in particular, there were the manoeuvrings of the military camarilla round the ageing President Hindenburg as well as the machinations of General Schleicher, both in his role as minister for the Reichswehr and later as short-lived chancellor. But the various manoeuvres were in the nature of a high level deal: how to keep Hitler out or, alternatively, on what terms he should be allowed in; the military did not itself seek direct political power.

Although by 1933 many of the junior officers were affected by the Nazi enthusiasm, the High Command was not. Nevertheless, a general transfer of loyalties was enforced, from the values of Imperial Germany to the personal oath of loyalty to Hitler – in the end an élite subservience. Earlier we referred to the 'liquidation' of the German military élite as one of the consequences of fascism, and the effects of this can be seen in post-war Germany. The pattern of recruitment has moved decisively in favour of the lower middle class, and the 'double rupture' suffered by the German military in 1918 and 1945 left its traces in the career patterns and social outlook of its élite, and the 'retired' officers got themselves permanent civilian jobs, unlike their predecessors in 1918 who flocked to the 'Free Corps'. The new army personnel is largely conscript, and the Bundeswehr does not enjoy the high status of the Reichswehr in West German society. There can be no doubt that the Federal Republic is one major country where the military is least influential, and there has been a dramatic drop in the status of officers, in the public view, in relation to comparable professions. In all three respects: social composition, ideas of legitimacy, and in its lack of social isolation, the German Army has lost the basis for an independent political role.

There are important points of difference between the French and German experience of the military. The estrangement of the French Army was not primarily caused by its social composition; a statute of the Third Republic required the officer intake to be made up by the promotion from the ranks of a third of the total, and generally, up to the Second World War French recruitment was more middle class than that for the German Army. For all that, the conflict with the ruling political authorities was more long-lasting. The French Army's loyalty to the Third Republic was suspect in its early years, and its attitude was shared by all the conservative forces in France. The line-up of pro- and anti-republican forces was shown with sharp relief by the onset of the Dreyfus Affair at the end of the century; here were the 'dual legitimacies' in their French context. But the showdown was averted, and it was only in the collapse of the Third Republic in 1940 that the bulk of the French Army threw in its lot with the conservation-authoritarian Vichy regime. Thus on the counts of social composition and legitimacy, the army for the most part learned to live with political democracy.

A new phase was evident after 1945. The normal post-war retrenchment made the officer class socially more homogeneous, for there was a sharp increase in those having a military background, and the temporary influx of non-professionals during the war was reversed. It is in this situation that the isolative tendencies of the military can become apparent, and the trigger to this process was the long and painful phase of decolonisation in which the army bore the full brunt in the decade of the 1950s. Mauled in Indo-China, and robbed of success in the Suez escapade, the French Army had no intention of facing a further drubbing in Algeria. And it was there that the army was able to develop its own conception of its role. Answerable to no one, and certainly not to the politicians of the Fourth Republic, it proceeded to rule Algeria and fight the Algerian war in its own way; in a limited sense, the French armed forces in Algeria constituted a 'state within a state'.

Like the German Army at the end of the Weimar Republic, the French military was in a unique position to influence events – but likewise unable to control them – as the attempted putsch in Germany of 1944 and the abortive Algerian rising of 1961 were to show. Having once handed power over to de Gaulle, the rebels were powerless to prevent the complete reversal of the army's Algerian policy. Their 'moment' had been in 1958, at a time when the army's isolative role had reached its full expression and when the legitimacy of the Fourth Republic had reached its lowest ebb. Once de Gaulle had assumed legitimate power, he was quite able to deal with the army, just as Hitler had squashed the German High Command as an independent force. The circumstances were entirely different, the effect was the same.[15] In neither case was the army able to rule alone, and in both the long term effect of military intervention has been to bring them into line with the other European states. In this, they appear not simply to be politically neutral, but politically neutralised.

If that is true, then the politicians in present-day Western Europe can 'forget about' the military to an extent not possible in the past. The military, like other state servants, may prefer to exercise a discreet political influence. Yet there is no guarantee that the conditions for active intervention may not later return.

Transitions from dictatorship

We can see how Organski's arguments – and the role played by the military – can be applied to cases of dictatorship which lacked pretensions to 'classic fascism' but which nonetheless showed the process of modernisation at work. Portugal, Spain and Greece have all emerged from dictatorship in recent years, and whilst none had an easy path to political stability, their democratic basis is no longer seriously open to question. In common they shared a low standard of living, economic and social backwardness, and a dependence on the agricultural sector. Those characteristics, although still discernible in comparative statistics, are far less pronounced than they were twenty years ago.* All these were alike in the kind of support which maintained their dictatorial regimes in being: privileged social élites backed by the armed forces. Towards the end they faced the same problem: how to come to terms with changing European circumstances and with the changes to their own societies, and they could not remain immune to pressures to

* See table on p. 310 for the main socio-economic comparisons.

liberalise political life. But could they guard against the threats to their privileged position once the process of liberalisation got under way?

The Portuguese and Spanish dictatorships were established much earlier than that in Greece, at a time when liberal democracy everywhere was reeling under the impact of fascism, whilst the Greek colonels took power as late as 1967, almost appearing as a European anachronism. The Portuguese coup, a fairly bloodless one, was initiated by the military in 1926; in contrast the Spanish Civil War, starting with a military revolt led by General Franco, was bitter and prolonged, from 1936 until 1939.

The Portuguese dictatorship, one of the most stable in modern history, lasted for almost fifty years, making 'pre-Salazar' an effort of historical reconstruction. It was a system combining minimal dictatorship with maximum sanctions. But its longevity was not simply due to the efficiency of the secret police; one also has to appreciate the 'national' justification for the rejection of democracy. Salazar took over from the military leaders, becoming head of government in 1932. His authority stemmed from the social groups which despised the former republic. Their distaste was for democracy in general and in particular for the corruption that had been rife in the dominant Democratic Party. The hatred for this 'demo-liberalism' was shared by both intellectual and class élites, and they found a unity in the Portuguese 'integralist' movement, a loose collection that included monarchists and those who were intellectually akin to the *Action Française*. These élites provided a stable identity and a source of political leadership, and the network extended to the hierarchy of the Portuguese Church and to the military leadership. Thus the Portuguese establishment was a unified one, and it subscribed to a common set of values which were given permanent expression in Salazar's 'New State' constitution of 1933: a state based on authoritarian, corporate, and nationalist principles.

The whole spirit of the system was firmly élitest. Salazar never sought a mass appeal, but rather emphasised his academic remoteness, a figure either to be respected or feared. Power rested with the tight-knit alliance between the military and the civilian rulers. The presidency was reserved for a leading figure from the armed forces, and all the paramilitary formations, including the secret police, were headed by army officers. This structure was authoritarian but had little in common with the fascist model. Indeed, Salazar specifically rejected fascism because it implied giving supreme power and legitimacy to the state, whereas his belief was that state power ultimately existed to uphold the place of the Roman Catholic Church in Portuguese society.

Both the civilian and military élites shared the same vision of Portugal which reached its most bizarre expression in their attitude towards Portugal's extensive overseas possessions. Whilst one after another the European powers had come to accept the change in world realities, Portugal clung to her empire, to her past glories, and to a belief in her 'manifest destiny'. At huge cost in money and manpower, Portuguese direct rule was perpetuated, even though the inevitable outcome was the loss of the territories and economic ruin for Portugal. From 1968 onwards, Salazar's successor sought to change tack and grant self-government to the colonies as well as attempting cautious liberalisation measures at home. But all dictatorships face their most severe test when they seek to dismantle their own powers, for popular expectations and long-suppressed demands outrun the willingness and even the ability of the regime to make the necessary concessions.

Portugal was no exception to this rule, but the trigger to the downfall of the old order did not come from a popular uprising. Instead, a line can be traced from the collapse of the colonial empire: the junior ranks of the officer corps became increasingly disillusioned with the hopeless cause for which they were fighting, even to the extent of absorbing ideas of the independence movements against which they were struggling. Thus it came about that the dictatorship was finally toppled by its leading prop, the armed forces. The military coup of April 1974 was engineered by some 400 officers, mostly junior in rank, and they formed the core of the revolutionary Armed Forces Movement (MFA) and constituted its Supreme Revolutionary Council. Whilst military intervention is usually associated in the Western world with right-wing reaction, in the case of Portugal the MFA stood for a left-wing solution to Portugal's problems. Nor at the outset was it particularly concerned with the niceties of securing democratic consent, for even though elections to a democratic assembly were held in 1975, the Supreme Revolutionary Council declared: 'We are going to have socialism in the next three to five years ... the country can choose something else afterwards.'

Undoubtedly, the MFA commanded widespread popular support, especially from the parties of the left. But it also underestimated the underlying conservatism of large sections of the population, and it could hardly hold national elections and at the same time ignore their outcome. Moreover, in the severe economic crisis facing Portugal, civilian rule was called for; gradually the military 'returned to the barracks': party government was installed after a further election held in 1976, and the military had to be content with holding a watching-brief in a Council of the Revolution. At first, too, party governments were of the left but the eventual transition from dictatorship to parliamentary democracy later also led to the formation of centre-right governments. By 1982, the 1976 'constitutional agreement' with its socialist aspirations and its institution of the Council of the Revolution no longer accorded with the facts of political life, and it had to be amended accordingly.

That is not to say that the role of the military ended up by being merely incidental: the experience of the years from 1974 until 1976 was vital for the Portuguese people – both in sweeping away the values of the old regime and in selecting for themselves the path of liberal democracy. Increasingly, that path has indicated a preference for conservative consolidation, with the right-wing Social Democrats (PSD) winning an overall majority in 1987.

Superficially, Spain always appeared to be closer to the ideas of fascism than Portugal, but in reality the Portuguese 'Integralismo' stood for a more coherent intellectual tradition. In contrast, Franco was quite content to assume a pseudo-fascist camouflage for as long as it suited him, and Francoism showed itself to be no more than a re-vamped model of the traditional type of conservative-nationalist dictatorship, with ingredients of 'clerical conservatism'. At the time of the Civil War, the Falange movement provided a suitable cloak for Franco, but it was always quite peripheral to his power base which was the army. The Falange movement, with its specifically fascist elements, was effectively 'taken over' by Franco after its leadership had been decimated during the fighting. But once Franco was securely in power and all the paraphernalia of party uniforms and personal adulation had served their purpose in lending the regime legitimacy, the Falange and its leadership was allowed to deteriorate and kept firmly away from positions of real power. If we recall the traits of a true fascist movement – its totalitarian nature, revolutionary spirit, the mass following – it is obvious that the *Movimento Nacional*, no longer even graced by its Falange title, was a non-starter.

The role taken by Francoism was to paper over the deep divisions that existed in Spanish society. The political system of the republic has given these full expression: economic and social cleavages, together with the fragmenting effects of regional loyalties and national minorities. Francoism, plus Castilian hegemony, suppressed these conflicts by imposing a centralist-authoritarian regime, but it did not eradicate them. The dictatorship helped to shore up the position of the pre-republican economic and social élite, and economic conflict was for long decently hidden by the imposed corporate unity of 'vertical syndicalism', with the state, workers and employers nominally serving as equal partners. The Church, too, put its authority behind the dictatorship, since the latter guaranteed the position of religion in Spanish society and stood as a bulwark against corrosive forces of the republican left.

The cracks in the edifice of Francoism did not appear until the late 1960s. They were diverse in character. There were numerous signs of industrial discontent, leading to the formation of illegal Workers' Commissions. Their impact was joined by the voice of the Church which became openly critical of the regime. From another direction, the Basque liberation movement, far from being permanently crushed by Francoism, began its resurgence in the 1960s. Behind all the discontents, other fundamental changes were occurring, for Spain was in the process of rapid economic modernisation: increasingly the restrictive weight of the dictatorship was perceived as holding back the development of a modern industrial society.

Franco ruled for life, 'Caudillo of Spain, by the Grace of God', the front-runner for the army and the established social interests. As long as he was in control, the system was never in serious danger, but – as for Portugal – the tricky problem of succession had to be resolved. Franco was fortunate – or perhaps unlucky – in his choice. If Franco had wished to restore democracy, his selection of Don Juan Carlos of Bourbon might even be described as a stroke of genius. But it is more likely that he believed the restored monarchy would perpetuate his values – and those of the military – even if in a slightly more liberal form. Yet the accession of the new monarch on Franco's death in 1975 heralded a fundamental change. Pessimists predicted that the disintegration of Francoism would uncover all the suppressed conflicts in Spanish society – economic and social cleavages, anti-clericalism, republicanism, and the claims of national minorities. These were after all the major fault-lines inherited from the 1930s; could a more liberal regime hope to contain them successfully?

Those doubts were for the most part quickly allayed. The course of liberalisation under the constitutional monarchy was remarkable both for its speed and radical nature: elections were held in 1977, with the Communist Party competing, an event quite unthinkable a few years earlier, and a fully parliamentary constitution was ratified by referendum in 1978. With the restoration of party government, rapid strides were also taken to meet regional claims by granting substantial autonomies, satisfying most except the Basque extremists. All those changes presuppose a large degree of consensus, but how did that consensus arise? One of the errors of those who believed in a post-Franco chaos was to suppose that all the cleavages of Spanish society had remained intact, whereas in fact the passage of time had made them less relevant, especially with the effect of economic modernisation. There was also another potent influence at work: all groups who looked for benefits under the new regime were wary of pressing demands too far, for that might well invite right-wing reaction. That was not an idle fear, since there was still one major 'unreformed' element inherited from the Franco era: the military. The fear that the armed forces would once again intervene forced the parties, organised labour, and the business world to concentrate on creating a climate of political stability. That their fears were not unjustified was shown by the abortive army coup of February 1981. Yet the Spanish military no longer wielded the influence it once did, for as a political instrument, for it lacked the backing of key social groups.

Although the transition from dictatorship has been successfully completed in Spain, the armed forces still have a political potential. It is a potential which is best realised in times of uncertainty and where other destabilising factors are present. One such factor is the continuing presence of Basque extremism – especially to the extent that it chooses the armed forces as a principal target. However, one also has to take into account other factors fostering stability, especially at a governmental level. In this connection the 1982 election (confirmed in 1986) was significant, for it resulted in an outright majority for the Socialist Party, and given its legitimacy coupled with the party's expressed moderation, the chances of a reversion to an unstable situation have sharply diminished.

Whilst the Portuguese and Spanish dictatorships acquired a certain patina of respectability over the years, the brief Greek experiment of military rule from 1967 until 1974 appeared as a rather weak interlude. Yet the 1967 coup was itself one late manifestation of the Greek army's political involvement dating back to the 1920s and 1930s, culminating in a military dictatorship from 1936 until 1940. And alone of the West European states in recent times Greece has suffered from a prolonged bout of civil war, from 1944 to 1949. Engaged in that struggle, the army saw itself as the country's saviour from communism.

The Greek army showed itself to be a peculiarly independent élite, able to define its own position in society. Partly that was due to the lack of unity in the traditional élites, but it also arose from the fact that the armed forces felt no strong loyalty for the monarchy. The fact that the monarchy failed to act as a unifying force for social conservatism, allowed the army to seek its own definition of the national interest, and lacking any immediate social reference group, the military concentrated instead on a value system that combined nationalism with religion – the Greek Church. That trait was already evident in the earlier military dictatorship which combined national socialism with religious fanaticism. It would be wrong to regard the Greek military as an entirely independent force, for it was significantly content with civilian rule for a long period after the civil war as long as that was based on an assured conservative majority and the left was still in disarray. Yet by the mid-1960s that was no longer the case: the moderate Centre Union obtained a majority of the vote in the 1964 election, and by the time of the 1967 election it seemed certain that the Centre Union with the United Democratic Left would obtain a large majority. Yet the military could not accept this prospect, for it regarded a centre-left government as incompatible with its own position. Consequently, the army struck before the election could be held, and its coup in April 1967 met with no immediate opposition from the monarch. The fact that the king himself was involved in a loyalist counter-coup a few months later did not disturb the military junta overmuch – since the monarchy was not central to their conception of legitimacy. The Greek colonels deeply mistrusted the parties and politicians and prepared themselves for a long period of direct rule. Their political mission was to eradicate the existing political establishment (especially the parties) and in some undefined way to lead the country back to a purer democracy. Despite their grandiose pretensions, the military had little idea how to use power to win support from the general population. Thus the military increasingly began to operate in a void, without active support from any key social groups. The end came ignominiously, for in the course of the sudden confrontation with Turkey over Cyprus in 1974, the armed forces proved unable to match Turkish strength. The military had no option but to call back the 'despised politicians'.

The short episode of the Greek dictatorship may not seem of great importance. Yet we should also appreciate the peculiar way in which it operated actually to place Greek democracy on a surer footing, its 'modernising' effect. Prior to the coup, the political system operated an uneasy balance: the monarchy, the army and the parties. Its unstable nature was compounded by the character of the party system – 'acceptably stable' only as long as the right was in power. The transformation in the period after 1974 was remarkable. In the first place, the claim to a superior 'national identification' on the part of the army was irretrievably shattered. Secondly, the decision made by popular referendum in 1974 to dispense with the monarchy placed constitutional authority firmly with the political parties. The new republic is a 'party democracy', and that change has also led to a transformation in the nature of the party system. At first, power resided with the moderate right, 'New Democracy', but the rise of the Socialists (Pasok), their outright victory in the 1981 election and their hold on office since then show the first genuine switch in political power, besides bringing about a substantial modernisation of Greek society. One might even conclude that the dictatorship actually helped to facilitate the changes that it sought to prevent.

Extremism today

In the previous sections we have been concerned with extremism at the government level as an alternative to constitutional democracy; the other perspective is that of extremism as a minority and oppositional movement. By 'extremism', whether of the right or the left, we mean that the goals of the party or movement include as a *minimum* a radical change in the political structure, and possibly radical changes in the economic and social basis of society as well. In Western Europe it is apparent that such challenges to liberal democracy have not originated from within the party system. The electorate has largely failed to express extremist sympathies, and the political parties have faithfully reflected this moderation. Threats have come from outside the established political structure on occasion, but there is also the possibility to be considered that the system *as a whole* can lurch towards illiberal solutions, irrespective of the nature of the individual parties.

1. *Right-wing extremism.* Outside of Italy and latterly now France, extremist right-wing parties are virtually non-existent as political forces in Western Europe; the most that can be said is that they are perhaps in a state of suspended animation, awaiting the spark or catastrophe to bring them into the political reckoning. The appeals which they can make are diverse: to nationalism, race, militarism, simple anti-communism, and anti-democratic sentiments generally. These seeds can germinate individually, but they are more likely to appear in combination; it is difficult, in fact, to assess whether such a fascist-type syndrome is made up of genuinely independent factors. One facet tends to entail the others: a rabid nationalism is normally both expansionist and explicitly militaristic; it is also bitterly mistrustful of 'anti-national' elements in society: racial minorities and international communism; and liberal democracy is seen to be infected by them, so a resort to non-democratic means is the only way to make the country secure.

Whatever the activating reason for such extremism, its full flowering probably requires all these issues to become part of the party's appeal, but they may not be central to the support which such a party obtains; the underlying reason is more likely to be the economic and social threats which middle-class groups see to their status and class position. The continued failure of right-wing movements in recent years cannot be dismissed as fortuitous, so that these threats to the middle-class or to important social élites have presumably been absent.

Germany provides us with a leading test case because her past history showed a proclivity for right-wing extremism, and the imprint of the Nazi dictatorship is sufficiently recent to provide a model for disaffected groups. Yet the absence of any strong right-wing movement has been the notable feature of the West German political system. Briefly, in the late 1960s, the German National Democratic Party (NPD) seemed on the verge of winning Bundestag representation, but the party rapidly dwindled into insignificance, leaving behind a host of tiny right-wing organisations, capable of sporadic terrorist activity it is true, and perhaps keeping alive some aspects of Nazi mythology, but quite unable to raise a sympathetic response in the general population.

Their failure has not been because of the absence of suitable issues in the post-war era. There was, after all, the fundamental question of the division of Germany and the loss of the eastern territories – and it has to be remembered that a large section of the electorate originated from the 'lost provinces' and East Germany, and many still have relations in the German Democratic Republic. Brandt's *Ostpolitik* in the early 1970s was deliberately aimed at reconciliation with the communist states of Eastern Europe, the treaties he made effectively wrote off large parts of the former Reich, and the Basic Treaty he concluded with the German Democratic Republic was tantamount to accepting the permanent division of Germany. Yet all that caused no more than a fluttering in nationalist dovecotes.

A realistic appreciation of development in the Federal Republic has to take account of Western Germany's remarkable economic recovery and continuing prosperity. In the early years, the so-called 'economic miracle' was a powerful agent in dissolving old antagonisms, but it was also a means whereby those uprooted and dispossessed were integrated into the 'new' West German society and its prospering economy. On a political level, the agent of their integration was to be the moderate catch-all party, the Christian Democratic Union, and its resilience over the years is an index of the failure of right-wing extremism. Questions naturally remain:

What would be the consequences of a fierce economic recession? Would new discontents and objects of attack then become apparent? One only has to focus on the problem of the migrant 'guest workers' in West Germany to see that they could provide the basis for a 'flowering' of right-wing activity, as to some extent has been the case for other countries.

If this picture of muted right-wing extremism is corrected for Germany, we should hardly expect other West European countries to offer much more, for their 'national' problems are arguably fewer. Only in Italy does the ultra-right have any kind of secure place in the party system, where the *Movimento Sociale Italiano* (MSI) is active as a neo-fascist party. The fortunes of the MSI have fluctuated over the years – almost nine per cent of the vote in 1972, and just under six per cent in 1987, with strongholds of support in Rome and Sicily. How is one to interpret the survival of neo-fascism in Italy? Undoubtedly it is linked to the Mussolini epoch, and – in contrast to Germany – the reaction from fascism was not quite absolute, for it still persists as a part of the political culture of certain sections of society: but it is a persistence rather than a dynamic element, representing the 'old guard' of Italian society. For some, too, Christian Democracy does not offer a suitable alternative, since the DC only has a weak ideological base and for many years the party has cooperated in government with the parties of the moderate left. Moreover, the strength of the PCI can easily be interpreted as a challenge to the existing system and its values – against which only authoritarian solutions suffice. The MSI manages to maintain a core of voting support and act as a focal point for various groups which are quick to exploit social grievances, seek confrontation with the extreme left, and bring the republican order into disrepute. Their activities have brought a 'counter-terrorism' to the Italian scene in parallel to that of the 'red brigades', and the extreme right was behind planned coups involving the armed forces. Yet nefarious as the ultra-right shows itself to be, it is also a marginal political force – hoping to destabilise the republic but never succeeding in attracting widespread support.

Of most contemporary significance during the 1980s has been the progress of the far right in France. Under the leadership of Jean-Marie Le Pen, the National Front made a considerable impact on French politics, both for the support the party obtained and for its effects on the traditional parties of the right. In the 1981 election the National Front received derisory support, but fared much better in the mid-1980s, with around 11 per cent in the 1984 European elections and 10 per cent in the 1986 assembly election –

a result that, with proportional representation then in force, gave the party sizeable representation in the National Assembly. That achievement could not be repeated in 1988, since with the return to the second ballot system the National Front stood little chance of winning individual constituencies and was virtually eliminated from parliament. However, historical experience suggests that extremist parties depend less than moderate parties on elections and conventional politics for their survival and influence, so that the National Front still has to be treated as a force in French politics.

The question is: what kind of label should be attached to the National Front?[16] Its sharp focus on anti-immigrant themes makes it appear as a single-issue racist party, but the nature of its support suggests that the National Front has a potentially wider appeal and could sharpen the ideology of the right, especially in reaction against the prospect of a long period of Socialist rule under President Mitterrand. Le Pen's populist style of leadership and effective rhetoric has to be seen in the context of a disarray affecting the parties of the moderate right. The élites in those parties are divided in their attitudes towards the National Front: those near to the centre regard it with anathema, whilst those closer to its views see the Front as a dangerous competitor. Either way, the intrusion of race-issues – if not yet a coherent extreme right ideology – has introduced a polarising element into French politics.

Successful parties of the far right are notably absent in all the smaller countries. Here, one should exclude right-wing 'protest' parties of a more conventional right-wing colouring: the content of their protest is usually related to the level of taxation and scale of government intervention, rather than being seriously 'anti-system'. Nor do they usually have an anti-parliamentary ethos or attempt to generate a mass social movement. A typical example of such a parliamentary protest is the Progress Party in Denmark. It arose in the early 1970s as an 'anti-tax' protest party with a vote of almost 15 per cent in 1977. It was treated as an 'untouchable' by the other parties, but gradually moderated its position in the 1980s, and has now to be treated more as a conventional, if still a peculiar right-wing party.

Of the countries which did not experience fascism, Britain has perhaps been more affected than most by political extremism, although this impulse does not show through at the parliamentary level. The sharpening of the national question in Northern Ireland, and the rise of the ultra-loyalist Vanguard Movement in the 1970s – and of other factions bent on upholding Protestant dominance at any cost – can best be described in terms of being a right-wing reaction, although it is considerably displaced by the religious basis of the conflict and by the complexities of the national issue itself. In mainland Britain the far right, principally represented by the National Front, belongs to the conventional pattern of extremism. Admittedly, if one were to judge the National Front merely by its electoral performance, it would be quite insignificant: the party scored only 0.6 per cent of the vote in the 1979 election and virtually disappeared as an electoral force in the 1980s. However, the British electoral system works greatly to the disadvantage of very small parties – since votes given to them are entirely wasted, so that would-be supporters are much more likely to vote for one of the larger parties, and right-wing extremism has to be treated exclusively as an extra-parliamentary fringe group. The National Front is typically neo-fascist in its hankering after the old-style fascist style and formulae, and it traces its antecedents to Moseley's pre-war British Union of Fascists. The basis of its appeal is firmly racial, that is, pitched against the coloured immigrant community. From that basis, the typical fascist-type syndrome is built up, although the National Front is largely content to stay with its prime target. High unemployment, together with the concentration of immigrant communities in industrial areas, means that the National Front plays principally on the fears and prejudices of those in closest proximity – that is frequently those whose own social and economic position appears most under threat. Thus the tactic of the National Front has been to create provocation – by demonstrations or more violent ventures – at a local, 'affected' level. Undoubtedly, the impact of the National Front made race relations more difficult, but on the level of creating a coherent and broadly-based appeal, this form of extremism has failed to gain a worthwhile following.

Taking Western Europe as a whole, we can conclude that the extreme right has consistently been impotent – if measured in electoral or party terms. It is stronger as an extra-parliamentary force, but principally in the form of terrorism rather than as a social movement. Others may argue that it hides neatly in the folds of conventional parties and that potentially it is that connection which carries a greater threat. We shall look at this aspect in considering 'extremism of the middle' subsequently.

2. *The decline of European communism.* The relation of the far right to the far left may be through the heightened consciousness which one successful movement arouses in its polar opposite. Yet the weakness of right-wing extremism is not quite balanced by a

waning on the left, that is, if we count the Communist parties of Western Europe as being in any way 'extreme' in character.* The relevant parties especially in France and Italy show that the left can rely on a large following in competition with the *proven* moderation of social democratic alternatives. At the same time, however, it appears that European communism is moving towards an irreversible decline – and that is true whatever course the individual parties choose to follow.

The idea of 'Eurocommunism' which gained currency in the mid-1970s pointed to a new and moderate course for the Communist parties of Western Europe. The description drew attention to a number of related features: a belief that the transition to socialism could be effected by peaceful rather than revolutionary means, the relinquishment of the claim to be the sole, authoritative voice of the working class, disavowing the basic dogma that the building of socialism required the imposition of a 'dictatorship of the proletariat' – a euphemism for the dictatorship of the Communist Party. These admissions were reinforced by a loosening of party ties with the Soviet Union: no longer was her leadership or interpretation of 'proletarian internationalism' decisive for the policies adopted by any of the West European Communist parties.

Several important consequences resulted. One was that a Communist party became free to interpret *national* conditions and priorities in its own way. Another was that no barrier prevented the party joining in normal governing coalitions, both from its own point of view and that of its possible partners. Their compatibility stems from the less dogmatic position especially the implied acceptance of the principle of 'reversibility': the willingness to admit that the party's policies, once implemented, could subsequently be countermanded by the electorate and by a change of government. In effect, the Communist parties therefore moved to a fully *parliamentary* position, an acceptance of the tenets of liberal democratic politics.

These developments all cast doubt on whether the Communist parties of Western Europe can still be regarded as 'extremist'. Whilst their ultimate goals continue to require a radical transformation of society, the means to those ends no longer present a challenge to the existing order. Nonetheless, the umbrella description of 'Eurocommunism' was open to criticism on a number of counts. Firstly, it misleadingly gives the impression of a unified movement, whereas it was a piecemeal adaptation to

* For the fluctuating fortunes of Western European Communism see 'Party Representation in Western Europe since 1946', pp. 378–89 below.

changing circumstances. Nor is it entirely correct to suppose that a close and harmonious historical evolution marked their earlier development: the differences between the parties were masked by official ideology. In the wake of destalinisation in the 1950s even that common identity was lost. The 'Eurocommunist' label was also deceptive if it is implied that the changes took place almost simultaneously. In fact, the process was quite uneven in application. The 'polycentrism' advocated by Togliatti in the 1950s showed that the PCI was far in advance of the French Communist Party which well into the 1970s continued to adhere to a strict 'Moscow line'.

The earliest signs of a real transformation actually occurred in a number of Scandinavian countries. A prime example is the Finnish SKDL (Democratic Union of the Finnish People) which since its formation in 1945 claimed to be a party of general left unity. The Communists are only one element in the party which avoided becoming a mere 'front' organisation or too close an identity with the interests of the Soviet Union. The SKDL consistently won up to a fifth of the vote, and often participated in coalition government without jeopardising the parliamentary system. Yet the SKDL began to disintegrate in the 1980s, falling below 10 per cent in 1987, and the hard-line Stalinist faction split off to form its own party. The Icelandic Communist Party (People's Alliance) is, relatively speaking, a 'mass' party (with up to 20 per cent of the vote) and it has also joined in coalitions, but disintegration is also evident – in 1987 the party lost heavily to the Feminists, a good indication of the weakening hold of old ideologies. Willingness to support parliamentary government is shown too by the Swedish Communists: in the early 1970s after the Social Democrats had lost their absolute majority, the Communists – themselves with a tiny share of the vote – helped to keep the minority Social Democratic government in power, and that has largely been true since the Social Democrats returned to office in 1982.

The position in Spain and Portugal was more difficult to assess in the course of transition from dictatorship. Whilst the Spanish Communists enthusiastically embraced 'Eurocommunism' and actively cooperated with the Centre-Democrat minority government, the Portuguese Communists remained intransigent; their leader, Alvaro Cunhal declared in 1975 that there was no place in Portugal for 'Western-style democracy'. One can appreciate the motivation behind the divergent strategies: in the case of Spain it was necessary for the Communists to demonstrate their contribution to the democratic consensus, since the perils of sparking off a right-wing and military reaction were a leading consideration. In Portugal, however, the 'revolutionary spirit' fostered by the Armed Forces Movement encouraged the Communists to make a bid in line with their traditional ideology. Paradoxically, the Spanish Communists did not at all benefit from displaying a democratic commitment and fared badly in direct competition with the Socialists: in the 1979 election the PCE won almost 11 per cent of the vote, but collapsed to only four per cent in 1982 and 1986 – with the Socialists capturing almost half of the popular vote. At first, in contrast, the Portuguese Communists, despite or because of their hard-line course, stabilised their share at around 18 per cent. That different experience seemed to indicate the danger for Communist parties in too readily embracing a 'soft' strategy – but the Portuguese party, despite its die-hard line, none the less lost support, falling to 12 per cent in 1986.

Those examples exhaust the Communist potential of the smaller countries. In some, their sheer unimportance enabled them to maintain a rigid orthodoxy – as in Denmark, Luxembourg and the Netherlands – but, hesitatingly, they moved with the general tide. The Belgian Communists managed to halt a long-term decline by taking up the Wallonist cause, but for other countries – notably Austria, Britain and West Germany – the Communists are unable even to reach the starting-post; whether they count as 'extremist' or not is scarcely worth the argument.

The real crux of Communist development concerns Italy and France, for the sheer size of the Communist vote in these two states has put them in a qualitatively different situation: the outlook and strategy of the *other* parties has been decisively influenced by the Communist presence. Yet like the smaller editions in other countries, they were also faced by the challenge of a necessary evolution if they were not to be condemned to a static and sterile oppositional role.

The situation of the Italian Communists always appeared the more hopeful, largely because the party had long been conspicuous for its independent thinking, especially in the writings of its early leader, Antonio Gramsci. The party's fluidity – as well as its somewhat weaker 'international' commitment (to the Soviet Union) in the post-war period owes much to the leadership given by Togliatti, both in his positive attitude towards inter-party cooperation and later, from 1956, through his advocacy of polycentrism – the view that communist parties in individual countries had to modify policies in accordance with national circumstances. The national orientation of the PCI – being 'of' Italian society and not merely 'in' it – gave the party the chance to work positively from within the existing social and political framework without simply becoming involved in reformism. Summed up in the idea of 'structural reform', the position was that the PCI should – by alliance, permeation, and strategic compromise – assume an active leadership role in the renewal of Italian society, and at all costs it should avoid adopting an isolationist mentality.

That the Italian Communists could not rely on the bare insistence of an 'hegemonic' claim to leadership was made very clear as a result of the strategy pursued by the Christian Democrats in the 'opening to the left' policy beginning in the early 1960s. The success of the DC ploy was quickly made apparent, for the result was to split the Socialists and leave the PCI almost isolated. The threat was in some measure responsible for the PCI's own 'historic compromise' enunciated in the early 1970s. It was specifically an olive branch proffered to the DC, an offer to cooperate in parliament, in government, and in society. The PCI leader, Enrico Berlinguer, made it clear in 1972 that the offer was made in order to ward off the danger of right-wing reaction and to implement a genuinely popular programme. But why should the PCI have been so anxious to placate the DC? One obvious answer is that the PCI could hardly ever hope to get into a position of power without some positive help from the DC, for a straight 'leftist' majority would not be forthcoming. That view is reasonable, but it does not give full justice to the PCI's position: that in Italian circumstances bare majorities for social change would simply be divisive: the transformation of Italian society had to be based on a substantial, even overwhelming consensus.

From many points of view the 'historic compromise' was an undoubted success. The PCI was substantially 'rehabilitated', all kinds of practical cooperation with the DC government did follow, and the party benefited substantially at elections: in 1976 the PCI with a record 34.4 per cent of the vote seemed on the brink of reaching a parity with the DC. Yet by the 1980s the mood had turned sour. In the 1979 election the PCI vote dipped for the first time in decades (to 30.4 per cent) and the decline continued in the 1980s, to around 27 per cent in 1987. The PCI may have suffered from its own moderation and its behind-the-scenes identification with DC-rule, but the steady rise of the Socialists, in competition with the PCI, shows that the weakness of Communism is a matter of historical *identity* rather than of faulty *strategy*. Moreover, the party's major objective, that of sharing in governmental power, has still not been realised. Generally disturbing, too, although not as electoral competition, has been the impact of the 'Red Brigades': it appeared that a moderate course taken by the PCI would just lead to violent methods on the part of the extreme left. For all these reasons, the historic compromise was quietly abandoned by the PCI, although that did not necessarily mean that the party would take a more conflictual path in the future.

In contrast with the situation of the PCI that of the French Communists always looked less hopeful, and yet the PCF did at last win a share of government power in 1981 against all the odds. The French party was more traditional, more 'Stalinist' in outlook, less willing to promote an independent national line, less able to accept revisionist ideas from within its own ranks. Yet the party's ideological and organisational inflexibility was combined with a surprising willingness to make bargains with other left-wing parties in order to fight the bourgeois-bloc for the presidential majority. The need to make such bargains was evident – both because of the nature of a presidential election and the second ballot used for assembly elections – since no single party is likely to succeed entirely unaided. The PCF found a worthwhile ally in the Socialist Party which had undergone a successful process of 're-founding' in 1971 under the leadership of François Mitterrand, and Mitterrand became the joint candidate for the 1974 presidential election. Yet the compatibility of the two parties has always been strained since they compete substantially for the same vote, and there is the rivalry for the leadership of the left. The new Socialist Party was better suited both to win the voters and to supply an acceptable leadership. Despite the PCF's lip-service to change and efforts to appear less hidebound and dogmatic, its old image still persisted, and it was the flexible Socialist Party which gained electoral trust. Yet, of course, the PCF could not afford to break with its now more popular partner, really having no choice but to help in Mitterrand's 1981 presidential victory, and its poor vote in the following assembly election (16.1 per cent compared with 20.6 in 1978) confirmed its subordinate position. The PCF served as junior partner in coalition from 1981 to 1984, in itself a remarkable concession to parliamentary democracy, but return to opposition did not restore the PCF's fortunes: it fell to below 10 per cent in the 1986 assembly election. Yet once more in 1988 the Communists had to support Mitterrand's re-election: the 'presidential squeeze' both demoralised and decimated the PCF.

Even though the Eurocommunist label was patently inadequate and implied a unity of strategy and outlook for the various parties which simply was not there, it was useful as a general descriptive term indicating a loss of extremism, the willingness to make substantial compromises, to participate in normal parliamentary government – all of which is in contrast with their historic belief in the 'final' capitalist crisis, but despite their moderation, their hopes are based on a Micawberlike-stance of 'waiting for something to turn up'.

Zeal for revolutionary change, insistence upon its necessity, comes now only from the ultra-left. Its weaknesses are manifold: the extreme left is not a homogeneous grouping, but rather a host of rival splinter groups all competing for the Marxist ideological inheritance; these groups are also notable for their lack of any organic connection with the working-class movement – in sharp contrast to the concerns of orthodox Communist parties – and for their ideological preoccupation, reminiscent of a university-trained élite stratum. The resulting lack of electoral appeal – the absence of any kind of mass base – increases the attraction of alternative, 'direct' strategies. At the limit, that involves provocative political terrorism – the state should be 'provoked' into displaying its repressive character, and then the expected mass reaction will lead to the overthrow of the existing system. However, that form of confrontation is the limiting case, and it is evident that the provocation/response/mobilisation sequence is one which can be applied to all aspects of social life, but always at the expense of liberal democracy and the parliamentary system and its style of political competition.

3. *Extremism of the middle.* The third type of threat to liberal democracy is said to emanate from the established parties of the system; what we may dub 'creeping authoritarianism'. The implication is that it is not these constitutional power holders who are under attack, but they themselves change to a more authoritarian bent. The suspension of liberal democracy and its guarantees is easily accomplished in time of war; the argument is that tensions of a similar order, prolonged economic crisis or social upheaval, can have the same effect. And the root cause is seen in the nature of the socio-economic system. Thus Ralph Miliband has argued: 'The point is not that "bourgeois democracy" is imminently likely to move towards old-style fascism. It is rather that advanced capitalist societies are subject to strains more acute than for a long time past, and that their inability to resolve these strains makes their evolution towards more or less pronounced forms of conservative authoritarianism more rather than less likely.'[17]

This view would see the very success of the established parties in monopolising the electoral field as acting to squeeze out minority dissent. This dissent, perhaps manifesting itself as a form of 'extra-parliamentary opposition', then brings a predictable reaction from the ruling parties concerned to maintain the status quo. Precisely in the name of democracy: 'The State must arm itself with more extensive and more efficient means of repression, seek to define more stringently the area of "legitimate" dissent and opposition, and strike fear in those who seek to go beyond it.'[18] The degree of stability of a liberal democracy is then no measure of its democratic content.

This view is open to criticism on a number of counts. After all, it has been the West European *illiberal* dictatorships which have crumbled in the recent past. There is also little *evidence* of an authoritarian direction taken by the liberal democracies in Western Europe; the gulf separating them from illiberalism is still enormous: political opposition, trade union activity, legal and civil rights, do not yet show the impress of authoritarian government.

It is true that developments in various countries have been widely interpreted by critics as presaging active repression – the regulation of industrial relations, the endangering of civil rights through measures to maintain 'law and order', the difficulties placed in the way of minority political movements, especially those of a radical nature, by the 'siege atmosphere' which measures to combat political terrorism inevitably engender. Yet, even if one is ready to admit the evidence concerning particular cases, there is little to support the view of a *general* tendency.

Undoubtedly, Britain under the Thatcher Government since 1979 is widely regarded as showing authoritarian traits, although it is important to distinguish between the domineering style of leadership and the content of government policies. It is somewhat ironic that the market philosophy of neo-liberalism should have become associated with growing authoritarianism. It may be the case that Britain in the 1980s has become a more unequal society and a more divided one, but that is an entirely different proposition. Legislation has detrimentally affected the power of trade unions, but as a matter of fact such regulation only brought the British situation closer to the position long established in other European countries.

The conflict in Northern Ireland has entailed the greatest threat to civil liberties because of the wide powers enacted to counter terrorism and armed insurrection, and the latent danger is that police powers, once assumed, are not readily relinquished. West German anti-terrorist legislation was widely attacked for its threat to individual liberties, but the measures were not as wide as those enacted in Britain – against which there had been relatively little protest. Attempts to promote political change by violent means have been experienced in all the larger European states, but the reaction has not been to limit the rights and activities of parties and groups committed to peaceful change – indeed, the growth of 'new politics' is sufficient evidence of the relatively flourishing state of democratic society rather than proof of the contrary. But of course, even if one is prepared to accept these judgements that 'bourgeois democracy' has not become authoritarian, that does not prevent critics postulating an underlying 'fact' of crisis, making an authoritarian trend in the future 'more rather than less likely'.

A second ground for querying the analysis lies in the special treatment reserved for 'bourgeois democracy', as if that form of regime were especially prone to authoritarian tendencies. Our experience of the proliferation of state systems in the modern world over the past half century shows that advanced capitalist societies have a rather better record than others with regard to individual rights and political freedom. In other words, it is a rather slanted exercise to single out the sins of the state in capitalist society without maintaining an overall comparative perspective.

A third counter-argument, whilst accepting the close connection between liberal democracy and capitalism (as a matter of fact as well as of origin), holds that the future performance of liberal democratic institutions is not for that reason predetermined: borrowing from Marxist terminology, there can be an 'autonomy of the superstructure'. If this view is valid, then the character of political institutions is important for the future of the liberal democratic state. Thus, unlike other political systems, liberal democracy does provide a compensatory balance through party competition, although its nature and extent may be insufficient to prevent a 'lurch' of the whole system – a *general* movement towards a more illiberal society. Nonetheless, some balance is provided on an inter-party level, and that surely is the historic contribution of the balance between the moderate European left and the moderate right: the opposing forces offer real, if limited alternatives, and neither is likely to connive in repressive, authoritarian policies promoted by the other.

Finally, we should note that the vulnerability of liberal democracy to supplantation – as a question of pure technique – is neither greater than in the past nor essentially different from that faced by all kinds of regime. As far as military intervention is concerned, Western Europe is in a specially favourable position – the armed forces show a high level of integration with the rest of society and the advanced level of political culture and social organisation would deny legitimacy to military rule. But vulnerability has to be treated on a somewhat wider canvas – allowance for erosion rather than only for frontal assault. In that respect, the data-gathering propensity of the modern state is more serious, for there are numerous unintended consequences which in the end may be difficult to control. However, that is a problem of modern society – not a particular feature of liberal democracy.

The question of vulnerability can also be examined with regard to the phenomenon of 'terrorism', that is, the use of violence as a means of attaining political objectives by creating an atmosphere of fear in the general population with the aim of encouraging political destabilisation. Terrorism should be distinguished from 'revolution', since the latter involves a direct bid for power whereas terrorism, in the first instance, is concerned to erode political authority rather than immediately seek its supplantation. Whatever the motive force behind the use of terroristic methods – nationalism, the ideologies of the far left or right – they share a number of features. One is their presumed inability at the present stage to question the legitimacy of government at a mass level. A second characteristic they share is that of 'provocation'. The immediate aim is not to weaken the force of government but to provoke it to retaliation, thus to encourage a repressive response and eventually to sow dissension in the ranks of those upholding the existing system: some groups will be increasingly prepared to concede the terrorists' claims while other groups will become impatient with the restrictions imposed on strong government by liberal democracy. That disunity will be exacerbated if, as a result of a long-continuing terrorist campaign, the governments are shown to be impotent in dealing with the problem. A third feature terrorist movements in liberal democracies have in common is their ability to operate on two levels – one illegal and the other politically acceptable, as an underground organisation and as a more or less legitimate political organisation or party, reminiscent of the 'double strategy' employed so effectively by the Nazis in the Weimar Republic. That ability points to the central dilemma faced by a liberal democracy: how far can it tolerate movements dedicated to its overthrow? How can it guard against them without at the same time jeopardising its own principles? Unfortunately, there are no definitive answers to those questions.

Notes and references

1. The arbitrary nature of German fascism was well caught by Hans Frank, Nazi legal expert: 'Formerly, we were in the habit of saying, "This is right or wrong"; today, we must put the question accordingly: "What would the Führer say?"' That was, indeed, the question!
2. The process of *Gleichschaltung*, the 'synchronisation' of all secondary organisations, brings the individual at every turn into a direct relationship with the state, precluding any intellectually-watertight compartments: 'The

distinguishing feature of every totalitarian concept lies precisely in the establishment of a rigorous interdependence of all questions, with the result that an attitude to one necessarily involves an attitude to all others.' M. Duverger, *Political Parties*, Methuen, 1954, p. 233.

3. A. F. K. Organski, 'Fascism and Modernisation', in S. J. Woolf (ed.), *The Nature of Fascism*, p. 25.

4. See Barrington Moore, *Social Origins of Dictatorship and Democracy*, Penguin Books, 1967. Moore says, 'The taming of the agrarian sector has been a decisive feature of the whole historical process . . . getting rid of agriculture as a major *social* activity is one prerequisite for successful democracy.' p. 429 (italics added).

5. For different viewpoints on the critical reasons why some countries avoided the non-democratic route see, Barrington Moore, op. cit.; A. F. K. Organski, *The Stages of Political Development*, New York: A. Knopf, 1965; S. M. Lipset, *Political Man*, Heinemann, 1960; H. Daalder, 'Parties, Elites and Political Developments in Western Europe', in J. LaPalombara and M. Wiener, *Political Parties and Political Development*, Princeton University Press, 1969.

6. The weak ideological basis of Italian fascism was admitted by Mussolini in 1921: 'If Fascism does not wish to die or worse still, to commit suicide, it must now provide itself with a doctrine. . . . I do wish that during the two months which are to elapse before our National Assembly meets, the philosophy of Fascism could be created.' Quoted by Barrington Moore, op. cit., p. 451.

7. S. J. Woolf in S. J. Woolf (ed.), *European Fascism*, Weidenfeld and Nicolson, 1968, pp. 58–9.

8. Organski, op. cit., p. 41.

9. S. Andreski, *Elements of Comparative Sociology*, Weidenfeld and Nicolson, 1964, pp. 131–5.

10. Morris Janowitz in Jacques van Doorn (ed.), *Armed Forces and Society*, The Hague: Mouton, 1968, p. 25. The élite to which Janowitz refers was an aristocratic one.

11. C. B. Otley, 'Militarism and the Social Affiliations of the British Army Elite' in *Armed Forces and Society*, pp. 84–108. Otley gives a summary of class backgrounds of British, Dutch, German, Italian, and Swedish army élites.

12. S. Finer, *Comparative Government*, Allen Lane, 1970, p. 536. Finer distinguishes four levels of political culture, of which two, the 'mature' and the 'developed' are relevant to European conditions; he relates the four types of variations in per capita GNP; this shows an inverse relationship of the level of GNP and the likelihood of a military coup.

13. J. Blondel, *An Introduction to Comparative Government*, op. cit., p. 417.

14. C. B. Otley, *Armed Forces and Society*, p. 107.

15. The preceding argument is based on Kurt Lang, 'The Military Putsch in a Developed Political Culture: Confrontations of Military and Civil Power in Germany and France', in *Armed Forces and Society*, pp. 202–28.

16. For an analysis, see S. Mitra, 'The National Front in France – A Single Issue Movement?' *West European Politics*, April 1988.

17. R. Miliband, *The State in Capitalist Society*, Weidenfeld and Nicolson, 1969, p. 268.

18. *ibid.*, p. 272.

Additional references

K. von Beyme (ed.), 'Right-Wing Extremism in Western Europe', *West European Politics*, April 1988 (special issue)

K. D. Bracher, *The German Dictatorship*, Weidenfeld and Nicolson, 1971.

M. Broszat, *The Hitler State: The Foundation and Development of the Internal Structure of the Third Reich*, Longman, 1981.

R. A. Brady, *The Spirit and Structure of German Fascism*, Gollancz, 1937.
A. Bullock, *Hitler: A Study in Tyranny*, Penguin Books, 1964.
G. Carocci, *Italian Fascism*, Penguin Books, 1974.
F. L. Carsten, *The Rise of Fascism*, Methuen, 1967.
A. Cassels, *Fascist Italy*, Routledge and Kegan Paul, 1969.
C. Delzell (ed.), *Mediterranean Fascism, 1919–1949*, Macmillan, 1972.
F. Ferranesi, *The Radical Right in Italy*, Polity Press, 1988.
J. Fest, *Hitler*, Penguin Books, 1977.
N. Fielding, *The National Front*, Routledge, 1981.
R. Hamilton, *Who Voted for Hitler?*, Princeton University Press, 1982.
C. Husbands, *Race and the Right in Contemporary Politics*, Pinter, 1988.
Journal of Contemporary History, (various contributors), 'International Fascism, 1920–1945', January 1966.
I. Kershaw, *The Nazi Dictatorship: Problems and Perspectives of Interpretation*, Edward Arnold, 1985.
I. Kirkpatrick, *Mussolini: Study of a Demagogue*, Odhams, 1964.
W. Laquer (ed.) *Fascism: A Reader's Guide*, Penguin Books, 1965.
K. Lunn and R. Thurlow (eds.), *British Fascism*, Croom Helm, 1980.
D. Mühlberger (ed.) *The Social Basis of European Fascist Movements*, Croom Helm, 1987.
E. Nolte, *Three Faces of Fascism*, New York: New American Library, 1969.
N. Poulantzas, *The Crisis of the Dictatorships: Portugal, Spain, Greece*, New Left Books, 1976.
D. Schoenbaum, *Hitler's Social Revolution: Class and Status in Nazi Germany*, Weidenfeld and Nicolson, 1967.
M. Walker, *The National Front*, Fontana, 1978.
P. Wilkinson, *The New Fascists*, Grant McIntyre, 1981.
E. Wiskemann, *Europe of the Dictators, 1919–1945*, Collins, 1966.
E. Wiskemann, *Fascism in Italy*, Macmillan, 1969.
R. S. Wistrich (ed.), 'Theories of Fascism', *Journal of Contemporary History*, October 1976.
S. Woolf (ed.), *Fascism in Europe*, Methuen, 1981.

D. Blackmer and S. Tarrow (eds.), *Communism in Italy and France*, Princeton University Press, 1975.
S. Carrillo, *'Eurocommunism' and the State*, Lawrence and Wishart, 1977.
S. Clegg, G. Dow and P. Boreham (eds), *The State, Class and the Recession*, Croom Helm, 1982.
D. Cohn-Bendit, *Obsolete Communism: The Left-Wing Alternative*, André Deutsch, 1968.
A. Crispin, *Who's Watching You? Britain's Security Services and the Official Secrets Act*, Penguin Books, 1981.
R. Garaudy, *The Turning Point of Socialism*, Fontana Books, 1970.
R. Godson and S. Haseler, *Eurocommunism: Implications For East and West*, Macmillan, 1978.
W. Griffith (ed.), *The European Left: Italy, France and Spain*, D. C. Heath, 1979.
R. Kindersley (ed.), *In Search of Eurocommunism*, Macmillan, 1981.
B. Kohler, *Political Forces in Spain, Greece and Portugal*, Butterworth, 1983.
P. Lange and M. Vannicelli (eds.), *The Communist Parties of Italy, France and Spain*, Allen and Unwin, 1981.
J. Lodge (ed.) *Terrorism: A Challenge to the State*, Martin Robertson, 1981.
H. Machin (ed.) *National Communism in the Western World*, Methuen, 1983.
N. McInnes, *The Communist Parties of Western Europe*, RIIA/Oxford University Press, 1975.
R. Miliband, *Capitalist Democracy in Britain*, Oxford University Press, 1982.

A. Ranney and G. Sartori (eds.), *Eurocommunism: The Italian Case*, Washington: American Enterprise Institute, 1978.

R. L. Tokes (eds.), *Eurocommunism and Detente*, Martin Robertson, 1979.

A. F. Upton (eds.), *The Communist Parties of Scandinavia and Finland*, Weidenfeld and Nicolson, 1973.

P. Wilkinson, *Terrorism and the Liberal State*, 2 ed., Macmillan, 1986.

The European military

J. S. Ambler, *The French Army in Politics*, Ohio State University Press, 1966.

F. L. Carsten, *The Reichswehr in Politics, 1918–1933*, Oxford University Press, 1966.

R. Fields, *The Portuguese Revolution and the Armed Forces Movement*, New York: Praeger, 1977.

S. Finer, *Man on Horseback*, 2nd ed., Frances Pinter, 1987.

W. Goerlitz, *History of the German General Staff 1657–1945*, Pall Mall Press, 1969.

G. Harries-Jenkins, 'Armed Forces in European Society' in S. Giner and M. Archer (eds.), *Contemporary Europe: Social Structures and Cultural Patterns*, Routledge, 1978.

G. Harries-Jenkins and J. van Doorn (eds.), *The Military and the Problem of Legitimacy*, Sage Publications, 1976.

A. Horne, *The French Army and Politics 1870–1970*, Macmillan, 1984.

S. P. Huntington (ed.), *Changing Patterns of Military Politics*, New York: The Free Press, 1962.

K. Medhurst, 'The Military and the Prospects for Spanish Democracy', *West European Politics*, February 1978.

O. D. Menard, *The Army and the Fifth Republic*, University of Nebraska Press, 1967.

S. G. Payne, *Politics and the Military in Modern Spain*, Stanford University Press, 1967.

A. Perlmutter and V. Bennett, *The Political Influence of the Military: A Comparative Reader*, Yale University Press, 1980.

R. Porch, *The Portuguese Armed Forces and the Revolution*, Croom Helm, 1977.

D. B. Ralston (ed.), *Soldiers and States: Civil Relations in Modern Europe*, Boston: D. C. Heath, 1966.

J. Wheeler-Bennett, *The Nemesis of Power: The German Army in Politics, 1918–1945*, Macmillan, 2nd ed., 1964.

7 Assemblies and Governments

Parliamentary decline

'A Theatre of Illusions' is how one disgruntled member described the French National Assembly in the Fifth Republic. His cynicism no doubt echoes the views of parliamentarians in other countries. The 'illusions', if they are such, are especially relevant to the assemblies of unified systems: the simple corollary of government responsibility to the assembly is that the government should be able to control its decisions – by virtue of its hold over the majority parties. The trappings of legislative power help to sustain the illusions, and it becomes a vexed question to determine just how important such assemblies are in relation to the power of government.

There is another point of weakness evident in unified systems beyond that of straightforward party control: the powers of assemblies over governments are all double-edged. What appears as, and may actually be, a potent parliamentary control can be used by the government to further its influence over the assembly. In fact, we can say that inherent in this version of a balanced system is the underlying theme that no controls are ever completely one-way. In its most elementary *constitutional* form, this is apparent where the assembly has the power to bring down a government, but itself then faces the peril of dissolution; yet as we shall see the *political* implications of this reciprocal control are of greater importance. Where a system of separation of powers is enforced quite different considerations apply, and the demarcation of functions and personnel can make it easier for an assembly to stem the influence of government.

However, there is, too, the more general impression that *all* parliaments have declined in stature, that as the scope of government activity has widened, so parliamentary influence has waned. The conclusion: the basis of liberal democracy is threatened. Contrast this sense of decline with the undoubted prominence of European parliaments in the nineteenth century – the 'golden age' of legislatures.[1] Two factors may explain their special importance then, both at different times helping to secure legislative pre-eminence, but in fact mutually opposed. The earlier of the two was the relative insulation of legislatures from wider social forces; later there occurred the once-for-all, mass entry into politics as the working class won the franchise. In different ways, both phases served to make assemblies the focal point of political life, and the term 'liberal democracy' is a precise indication of the gap between them. The *liberal* state, '. . . was designed to operate by competition between political parties responsible to a non-democratic electorate',[2] and the narrow social base of the electorate meant that political choice could be maintained exclusively within the legislature. The absence of mass parties, party discipline, and even of meaningful party labels, gave the members of the assembly a unique freedom to control government, and since the ruling élite came from broadly the same social classes, changes of government did not indicate political instability. Thus legislatures were of central importance to the process of government, but the particular circumstances were not to last.

The fundamental shift occurred with the addition of democracy to the liberal state. The demand for a popular voice in government concentrated naturally on securing popular representation in the legislature as the best means of securing government by the people. As the initial battles were fought and won, so parliaments became synonymous with popular sovereignty, and they achieved an enormous symbolic importance. But at the same time the need to organise the popular vote gave rise to national and mass parties. No longer were assembly members able to act as individuals; party government and party discipline meant that the legislature lost its substantial power over government, and gradually, too, its reputation as a 'spearhead' of popular sovereignty. In both of these developments we see that the reasons for legislative pre-eminence were not lasting, and that comparisons with nineteenth-century ideal-pictures can be misleading; the heritage still persists – assemblies remain symbols of power and legitimacy. But the powers and functions of modern assemblies now have to be interpreted in an entirely different context, within the dictates of party democracy and contemporary government. Of course, that raises a further problem: assemblies as *symbols* of power and legitimacy must mean that other interests or forces are being indirectly legitimised – the 'parties' or 'the system' as a whole, or even perhaps legitimising the latent reality of 'executive dictatorship' which without the top dressing of legislative consent would simply be too unpalatable for the electorate.

The usual functions of assemblies continue unaltered in their form – the power to legislate, to vote and control expenditure; yet these traditional weapons are nowhere in Western Europe regarded as of prime importance, and there is a consequent sense of loss:

that legislatures really should legislate, otherwise they must be 'weak'. We can call these traditional functions of assemblies the 'direct controls', and they were historically the strong ones. They are 'direct' since it is around them that the work of an assembly is organised. The efforts of, say, the Opposition in Britain are geared to fighting controversial government legislation step-by-step, clause-by-clause, on the floor of the Commons and in committee, even though the final product may not look much different from what the government had originally intended. The apparent 'failure' to secure this control in its direct sense does not preclude the Opposition from securing indirect successes. This can be put another way: without the framework which the exercise of these direct controls gives, the work of Parliament would lack any coherent structure.

The important point is that certain indirect controls are operating alongside the direct ones, and they are only given expression in the course of assembly preoccupation with its allotted functions; they are used latently – but not, of course, unknowingly. First summarising the direct controls:

elective: the power to decide on the duration of governments, and providing for orderly succession;

personnel: the individual and collective responsibility of the members of the government to the assembly gives the latter a power to determine the composition of government; as a corollary, in unified systems the personnel of government are normally recruited from the assembly.

rules: the power to make laws and other decisions which are binding on governments, and to see that these decisions are observed;

And within these same areas there are a number of indirect controls:

elective: the necessity for the governing party (or parties) to impose discipline to ensure government duration requires also that governments foster continued support – they must heed the wishes of party groups;

personnel: members of the government normally start as members of the assembly – and eventually return there; this common origin, and prolonged experience of assembly life, acts as a strong *socialising* influence modifying the actions of government.

rules: the process of rule-making diminishes in importance (in the bounds of what is possible for the legislature), but otherwise peripheral aspects now come to the fore: the assembly is an important channel of *communication*, one allowing for the input of demands and linking all the participants – including the electorate;

To complete the picture, we should also draw attention to the *double-edged* nature of all these controls. Most obviously, the governments must seek to control the elective function of the assembly in exercising power over the government parties. At the ultimate, this would nullify the elective function, giving the government an almost permanent life, but the constitutional rules impose minimum standards. Secondly, a government recruits its members principally from the assembly, in doing so it exacts a loyalty from those it promotes and, additionally, encourages support from those who may be recruited in the future – the power of patronage. Finally, and as a matter of fact, the great bulk of law-making (more accurately, rule-making) belongs exclusively to governments in Western Europe; even the indirect aspects of this power, input and communication, governments will naturally seek to control for their own ends.

These general statements about the functions of West European assemblies make it apparent that there is a complex balance involved. Whilst the 'decline' of assembly power can be measured in terms of an idealised past, simply to write it off as no more than a convenient 'setting' for the display of governmental legitimacy would be wrong. The assembly remains a key factor in securing political balance; we can appreciate this contribution, first by examining how the various European parliaments operate in relation to our broad groups of function and then by viewing the general significance of assemblies in relation to political communication.

Elective functions

The duration, party composition, and the orderly succession of governments – the elective aspect – is partly determined by constitutional ground-rules. The nearest to complete constitutional determination in a unified system occurs in Switzerland. There, the written constitution fixes the life of the Federal Council, and strong constitutional convention decides the composition of the federal government as well as succession (or rather non-succession) by the institution of permanent collegial government. In other countries, the life of a government is left indeterminate, but with rigorous attention paid to the maximum life of the assembly – sometimes five, normally four years – as the critical constitutional factor. At root, the assembly's elective function depends on shifts of support in the electorate from one election to another. The nature of the British party system is such that it reacts passively to these shifts; the elective function is a formal one performed by a mandated college of electors, and an outgoing prime minister usually concedes the election to his opponent before the election returns are complete.

The British party system is atypical. In almost all other

countries, the election results offer a number of possibilities. In the simplest situation, where there are three parties and none with an absolute majority, there are four quite feasible outcomes, including all-party government, and the permutations rise quickly with the number of parties. A prime minister from a party losing support at an election is by no means inclined to throw in his cards. However, quite apart from the number of parties and coalition possibilities that may be present, we can distinguish between two uses made of the assembly's elective function. One approaches the British example by making changes in government dependent on party fortunes at a general election; the other shows little or no relation to election results: governments come and go, at times quite irrespective of how the individual parties fare.

A corollary is that in some countries changes of government between elections are rare, whilst in others there is a high potential for coalition change at any time. In the first category the premium placed on coalition stability means that governments will either last for the normal life of the assembly or that there will be a premature dissolution, but a simple change of government without reference to the electorate will be treated as deviant even though constitutionally allowable. It is doubtful whether constitutional provisions help account for the differences. Thus the idea was at one time prevalent that the power of dissolution, that is to enforce an early election, enhances government stability. But such a 'dissolution-centred' interpretation has to be related to the actual position of those in control – the party leader as prime minister or the coalition parties in conclave.

In fact, it is the constellation of political forces which gives the power of dissolution meaning. Only where, as in the Fifth Republic, it was deliberately fashioned as a weapon operating externally to the party system (in the hands of the president) can it be regarded as a separate, constitutional factor. It seems unlikely that the threat of dissolution – from whatever source – will have much effect in increasing governmental cohesion by itself. Thus the Norwegian constitution has no provision at all for the early dissolution of the Storting which always has to run its full four-year term. That, however, has not made governments any the less stable, and it can plausibly be argued that, since there is no prospect of an early election, there is little to be gained in chopping and changing governments.

We can first look at those countries where governments are stable from one election to another. Naturally, that stability is most likely to be found in situations of single-party government, usually associated with a two-party system, with Britain as the exemplary case. The fact that, in contrast to British practice, most assemblies run nearer their full term is not really a substantial difference, since the unrestricted power of the British prime minister to decide on the date of an election is largely a useful tactical weapon which secures an advantage for the majority party in the *timing* of an election; it is not a reflection of government weakness or instability. Of course, there are wide variations in how long governments last even if single-party government obtains. All kinds of accidental factors can intervene, and a government's majority may be very small: the three elections in Ireland from 1981 to 1982 were caused by the fact that there was no real majority government, and – similarly – the British election of 1979 had to be called because, through by-election losses, the Labour Government was reduced to a minority status and eventually defeated. At the other end of the scale, Austria for long provided a good example of single-party government combined with maximum assembly life: the secure, absolute majority enjoyed by the Austrian Socialists for more than a decade ensured the stability of government.

It is clear that in such cases the elective function is only nominally exercised by the assembly parties, for in reality the composition of the government has been determined previously as a result of the election. That must obviously always be so where a 'pure' two-party system exists, and almost always so when there are only two major parties. But the position rapidly becomes more complex when there is a genuine three-party system and in principle becomes indeterminate in a multi-party system. In practice, however, the number of parties – and the combinations that have to be tried in order to produce majority coalitions – is usually restricted by the problems of compatibility. Yet the fact that there are various feasible combinations means that the assembly must possess a real share in the elective function, since the election itself will not have provided an absolutely decisive outcome. It is at this point that a distinction should be made between two types of tradition in coalition formation. One resembles the functioning of a two-party system in that the electorate is given a clear choice of governments since the party alignments are made known in advance, and the commitment to form a particular coalition forms the basis of party campaigning. Thus the elective function is kept by the electorate – as long as the parties keep their promises! The alternative possibility is to keep the elective function firmly in the hands of the parties. This option is not necessarily a 'less democratic' solution, although it naturally gives much more power and freedom of manoeuvre to party leaders. The arrangement can work precisely if the party leadership is united and members and supporters trust it, and because leaders do have a flexible negotiating position with possible partners the party is able to make good bargains. We can appreciate that in a multi-party system, where all the parties have a fairly sure, if restricted clientele, 'making bargains' is a vital part of the process of government formation, and there are so many permutations involved that it is much better to wait until after the election: not only will some clarification result with regard to what is numerically feasible, there will be in addition a new deciding factor –the number of seats that each party controls, and that again will influence the nature of the bargains struck, especially in the share-out of the government ministries.

West Germany provides an excellent example of both types of tendency. Her three-party system in the 1970s took on the 'balanced' form similar to that of a two-party system: the SPD and the small FDP on the one side and the CDU-CSU on the other. In the elections of 1972, 1976 and 1980 the SPD and FDP committed themselves in advance to a continuation of the coalition thus giving the voters an absolutely clear choice of government. That picture was suddenly transformed in 1982 when the coalition between the SPD and the FDP abruptly ended and the FDP decamped to join a CDU government. This action – absolutely acceptable on a constitutional level and typical of party behaviour in multi-party systems – drew widespread criticism on the grounds that the switch had been in blatant disregard of the voters' choice and party commitments made in 1980. The discord was a major reason for deciding to opt for an early election in 1983, and the episode neatly illustrates two differing views as to where the elective function rightly belongs.

The case of the Netherlands provides a different perspective on the discussion, for it involves the operation of an entrenched multi-party system, and in most respects the Netherlands belongs to the second model – that with the elective function residing in the assembly. However, there has been dissatisfaction of long standing with this form of party élitism and a frustration on the part of voters in that they were effectively 'not allowed' to choose a government, only a party. Impatience and disquiet with the prevailing system led to the formation of a new political party, Democrats '66, as a protest against the game of coalition 'musical chairs' played by the parties, demanding instead that the political composition of the cabinet should express the explicit will of the voters – proposing among other things that the prime minster should be directly elected in order to achieve that aim. Democrats '66 also acted as a catalyst on the party system in trying to forge a 'progressive bloc' to contest elections, allowing the choice of *government* (if the bloc were successful), not just a party preference. In fact, however, the Dutch party system has thus far not proved amenable to such a change. Partly, the reason is that it is still a multi-party system and old habits die hard, but the Christian Democratic Appeal, formed in 1976, is also a complicating factor: although on one level the emergence of the CDA through the fusion of three religious parties helped to cut down the plethora of coalition possibilities, the CDA – partially cutting across the left–right axis – is free to ally itself with either pole (Liberal or Labour) and it is therefore impossible for it to express an unequivocal preference before the election.

Belgium also illustrates the effects of entrenched multi-partism on coalition formation, with the addition of the linguistic divide superimposed on the left–right axis. As a result of the 1987 election no fewer than eleven parties were represented, and it took all of five months for an agreement on the basis for a five-party coalition to be struck. The coalition – an over-sized one – was formed with the overriding aim of resolving the Brussels question, and the constitutional change necessitated a two-thirds parliamentary majority. Precarious as the coalition formula was, and over-sized coalitions tend to have a much shorter life than minimum-winning ones, it is clear that the delicacy and complexity of the linguistic-issue make it impossible for the parties to make absolutely binding pre-election declarations as to policy-details and coalition intentions.

Another type of example of electoral choice not being an important factor is seen in the permanent coalition between the Austrian People's Party and the Socialists from 1945 until 1966. Since these were the only two parties of any significance at all, their inter-party agreement, the *Koalitionsvertrag*, made it quite impossible for any section of the electorate to have any influence on the outcome of the election – except that the *Proporz* principle of sharing out the ministries according to party strength did make some concession to the electoral will.

The examples so far examined have been of systems which are relatively stable, and one may well conclude that not too much is at stake, at least in the short term, whether the elective function is exercised by the assembly parties or not. But more than questions of political style may be involved, as becomes evident when the political system shows signs of instability. In fact, the phenomenon of 'unstable government' is directly related to the active use of the assembly's elective function, although that does not tell us why the instability occurs. It is usual to regard unstable government as occurring over long periods and with governments lasting less than a year on average. Such a measure of instability would include Italy certainly, along with the French Fourth Republic, together with Finland, the Netherlands and Denmark. Two points should be made. The first is that there is no necessary connection between short-lived governments and a deeper political instability. It was the case for the Weimar Republic and the French Fourth Republic, but does not apply to Italy or to the other countries mentioned. Naturally, parties and politicians 'regret' the frequent break-up of coalitions, but they are also aware just how far they can go and how much they can ignore rumblings of electoral discontent. The second point to note is that the shortness of government life does not automatically mean that assembly life will be concomitantly brief. In some cases, there may even be an inverse relationship, that is, frequent changes of government combined with a longer life of assembly than enjoyed by many systems with stable government. That particularly applied to Fourth Republic France where a majority existed for keeping the assembly in being but not one to sustain governments. The electoral system was rigged to favour the moderate parties and they had no interest in returning to the electorate because the distortions in their favour might not be so great next time, and in that situation there was little connection between the government people wanted and the one they received: prior to the 1956 election only 2 per cent of a survey poll favoured the Socialist leader as the next prime minister; subsequently he emerged as just that! The parties also 'managed' the constitution: the constitution required an *absolute* majority to bring down a government, with automatic dissolution if that occurred twice within six months. But the clause remained almost inoperative: governments simply failed to get the *relative* majorities they required for essential measures – and it was to such hostile votes that they succumbed, leaving the constitutional formula inoperative and the assembly itself intact.

A basic reason for preferring the calculable effects of government instability to the less certain outcome of frequent reference back to the electorate could well be the presence of strong extreme parties of an anti-system nature. Thus the DC in Italy had no wish to see the PCI benefit from government instability, and Italian parliaments tend to run near their full term. As the Italian electorate has become more volatile, the disinclination to hold early elections persisted into the 1980s when the centre-lay parties come to occupy a pivotal position. Even if one of these smaller parties thinks it will benefit, the others can be relied upon to stave off an election by re-jigging the coalition. But there is a price to pay: the *immobilisme* of government may in the end increase electoral disaffection and a reckoning cannot be postponed indefinitely.

Personnel functions

The function of recruitment to government is almost exclusively performed by the assemblies in unified systems. The doctrine of 'responsibility' is that much easier to enforce if ministers not only appear in the assembly to answer for government actions, but also really 'belong' there as well. There is little doubt that the influence of recruitment – as well as the process of socialisation involved – is one of the most important of assembly controls.

Typically, European assemblies provide a base from which a governing hierarchy emerges, whether or not this is a strict constitutional requirement. In this respect, the British system is the most stringent, but in practice the exceptions turn out to be minor variations. Thus there are 'incompatibility' rules in both France and the Netherlands; a person joining the government simply relinquishes his assembly seat, but apart from losing his vote, his position in the assembly is hardly altered. In France, the situation has become somewhat blurred; roughly a quarter of the members of the government were not deputies following the 1981 Assembly election. There are sporadic exceptions to assembly recruitment. Caretaker governments in Finland avoid prejudicing delicate coalition negotiations if they are made up of non-political figures, largely civil servants. In several countries, the occasional non-party person is given a portfolio, and the British system can be 'bent' by awarding a peerage. De Gaulle's first governments contained a number of non-parliamentary 'technocrats', but later de Gaulle himself was to insist that his ministers, even if they were not party politicians, should fight for a constituency seat at elections – promptly resigning the seat, if successful, in order to maintain the incompatibility rule. The fact that the constitutionally unnecessary course of ministers contesting elections was adopted shows the legitimising power which the assembly carries, and the 'greyness' of non-political figures who are simply co-opted.

The most obvious effect of assembly recruitment to government is the strength of the link forged between the majority parties and government. But there is no formal process by which this is achieved. Instead, the composition of the government, as in Britain, remains the prerogative of the prime minister. However, the realities of coalition-building are such that the influence of the party will vary from one country and one situation to another. Where the coalition parties are of comparable size, coalition negotiations involve a hammering-out not only of policies, but the party share-out of the ministries and the names to fill them as well. If a party stakes a claim to a particular ministry, then the incumbent becomes virtually the nominee of the assembly caucus of that party, and the prime minister will only have a decisive say in the ministers coming from his own party. Thus it was a novelty in Norwegian politics in the 1965–71 coalition, that the member parties nominated people to fill government vacancies, not the prime minister. Inevitably, ministers who arrive in this way will see their main loyalty to their parliamentary party rather than to the head of government. The loyalty of ministers may even be shared between their party, as a parliamentary and governmental élite, and their party as a national political organisation, especially where sub-federal or regional organisation is strong, or the party is intensely factionalised. The position of Christian Democrat ministers in Italy exemplifies this split loyalty. A single powerful figure has rarely been able to dominate the party, and consequently DC prime ministers have had to share authority, often in a subordinate position, with the party secretary. Since cross-currents in the party and the numerous entrenched factions (the *correnti*) prevent a unified leadership emerging, governmental crises result not only from party competition but also from internal factional dispute. In the course of prolonged governmental 'crises' a selection of prominent Christian Democrats, usually former ministers, will in turn try to form a new government. The decisive merit of any one of them rests on whether he has a broad acceptability in the party *and* whether he can come up with a workable coalition formula, so that successful Christian Democrat leaders are also faction and coalition leaders, first seeking to control the secretaryship, and subsequently the premiership and ministries. The dispersion of the personnel function to party secretaries and faction leaders is taken to such an extreme that the formal institutions of parliament appear to be by-passed.

Usually in situations where one party is dominant, the prime minister's power is much greater. Thus the political scene in West Germany between 1953 and 1961 was dominated by the CDU and Chancellor Adenauer – in 1953 the CDU almost, and in 1957 actually, gained a majority of votes on its own account. There was no question that in this period Adenauer firmly controlled his own party, and the fate of the junior coalition partners was in his hands. Federal ministers were 'his' ministers, and the terms of the Basic Law by which, 'The Federal Chancellor determines, and is responsible for, general policy' (Article 65), helped to foster the concept of 'chancellor democracy'. In fact, this expression is remarkably similar in connotation to the idea of 'prime ministerial government' in Britain – the view that the accretion of powers in the hands of the prime minister and the nature of modern elections (in which all issues polarise around two rival candidates for supreme office), have together made parliamentary, even party government an outmoded expression. Yet both concepts are open to serious criticism. In West Germany it proved to be no more than a label for a particular period, and ended when Adenauer's authority visibly crumbled with the onset of the Berlin crisis in 1961 – the occasion of the erection of the Berlin Wall. Shortly afterwards, the CDU lost its Bundestag supremacy, and Adenauer had increasing difficulty with his own party and with the coalition partner, the Free Democrats. No more was heard then or subsequently of chancellor democracy, and that may be considered strange if one thinks that Helmut Schmidt (chancellor from 1974 until 1982) was widely regarded as a strong and forceful leader. Yet he, like other post-Adenauer chancellors, proved to be in the party and parliamentary mainstreams – and they were prepared to exercise their authority *through* the parties and the Bundestag, not regardless of them.

Where no one party has much of an edge on the others, the paramount influence on ministers will be their own parties, not the government leadership. This factor applies with all the more force in situations of unstable coalition; ministers know that their political future rests with the party, and the fall of the existing government will not preclude them from having another (or even the same) post in the next one. Certain parties, certain people, become indispensable – the Centre Party in Finland, the CDA in the Netherlands, the Christian Democrats in Belgium, the Radicals in the Fourth Republic. Contrast this with the period of Adenauer's rule in West Germany: on more than one occasion, the effect of a small party leaving the CDU-led coalition was that the ministers hung on to their posts when their party went into opposition. This 'treachery' is highly exceptional; party loyalty usually comes first. In several countries, party leadership is strictly divorced from those who accept ministerial office. The reason is apparent: a party serving in coalition has to maintain its identity and morale. One way of doing so is to underline the independence of the parliamentary party – and at the same time reduce the status and authority of those members who become ministers.

In all we have been saying about government leadership and ministerial recruitment, there is a clear point at issue: if there were a general trend towards 'chancellor democracy', or its national equivalent, then the personnel functions of assemblies would be declining. Yet there is no evidence that this is the case in Western

Europe, and recruitment to government remains an important assembly control weapon. All countries have a period when a gifted leader can impose his own pattern for a while – a combination of factors, involving his own relative ability, the structure and traditions of his party, and its strength in relation to others. His lasting influence may be important, but to take the experience of de Gaulle: in order to impose his own pattern he was forced to break up the existing unified system quite deliberately. The quasi-presidential system he bequeathed to his successor – a 'routinisation of the charisma' – represented a determined and successful attempt to loosen the hold of assembly parties on government. But other outstanding leaders have been content to work within the parliamentary framework, and consequently when they depart the old practices and controls are reasserted.

A less obvious aspect of the personnel function is the process of socialisation. It is no small matter that prior to taking office, ministers may spend several years as full-time professional politicians with seats in the assembly. The values and attitudes they bring with them correspond to their party labels, but they are also subject to an assembly 'embrace' – as their whole parliamentary party has been for decades before them. And the rules of the parliamentary game are too well learned to be forgotten by those who become ministers. There is an element of self-regard: ex-ministers will have to return to the assembly one day, or retire from politics. The net result is to moderate the antagonism inherent in the relationship between assemblies and governments. Codes and practices vary, but two essentials are the 'rights' of opposition and the trust necessary between a minister and his parliamentary party. To ride roughshod over both is to court eventual disaster.

One has to introduce a number of reservations to this model picture. It does not apply to all politicians nor to all parties. The longer a party has had parliamentary representation, the more it has shared in office, the less the likelihood it will break the 'rules' when it is in a position of real power. The classic example of non-socialisation is the Nazi Party in the Weimar Republic; it fulfilled its promises. We have seen how in a few years the tiny party in the Reichstag suddenly became the largest of all – in uniform and more of a military formation than a political party. It can be reasonably argued that had the NSDAP shown instead a slow growth throughout the 1920s, a greater willingness to play the party game, even to take a minor place in government, might have been evident. It can be objected that such considerations are irrelevant for an extremist and anti-parliamentary movement. This, however, is to ignore the changes that are apparent in European Communist parties. They see a parliamentary solution as the best that can be hoped for, and this road requires them to engage in a long-term parliamentary strategy, electoral pacts with the Socialists, participation in government even in a subordinate capacity – as with the French Communists, the junior coalition partner of the Socialists from 1981 to 1984. This attitude is a far cry from the purely tactical share in government that many took at the end of the war, further still from the splendid isolation of the Communist Party in the Weimar Republic: 'After the Nazis, our turn will come!' All the same, to the extent that a Communist party is still rigorously excluded from government the parliamentary socialising process works in reverse. Permanent opposition becomes an acceptable mode of existence; it is hardly likely to engender any respect for the problems of government. But changes have gradually become evident: government participation in Finland and Iceland, active 'support' in Sweden, signatories to multi-party 'pacts' in Italy and Spain culminating in the 'arrival' of the French Communists in government. All these are signs of a 'parliamentary communism' still awaiting a rigorous test.

Beyond the obvious socio-economic differences in recruitment from party to party, there are national variations evident in the source of politicians. Most significant of these is the place of the public servant in politics. Once again Britain is quite untypical; it is not a question of the Civil Service being politically neutral in its dealings; British civil servants are politically emasculated as well – besides the position of the judiciary, the one real element of the separation of powers. For historical reasons, and with a different conception of civic rights, the situation in mainland Europe is in sharp contrast. Many nineteenth-century assemblies contributed very few government ministers; these were recruited directly from the government service. Whilst Bismarck was chancellor in Imperial Germany, he was the only minister with a seat in the Reichstag. In Sweden, public officials formed a high proportion of the multi-cameral assembly before 1866, and the Finnish 'caretaker' governments are largely composed of civil servants. The undoubted blurring of function has meant that public officials are often free to pursue an active political career. This is written into the Austrian Constitution (Article 59/2): 'Public employees, as well as members of the armed forces, do not require release from their posts in order to serve as members of the National Assembly. Should they wish to stand for election to the National Assembly, they are to be granted the necessary free time.' Norway is exceptional in excluding higher civil servants from the Storting, but in many countries it is quite unremarkable to have a proportion of public employees in parliament. In West Germany, this tradition extends to the Land assemblies; an established state official, with a seat in the Landtag, may well find himself speaking in opposition to the Land minister who heads the official's own department.

In former times, the presence of a number of serving officials in a parliament would be an obvious index of weakness in the face of government; now they are certain to be 'party men'. It can mean that the public service is overtly politicised – in Austria, the influence of party reaches fairly deep; this 'political' aspect of the civil service is one we take up in the following chapter. In the parliamentary context, the level of expertise of officials can be a source of talent covering the whole range of government activity, and with a higher degree of competence than possessed by the average parliamentarian.

Nowadays, it seems unlikely that the origin of assembly personnel is a matter which governments can turn to their advantage. The real power of governments is found in the disbursement of ministerial posts. In this, the power of the British government exceeds others. By most standards Britain has a large assembly, yet a high proportion of its members, and up to a third of the majority party, can be recruited for government service. A massive array of senior and junior ministers results. In one way, this dependence makes an assembly stronger, but the reverse is also true – a government can control a key proportion of its voting strength which in Britain even extends to the ranks of Parliamentary Private Secretary, and the promise of eventual preferment goes far wider. This influence of the government is probably more important in Britain since the ministerial team is concentrated in one party; in other countries, fewer posts are available, and the loyalty exacted is to the party in coalition rather than to the government leader.

Rule functions

Law-making was historically a central function of legislatures. The ability to impose binding restrictions and commitments on governments in one area after another was the means by which they rose to a pre-eminent position, especially if those 'restrictions and commitments' are made to include the whole gamut of financial and taxation powers. But important as the legislative arena was as a lever to enforce parliamentary authority, it has to be remembered that assemblies actually have very little direct say in most aspects of what might be called the totality of 'rule making', since formal legislation – passing laws – is only a small fraction of the whole. That is evident if one thinks of all the various forms of delegated legislative authority and subordinate decree-making powers.

This loss does not alter the fact that most assemblies behave as if the legislative process was still the prime function. Parliamentary behaviour continues unchanged even though the outcome of any particular piece of legislation may have been long decided in the cabinet or in inner-party cabals: its safe passage through the legislature has been pre-ordained. The process of legislation may seem to be a surviving piece of symbolic ritualism – as long as governments have majorities and where party discipline can be counted on to produce a favourable result. Yet even if one concedes that much legislative activity has no great weight or function, nonetheless it is this activity which serves as a *framework* for party and parliamentary politics. Thus legislation – perhaps more generally 'government business' – should be seen as providing a context within which demands can be voiced and communications passed to the various parts of the political system.

As an extreme example of legislative downgrading to virtual non-competence, we can take the position of the French Assembly of the Fifth Republic in contrast to the Fourth. In the old republic, the Assembly was the fount of all legislative authority, a power which went to it largely by default, since governments foundered one after another in their inability to push through fundamental legislation, and the reaction of the National Assembly was to become excessively concerned with minor measures – understandable in view of the party stalemate and the activity of pressure groups. Philip Williams commented: 'Indeed, it is a sign of the triviality of members' preoccupations in the Fourth Republic that nine-tenths of the bills introduced in its last year, and half of those passed, would have fallen into the domain of regulations.'[3] This 'domain of regulations' is one of the areas of legislation created in the 1958 constitution in an attempt to cut through the tangled web of assembly legislative power.

Essentially, the 'rationalisation' of legislative authority in the Fifth Republic shows a parallel with its division in a federal state, though the division is not territorial but between government and assembly. The constitution, mainly in Article 34, gives a comprehensive list of headings under which an assembly can legislate, either to establish 'rules concerning' or 'fundamental principles', but the implementation of these and their detailed expression is achieved by government 'regulation' – in other words, an enormous increase of what in other countries would be delegated legislation. Besides the definition of ordinary law by a number of headings, there is a further category of 'organic law', which although not as fundamental as the constitution, still requires special procedures under Article 46. As in a federal system, the definition of competence and procedures has to be given to an outside body, not the government or assembly. A reading of the constitution would not be of much help in distinguishing a 'principle' from a 'rule' and both from a 'regulation'. This delicate task was laid at the door of the Constitutional Council which can rule on the constitutionality of laws and the appropriateness of procedures, either before a measure comes into force or afterwards.

The government's sweeping powers are made explicit by Article 37: 'Matters other than those regulated by laws fall within the field of rule-making'; thus all residual areas are the responsibility of government, and 'laws' too can be modified by regulation. If this were not enough, the government can also ask the assembly for powers to issue ordinances which encroach on the law-making domain. Shorn of its prime legislative powers in this way, an assembly loses any real pretension to the function of rule-making. It is no longer in a position to haggle over the small print or even to read it; as a consequence, there is a further loss: there is little 'legislative context' for the passing of communications or the voicing of demands. Only with the President unable to control a majority in the Assembly might the Assembly be able to win back its former position. This was the case between 1986 and 1988, with the parties of the right having an assembly majority, thus restricting the power of President Mitterrand.

Fortunately, the complexities of the French provisions are not reproduced elsewhere. But the absence of such severity in other countries does not necessarily make their assemblies that much stronger in relation to rule-making. The sheer amount of legislative activity is a poor guide to its significance, nor can assembly power be inferred from the number of bills sponsored by private members or opposition parties (between 5 and 10 per cent of all legislation in Western Europe). One can even say that a government's readiness to accept assembly initiative is a convenient form of tension-management, giving it an 'illusion' of power. Even if it is conceded that resulting measures are highly worthy, it is hardly a serious index of assembly power. For that matter, it would be difficult to conceive of an index which could be satisfactory in giving an undistorted measure of assembly power expressed through the legislative function. It is important, obviously, not to confuse dedication, application, and expertise with the exercise of power – they may be an indication, but it is just as possible that apparent 'busyness' conceals impotence. It may be the case that one legislature is very successful in terms of forcing through amendments whereas another is apparently far less so. Yet a qualitative judgement has to be made: a large number of trivial and detailed amendments may not equal one case where the parties in the legislature have forced the government to change its mind over an important issue. Thus, unless we select our legislative cases to ensure that we are comparing like with like (for instance a study of legislation dealing with a specific industry or problem) the compilation of data is virtually meaningless. A further problem is the area of 'non-legislation' – that is legislation either not introduced by the government at all because of its fear of hostile reaction or quietly dropped or shelved as the extent of the opposition (particularly in the majority party) became apparent. Finally, one might refer to the extensive legislative debates in the House of Commons, especially to the time taken in plenary session. Does this devotion make British control over legislation better or does it rather lead to an improvement in debating skills? In Sweden, usually counted as a strong legislative assembly, such debates are of far less importance, and also the government takes a much less prominent role.

The style of legislative activity in Sweden makes it apparent that we also have to take account of the activities which lead to bills being introduced – the input of demands and ideas which promote legislation; there may be less need for conciliation or the airing of views in the formal passage of a bill if this has taken place earlier. Normally, the basis of legislation is taken to be the prerogative of the ruling parties, but in Sweden the Riksdag itself plays an important part; the emphasis is on the introduction of 'propositions' to be investigated rather than on the government's presentation of ready-made bills. Briefly, any Riksdag member can raise a matter of public importance, requesting government action. A committee reports on this matter, and with Riksdag approval, the proposition is brought to the attention of the government. The normal course is then to set up a Royal Commission whose report is circulated widely for comment by interested parties, the government is then in a position to place detailed legislative proposals before the Riksdag. Even allowing for the fact that a high proportion of the 2,000 propositions which may be made in the course of a year relate to detail, simple electioneering, or to the scaling-up or down of government expenditure, there remains a hard core of proposals which can lead to fundamental legislation. This process makes for a diffusion of the rule-making function in comparison, say, with the British system, not only through the inter-party co-operation involved (perhaps a better word would be 'interaction'), but also in the wide consultation with affected interests. A proposition may fail eventually and yet spark off wide discussion and inquiry – supplementing the even more numerous official inquiries that the government conducts on its own account.

The Swedish pattern contrasts with the usual form whereby the government majority provides the basis for an announced legislative programme. But there are substantial differences between assemblies here as well. Some of these relate to procedure: the relative importance attached to plenary sessions as opposed to committee; however, it is the variation in the party basis of government which is all-important. Only where single-party government results is it possible to say that the legislative programme is directly related to an electoral mandate. A coalition government can claim no such clear-cut authorisation, and actual legislation is the product of difficult negotiation and compromise. The result will vary from a coalition that is little more than a holding-operation, securing only a minimum of essential government business, such as the budget, to one where a detailed programme is decided upon in advance. This latter situation is well-illustrated by Clause 4 of the 1956 Austrian coalition pact: 'Government proposals, about which both coalition parties represented in the government have already agreed in matter and form, are binding for the parliamentary groups of the two coalition parties. Basic agreements to amend them need the agreement of the coalition committee.' Rarely would one expect to see decision-making taken so explicitly outside the realm of parliaments, but it is frequently such a coalition committee (rather than a cabinet) which wields the real power in determining the laws to be passed.

Structural differences are also relevant in assessing the rule function of assemblies. In particular, one gauge of their power, not only in legislation but also as a general control mechanism, lies in the strength of their committee systems. This was one conclusion reached by Blondel: 'The maximum effectiveness of assemblies is obtained if small groups are created.'[4] One might almost say that there is an inverse relationship between the number of assembly committees and the power of government. In general terms, it is not difficult to see why this should be so. A number of small groups is less amenable to government control than a single, large one. A degree of specialisation results, and a committee expertise is generated which can soon run counter to party or government policy, a characteristic which is well illustrated by the development of the committee system in the House of Commons over the past decade. We should expect strong committees in the following conditions: where the composition of committees does not reflect the majority in the assembly – alternatively where party discipline is weak; where committees are relatively small and specialised, rather than large and ad hoc, and on which members serve together for long periods with a chairman who is independent of government pressure; finally, where committees have the right of independent access to the bureaucracy and other experts, and themselves have considerable research facilities.

It will be obvious that the foregoing conditions are exactly met by the United States Congress. For these reasons and, of course, because it enjoys a life independent of the president, the American assembly is more powerful than any in Western Europe. Although it has been breached in recent years, the 'seniority rule', by which chairmanship of a committee goes by convention to the member of the majority party with the longest continuous service on that committee, concentrates power in a man who is not susceptible to party discipline or presidential blandishments – his long congressional service presupposes that he has the safest of safe seats in Congress. One should also add the power of committees effectively to 'kill' bills, and for the committees themselves to spawn sub-committees. And then there is the existence of the key 'gateway' committees: the Rules and Appropriations committees plus the joint committees of the two houses; through all of these, bills will normally have to make their perilous journey.

On this formidable yardstick, the committees of European assemblies achieve a low rating. Party control at all levels is much more in evidence, and a government committed to a legislative proposal is unlikely to tolerate committee 'obstruction' for long. Yet there are important differences in the systems that have evolved; for illustration, we can take West Germany, Sweden, and France as representative of the possibilities. The West German committee system in the Bundestag is typical of many assemblies in relying on specialised committees. These are fairly numerous, around twenty, and are fairly small with from fifteen to twenty-seven members; almost all have a legislative and inquiry function, and thus have a 'hybrid' character. They cover the whole range of government activity, and the great majority pair neatly with corresponding federal ministries. It is important to realise that the centre of gravity of the Bundestag is to be found in the committee system and not in the plenary sessions – less than a third of the time spent on them compared with the House of Commons. Committee membership depends on qualified expertise; a member may owe his place on the party list, and hence election to the Bundestag, to the fact that his party felt that he could make an expert contribution. And it is in a committee that he will make his parliamentary reputation, not on the floor of the house. Party discipline is strict on most issues and the committees exactly reflect party strength. Nonetheless they are highly effective; sitting in private and with their own secretariat, they hear the evidence of government officials and independent witnesses; ministers attend, though not as chairmen. The net result is to make the committee a focal point for government and opposition, as well as the object of interest representation.

In other systems the division of labour is not so marked. Scandinavian assemblies differ in two respects. Firstly, there are far fewer committees; secondly, there is little attempt to align them with particular government departments. They are still of fundamental importance; thus the basic Finnish Parliament Act of 1928 devoted sixteen detailed articles to their power and composition, although there are only eight specialised standing committees. The present Swedish Riksdag has three of its eleven committees concerned with legislation and only the finance and foreign affairs committee of the others match the relevant departments of state. The Swedish system also goes far in dissociating the government from the committees by the rule of 'ministerial disability' – ministers are firmly excluded from taking *any* part in the deliberations of committees. It may be true that this rule is simply a hangover from a strict separation of powers doctrine, but ministerial exclusion and the fact that a chairman need not come from the majority party, may have helped foster the spirit of informed objectivity, *Saklighet*, and in practice this gives opposition groups and parties the chance to argue the merits of their case and helps avoid the sterile duality of government and opposition which is often the alternative.

In case one should doubt the potency of committee power, it is salutary to contrast their position in the Fourth and Fifth Republics. In the Fourth, the heart of any government's troubles was to be found in the activities of committees. Once a bill had been sent to one of the twenty specialised committees, the government virtually lost control over its ultimate fate. In the end, an unrecognisably mangled version could be reported out to the Chamber, and there the government would have to use all its resources to bring back deleted clauses or to remove various provisions added in committee. Even though the party composition of the committee reflected that of the Assembly, few of its members, and quite possibly not its chairman either (who, after all, could reasonably hope to receive the relevant ministry himself once the government fell) would feel themselves bound by the wishes of the government

– especially not when opportunities arose to further their particular interests. A further handicap was that ministers did not pilot their own bills through committee and assembly; this latter task would be entrusted by the committee to a rapporteur who could well be hostile to the bill.

The Fifth Republic changed all that. In place of the numerous specialised committees, the constitution set up six very large ones on a broad functional basis, some with as many as 120 members – on the clear supposition that, as a virtual mini-assembly, government control would be that much easier. This move was over-ambitious, and sub-committees have naturally resulted to deal with detailed aspects of bills. Government powers were greatly strengthened: the minister now pilots his own bill through committee and Chamber, and the plenary session considers the government's version of the bill with the committee's view merely as proposed amendments. As an additional precaution, to prevent delaying tactics, the government can call a bill out of committee before it is reported. Finally, the convention whereby the chairmanship of committees bore some relation to party representation was broken after the 1968 election when the Gaullists, enjoying an absolute majority, took them all.

These measures have brought the French system quite close to British practice – the priority given to government measures, the means to secure their passage through committee, and the move away from highly specialised committees. The British approach has naturally been to reproduce the dualism between Government and Opposition in the committees, and that dualism is most easily perpetuated in large, non-specialised bodies in which the government has the majority and ultimately the whip-hand. Although this approach is still true for purely legislative matters, a quiet revolution has taken place in House of Commons committee structure since 1979. The reforms have led to the establishment of a whole range of select committees which systematically monitor and shadow all the leading government departments. These departmental committees represent a major innovation in British parliamentary practice, not least because they show a bi-partisan approach which challenges the adversarial, Government versus Opposition, style of parliamentary procedure. This development reveals a modest reassertion of the power of Parliament against the heavy weight of single-party government, and in a sense, the new committees represent an embryonic 'parliament-in-waiting'. The critical examination of departments such as the Ministry of Defence, the Departments of Trade and Industry, and of Health and Social Security, and the Home Office, has given Parliament a power of scrutiny of the civil service that it never previously enjoyed. This scrutiny has also caused some discomfort to government ministers, since the work of the committees has become an important object of media attention. Moreover, attention is focused on the *issues* themselves, rather than on party conflict, which tends to be the case for plenary debates.[5]

Whilst the range of European committee systems show different and characteristic emphases, only the American manages to preserve a sharp demarcation between government and assembly. European versions vary from the dualism in Britain to the Swedish emphasis on a genuine assembly input function. Between the two is the West German type, combining expertise with a strict party orientation. The basic choice is whether to insist that control functions are best exercised by securing a 'distance' from government or not. This problem comes to a head in the question of foreign affairs and defence committees. The presence of these is natural if one agrees that control functions are best furthered by an association of the assembly with government, but the counter-argument – at least for unified systems – is that participation in such committees means that the opposition parties, since they must be taken into the government's confidence, lose their freedom of action; the emergence of bipartisan policies is poor compensation for an unfettered right of criticism.

It is helpful in this discussion to regard second chambers as an extension of the committee idea. In their own right, as a separate mode of class representation or an overt check on the popular assembly, they are largely anachronisms, and the evolution of party government has tended to leave them high and dry, with the important exception of the West German Bundesrat.* Both Denmark (1953) and Sweden (1970) have rid themselves of their upper houses, and this would have substantially been the effect of de Gaulle's ill-starred referendum in 1969. A second chamber does have a live function where there is a marked territorial power dispersion, providing a political means of resolving differences of view regarding local-central competence. For the rest, powers of an upper house usually appear greater than they are in reality. The superficially strong bicameralism in Italy, with the government responsible to both houses, is negated by the fact that the party line-up is roughly the same in both. The same double responsibility exists in theory both in Belgium and the Netherlands; in practice, they are appendages, and both reflect the party situation in the lower house. The British House of Lords, with its built-in

---

* For the role of the Bundesrat, see under 'European Federalism', p. 262-82 below.

Conservative majority is always an implied threat to a Labour government especially at the tail-end of a parliamentary term. In contrast, Austria, a nominally federal state, has an upper house so weak that one can hardly speak of a genuine two-chamber system; its veto can be overcome by a simple majority vote of the National Council. Perhaps one of the last attempts to reassert the second chamber as a control on the lower house will prove to have been the French Senate; the constitution made it a mechanism which, on occasion, could be used by the government to circumvent a hostile vote in the Chamber of Deputies.[6]

The idea of a second chamber as a glorified committee of the lower house comes to reality in three Nordic countries: Norway, Iceland, and Finland. In all three, there is no second chamber as such, but the assemblies constitute themselves into two divisions at the beginning of each parliament. In Norway and Iceland, they then function as distinct bodies. The Norwegian Storting elects a quarter of its members to sit separately, but a common membership of committees is retained. The Icelandic Althingi operates as two distinct entities, except for two key committees, and disagreement between the two divisions results in a combined meeting (as in Norway) decided by a two-thirds vote. In both countries, the party proportions are preserved so that the likelihood of confrontation is remote. The Finnish Eduskunta elects somewhat less than a quarter of its members to a Grand Committee, but they still retain their position in the full assembly. The Grand Committee reviews all legislative proposals, but with scrutiny powers only, since the views of the whole Eduskunta finally prevail.

The modest end-point of second chambers in Scandinavia should not obscure one relevant fact: the organisation of an assembly into two or more operating parts may be the best way for assemblies to preserve a 'zone of independence', especially in rule-making functions, which is not incompatible with majority party rule. It is, in fact, an extension of the idea of 'internal checks' based on an increased differentiation.

Communications
One way of assessing the political function of assemblies is to regard them as devices for providing and passing on information which will form the basis of decisions reached in other parts of the political system. Indeed, the more one emphasises the communication function of assemblies, the less one is inclined to see them as decision-making organs at all. This view applies with force to unified systems and to all the functions we have considered so far: where the elective function has increasingly shifted to the

electorate, and rule-making has become an aspect of majority party power, as has the personnel function in unified systems because of common membership; assemblies are uniquely suited to communication rather than to detailed control.

Various writers have expressed the importance of communication in different ways. Dahl, speaking of Britain, found that Parliament is not a site '. . . for encounters, so much as it is a forum from which to influence the next election.'[7] Or as Blondel stated, more generally: 'The primary function of assemblies is one of communication between inputs and outputs, as well as one of feedback from outputs on to inputs.' The most he would allow for traditional rule-making is a 'streamlining' of inputs or a 'clarification of demands, which entails as its by-product a rather greater publicity given to these demands'.[8] European assemblies can be seen as 'nodal points' of communication: the meeting-place of a number of routes issuing from and returning to the electorate, but others as well which link the parties, organised interests, and the government.

Another associated contribution which assemblies make to the political system is to give the seal of legitimacy to those groupings whose activities relate to the assembly – government and party. And this effect applies even if its functions are performed quite passively. The legitimising power of parliaments is well-shown in the lip-service paid to them by dictatorships. But unless an assembly does have a *potential* for active control – beyond the passive function of a downwards communication – it is unlikely either to be able in the long term to maintain respect for itself or to act as a legitimising prop for political rulers and contestants.

It is clear that there is no 'pure' communication function, that it is more a bundle of functions, a resultant of others. Direct comparison of assembly performance in this respect is therefore difficult. Assemblies not only develop individual styles, there is also the probability that no two assemblies, even in unified systems, handle the communication function in the same way. Whatever the particular content, it will be an index of performance for the political system as a whole, and failure in communication can lead to a rapid decline in effectiveness throughout. The British system scores highly in being able at times to achieve a 'sense of occasion' in the momentous 'great debate' which has an immediate impact on the nation. It is argued that multi-party systems in contrast, are necessarily more muffled in their effect, and that they become inward-looking since they must concentrate primarily on the give-and-take of coalition government. But it would be rash to regard the British Parliament as superior just for that reason. The natural concomitant of a multi-party system is that the assembly parties have more power to make fundamental decisions. Answers to the questions: 'Which parties will be in the new government?', 'Will this controversial measure be carried?', 'Will the government fall?', all result in immediate and effective communication, and an informed electorate; the occasional 'great debate' may only be a partial compensation.

Even on a more subdued level, the Swedish style of legislation, with the particular attention given to inputs, is likely to draw in a cross-section of opinion only on the fringe of political activity. Again, the Swiss use of the referendum offers a direct means of communication which is often only weakly performed by the parties in exclusively representative systems. An alternative argument is that the sharp dualisms encouraged by the British dichotomy of Government and Opposition (in emphasis, if not in content) are at times counterproductive. The 'informed and rationally-active citizen' can deal with the ploys and counter-ploys involved, but the overall effect on the electorate may simply be confusing, even alienating. The 'adversary style' of British politics possibly owes much to the traditions of the House of Commons which itself verges on a gladiatorial style in the confrontation between the leaders of the major opposing parties, and this cultivated polarisation may give a false impression as to the real alignments in British politics.

The development, since 1979, of the House of Commons select committees in Britain may work against that tendency, but the media have become a significant intervening variable. Rather than competing with Parliament, and, however, thus challenging its rendering of the communications function, they should be seen almost as being drawn into the parliamentary process itself.

If this emphasis on the positive role that public communication can play in promoting and popularising the work of assemblies seems over optimistic, the effectiveness of assemblies in more detailed aspects of communications should not be undervalued. The political homogeneity of single-party government gives the members of the majority party the chance of securing the government's undivided attention. For all unified systems, a key aspect of communication is in the contact of party and ministers; it is in the party committees that rank-and-file views can be forcibly expressed to ministers, rather than in the open assembly. For good reasons this type of communication receives minimal publicity, and the same type of process is evident in the coalition committees of multi-party government. This semi-private communication functions as a feedback to government, and is complementary to the public side of assembly transactions. The criticism of public debate is that the proceedings are followed by relatively few, but this objection misses the nature of most political communication: it is rarely direct in the first instance; to begin with, messages are passed horizontally – that is, between élites – and only later do they move vertically, to the general public. In this sense, assemblies are not 'popular', but firmly élitist in their make-up.

All that we have said does not point to a general parliamentary decline. This is not to say that assemblies are powerful in their own right, but indispensable as 'sites' available to all active political participants; that they are élitist is inevitable, since this élitism is a major characteristic of liberal democracy, but the parliamentary system functions to prevent a single unified élite from emerging.

Notes and references

1. For a representative early view, see Sir Henry Maine, *Popular Government*, 1885.
2. C. B. Macpherson, *The Real World of Democracy*, Clarendon Press, 1966, p. 35. 'There was nothing necessarily democratic about the responsible party system ... The job of the competitive party system was to uphold the competitive market society, by keeping the government responsive to the shifting majority of those who were running the market society.' p. 9.
3. P. M. Williams, *The French Parliament: 1958–67*, George Allen and Unwin, 1968, p. 57.
4. J. Blondel, *An Introduction to Comparative Government*, p. 362.
5. See, G. Drewry (ed.), *The New Select Committees*, Oxford University Press, 1985.
6. In the words of Michel Debré, the upper house was to be, '... a Senate whose principal role is to support the government in case of need.' Quoted by P. M. Williams, op. cit., p. 29.
7. R. A. Dahl (ed.), *Political Opposition in Western Democracies*, New Haven: Yale University Press, 1966, p. 339.
8. J. Blondel, op. cit., pp. 321 and 325.

Additional references

D. Arter, *The Nordic Parliaments: A Comparative Analysis*, Butterworth, 1983.
K. Bradshaw and D. Pring, *Parliament and Congress*, Quartet Books, 1973.
D. Coombes and S. Walkland (eds.), *Parliaments and Economic Affairs*, Heinemann/Policy Studies Institute, 1980.
P. Furlong, *The Italian Parliament*, Butterworth, 1983.
A. Grosser, 'The Evolution of European Parliaments', in M. Dogan and R. Rose (eds.), *European Politics*, Macmillan, 1971.
H. Hirsch and D. Hancock (eds.), *Comparative Legislative Systems*, Glencoe: The Free Press, 1972.
Inter-Parliamentary Union, *Parliaments of the World: A Comparative Reference Compendium*, Gower, 1986 (2 volumes).
J. Lees and M. Shaw (eds.), *Committees in Legislatures: A Comparative Analysis*, Durham, North Carolina: Duke University Press, 1979.
G. Loewenberg, *Modern Parliaments – Change or Decline?*, Princeton University Press, 1966.

G. Loewenberg and S. C. Patterson, *Comparing Legislatures*, Little, Brown, 1979.

M. Mezey, *Comparative Legislatures*, Durham, North Carolina: Duke University Press, 1979.

J. P. Morgan, *The House of Lords and the Labour Government, 1964–1970*, Oxford University Press, 1975.

P. Norton, *The Commons in Perspective*, Oxford: Martin Robertson, 1981.

P. Norton (ed.), *Parliament in the 1980s*, Basil Blackwell, 1985.

A. Petrie, *The French National Assembly in the Fifth Republic*, Butterworth, 1983.

N. Polsby, 'Legislatures' in F. Greenstein and N. Polsby (eds.), *The Handbook of Political Science*, Volume Five, Reading, Massachusetts: Addison-Wesley, 1975.

S. A. Walkland, 'The Politics of Parliamentary Reform', *Parliamentary Affairs*, Spring 1976.

S. A. Walkland and M. Ryle (eds.), *The Commons in the Seventies*, Martin Robertson, 1977.

K. C. Wheare, *Legislatures*, Oxford University Press, 1968.

8   Executive Power

Political leadership
All governments are concerned to meet two widely different requirements: to provide for efficient administration and the need to secure political direction. Just how these two requirements are fulfilled, and combined, will result in a distinctive government form. The solutions favoured in Western Europe follow a similar pattern: parliamentary systems to give political direction, and a 'constitutional bureaucracy' to provide efficient administration – a term which we examine in the following section. A parliamentary form results in a cabinet system of government which supplies a *general* political leadership; at the same time it sets up a number of *specialised* leadership positions, also of a political nature, through a wide range of ministerial appointments. The doctrines of collective and individual ministerial responsibility incorporate both forms of political leadership; whilst they are analytically and often in practice distinct, they are exercised by the same group of party politicians in power.

The alternative, a non-parliamentary one, is to rely solely on a general political leadership, in which case leaders may or may not come to power by democratic means. We can take three representative examples. Thus the president of the United States exercises all the general leadership functions himself; the heads of the various departments of state, his nominees, are responsible to him alone, and the separation of powers operates to make them non-political in origin in that they are not recruited from Congress; their status in presidential cabinets in the final resort is only advisory. General Franco, the Caudillo of Spain, was the only source of political authority; his governing ministers consisted of non-political technocrats along with army officers, and they were responsible to him alone. In the Soviet Union, the presidium of the Communist Party supplies a permanent collective leadership – though this can be usurped by one man – whilst the Council of Ministers has virtually no collective functions and individual ministers have only a technical competence. In their different ways, all three types of government show a greater concentration of political leadership than in parliamentary systems, and none of them enforces collective or individual responsibility to an assembly.

The evolution of the general and specialised political functions in parliamentary systems has resulted in a broad band of leadership roles which span the administrative system, and this structure has led to the necessity of determining a line of demarcation between political oversight and executive administration. But in practice the division is blurred. The sharp dichotomy between the apolitical civil servant and the political minister cannot always be maintained. That is evident in the appointment of 'technocratic' figures, often civil servants, to head ministries. More significant is the practice of finding key places in sensitive departments for top-ranking civil servants known to be sympathetic to an incoming government, or bringing in people outside of the civil service entirely to take up positions within a department working alongside the permanent officials. Even those who regard the civil service as politically neutral would nevertheless see its function in terms of securing the continuity of the state, and at times that role must imply a basic political competence. One has to admit that the distinction between politics and 'pure' administration must break down in practice. The intimate relationship between political leadership and the highest rungs of the administration means that there is a constant interchange between the two, and the problem of all governments is to retain a firm hold on the political reins.

We can usefully mention one approach to this problem of securing political primacy which, in its broad sweep, provides a basis for comparison, namely the theory of 'parallel hierarchies'. It involves creating a *second* bureaucratic hierarchy, exclusively at the service of the political leaders so that they can control the activities of the administration; at the logical extreme, it requires that for every unit and level of administration there should be a parallel control section, with a comparable level of expertise but not duplicating the routine administrative tasks. The reason for its leading importance in communist administrative thinking has been that the parallel hierarchy would serve to underpin the primacy of the party. Party control is mandatory at all levels and this approach is one way of ensuring that it remains a reality. But such a solution requires a large outlay of resources and manpower, and that is only feasible if the party is assured of permanent power. The possibility of frequent government alternation in western systems makes control impracticable on this scale, although the institution of 'ministerial heads' is similar in principle. Indeed, what is remarkable about these systems is that the party, as a *national organisation*, contributes very little to the maintenance of political leadership once its leaders gain power. The party leaders not only experience a loosening of party control over their actions once they attain office, but the party also relies on this small band of men to secure political leadership without any other precaution or intervention. The party itself does not come to power, only its government representatives.

Yet is is possible to construct a model of liberal democratic politics in which this did happen. It would involve, for instance, the party machine supplanting the policy-making functions of the entire higher civil service and some of the administrative tasks as well; only the lower reaches of the administration would be left intact. A 'superimposed' hierarchy, rather than a parallel one, could result.

It is in the objections to such an arrangement that one appreciates the basis of the system that has evolved. Firstly, it is clear that the frequency of changes in the party complexion of government could lead to a disruption of policy output and a lowering of administrative efficiency. Secondly, it can be argued that the quality of administrative expertise would suffer (although this reservation assumes that the capability of party machines remained at their present level). Thirdly, there is the possibility that an unmitigated spoils system would result, that connections would prevail over merit; this is not a necessary consequence if the party machine were already organised on a merit-hierarchy basis. Finally, it can be said that the cabinet system of government achieves the same effect as a superimposed hierarchy, but in a much more economical way: it is sufficient if the controlling government positions are taken over by the party, since the administrative machine is geared to political control exercised in such a fashion.

One can also refer to a number of factors which serve to strengthen this type of political leadership. The cabinet itself can be regarded as an insulative device. It is here that the general leadership functions are preserved, and it is in the cabinet that the performance of specialised leadership comes under scrutiny; political ministers in the cabinet are 'among themselves', and high-level decisions are taken with the widest considerations of government and party benefit in mind without the direct influence of the permanent administrators being apparent. Where coalition government is the rule, the cabinet is not a protection against the various party pressures, but in the case of single-party government the cabinet system ensures a partial insulation from both party and administration.

The presence of a party dominant in government for long periods does not necessarily result in strong political leadership vis-à-vis the administration, as the example of the Christian

Democrats in Italy shows. Although the bureaucracy is 'colonised' by the permanent governing party, the client relationship favours the party and its affiliates as a whole, not just the national political leadership. A large number of related groups enjoy a special relationship to government power, even showing their influence in the composition of the bureaucracy. This accommodation to a range of party interests means that the national leadership is in competition with its own party. A remedy would be a general party reform, centralised and cadre-oriented rather than dispersed and mass-based. Yet to do this could weaken the party's attractions, and its first priority is to maintain its hold on power at elections.

Two administrative devices can be mentioned which have the effect of concentrating policy functions within the political leadership. One is to make a clear distinction between the policy functions of departments and their 'agency' functions. In principle, this division is a clear-cut distinction, yet only in Sweden is it carried through to the extent that most ministries are concerned solely with policy formulation and oversight, whilst numerous agencies and boards are responsible for detailed administration. But this system does not supply any guarantees: agencies can become very independent and evolve their own policies, and within the ministry the political heads are still subject to the direct influence of the permanent administrator.

It is precisely to avoid this direct influence that the ministerial *cabinet* operates in France. It has the character of a superimposed hierarchy in miniature: the minister's *cabinet* consists of up to a dozen members appointed by an incoming minister, each with a specific function, partly political and partly administrative. They exercise a collective advisory function to the minister in respect of policy formulation, departmental supervision, and coordination of the work of the ministry with other departments. One has to bear in mind that French ministries lack the powerful unifying influence of the permanent secretary in control of British government departments, so that the unification is largely supplied by the *cabinet*. In practice, the staff of the *cabinet* is mainly recruited from the civil service, especially the *grand corps*, so that the political role of the official is not necessarily weakened. However, it may be the case that their freedom from departmental loyalties and their greater personal commitment to the minister does make a contribution to political supremacy exercised by the minister.

Ultimately, the question of political leadership has to be evaluated by reference to the chief office holder, the prime minister or equivalent. It is the leader of the government who is widely regarded as providing the mainspring for political initiative, implementing party policy by settling priorities, selecting and dismissing individual ministers. There is no doubt that the liberal democracies of Western Europe all provide maximum scope for such a leader to emerge on a constitutional level, but the political conditions have to be favourable as well: unstable and broadly-based coalitions are unlikely to allow a prime minister more than a coordinating role, and typically strong leaders have emerged where one party has been in undisputed control and where the leader has been able to ignore or suppress dissident factions within the party. Candidates for the appellation of 'strong leadership' would include Adenauer in West Germany, Kreisky in Austria, Thatcher in Britain, and Mitterrand in France – although the presidential 'injection' complicates the French case. However, the important point to note is that such leadership is associated with a particular person at a particular time rather than being a feature of the system. We saw earlier that in West Germany the idea of 'chancellor democracy' was a transient phase as is the term 'prime ministerial government' applied to Britain. In other words, parliamentary systems – as opposed to presidential ones – do not favour the institutionalisation of strong, personal leadership. One might also query the extent to which a prime minister actually does provide a pervading influence over policy decisions save in exceptional circumstances. The apparently 'strong' leader undoubtedly has that reputation, but the concentration on 'style' may be misleading since it may have little to do with the actual content of decision making. Indeed, the greatest virtue of a leader from the point of view of the party may well reside in electoral appeal, and the all-powerful reputation of the leader has to be seen as much in terms of electoral image as in executive content. Furthermore, a prime minister frequently lacks the detailed knowledge to which departmental ministers have access when decisions have to be made, and the lack of expertise can be a decided handicap in asserting authority. One remedy is to build up a 'department' solely at the disposal of the prime minister which effectively shadows the work of the most important ministries and hence gives the prime minister specialist backing at cabinet level. Thus the West German *Kanzleramt* has become an important adjunct to the chancellor. In Britain, the Prime Minister's Office has a similar function; although on a much-reduced scale and more in the nature of personal advisers, there is no inherent reason why it could not become a full-blown department, and – once firmly established – such a super-ministry could permanently enhance the power of any future prime minister.

The general problem for parliamentary systems is to ensure that political control is maintained, but there is always the inherent possibility of a 'reverse osmosis' – that the values and aims of the bureaucracy will infect the political leadership. This tendency will be shown in the readiness of ministers to accept the advice of the permanent officials rather than that of the party, to put forward departmental policies rather than party ones, or at least seriously to modify the content of the latter. The question of how a bureaucracy can come to have its own 'values' is one which we consider in a succeeding section on 'administrative élites'; first, the historical context of a civil service should be taken into account.

Constitutional bureaucracy

It is through its historical evolution that the status and role of a country's administrative personnel can best be appreciated. The key development in western societies has been termed the 'depersonalisation' of the state. The changing nature of state power, away from the personal authority of a particular ruler towards the exercise of an abstract and 'rational-legal' authority, was seen by Max Weber as one of the typical features of capitalist society, one which replaced the authority of traditional and charismatic rulers. It was in the implementation of this rational-legal power that, according to Weber, a bureaucracy came into its own as the one perfectly rational instrument of government.

For Britain in particular we can say that this evolution led at a fairly early date to the emergence of a 'constitutional bureaucracy'. As the idea of the circulation or alternation of governments became an integral part of the liberal democratic order, so as a corollary there came about a virtual separation of an important part of the government machine: 'From being one strand in the unified executive, the civil service had become a distinct entity, at the service of each successive cabinet.'[1] This status implied a permanence for the skilled administrators, but it also meant that they had to be removed from the political arena as a substantive requirement for their continued employment. It is reasonable to say that the idea of a constitutional bureaucracy which this removal caused is a common end-product for the European democracies, whatever particular route was followed. The important differences that still exist derive from the ways in which the civil service became a 'distinct entity' in government. The most notable contrast is, in fact, between Britain and most of the other states in Western Europe.

There are two reasons which we can put forward for the different pattern of British central administration, and each has left is own stamp. One lies in the development of public law, the other in the *phasing* of constitutional development. Britain was outside the European mainstream in not participating in the rediscovery of Roman Law; this divergence was due in part to the fact that the rediscovery from the sixteenth century onwards coincided with the emergence of absolute monarchies in many European states, and Roman Law provided the legal doctrines which could be used to bolster up absolutist claims. And the use of one type of legal system also came to colour administrative styles: 'There are parallels between Roman and modern European administrative traditions, and Roman Law has exerted a great influence on continental jurists and is the fundamental European tradition.'[2]

The development of modern absolutist states required a high degree of centralisation which could only be operated by expert administrators, and with the growth of trade and industry, active government intervention necessitated the specialisation of administrative services. By the mid-eighteenth century these administrative techniques had been well-developed in Prussia; her rationalised administrative system, developed by Freiherr vom Stein, was complementary to her military strength and quickly compensated for her late entry as a European power. In France, Napoleon's contribution was of greater import because he created a blueprint which could be, and was, run off for many other states. The Napoleonic system harked back to the Roman system of administration in various ways: the provision of a systematic legal code, the organisation of central government along functional lines, the insistence on employing skilled personnel of proven ability. In many ways he reinforced the royal administrative system he inherited: the idea of technical training for specialist administrators, and the prefectoral system had much in common with that of the former royal *intendants*.

Besides developing quite dissimilar legal doctrines, Britain took a different line in her constitutional development. First there was the much earlier establishment of constitutional government than elsewhere. Subramaniam has indicated the development of responsible government in Britain as emerging in distinct phases: there was a two-step climb from original absolutist rule to the fully democratic order – the critical intervening phase was the rule by a wealthy oligarchy; in contrast, other European states took a single step only from absolutism to democracy: 'When Britain settled for government by enlightened gentlemen of means, the leading states of Europe evolved into absolute monarchies and developed an efficient modern government machine to make it effective.'[3] This build-up of a powerful state bureaucracy was then carried straight over into the fully democratic era. Even though some states developed wealthy oligarchies at a later date, the administrative framework was by then fully established.

Thus it was the timing of the intervening period which had a decisive influence on the nature of the British civil service, especially as it coincided with a re-awakening of the generalist ideal in education. Both the nature of government and the implanting of a liberal educational tradition were sufficient to impede the growth of a specialist civil service, and this feature has remained as a permanent influence on the nature of the higher civil service in Britain, favouring the 'generalist' rather than the 'specialist' – a contrast we shall examine shortly.

The rather natural growth of the British system, its lack of purposive modelling at least until the latter part of the nineteenth century, made changes consequent upon immediate needs. This gradualism enables us to detail the steps by which the civil service came to be depoliticised. It was a halting process, in the nature of successive approximations, and necessarily so, since the parallel establishment of the principle of ministerial responsibility was equally long drawn-out. In the end, the British version of constitutional bureaucracy was clear: there was a sharp distinction between two types of state service. State servants were either political (hence removable) or civil (permanent as long as they remained non-political). In the phase of transition each individual office-holder had to be assessed; would he serve the incoming government as loyally as he had the last?

The nature of the cut-off finally arrived at left no room for a spoils system as it did in the United States where the desire for the spoils of office ensured that a large number of otherwise 'non-political' appointments were available to a victorious party. Jacksonian democracy, with its popularisation of the spoils system, can be contrasted with European experience in that the United States reached a fully participatory system much earlier. Parris, in answering the question why no spoils system came about in Britian, advanced a number of reasons of which perhaps the most important was the nature of the dominant value system: 'Office was regarded as something closely akin to freehold property. To deprive a man of it seemed only less shocking than to deprive him of goods or land.'[4] Here we see values which were fundamentally opposed to achievement-orientated American society.

Continental practice emerged as not all that different from the British, but for rather different reasons. The permanent nature of absolutist, or at least non-responsible government, made wholesale changes in administrative personnel less likely from the start. A greater reliance on expertise at all levels meant that people would enter the state service as a career for which they had often had specific training in advance. The claim of the civil servant to a permanent post did require of him a special loyalty to the state, but in return he enjoyed a high status in society. There was an additional twist arising from the late development of responsible, parliamentary government: the lack of responsibility meant that there was no good reason for excluding civil servants from top ministerial appointments; indeed, their skill and experience were an added recommendation. We have seen earlier that it was common practice throughout the nineteenth century to appoint civil servants as ministers; theirs was not so much an acknowledged political function as a bureaucratisation of politics – a tradition that lies not far from the surface and which naturally comes into its own again whenever parliamentary government shows signs of faltering. Such discontinuities of the parliamentary system have not affected Britain in modern times, and the easy conclusion to draw is that a completely non-political service shows the virtues of British government stability to be rewarded.

This idea can be challenged. Anyway, it is agreed that in those West European countries where leading civil servants do have some political function, the situation could never lead to a spoils system – all European bureacracies are too well-protected for that to happen. The British view is that absolute loyalty can be maintained on the basis of absolute neutrality – as a statement of faith on the part of the civil servant. That view rather slurs over the distinction between a passive loyalty and an active commitment. If British parties had less common ground, in particular if the Labour Party had sought to make 'revolutionary' changes, then doubtless ideas of civil service neutrality would have been modified. Other countries acknowledge that their senior servants do have political views, and their services are made use of accordingly, even if this entails a switching-around of top-level administrators after a change in government. Even in Britain there is a growing tendency to accept the role of 'political advisers' to ministers, although the civil service would resist the making of appointments of a political character within the hierarchy of established officials.

Ferrel Heady contrasted the British and American administrative systems with the majority of those in Europe; the former he saw as being firmly in the 'civic culture' tradition, the main traits of which he regarded as the effects of 'the gradualist pattern of political development on public administration', and as a result: '. . . the administrative system was also able to shape feature by feature in a way that reflected political changes and was consonant with them.

Political and administrative adaptations were concurrent and fairly well-balanced, but the political theme was dominant.'[5] This view, that the predominance of the political element early on made civil services more dependent on social development is echoed by Hans Daalder with particular reference to the possibilities of party control over bureaucracy: 'The British civil service was from the outset below party; the French and German bureaucracies were to a very real extent above it.'[6] The power of such bureaucracies meant that when party government did come the political function of the bureaucracy continued.

It is this question of political predominance which Heady regarded as a cardinal difference between the civic culture tradition and continental bureaucracies cast in the Weberian form. But as David Coombes has pointed out, in terms of objectivity, impartiality, and discretion, 'The standards of the British civil service have been far closer to the classical type of career service than those of its Continental counterparts.'[7] One unfortunate consequence of taking a 'classic' view of *any* bureaucracy is the tendency to play down the links which civil servants have with the rest of society. The view that they can be insulated from social life or become what Michel Crozier termed 'closed systems of social action' is only true for limited periods. Such a role as that of an independent agent of social and political renewal is also likely to be transient. The more permanent position is that of an élite which reflects the distribution of power in wider society.

Administrative élites

Constitutional bureaucracies in the European tradition conform to a similar pattern in the way a civil service is run. A first requirement is that the conditions of service should be standard throughout. Within these conditions, uniformity is best ensured where recruitment is centrally organised, and quite separate from the individual ministries. Hiring and firing at will is unthinkable, and promotion according to personal whim scarcely less so. Successful candidates are chosen on merit alone, and once appointed at a relatively early age, there is little likelihood that they will ever be dismissed. Promotion strikes a balance between merit and seniority. In return for this favourable treatment civil servants are expected to abide by the formal rules and procedures, and never to challenge (or undermine) the political authority. These conditions of service dovetail with Weber's itemised definition of bureaucracy,[8] and the process of bureaucratisation since the nineteenth century represents the successful imposition of those terms of service. The bureaucracy becomes a 'closed', career service from which 'outsiders' are excluded, and an administrative élite runs the state machine.

Before we look at the social and political implications of this élite, we should appreciate the importance of individual variations which make for differences in the type of bureaucracy which emerges. These variations occur in several ways: the degree of centralisation, the extent of competitive recruitment, the nature of training, and the forms of post-entry specialisation all have an effect.

Britain has a highly-unified service, and is in almost every respect fully centralised. This homogeneity applies to the method of recruitment, to Treasury control, and to the relative lack of 'field' or regional deconcentration. A leading contrast is with the civil service in a federal state where the federal service will be quite small in comparison with the state services, each of which will be responsible for its own recruitment. Thus each West German Land is directly responsible for its own civil servants, a term which also includes teachers and judges, and well over 80 per cent of public administration personnel (that is, excluding those engaged in public enterprise) are employed by the Land and local authorities. However, overall conditions are fixed by federal law, and strong trade unions ensure that none of the Länder gets out of line in respect of remuneration and grading. The dispersion necessary in a federal state is an important component of European 'administrative' federalism which we look at in the following chapter; in the unitary states, the civil service is never broken up in this way, but only geographically dispersed for administrative convenience. Only a small proportion of the French civil service is located in Paris, the majority dispersed to the departments. This geographical dispersion possibly makes for a greater independence of the individual ministries rather than for the local units.

The Swedish alternative, as already indicated, does give subordinate units greater independence. Administration is in the hands of numerous agencies, and their independence from the parent ministry is further underlined by the fact that recruitment is not centrally organised, though other conditions of service are laid down nationally. Decentralised recruitment can work two ways: it can lead to an undesirable local nepotism at its worst, but at best it can lead to a more open type of recruitment, possibly with less social bias. Sweden perhaps accords to this latter type, and Italy to the former.

The way in which people enter the civil service varies considerably from one country to another: according to whether it is by means of competitive selection or by the possession of prior qualifications, and allied to this, whether provisions are made for training, preceding formal entry, post-entry, or not at all. Sweden relies on qualification only, with little specific training except in the trading agencies. In Italy, entry is competitive with no prior or post-entry training. British entry is highly competitive, but with less developed in-service training as yet. The German system has a developed scheme of advanced pre-entry training, but non-competitive entry. And France operates in reverse – intensive post-entry training with highly competitive entry. From this variety, it is doubtful if any sure conclusion could be drawn, but the really fundamental similarity is the tie-in of civil service recruitment with the system of higher education for all countries, and an examination of the relationship to education helps to explain some of the variations.

In neither Sweden nor Germany is competitive entry a feature, but in both countries there is a tradition of strong government influence on the content of university training. For the majority of German students the final educational qualification is the 'state examination' in the relevant faculty. In effect, this is a passport enabling them to enter state service in a capacity determined by their specialism. It is not vocational training, but vocationally-relevant, with the needs of government influencing the content of the course. The same is true for Sweden, especially in relation to university law courses, and we shall see that this is still the prime source of recruitment for the majority of services. The German emphasis on pre-entry training is, however, probably unique. Typically, and especially for those seeking a legal qualification for state service, a first state examination is followed by an extended period of pre-entry, practical training lasting for three or more years. In this time the *Referendar* (probationer) spends some time in each of a number of administrative departments and in the courts. Finally, he takes his second state examination, and, if successful, becomes an established civil servant. The ambit of such training is wide for it takes in future high officials in federal and state service, the judiciary, local government and the legal profession itself. Chapman drew attention to the effects: 'This common background produces a closely knit and cohesive governing cadre with ramifications in all fields of public life ... In most other countries it would be unbelievable to find people capable of going through this training process working in local government.'[9]

The contrast with the French system is striking, all the more so when one considers that at least for the senior civil servants just as cohesive a governing cadre emerges. The relationship of the state to the universities is markedly different. We can say in fact that the state does not place a reliance on them; instead it has built up its own parallel educational system which in some fields is more highly regarded than what can be offered outside. One should distinguish here between those candidates who will finally be placed in one of the most important of the technical corps and those who will join the general administrative corps. The former will normally qualify first by winning a place in fierce competition to an institution such as the *Ecole Polytechnique* – this as an alternative to university entrance which is *not* competitive. From there, if the successful student wishes to have a career in the state service, he will go to one of the specialised colleges associated with particular technical corps as a form of postgraduate training before receiving his first posting. Thus the decision to enter state service usually has to be taken in the final years at school, but such is the reputation of, say, the *Ecole Polytechnique* that a 'polytechnician' can always switch on completion of his training to private industry – and be welcomed as a valued acquisition. The French term, *pantouflage*, neatly expresses the facility with which a civil servant can safely 'parachute' to a leading post in the private sector.

Parallel with the great technical schools is the *Ecole Nationale d'Administration* (ENA), providing an in-service training for those who have already graduated at a university in law, economics, or politics. Highly-competitive entry requires additional, specialised preparation at one of the Institutes of Political Science attached to the universities. The ENA course itself is once again competitive, and those who pass out near the top have the pick of which of the *grand corps* they will enter. Thus the administrative élite, whether from the ENA or the technical schools, is based on intellectual excellence over a broad range of disciplines.

In Britain, the complete divorce that existed between the needs of state administration and what the universities provided, led to the university traditions themselves coming to dominate the civil service, with particular emphasis on an education in the humanities. The generalist ideal assumes that academic background prior to entry is irrelevant to administrative arts, but that general excellence is ensured by competitive entry. Even though the post-Fulton reforms weakened the generalist–specialist dichotomy that runs through the service, the fact that this problem has not emerged in other European countries is worth noting.

The continental equivalent to the British generalist is the civil servant who has had a legal training, for he will normally be found near the top of the administrative hierarchy. But this will not be because of the 'general' qualities which a degree in law will foster in him, rather it is that as an administrator he is expected to be well-versed in law as one of the tools of his trade. Thus the basic difference between a judge and a legal-administrator is that one applies the law in the course of litigation and the other applies it in the course of his administrative duties – hence the common training which they undergo in several countries. It is the state service which dominates the legal profession rather than the other way round: in Sweden, just under two-thirds of the legal profession are employed by the state, either as judges or administrators, and within the service the jurists heavily outnumber all other groups. But the importance of a legal training in Scandinavian and other countries does not mean that those who are technically qualified are thereby downgraded as 'mere' specialists, and we have noted the high status of the technical corps in France.

How significant are these differences? They may result in differences of technical competence, but against this one has to bear in mind the different administrative traditions of various countries: administrative legalism would be foreign to the British approach as would the British generalist be at sea in German administration. The real issue is the *social* function and origin of the administrative élite. Dahrendorf made this comparison: 'In principle, the law faculties of German universities accomplish for German society what the exclusive Public Schools do for the English, and the *grandes écoles* for the French. In them an élite receives its training.'[10] There is then a 'functional equivalence' between them, but the similarity does not stop there. Common to all the West European states has been the close connection between wealth, education, and administrative power; the line which can be drawn in Britain from the public schools, through the older universities, to the generalist administrators – at least until the very recent past – simply finds a different formula in other countries. Entry based on 'merit' only highlights differences in educational opportunity, and a civil service geared to a university training has always discriminated in favour of the middle class.

The discrimination was not entirely accidental, and this fact becomes apparent when one looks back to the nineteenth century: the large-scale reforms – including the merit system of open competition – did not really alter the balance which favoured the privileged, and were not intended to do so. At the time of the Northcote-Trevelyan reforms in England, Gladstone defended the introduction of open competition on the grounds that the new method, '. . . would not entail a lowering of social standards in the service – a substitution of *parvenus* for "gentlemen" – but would rather "strengthen and multipy the ties between the higher classes and the possession of administrative power".' Asa Briggs commented, 'The civil service was to be thrown open not to the "raw" middle classes but to the new educational élite of the public schools and universities . . . social stratification was to remain.'[11] This view of the social function of the civil service found a contemporary echo in France: 'The higher classes, as they call themselves, are obliged to acknowledge the right of the majority, and they can only maintain their political dominance by invoking the right of the most capable . . . The tide of democracy must encounter a second line of defence . . . of superior qualities whose prestige cannot be gainsaid.'[12]

The bias has not been eliminated with the passing of the years, only the middle class is no longer 'raw'. Sweden may be regarded as one of the more socially-progressive of the European states, yet the composition of the civil service means that the highest social group with only 5 per cent of the population supplies some 50 per cent of the senior officials.

Obviously changes are taking place. In Britain, with the abolition (in 1971) of the three traditional classes – administrative, executive and clerical – each linked to a certain educational stardard increased fluidity to a limited extent; in the past, inter-class mobility was limited since each class had its own career structure. The new system, at least in theory, did not make lower, formal educational attainments an absolute bar. But the willingness to make reforms does not ensure their success. The French ENA was set up in 1945 partly to end the nepotism of individual corps recruitment and also to make the intake more socially representative. Yet students of a direct working-class origin are still a rarity. A certain social narrowness accompanies the schools' reputation for fostering 'meritocratic' ability, and effectively provides a short cut to high office for the middle class. To a lesser extent the same is true for the technical schools: the French civil service is firmly rooted in the Parisian middle class.

The social élitism is enhanced by the amount of inbreeding which takes place. Often the family traditions show a constancy for a considerable period, thus maintaining the social composition of the service intact. Dahrendorf records the 'overwhelming' fact that, 'In Imperial Germany, the Weimar Republic, and the Federal Republic about one half of all civil servants were recruited from the families of civil servants. This is the real inner continuity of German officialdom.'[13] Similarly, up to a third of the successful candidates to the ENA are the sons of higher officials, and a greater proportion if one includes all grades of public official.

Whilst the social composition of many services is not at all representative of their communities, the bias is passive and the general quality of the services is not open to dispute. This contrasts with the situation in Italy, still in the stage of positive discrimination where offices in various ministries appear to be populated largely by individuals coming from a particular province or a particular private group. The malaise of 'job colonisation' goes deeper. Lack of respect for Italian officials is often apparently confirmed by the number of scandals involving civil servants. The aspiring candidate sees the security offered by state service as the summit of his ambition; lacking is a further sense of public service: his authority is for use against a disrespectful public. Almond and Verba showed the wide range of attitudes towards bureaucracy; whilst the overwhelming majority of British respondents believed they would receive fair treatment from civil servants, and almost two-thirds of the West German sample thought so too, barely half of the Italians thought that impartiality was likely.[14]

Quite opposed views are held about the *political* power of civil servants. The terms on which a constitutional bureaucracy was established in the first place seem to exclude the overt use of political power. In Britain, the civil servant is regarded as a political cypher, and where civil servants are admitted to be at all influential, this ability is applied to their individual characteristics rather than to the nature of bureaucracy. At the other extreme, Max Weber advanced the view that, 'Under normal conditions the power position of a fully developed bureaucracy is always overtowering'.[15] Part of the confusion arises from the *way* an administrator treats a political problem; he does not offer a political solution but an administrative one, as Mannheim put it: 'The attempt to hide all problems under the cover of administration may be explained by the fact that the sphere of the official exists within the limits of laws already formulated. Hence the genesis or the development of law falls outside the scope of his activity.'[16] This does not at all prevent him from engaging in legislative activity or any other political decision-making, but it will not be expressed by him in these terms, and since the problems are defined administratively, an issue will inevitably be played down by him, though his power is not less for not receiving open recognition. One can go too far in this direction and build up a composite picture of the all-powerful civil servant, a 'fallacy of aggregation' in which as Parry observed, '. . . evidence of the planning powers of French officials, the policy forming opportunities of British civil servants and the independence of the old German officialdom are compounded to produce a picture of the political power of the bureaucracy as such.'[17]

We can, however, postulate four major conditions under which a bureaucracy is likely to be strong, although no one by itself will lead to an independent power position:

- if the political authorities are weak and governments are unstable;
- if the service is unified, grounded in a common pattern of recruitment and training;
- if it is socially homogeneous – though one should note here that when it is fully representative of a dominant social class, the harmony which results will not give the bureaucracy power in its own right;
- if, conscious of its corporate identity, the service can develop an autonomous sense of purpose.

It is clear that most European bureaucracies have some of these conditions in their favour, and if we add as an alternative to the first of these that the government may actually favour active intervention by civil servants, then one can appreciate that the exercise of bureaucratic power is a real eventuality. Blondel, in fact, concluded that France, '... seems a country where the possibility of "technocracy" is not remote.' He used the term 'technocracy' in regarding bureaucracies as 'managerial enterprises with an autonomous sense of purpose that sets them aside from the rule-makers', and the administrators are regarded as the 'technicians'. The French situation in the 1960s was one in which all our conditions for bureaucratic power were met. Blondel argued that the French and British bureacratic models were at the two extremes of a spectrum, and that, '... the question of managerial influence has been minimised in the UK and other Anglo-Saxon countries and maximised in France and some other Continental countries because of the relatively lower status of technicians in the managerial hierarchy of the former countries.'[18] The acceptance of a lower status depends on various factors. The 'sectional demands' of the technicians will be weakened by strong parliamentary pressures, but also where, as in Britain, the humanistic university training weakens the technical ethos. The weak substitute for this ethos, membership of a professional association, does not offer a sufficient stimulus within the public service; the influence of the technician is simply dispersed to a number of administrative agencies.

In Britain a more sceptical assessment of the influence of the civil service than that advanced by Blondel emerged in the 1970s, as political élites engaged in a policy polarisation that lacked support within the administrative élites. But the subordination of the civil service to broader, politico–cultural, and specifically party influences in Britain, was emphasised in the 1980s by Mrs Thatcher, who sought to ensure that the civil service conformed to the will of its political master. Nevertheless, the proposals for major reforms along Swedish decentralist lines floated in 1988, demonstrated not only the weak corporate position of the civil service vis-à-vis government, but also a desire to establish a strong policy-analysis role for a Whitehall-élite, a role which had been largely expropriated by party-related 'think-tanks' during the mid-1970s.

The contrast between Britain and France is marked. Unity of the technicians is bolstered by the pre-eminence of certain forms of technical training, by the solidarity of the technical corps, and by the fact that the products of this technical élitism spill over into wider society, making social control that much more difficult. And in the French circumstances these effects were multiplied by the government instability of the Fourth Republic, and by the search for administrative solutions in the Fifth. All the same, if Britain and France represent polar points with respect to the exercise of 'technocratic' power, the dissimilarities are not so pronounced when one considers only the social-class 'representative' nature of the two, and many would hold that it is the social composition of a civil service which in the end is decisive for the role which it plays in society.

Policy styles in Western Europe
What takes place within the 'black box' of the government-administrative complex – how policies are formulated and implemented – shows considerable differences in the various national political styles. Whilst both the élite social origins of the European bureaucracies and the interventionist tendencies of West European governments are comparable in the functioning of their administrative systems, the differences between them are significant.

The rise of protest politics in the later-1960s, demands for greater participation in the governmental process, and the promotion of new issues were combined with the subsequent oil-shock and depression of the 1970s; they led to theories of overloaded government and of legitimacy crisis. It was precisely the political and administrative élites which became the focus of critical attention. Since they were regarded as the key targets of increasingly vociferous interest groups, these élites were vulnerable to the new pressures. Their susceptibility stems from the relatively free means of access available in pluralist societies, and the absence of any effective protection from these pressures. This combination of more demanding Western European publics and simultaneously declining resources led to increased interest in the nature of state and governmental élites; their response to this new situation was critical to future developments. Some observers thought that the differences between them might lead to different responses to the new situation – would the Swedish state, for example, with its record of radical and innovative policy implementation, find ways of coping with these problems more successfully than states whose political and administrative élites had more reactive and piece-meal approaches to problems? Marginally divergent approaches could lead to increasingly great variations in the style and content of the West European liberal–social democracies.

Before this possibility can be established, however, it is necessary to ask a series of preliminary questions. If governing *per se* is becoming more difficult, to what extent is this problem due to the nature of the new issues themselves? Is there a general move away from bargainable, economic issues towards non-bargainable issues based on value judgements, for instance, about the importance of popular participation in its own right, or the viability of nuclear power? Does the nature of the relationship developed by government departments with interest groups depend on the origin of the interest group itself, so that a restriction of the policy-making community to socially-exclusive and mutually accommodative élites was necessary for policy-making to be at all possible? Does the successful handling of issues depend on keeping their resolution firmly within a narrow arena, such as the bureaucratic–corporate one, rather than including the representative institutions and the general public – thus cumulatively enlarging the arena within which the decision-making process takes place? Only after questions such as these have been addressed is it possible to determine whether the nature of government–administrative relations with society is significantly different in the individual West European states.

In an analysis of policy-making and implementation in West Germany, Dyer suggested that, whilst at first new issues seemed less open to resolution because they were less amenable to bargaining, the handling of the nuclear-energy issue showed that there had nevertheless been a change in policy style away from a confrontative, zero-sum approach, towards a consensual approach in which bargaining was encouraged and brought benefits. All four 'ideal-types' of policy style, which Dyer identified as useful for analysing the German policy-making and implementation process, were applicable to the nuclear-energy issue, indicating that not even the apparently most intractable of issues exclusively determined the policy style adopted. Thus, from *regulation*, that is, the authoritative imposition of policies, and *status maintenance*, a style involving only the interests of officially recognised insider-groups, both of which neglected the larger social questions, the government moved first, in the 1973–76 period, towards *activism*, that is, with an attempt to act innovatively and impose decisions on society, and then, subsequently, towards a search for *concertation* – an attempt to involve all interested pressure groups and to reach enlightened and rational solutions through a sort of interactive domestic diplomacy.[19]

This example indicates several major themes in the analysis of policy style. The first is how several styles may be relevant to one issue and how these can combine and change in salience over time. The second theme is how an initially restricted policy-making community was challenged by direct action, often of a disruptive nature, alternatively by unconventional participation in the policy process. In some instances, this development can be negative and lead to the overcrowding of the policy environment – an indecisive policy network, where diffuse interests apply a mutual veto, leading to immobilism. Yet the sometimes slow and difficult transition from authoritarian to consensual styles of policy-making and implementation may be positive in reinforcing democratic stability and promoting efficiency by breaking up narrow, self-serving coalitions.

Widening the scope of participation adds a beneficial dynamic to the policy process by weakening vested interests, and it educates a wider public in appreciating the complexity of the issues involved. The quality of policy formulation and implementation is affected by the manner in which policies are arrived at in shaping their rationality and in fashioning an optimal outcome. The benefits of broadening participation are particularly applicable to those administrative systems which have traditionally been accessible to a host of interests, yet still able to encourage the leading groups to adjust their demands on a consensual basis. Such traditions are found in the 'consensual' democracies of Scandinavia, but also in other countries where ideas of common interest and 'rationality' found institutionalised expression, such as Germany or the 'consociational' democracies of Austria, Switzerland, Belgium and the Netherlands. The establishment of *Konzertierte Aktion* in Germany in 1967, to co-ordinate the collective bargaining of major economic interests with the government's own expectations, underlined the importance of attitudes of élites towards interests in society and the management of conflict. In the German case, the explicit normative code, and the value attributed to *Sachlichkeit* (objectivity), in conjunction with the institutional dispersion of power (for instance, the federal nature of the state, reflected in the parties as well as in the formal state machinery, the inevitability of coalition government, the strength of associationalism in German civil society) is reflected in political and administrative behaviour. These attitudes can even restrict the impact of neo-liberal change which many forecast as a consequence of the return of a conservative government in 1982.

More authoritative decision-making styles may also cope with the new conditions. For example, the possibly more autocratic French system of policy-making and implementation managed to cope with rising popular demands since it was clear that infringement of the state's autonomy would not be tolerated. In contrast, the British system, unable to establish a political or cultural basis for mutual adaptation, proved both too accessible and too conflictual, encouraging inflation and the aggravation of social tensions. The necessity for British interest groups and the public at large to adjust their expectations may have been achieved through the rhetoric and actions of successive Thatcher-led governments, simply because a mutually-adjusting social democratic consensus was not available.

Heisler and Kvavik[20] have followed the 'optimistic' consensus approach expressed in the ideas of a 'virtuous circle' and widening participation. According to their thesis, the liberal democracies of Western Europe have developed complex institutional arrange-ments of consultation between the political-administrative élites and interest groups so that, in effect, democratic participation in all these pluralist societies far from being restricted to electoral politics (the input-side of the political system) has increasingly involved direct links with the policy-making and implementing branches of the state (the output side). This viewpoint stresses not only the importance of the participatory and democratic political culture, but also its institutionalisation and self-reinforcement. The expansion of governmental and administrative machineries and the plethora of interests which they attract are indicative of the democratisation of the modern Leviathan. Such interweaving of state and society and the resolution of conflict in specialised sub-governments is the basis of the 'European polity model', and in the view of its proponents it is a key to modern democratic stability.

At its extreme this argument, advanced by Richardson and Jordan[21], suggests that the conflicts of the parliamentary and party system are no more than a façade, which is even applicable to the adversarial system of politics in Britain. Nevertheless, even though this model stresses the convergence of policy styles in Western Europe, albeit with differences according to the issue and the interest groups involved, specific national policy styles are still identifiable.

The British policy style has been described as one of 'bureaucratic accommodation'. This pattern stresses the receptiveness of government to interests and hence the dominance of sub-governments in the actual process of formulating and implementing policies and not the confrontational rhetoric of party élites. According to this argument, even the reform radicalism of the Heath administration (1970–74) was less significant than the undercurrent of technocratic, consensual reform. Similarly, the radicalism of the Thatcher governments has to be placed in the context of the historical absence in Britain of any stable policy framework within which economic performance could be maximised. The bureaucratic nature of the British establishment means that consultation does not take place within an arena that encourages a consensually-established rationality, as in Germany or the smaller European democracies. It is a style which reserves to government the right to decree authoritatively what is in the 'national interest'. In the end, of course, this power must reside in all governments: there is a tension between the need for democratic government to be based on consensus and the imperative for governments to govern. The stress on the bureaucratic nature of British accommodation shows that the dominant tendency is for interests to be taken into government rather than the latter moving towards society.

Some analyses of policy tend to overstress ideal, normative procedures as the basis for distinguishing national policy styles, and they neglect the vital institutional aspects of administrative behaviour. In the British case, the failure to establish a dominant economic policy framework, with the absence of the institutional dispersion of power found elsewhere, means that resistance to activist government in Britain is weak, fragmented, and polarised. In these circumstances policy failure, together with social and political antagonism, came to be blamed on the structure of government itself. Analyses of this kind led to the demands for constitutional reform and to the founding of an avowedly 'centrist' party as a remedy for British problems in the 1980s.

The Swedish policy style differs from the mode of activist government and the rigid distinction between state and society. Here the policy-making core is kept small and is formally differentiated from the bulk of the administration responsible for implementing policies which itself is markedly decentralised. This distinction is combined with wide interest-group participation in the formulation of policies. As a result, the distinction between the core administration and its devolved agencies is blurred, and the relationship between grass-roots and élites is close and egalitarian in outlook. Priority is given to reaching consensual solutions; even when this proves impossible the strong belief in a rational approach to policy serves to moderate the behaviour of participants. The Swedish policy style has been described as 'radical/consultative' to the extent that the close contact between élites and grass-roots combined with the highly organised nature of Swedish society has permitted governments to be innovative rather than merely reactive.[22]

Although the brief period of bourgeois government from 1976–82 showed continuity with the previous period in overall policy style and policy objectives (such as an active labour-market policy designed to keep unemployment to a minimum by encouraging retraining and labour mobility) conflict in Sweden did become adversarial in the 1970s. The dominant policy style was being challenged and was judged to be ineffective. In 1980, a referendum on the nuclear issue was necessary because the parties were unable to resolve the problem, and in 1983 the largest-ever demonstrations seen in Sweden took place in Stockholm, when marchers protested against the imminent introduction of the so-called wage-earner funds. These funds, regionally-based with majority trade union representation on their boards, were designed to increase the availability of investment capital, although opponents saw them as a form of back-door socialism. Because these funds related to the core issue in the continuing debate about capitalism and democratic socialism in Sweden – who should control resource allocation and investment – feelings ran high. In the same period, the system of centralised bargaining between the Swedish Employers' Federation and the Swedish Federation of Labour, broke down, but the confirmation in office of the Social Democrats in 1985 underlined the persistence of social democratic hegemony, as long as the party was able to retain its strong links with the trade union movement.

An element of confrontation has always been a part of Swedish political life, and arguably it is a necessary component of political and social stability. The change of government in 1976, after many years of one-party domination was perhaps beneficial. The conflicts over nuclear policy and economic issues, with which the political changes of 1976 and 1982 were associated, had much of their potentially disruptive content defused. The political victories and defeats have to be seen in a context of political values in a country where feelings for national unity and consensus are basic to the policy-making and implementation processes. Those values have to be reasserted once decisions have been made by the electorate. The Swedish polity is one in which policy style determines the political style: political confrontation takes place, but the dominance of the consensual policy style permits conflict to be positively integrated into the wider framework of government–society relations. The British system differs entirely since the political style has a dominant influence over policy style.

Norway, one of the archetypes of the European polity model, also reveals the importance of political conflict, for strife between the parties of left and right has been prominent, despite the designation of Norway as a consensual democracy. The combative nature of party politics in Norway right through the early postwar decade was reinforced by the rise of the Conservative party vote in the later 1970s.[23] Yet, whilst fierce political battles were fought, defeat or victory in the parliamentary and electoral arenas were accepted as authoritative, and the prevailing consensual policy style was unaffected.

Norway also provides an important example of the way in which an independent and highly legitimate judicial apparatus can be as important as electoral verdicts in maintaining the domination of official policy processes over political confrontation. The so-called 'Alta valley issue' of 1978–82 came to a crisis when a planned hydro-electric power station threatened the devastation of a region and led to a confrontation between the government and the new forms of unconventional participation. There were mass demonstrations in defence of the minority-rights of local Lapps and ecological and cultural preservation forces against the forces of economic growth. The conflict, however, came to an abrupt end in 1982 when the Supreme Court issued an authoritative decision against the protesters' legal claims. Instead of continuing with their direct action, or even becoming more violent, the protesters simply dissolved their organisation.

The distinction, or lack of it, in this case, between policy style and political style can be related to a final example of policy-making and implementation – the 'dual style' of the French Fifth Republic. In France, it is not a matter of which is dominant, politics or policy-making, for they are not clearly separated; rather it is the ambiguity in the attitude of society and the electorate towards authority in both areas. It is the relationship between the government's need to govern and the need for the government to govern consensually which is the core problem.

The dual style of the French state shows a routine and reactive approach to policy-making and implementation which is less successful when the country is in the grips of a periodic crisis.

Such a crisis, however, provokes both a cathartic reaction characterised by heroic, Napoleonic innovation and assertiveness, and with it a counter-reaction opposing any such Jacobin, authoritative interpretation of some supposed 'national will'. French political history has shown an ambivalence to the liberal democratic form itself: should it be 'heroic', activist and innovative, or participatory and plebiscitary? And what if plebiscitary democracy turns out to be demagogic and uncomfortably authoritarian?

The French state's traditional institutional autonomy has given it a capacity for innovative policy-making and implementation, whilst its heroic traditions ensure that its élites are ready to undertake such initiatives.[24] Increasingly, however, the state has found itself constrained by the decisions of other governments, by multinational companies, by the inadequacy of the state-machinery in the face of the demands made upon it, as well as by the power of societal interests, and they are backed by the growing constitutional and judicial institutionalisation of their rights. In the period 1981–83, under the influence of the first Socialist government of the Fifth Republic, the government attempted a series of radical policies in an étatist way, taking co-operation for granted and relying on its own executive powers. Only the defeat of its economic and educational policies caused the Socialist élite to realise its mistakes and instead seek co-operation with key functional groups as an essential element of the art of governing. The ability to govern authoritatively and the need to acquire supporting legitimation involves a recognition that governmental authority derives not only from the electorate, but also through encouraging participation in the processes of decision-making and implementation. The combination of Bonapartist and plebiscitary behaviour displayed by the Socialist governments under President Mitterrand was fully in the mould of the French 'dual policy' style.

These examples show that West European executives share certain constraints. They range from the challenge presented by technological developments, through the broader, more political problems such as the rise of the participatory challenge, to the need to acquire legitimacy for authoritative action. At the same time, they have different national traditions, so that, for example, the question of nuclear power in France is uncontroversial, since it is regarded as an essential ingredient of national sovereignty, whereas in Germany the issue became highly politicised. If there is a common trend towards a more democratic, or consensual style of policy-making and implementation, the need to secure administrative continuity in the face of political discontinuity is an important factor. In the contemporary era, an effective policy style has to take account of the positive contribution of constitutional complexity and institutional balance as against the unavoidable simplification associated with partisan political conflict.

Controlling executive power

There are two quite different aspects of the control of the executive; one is the *political* limit set on governments, the other is a *policing* function which acts on the detailed exercise of executive powers. Of the two, it is the political controls which are the more fundamental, since without them the possibility of calling a government to account is non-existent, and if that is the case then any other controls are only allowed by the grace of the government – by the nature of things it will always seek to protect itself and its servants. In the preceding chapter we have seen how, in parliamentary systems, the political controls are given expression in the relations between assemblies and governments; the life-blood of this relationship is the operation of the party system, and as a *control* function, the party system revolves around the twin pivots of 'government' and 'opposition'. In its constitutional form, the basis for the control is embedded in the principle of collective responsibility of government to assembly – a starting-point from which any parliamentary system must proceed to define the precise nature of its own political controls.

We can term the political controls the 'macro' aspect of the system, since implicitly it is the fate of whole governments and whole policies which are at stake. The policing function is naturally a 'micro' one: it questions particular actions of the executive, the implications of certain policies, and seeks redress for those who have been harmed. But it stops short of passing judgement on the government of the day. In principle, the distinction is clear-cut; in practice, there is a considerable blurring between the two: the questioning of a government's fitness to govern is partly a matter of regarding the activities of the executive as a whole, and the particular policies favoured by a government are bound to affect the *behaviour* of government; the only way to make the government behave may be to turn it out. The overlap is also evident in the actual working out of the two principles of collective and individual ministerial responsibility. Although a minister is in general charged with the sole responsibility for the work of his department, once he is on the parliamentary rack for the shortcomings of his civil servants, the issue can easily be translated – by government or opposition – to a question of confidence in the government.

Since we have dealt with the issue of political control in several contexts already, we can concentrate here entirely on the policing function, and how it is implemented. Really it is a problem of securing administrative rather than political responsibility, although it may entail the use of political institutions. In fact, we can make the fundamental distinction between devices for administrative control which are geared to political, usually parliamentary, techniques and others which operate explicitly to avoid such a connection. What is more, the European states differ considerably in the emphasis they place on one or the other.

The tradition of parliamentary control over administration is a strong one, and it is used in a variety of ways, ranging from the full plenary session to individual contact between assembly members and government officials. In the first category are the instruments of full debate and various methods of interpellation. Unless the issue is primarily of political importance, plenary sessions are expensive and blunt weapons for detailed control. But it is apparent from the British use of Question-Time that the 'details' are always potentially of wider importance. Formally, it is a request for information, possibly a demand for action, but questions have an implicit political function as well. Ministers are judged by the kind of performance they put up, and the use of questions is one aspect of the forum-like qualities of the Commons, articulated to highly-public exchanges. It is because Question-Time is not just about straight answers to specific questions that it does not transplant readily to other assemblies.

Generally, the more effective control of the administration is secured by the use of specialised committees with the power to interrogate officials, to send for 'persons, papers, and records'. The problem here is to differentiate between the work of the officials and the political responsibility of the government. As a control device it may simply be too effective; the searchlight of the politicians may be too blinding and result in officials lacking in nerve or alternatively, in officials who themselves become too well-versed in playing politics. The protective shield of *ministerial* responsibility is of use in averting both tendencies. The other way in which detailed control of the administration is possible within the parliamentary framework is through the work of individual members of the assembly, or through the work of their common agent, the Ombudsman – a figure who has come to symbolise the control of the executive by parliamentary means.

The Swedish version of this office is based on somewhat different considerations from the later imitations. Most obviously lacking in Sweden has been the full doctrine of ministerial responsibility, arising from the neat separation of the policy-making ministries and the executive agencies which are free from ministerial control, so that the latter cannot be controlled by the Riksdag via the relevant minister. The long history of the office covers periods when the Ombudsman was little more than a royal nominee; only since 1809 has he been securely a servant of the Riksdag, but in this time he has emerged not just as one more parliamentary official, but a person enjoying a popular standing in his own right, a protector against the abuses of those in authority.

What really marks out the Swedish Ombudsman is the considerable power of initiative he possesses. He has the power of independent investigation, that is to say, he can make unsponsored tours. His counterpart for the armed forces, the Military Ombudsman, is in this sense even more of a trouble-shooter, for the great majority of his cases arise in the course of his tours of investigation, but even for the civilian Ombudsman the proportion of 'discovered' cases, as opposed to those 'referred' to him, is as high as a third. The British version is very much watered-down. The main differences can be itemised: the Parliamentary Commissioner has no right of initiative – he must wait until cases are referred to him by Members of Parliament; large areas of the administration are excluded from his jurisdiction, the most important are the armed forces, the police, and the local authorities; he is answerable to a Parliamentary Select Committee, and this could conceivably blur the clarity and finality of his judgements. His terms of reference are more circumscribed and also less well-defined; his brief of 'maladministration' precludes judgements on the merits of a case, and the British system still has to grope its way forward. The fact is that the institution cannot yet be finally judged in the countries which have copied Sweden – Denmark (1953) and Norway (1962), and France now has the equivalent office of the *mediateur*. Even so, it is a mistake to regard the Ombudsman as simply a legislative offshoot, one way of plugging gaps in a deficient parliamentary system of control. Properly conceived, it is a political institution on a par with others, with the assembly only providing a protective base, but the office itself a legally competent entity. The institution can combine popular, legal, and bureaucratic elements, and it works well within the bureaucratic ethos. The Swedish Ombudsman has power to start court actions against officials and he relies heavily on the weapon of publicity. Both of these features are notably absent in the British case, and it is not unfair to conclude that there the office is a prop to Parliament, rather than an attempt to secure a genuine innovation.

Typically, those countries which favour parliamentary control also favour strictly legal controls on the executive, that is to say controls by the ordinary courts to check the misuse of executive power. Like Britain, the states of Ireland, Denmark, the Netherlands, and Norway have no developed system of administrative law. It may be that for most of the monarchies, there has been a greater tendency to insist on parliamentary and external court jurisdiction, avoiding royal influence and the apparatus of a 'star chamber' where possible. However the differences arose, there is now a considerable contrast between those countries which operate a parliamentary plus legal check and those which seek administrative solutions to the problem of controlling the executive.

The idea of 'administrative law' needs some explanation and illustration. We can take the French *Conseil d'Etat* as the model of administrative law in action, and as an example of a type of body which in one form or another is common to most West European states. As is the case with the other Councils of State, the French *Conseil* combines in one organ advisory, legislative, and judicial functions. We are not concerned here with its substantial powers of vetting draft laws and controlling delegated legislation, but all the functions are linked. France was exceptional in having developed, almost by accident, a general administrative court in the nineteenth century, and its general nature meant that detailed application was left to a large number of minor, specialised courts. The result was that the Council of State emerged at the apex of an appeals system, the infrastructure of which remains the specialist and provincial courts. The consequence is a dual judicial system, both with their well-defined competence: the ordinary and criminal courts co-existing with a system of administrative courts.

At a maximum, and as it exists in France, a developed system of administrative law, with its related court system, involves the following features. There must be a *complete* jurisdiction over the public service, and correspondingly a rigorous exclusion of the ordinary courts. There has to be the power to judge whether a public authority has acted within the law or regulation, to see that discretionary powers are not misused, and that there is no wilful misuse of power. Complementary to these powers, the administrative courts should have the ability to award damages and ensure that adequate redress is made to those who have suffered through the fault of officials.

This is a 'model' view, and various deviations are evident in practice. The mere existence of a Council of State is no guarantee of standards. This is true of the Italian Council – a conservative body with recruits from prefects and other state officials near the end of their career whilst the French Council is a highly professional body. But one feature they must share if a bona fide system of administrative law is to exist: the decisions must be binding on governments, however unpalatable they may be. Thus the Netherlands, with no administrative law system, has only a weak Council of State with advisory powers. Its findings are made public, but this only forces governments to justify their decisions, not change them.

West Germany may be used as an illustration of the structure of administrative courts, though it operates without a Council of State. The Constitutional Court has a share in supervision over the administration, since the entrenched constitutional rights (especially those applying to individual liberties) may be infringed by the federal executive or those of the Länder. At the same time, there are a number of administrative courts running parallel to the main areas of public administration. The structure of the general administrative courts is three-tier, necessitated by the federal system: local courts, Land courts, and finally the Federal Administrative Court in Berlin. Besides the general courts, there are a number of specialised ones: Labour Courts, which include the private sector, Social Courts, concerned with social security questions, and the Finance Courts, with a jurisdiction in all taxation matters. The normal three-tier system gives a channel of appeal; a fourth-tier, the Supreme Federal Court, to iron out differences between the regular and administrative courts, has still not been set up.

Similar administrative court structures are to be found in other countries, such as both Sweden and Finland. Denmark differs, and her system is noteworthy in two respects. Firstly, there is an elaborate system of intra-departmental appeals, with a *de facto* independence from ministerial influence and a flexibility not enjoyed by formal administrative courts. Secondly, the Danes do not make the sharp distinction between ordinary and administrative law. In the Danish case, one sees that the possibility of moving to a system of control based on administrative law is not inherently difficult, and Belgium's Council of State was set up only in 1945. But the real issue is whether such controls are compatible with parliamentary and legal controls. The short answer from Sweden, which uses the full armoury, is that they are. In the final analysis, it is the independence of an administrative court which is in question; but there is little logic in recognising the independence of the normal court system and yet not appreciating that the 'administration' is hardly a monolithic block. Critics of the adequacy of parliamentary methods as controls argue also that the major effect is a downgrading of public law, and Mitchell put the case strongly: 'The question, quite bluntly, is whether we want to restore the place of law in government. That restoration demands a susceptible law and a susceptible body which administers that law, a body which at the same time is aware of the real needs of government and of the value of the individual. That is what, behind its technicality, *Droit Administratif* is about; it is what the Conseil d'Etat tries to be.'[25]

Behind the debate on the relative virtues of parliamentary and administrative forms of control is the fundamental issue of whether it is necessary to secure a 'political distance' between the agent and its control. One of the tenets of liberal democracy has always been of institutional separation and balance; yet we saw in our discussion of European constitutionalism that it is the internal checks which have been instrumental in fostering constitutional development. In a similar way, it can be argued that it is *within* the bureaucracy itself that some of the most powerful controls are to be found.

Such a conclusion – sound as the line of reasoning may be – does little to quell the concerns of those who see the increasing competence of the modern state as evidence of its growing autonomy from civil society. Yet the threat to the erosion of civil liberties arises in part precisely because of widespread demands that the state should intervene in all spheres of social and economic life. At the same time, the legitimate demand for standards of equal treatment for all has necessarily led to a strengthening of executive power – a bureaucratisation of society – in order to achieve equity. As a consequence there are confusing calls: for additional state responsibilities on the one side and for a more 'responsible' state on the other.

The problem of 'controlling executive power' raises the age-old question: *Quis custodiet custodes*? An answer in the form of 'internal checks and balances' does supply an interesting contribution, but a solution in the form of self-control is bound to be insufficient by itself. We have to look as well at the constraints imposed by democratically-based institutions and the independent power of the judiciary, although either of these alone will prove inadequate. The threat is not so much that those in control-positions within the state apparatus will necessarily flout or seek to circumvent external restraints, but rather that the traditional means of controlling executive action become inflexible and are inadequate in keeping pace with the widening scope of government activity and the rise of new social problems. Contemporary illustrations abound: combating modern terrorism, dealing with drug-abuse and social violence, tackling the 'permanent' high levels of unemployment, controlling the threatening Aids pandemic. All of these problems require the active involvement of governments, and any action they take may have serious implications for the liberties of the individual. What does emerge is that the control of executive power is not just a specific and static problem, but one facet of the changing structures and aspirations of the societies in which we live.

Notes and references

1. H. Parris, 'The Origins of the Permanent Civil Service, 1780–1830', *Public Administration*, Summer 1968.
2. B. Chapman, *The Profession of Government*, Allen and Unwin, 1959, p. 9.
3. V. Subramaniam, 'The Relative Status of Specialists and Generalists', *Public Administration*, Autumn 1968, pp. 331–40.
4. Parris, op. cit., p. 151.
5. F. Heady, *Public Administration: A Comparative Perspective*, Englewood Cliffs, N.J.: Prentice-Hall, rev. ed. 1979.
6. H. Daalder, 'Parties, Elites, and Political Development in Western Europe', in J. LaPalombara and M. Weiner (eds.), *Political Parties and Political Development*, Princeton University Press, 1966, p. 60.
7. D. Coombes, *Towards a European Civil Service*, Chatham House; PEP, 1968, p. 59. This does *not* imply that civil servants are to be 'impartial' as between government and opposition.
8. On the characteristics of bureaucracy and their relation to the conditions of service, see R. Bendix, *Nation-Building and Citizenship*, New York: Wiley, 1964, pp. 107–15. We can summarise the essential aspects of Weber's view of 'bureaucracy': organisation determined by rules, competence, and hierarchy; and the bureaucratic office is a 'vocation' based on special knowledge and training, with the office distinguished sharply from the incumbent.
9. Chapman, op. cit., p. 107.
10. R. Dahrendorf, *Society and Democracy in Germany*, Weidenfeld and Nicolson, 1968, p. 236.
11. Asa Briggs, *The Age of Improvement, 1783–1867*, Longmans, 1962, p. 443.
12. Quoted by T. B. Bottomore, *Elites and Society*, Penguin Books, 1966, p. 88.
13. Dahrendorf, op. cit., p. 252.
14. See G. A. Almond and S. Verba, *The Civil Culture: Political Attitudes and Democracy in Five Countries*, Princeton University Press, 1963, pp. 106–14.
15. H. Gerth and C. Wright Mills, *From Max Weber*, Routledge, 1948, p. 232.
16. K. Mannheim, *Ideology and Utopia*, Routledge and Kegan Paul, 1960, p. 105.
17. G. Parry, *Political Elites*, George Allen and Unwin, 1969, p. 83.
18. J. Blondel, *An Introduction to Comparative Government*, Weidenfeld and Nicolson, 1969, p. 405 and p. 402.
19. K. Dyson, 'West Germany: The Search for a Rationalist Consensus?' in J. Richardson (ed.), *Policy Styles in Western Europe*, Allen and Unwin, 1982.
20. M. Heisler and R. Kvavik, 'Patterns of European Politics: The "European Polity" Model', in M. Heisler (ed.) *Politics in Europe*, New York: David McKay, 1974.
21. A. Jordan and J. Richardson, *British Politics and the Policy Process: An Arena Approach*, Allen and Unwin, 1987.
22. G. Gustafson and J. Richardson, 'Sweden' in F. Ridley (ed.), *Policies and Politics in Western Europe*, Croom Helm, 1984.
23. D. Urwin, 'Do Resources Decide, but Votes Count – In the End?: A Review of some Recent Norwegian Literature', *West European Politics*, April 1987.

24. J. Hayward, 'Mobilising Private Interests in the Service of Public Ambitions: The Salient Element in the Dual French Policy Style?', in J. Richardson (ed.) *Policy Styles in Western Europe*, op. cit.
25. J. Mitchell, 'The Real Argument about Administrative Law', *Public Administration*, Summer 1968, pp. 167–8.

Additional references

J. Aberbach, R. Putnam and B. Rockman, *Bureaucrats and Politicians in Western Democracies*, Harvard University Press, 1981.

J. A. Armstrong, *The European Administrative Elite*, Princeton University Press, 1973.

P. Birnbaum, *The Heights of Power: An Essay on the Power Elite in France*, University of Chicago Press, 1982.

J. Blondel, *The Organisation of Governments: A Comparative Analysis of Governmental Structures*, Sage Publications, 1982.

S. A. de Smith, *Judicial Review of Administrative Action*, Stevens, 1973.

M. Dogan (ed.), *The New Mandarins of Western Europe: The Political Roles of Top Civil Servants*, Sage Publications, 1976.

G. Drewry, *The Civil Service Today*, Martin Robertson, 1983.

K. Dyson, *Party, State and Bureacracy in Germany*, Sage, 1977.

K. Dyson, *The State Tradition in Western Europe*, Martin Robertson, 1981.

R. Gregory and P. Hutchesson, *The Parliamentary Ombudsman*, Allen and Unwin, 1975.

V. Herman and J. Alt, *Cabinet Studies: A Reader*, Macmillan, 1975.

A. King, 'Executives', in F. Greenstein and N. Polsby (eds.), *The Handbook of Political Science*, Volume Five, Reading, Massachusetts: Addison-Wesley, 1975.

A. King (ed.), *The British Prime Minister*, Macmillan, 1985.

J. D. Kingsley, *Representative Bureaucracy*, Yellow Springs, Ohio: Antioch Press, 1944.

H. Parris, *Constitutional Bureaucracy*, Allen and Unwin, 1969.

B. Peters, *The Politics of Bureaucracy*, Longman, 1978.

R. Putnam, *The Comparative Study of Political Elites*, Prentice-Hall, 1976.

F. F. Ridley (ed.), *Government and Administration in Europe*, Martin Robertson, 1979.

P. Robson and P. Watchman (eds.), *Justice, Lord Denning and the Constitution*, Gower Books, 1981.

R. Rose (ed.), *Challenge to Governance: Studies in Overloaded Politics*, Sage Publications, 1980.

R. Rose and E. Suleiman (eds.), *Presidents and Prime Ministers*, Washington: American Enterprise Institute 1980.

D. C. Rowat (ed.), *The Ombudsman: Citizen's Defender*, Allen and Unwin, 1968.

R. Scase (ed.), *The State in Western Europe*, Croom Helm, 1980.

B. Schwartz, *French Administrative Law and the Common Law World*, New York University Press, 1954.

E. Searls, 'The Fragmented French Executive: Ministerial *Cabinets* in the Fifth French Republic', *West European Politcs*, May 1978.

P. Self, *Administrative Theories and Politics*, George Allen and Unwin, 1977.

P. Self, *Political Theories of Modern Government*, Allen and Unwin, 1985.

G. Smith, 'A Model of the Bureaucratic Culture', *Political Studies*, March 1974.

M. Walles and A. M. Hanson, *Governing Britain*, Fontana 1984.

European Journal of Political Research, 'Political Elites in Europe', March 1978 (whole issue).

9   The Territorial Axis

The resurgence of territorial identity

Until the recent past it was possible to paint a fairly uniform picture of Western Europe, one of increasingly unified states and society, centralised and homogeneous, responsive overwhelmingly to national political concerns and receptive to national planning needs. Yet it is obvious that such a portrayal needs radical amendment and that the supposition of 'national homogeneity' is often a fiction which neglects the realities of history: 'It has become painfully evident that minority dissatisfaction is a central problem of our age, and a dominant theme in the historic development of the uniformly organised modern state.'[1] That 'minority dissatisfaction' frequently has a territorial ingredient, as has been made evident in various parts of Europe with increasing impact over the past two decades or so. Even though such movements do not necessarily herald the 'break up' of the state and although extreme examples, such as that of Northern Ireland or Basque separatism, may give a distorted impression, nonetheless the politics of territory is a potent force in its own right.

A feeling of belonging and communality associated with a particular area, that is to say a sense of 'territorial identity',[2] has patently been an important influence in shaping political loyalties. In principle it can relate to a small locality just as much as to a large territorial entity. As far as the development in Europe is concerned, the most powerful expression of territorial affinity was embodied in the idea of the nation state; indeed the concept of the 'nation state' was itself largely a European innovation, even if it is now the general norm: in the twentieth century the principle of 'national self-determination' has proved to be the supreme justification of state formation. In making a virtual equation of state and nation, the nation-state formula had the effect of dissolving or subordinating most other politically relevant bonds, and although the nation did not necessarily provide a precise territorial delimitation of the state, it served as an approximate or minimal definition.

The rise of the nation state shows the significance of political territory, and the high degree of popular identification it enjoyed made the nation state stand at the apex of political loyalties.

However, its supremacy did not preclude other levels of territorial affinity persisting within the state – which can signify two quite opposed effects. Local or regional attachments may reinforce a more general, national loyalty, a complementarity most clearly displayed in federal states of long standing such as the Swiss Confederation, where the affinities for the constituent cantons are subsumed in the regard felt for the national federation. These are 'dual loyalties' but they do not conflict in any critical sense, even though diverging territorial interests have to be resolved. Peaceful co-existence need not obtain, for the dual loyalties may conflict and result in a destructive political impetus which in extreme cases can threaten to fragment the state. To explain why some countries have avoided these tensions while others have been beset by them requires reference to all the historical circumstances, but one important general reason can be advanced: the most potent cause of conflict is to be found deep within the original construction of the nation state, in that its 'national' basis was imperfect from the start: the 'nation' itself was not a homogeneous unity based on a common ethnicity or language, but possibly an amalgam based on a major grouping and several minor ones. That rendering is at odds with a view that the nation antedated the state and that the state arose from a pre-existing national infrastructure. It is true that the progression held good in many instances, but the contrary sequence could also be followed: nations create states, but states can also create nations.

The malleability of the 'nation' seen from this latter perspective means that the task of nation-building has been a central activity of the modern state, and it may have been imperfectly performed. In the Swiss case, the nation was moulded from disparate elements, but even where there was an initial cultural and linguistic homogeneity, there need not have been a strong awareness of it, nor need there be a firm attachment to the nation-state form and its political authorities. Where heterogeneous cultures are involved, forging a national identity is much more difficult. An obvious course may be followed: the majority culture simply dominates minority ones. But even if they are ignored or suppressed over a longer period, minority loyalties may prove especially tenacious if linguistic ties or other bonds are territorially rooted. Often quiescent for a whole era, they may suddenly appear as a dissident 'sub-state' nationalism, demanding concessions, regional autonomy or even complete detachment from the existing state.

Such forces are active or latent throughout Western Europe. The difficulty lies in explaining their varying incidence and why Western Europe has experienced an apparent upsurge in territorial discontent in recent years. In part, 'suppressed' minorities – suppressed in their eyes if not in the view of the central authorities – will press their claims when the state is least able to resist, and it will be especially susceptible in the upheaval consequent upon a change of regime. Alternatively, dissent may occur as a direct result of efforts to secure national uniformity in, say, language-use and education, bringing results quite the opposite of what was intended. Yet such explanations are not entirely sufficient in explaining the resurgence of territorial politics, and two further lines of argument can be usefully explored, one primarily economic, the other relating to the character of the modern state.

The economic argument can be variously expressed. At its most basic it refers to the extent of economic imbalance – certain regions are disadvantaged and impoverished compared with others. If the poorer regions have a distinctive identity, then a political reaction is to be expected. However, there are various objections to seeing the 'economic trigger' working solely in that way. In the first place, many culturally distinctive regions have experienced economic handicaps over a long period without generating a regional political movement, so that impoverishment by itself is an insufficient cause. Secondly, a prolonged decline can equally lead to a loss of regional identity – through large-scale emigration to more prosperous areas, through attempts at cultural assimilation as a means of securing economic and social advancement. Thirdly, and perhaps most notably, regional political movements are often associated with a substantial improvement in economic conditions. These considerations mean that the focus of the economic argument has to be shifted to an emphasis on economic change and the pace with which it takes place; in those circumstances of rapid transformation, the social effects will lend themselves to a political expression. The Basque region of Spain is not a 'deprived' area, and Flemish nationalism in Belgium began to have a wider popular attraction when Wallonian economic supremacy had commenced its decline. Undoubtedly the process is complex: the poverty of a region would be seen as a badge of its lowly status, and the effect of increasing wealth makes it imperative to win back self-esteem. Increasingly, national political restrictions appear irksome and discriminatory, and the winning of regional autonomy is seen as the only way of achieving a parity of status.

Regional loyalties cannot simply be stamped out of the ground. There must be a cultural-ethnic base in the first place, and most probably there will also have to be a cultural intelligentsia constituting the core of the movement and activating popular awareness. If these prerequisites are absent, regional interests will be expressed diffusely through existing national political institutions, and the national parties will take those interests into account without changing their orientation. The two types of regional effect can co-exist within a country – a few, if intense, regional claims along with a majority of muted regional expressions. Given that combination, the problem is to secure a workable and equitable form of decentralisation. If the entire constitutional structure of the state is remodelled in order to secure a uniform system and meet minority claims, it may prove an expensive and cumbersome way of dealing with the problem.

An entirely separate argument about the revival of territorial politics concerns the changing character of the modern state, applying with particular force to the old-established nation states of Western Europe: they no longer need to insist on the strict identity of state and nation, with the result that all shades of 'localist' sentiment are allowed maximum play. That situation arises because the 'external' functions of the West European states have been substantially eroded, that is, in strategic, political and economic terms. The states of Western Europe maintain a harmonious relationship with one another which would have been unthinkable in previous eras and right up to the recent past. No longer does the individual state have to provide a 'protective shell' against its near neighbours. The emphasis instead is on collective action, and the political and economic equivalents are evident in the process of European integration, even though the formal position of the nation state has as yet been relatively unaffected. This apparent loss of functionality does not itself lead to an upsurge of territorial politics within the state, but the weakening of the need to insist on the nation state as the 'apex of political loyalties' opens up all kinds of possibility for the expression of other loyalties, whether they are territorially based or not.

Modes of decentralisation

The discussion in preceding chapters centred on the question of the dispersion of power, or alternatively its concentration, at the *national* level; these aspects are seen particularly in the nature of assembly-government relations and in the organisation and control of central executive power, but the idea of 'balance' in the liberal democratic state permeates all political institutions. We should now see how this dispersion operates along the territorial axis and appreciate some of the theoretical perspectives involved. To start with, it would be incorrect to regard the territorial dispersion of power as necessarily of a lower order than what can be achieved at a national level – nevertheless the former is usually regarded as a quite subordinate issue, often merely as an appendage of 'local government'.

The essential parity of the two forms was demonstrated clearly by Arthur Maass.[3] He showed how all the major terms of a 'national', or as he termed it, a 'capital division of powers' – by process, function, and constituency – can be reproduced on a territorial level to give an 'areal division of powers'. The fact that it is at least feasible to construct a model of this kind in which power can be distributed territorially, makes it necessary to differentiate both between the various *levels* at which an areal dispersion is employed and between the *types* of dispersion used; taken together, these two give the characteristic features of any system of local-central relations. At the extremes, there will either be complete local autonomy or the wholly-centralised state, and Fesler points out the implications of both: 'Total decentralisation would require the withering away of the state, whereas total centralisation would imperil the state's capacity to perform its function.'[4] It is not difficult to see why both should be true: 'complete' local autonomy would make it almost impossible to hold the state together when differences of interest arose; total centralisation is likely to be an inefficient and expensive solution if all decisions have to be referred to the centre, and normally an unpalatable one for those who are so governed.

A first distinction to be made is between powers granted on an 'original' or on a 'devolved' basis. By powers granted to an area on original terms, it is implied that its structure and functioning exist independently of the central government – most obviously they will be spelled out in the constitution, and in most cases will be beyond the immediate reach of the government of the day. These guarantees of local autonomy may possibly have originated with the state itself or simply be added later by constitutional amendment. Clearly, original powers are most closely associated with some form of federalism, but in principle it could apply to any level of areal distribution. Later, when we examine European federal systems, we shall see that the term 'federalism' covers at least two quite different concepts and that although both can be labelled 'original', in fact, one shades off towards a devolution.

Devolution of power may be no less far-reaching in its effect than an original allocation, but the cardinal difference is that it is a grant of power by the national political authorities and as such its continuance finally depends on its acceptability to these authorities, central government and national assembly; the area unit has no entrenched rights. The devolution of power also involves two distinct types of power distribution: 'deconcentration' and 'decentralisation'. The *deconcentration* of power is a simple delegation of authority from one level of the administrative hierarchy to a lower one which is spatially remote from the centre. The delegation of such authority, which can take place at various levels, need not involve the use of marked discretionary power: the field services of the central government may be closely controlled in order to ensure a national uniformity. But where the central government maintains a single locally-based personage as its representive, his powers of decision making will often be very wide.

In contrast with the deconcentration of power, *decentralisation* implies some measure of self-government, or at least of self-administration, for the regional unit; it represents a sub-division of the national state, a segmentary structure with the control of the segments resting on local constituencies. Obviously, there can be varying degrees of decentralisation; at the minimum, elected assemblies will be restricted to decisions on petty local matters, have few financial powers, and be quite unimportant in comparison with the central government's field agencies. And at a higher level, regional councils may have little more than advisory planning powers. However, at the maximum a whole range of government activity will be decentralised and large areas may enjoy what is virtually 'home rule'. We can set out the requirements of a strong form of decentralisation as follows:

1. *direct* election of representatives to a regional or provincial assembly;
2. control over the subordinate local government organs in the area;
3. a provincial executive authority responsible to the assembly;
4. an area administration under the control of the executive;
5. powers to finance activities in the region.

If none of these is granted by the national authority, then what emerges can be little more than an advisory council. However, even if only one of these requirements is met, the basis for an effective decentralisation exists. The direct election of representatives is perhaps the critical ingredient, for as long as this element is absent, the legitimacy of a regional or equivalent body will remain incomplete; appointed or seconded members will owe their first loyalty elsewhere.

In practice, both government deconcentration and decentralisation exist alongside one another. They may even pass each other by: if the functions allocated to the two types of dispersion are quite distinct, then local field administration of the central government service need bear no relation either to the structure or the areas of the decentralised organs; this parallelism can be described as a system of 'dual hierarchies'. Alternatively, there can be a correspondence between the two so that not only are there similar areas for the field services and the decentralised government but the patterns of authority for the two hierarchies can be 'fused' at one or more points.* The fusion may take place around a single figure or office, and this authority represents both the forces of deconcentration and decentralisation. The two types, fused and dual, make for two quite distinctive patterns of local and regional government systems. Contrast the institution of a state-appointed provincial governor or the prefect of a French department with the complete dualism which characterises the British system.

From a consideration of the two main types of the areal distribution of power, original and devolved and their chief sub-types, we can turn to the number of levels to which power can be dispersed. Just as the arrangements at a national level are amenable to complex sub-division, so there is hardly any limit to the sub-divisions on a territorial basis. In practice, however, actual division keeps to a few, distinctive levels, not all of them represented in any one country; the full range of power distribution can be represented as:

1. Supranational authorities
2. National government
3. Federal state units
4. Regional government or administration
5. Upper-tier local government (province or district)
6. Intermediate government *administration*
7. Lower-tier local government (commune or municipality)
8. Sub-communal units (parish councils).

At one extreme, Switzerland has a very simple structure (virtually only 2, 3, and 7), whilst West Germany (with 1, 2, 3, 5, 6, and 7) has one of the widest spreads. Even within a country there is scope for variety with the main urban areas having the fewest levels – the city of Hamburg is a unit of local government and at the same time one of the component states of the Federal German Republic. And as already indicated, the same unit in a fused system combines decentralisation and deconcentration. At the highest level, that of supranational authority, some special considerations apply, but the territorial component is still present and supranationalism can

* See the diagram on p. 262, illustrating the 'fused' and 'dual' forms.

provide the basis for some form of federal association; we shall look at the particular features and problems of political integration in the following chapter.

No one country's arrangements can really be put forward as exemplary and the wide range of possibilities defeats a simple categorisation. But beyond the practical difficulties there is an added complication, since the apparent dichotomy of 'central' and 'local' authority conceals the fact that the arguments for centralisation are frequently of a *different order* from those favouring local power. Narrowly conceived, the argument could be one about 'local democracy' versus 'central efficiency'. Yet democracy, both in the sense of popular control and the dispersion of power, is compatible with a 'capital division of power' as well as its areal division. In turn, maximum administrative efficiency can only be attained by avoiding an undue concentration at the centre. Thus any move towards a central-local 'balance' is not necessarily the outcome of direct conflict between the two, and for this reason it is impossible to set up a particular areal division of power as a model. At the very least, account also has to be taken of the terms on which the capital division of powers operates.

A further twist is evident. The demand for local power, in the guise of 'freedom', may result in powerful local interests holding sway – and these will be directly opposed to the popular voice at the national level. The term 'efficiency' is also capable of holding different meanings. It can be interpreted in a purely static sense – current economy in the use of resources to achieve the goals of the community. However, one such widely-held goal is to secure the economic and social development of the nation, and this aim needs more than just efficiency; it also requires the promotion of popular participation as well as the integration of governmental activities. Whilst economy in supplying static services may require a high concentration of administrative resources and a minimum of duplication, the broad aim of 'development' may necessitate a measure of dispersal. Thus it can result that the dictates of democracy may be increasingly satisfied at the national level at the same time as the goals of the community indicate increased local power. From this it can be concluded that the apparently competing demands for 'efficiency', 'economic and social development', local 'freedom' and 'democracy' only partly impinge on one another; the realisation of one aim does not necessarily imply the others – nor preclude them either. A broad band of central-local relations, representing various actual systems, will show how the various optima are combined; the location of any one system depends partly on the nature of the national balance attained as well as on the priorities of the particular society.

The European countries have generally favoured a unitary system of government in which power is devolved to area units; the powers, structures, functions, even the existence of these units are matters which ultimately are decided nationally. Nor has the drift of socio-economic forces been particularly favourable to localist sentiment: nationwide markets, central planning, improved communications, accompanied by an increase in mobility from one part of a country to another, have led to a growing social homogeneity. These are all factors which give a national focus to political life; the consciousness of being a Bavarian takes second place to the political line-up at Bonn. But the pointers are not all one way. The pace of economic and social change is the cause of sharp national imbalance with hardship resulting for certain areas. The threat of social dislocation, the knowledge of being in an economic backwater, leads to demands for a local say in decisions. Furthermore, the planning undertaken by the central authorities has to be related to the requirements of the sub-national areas; the idea of 'regionalism' is one response – a recognition that national planning is likely to be neither adequate nor acceptable if it is dictated entirely from the centre. We have also seen that there has been a resurgence of territorial identity in Western Europe, in part as a reaction against the over-zealous centralisation pursued in the post-war era.

Patterns of local democracy
There are also strong European traditions of local self-administration to consider. Some of the extravagant claims for local democracy must be discounted, but the fact remains that local government in Western Europe has accumulated considerable expertise and prestige. At the level of local government, the picture of European systems can be presented as a choice between one of deconcentration allied to local government, typical of the 'fused' model, and the alternative of local self-administration in certain respects, quite divorced from the central government's field services, and giving a system of detached or 'dual' hierarchies. Despite the enormous number of individual variations, particularly with regard to the allocation of powers, both types of system work generally within a two-tier structure. Switzerland is the main exception, where the municipality is the only level below the canton; within individual countries, some urban areas are single tier, with the city acting as an all-purpose authority. Often the second, or upper, tier is the chief unit of government deconcentration, so that it is the commune or municipality – the lower, or first, tier – which is the real focus of local government.

The traditions of the commune are almost everywhere very strong, and as a consequence extremely resistant to change. The communes in most countries are often very small, but vary widely in size, and whilst they are frequently regarded as quite inadequate units of government, they insist on their continuing indispensability. In Switzerland, there are some 3,000 municipalities, ranging from only fifty people to over half a million inhabitants, and their existence is guaranteed in the constitutions of several parent cantons. Local attachment is an integral part of the Swiss political structure: it was after all the small, valley municipalities of central Switzerland which formed the nucleus of the original confederation. Likewise in Belgium, the myths of the commune are exalted: 'A student of Belgian history finds that the equivalent of the Magna Carta or the Declaration of Independence was a document of the Middle Ages assuring that the rights of the communes would be respected.'[5]

Root-and-branch reform of local government is a rarity, even where the existing structure is patently inadequate; stop-gap devices are used: ad hoc authorities are created, intercommunal co-operation encouraged, and voluntary amalgamation made easier. The apparent inadequacy of the small units arises from the greater number of services which local government is expected to provide, and the small units simply do not have the financial or administrative resources. It also arises from the changing patterns of settlement, particularly in the rapid growth of urban areas which can make nonsense of time-honoured communal traditions. We can trace three stages in the thinking about local government in its rural and urban context. The first stage, at the origins of local government, was the conception of parity, and this view naturally resulted in the nation-wide distribution of uniform communal government. With the growth of large towns, the second stage, the need for differential treatment became apparent – to encourage the urban and preserve the rural – and resulted in the urban-rural dichotomy; this is seen typically in the English county borough, divorced from its partially-rural county hinterland, with a similar pattern in Germany (the *kreisfrei* cities). The third, and current, stage is to reverse this town-country split and to make the city the focal point for a large local government area.

The pattern of reform has indicated both an increased size to secure functional competence and an end to the rural-urban dichotomy. To some extent, these reforms can be regarded as no more than a *technical* matter: the retention of a two-tier structure points to the particular problems of spatial organisation, with an upper level needed for wide planning and for the provision of services needing a large catchment area. The need for this upper tier in many countries is made greater by the requirements of central government, both as a unit for the deconcentration of government services and as a vantage point for the supervision and control of local government. The 'technical' argument for the lower tier is that as the size of the unit increases, so there are decreasing returns to scale beyond a certain point. The problem here is that 'decreasing returns' are particularly difficult to quantify; vague feelings of 'remoteness' may result in the serious under-use or even misuse of services. Thus, although in general terms it is clear that a two-tier structure can maximise economies of scale of two quite different orders, it is not so clear what the size of each should be, nor how the functions should be shared between them.

In comparing the impact of reform in 'dual' and 'fused' systems, it has to be taken into account that there is a substantial difference in the idea of what a 'commune' stands for in fused systems. There is inevitably a closer connection with the central government; communal officials are public as well as local officials, since the commune is an expression of government deconcentration as well as of decentralisation. Often the commune is treated (in theory) as having a *general* competence in law simply because it is a unit of public administration.

How sharply this view contrasts with the English position can be seen in a key sentence in the Redcliffe-Maud proposals for the reform of English local government: 'The only *duty* of the local councils would be to represent local opinion.'[6] Such 'no-power' councils were, in the event, rejected by the government in favour of a two-tier system with shared powers. The novelty of the Maud proposal that local councils, at the communal level, should act primarily as 'demand articulators' (though not precluded from exercising other functions delegated by the upper tier) draws attention to a polarity of views about the nature of local government. At the other extreme, the function of local government is seen to be to encourage a maximum of local commitment and active responsibility for self-administration – seen in its ultimate form in the *Amtszwang* (duty to take office) which still obtains in some very small Swiss municipalities.

The suitability of the commune as an administrative unit is related directly to the critical problem of size. And here we should look more closely at the argument that the efficiency of local government increases with the size of the unit, a view of larger units as the general panacea for the 'crisis' in local government. What stands out in contrast to recent British thinking, is the generally lower population-size acceptable as the basis for communal administration. The Redcliffe-Maud proposals for England envisaged a minimum population of 250,000 for the provision of all major services – far higher than that in most other countries outside their metropolitan areas. Few people would make a simplistic equation between size and 'efficiency', since efficiency has so many alternative criteria. The research studies carried out by the Redcliffe-Maud Commission failed to show a 'statistically demonstrable correlation' between population size and efficiency in terms of cost-effectiveness. And in his dissenting opinion Derek Senior concluded: 'The fact must be faced that no objective basis exists on which to attribute any material significance to population size as a factor in any way influencing the performance of existing major authorities.'[7] There are numerous ways in which the communal efficiency of relatively small communal populations can be enhanced: the potential of inter-communal co-operation, the widening of the financial tax base, a more generous interpretation of 'social' development, and, in fused systems, the possibility of government deconcentration to small local units, with a second tier providing a unit of co-ordination. Of course, it is precisely the flexibility of the 'tier' system which should be available to take account of low and high population for the requirements of different services. The over-ready acceptance of quantifiable scale-economies (with little attention paid to less quantifiable dis-economies) leads to mammoth second-tier authorities comple-mented by weak 'community councils' at the communal level.

At various points we have touched on the relationship of local government to the central administration, particularly in the idea of fused and dual systems of administration, and we can take this aspect as one of several ways in which English local government differs from most others in Western Europe; to some extent the causes of these differences are related. The most obvious contrast is found in the English reliance on the tradition of 'government by committee' – indeed, 'government by, of and through committees'. The committee system involves the local representative as a body (not just a few of them and not just the party in a majority) with the work and decisions of the permanent executive personnel. This association is not an accidental feature, for it is a natural expression of the detached as opposed to the fused hierarchy – a total responsibility for the functions of local government borne by the council as a whole. A consequence of the committee system is that there can be no unified executive, either political or administrative, only the unsatisfactory substitutes of a majority-party caucus and the town-clerk.

In other countries, the unified executive is the rule with the

Dual Systems

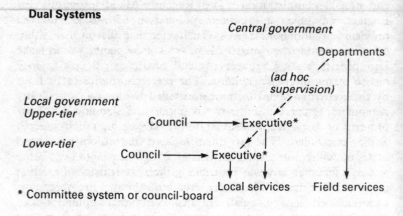

* Committee system or council-board

Fused Systems

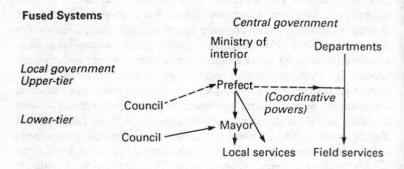

unification seen in one person who can come to office in various ways: direct popular election, election by the council, appointment by the council of a 'professional' administrator (e.g. the Irish 'manager'), appointment by the central government. The Länder in West Germany use all of these methods for their municipalities except the last; however, direct government appointment, especially at the upper-tier, is quite usual in many countries. Thus there is a contrast in the responsibility which the English system places in the council as a whole as against the vesting of this responsibility in a single individual where some degree of fusion exists – the prefect of a French department, the mayor of the commune.

A further major difference is in the absence of a *general* central government supervisory power in England. Central government ministers act individually in supervising the services provided by the local authorities which concern their departments, and the Department of the Environment has a co-ordinative and advisory rather than a directive function. The more usual practice is for a particular ministry to have strong regulative powers over local authorities, and this authority is usually underpinned by the presence of a government-appointed 'governor' or similar person at the provincial level. Even if the fusion is incomplete, some kind of government hierarchy is implied which at one point has to come to terms with the local representative system. An important result we have already noted: since the local–central antithesis is blurred, local authorities have wide powers, albeit under the umbrella of central government control. This wide local competence is evident for West Germany and to some extent for France, with an apparent difference in focus from that of British local government in that the French approach emphasises the community to be administered, rather than the services to be run.

The council-board system is prevalent in the Scandinavian countries, and at the lower tier a chairman is appointed by the council to head the board. At the provincial level, the picture is a mixed one, usually the governor is appointed by the government, but Sweden has changed to having an elected representative. These modes of selection of the executive are a fair indication of the degree of fusion which is in operation. As a general rule, there is less fusion of the local and administrative hierarchies where appointment at both levels is in the hands of the local councils. But this rule should not be taken too far; the principle of fusion is quite compatible with a degree of local freedom in the appointment of a council executive. This is true for West Germany where administration at the local level makes little distinction between decentralisation and deconcentration, and where the executive head (only rarely an appointment made by a Land government) enjoys a powerful position in relation to the elected board members, irrespective of how he comes to office. In the Netherlands, the local burgomaster is a career-official appointed by the central government, and a government commissioner heads each of the eleven provinces. But at both levels the official works alongside a board with executive powers, elected by the municipal or the provincial council. Formally, the same system applies in Belgium as well, but the established practice is for the council at the communal level to nominate its own executive head who is confirmed in office by the government.

The most complete expression of fused authority structures was found in the French prefectoral system, though substantial changes were effected by the Socialist administration in the early 1980s. It is still early to evaluate the full impact of these changes, and despite some radical developments there are many elements of continuity with the previous system. In that system the departmental prefect, a career civil servant, stood at the meeting-point of central and local pressures. As an agent and representative of the central government, he had both general and particular responsibilities for government services in his department. He also became responsible for the quality of local government in his area, and almost as much the department's representative towards the central authorities as the other way around. The prefectoral apparatus becomes a ubiquitous feature of departmental life: 'The prefecture is a focus of power: it is a combination of local Whitehall and County Hall. The citizen of the French provinces can look to the prefecture as a seat of government when in Britain he must look to London.'[8] Yet the prefect was not a miniature Napoleon. He was always at the centre of cross-pressures, those emanating from strong departmental interests and the central government ministries. The Socialist reforms have demonstrated that the prefect, now the 'Commisar for the Republic' with fewer formal powers, except in the case of emergency, had in fact become a useful legal and technical adviser to the bulk of the communes and departments which were too small to manage on their own. Protected by the *cumul des mandats* (multiple mandates) of French politicians, whereby most national figures were at the same time also local mayors, French localities successfully resisted central government attempts to reform their structure against their will. Rather than centre domination via the prefecture, the interpenetration of local and national élites had been effected through political channels, and the 'capture' of prefects by their political environment. A key aspect of the socialist legislation was to make local and élite administrative personnel interchangeable as well, and this aspect of reform, along with the reduction in the power of the prefects and the tendency towards the assumption of their tutelary role by regional government (see below) affect local government throughout France. Despite the alleged universality of the reform legislation, only the large departments and urban communes possessing adequate financial and personnel resources have been able to assert their independence and, in effect, the legislation has done no more than regularise a process that was already well developed.[9]

The basis of this fused, prefectoral pattern is seen in a number of countries that have been influenced by France. In one of these, Italy, the system has not resulted in a high quality of administration or uniformly-adequate local government. The system was a replica of the French one with the main difference that at the upper-level, the province, there was a form of dualism, that is, both a prefecture and a separate executive council, with a president, chosen by the provincial council. Much more than the French arrangements, the Italian prefect appeared to be a device set up against local government, though the degree of this opposition largely depended on the party-political composition of the local council; there was little antagonism between the two in Christian-Democratic strongholds, but it came to a head where local government was in Communist hands, and that has been the case for the great majority of large cities. Paradoxically, the balance of forces which then obtained may have resulted in better administration overall, since the chances of collusion were minimised, which is certainly not so in areas where the prefect developed a *clientela* relationship with the dominant Christian Democrats. In any case, the decrease in political polarisation in Italy has led to a significant decline in the tutelary role of the prefect, and this has tended, as later in France, to be taken up by regional government. In fact a series of reforms in local government was precipitated by the extension of regional governments from the five special regions to the fifteen 'normal' regions in Italy since the early 1970s (see below).

If the model of fused authority appears to have been given a new lease of life by regional reform in France and Italy, the dual system exemplified by Britain seems to have been subject to considerable challenge since the 1970s. For some observers this change has been closely related to the decline in Britain's international and economic position, so that central élites who previously ignored 'low politics' in the pursuit of 'high politics' were no longer able to do so.[10] Changes in the relationship between central and local government appeared under the Heath and subsequent Labour administrations, but it was only in the 1980s that this switch became apparent when Mrs Thatcher's directive policy style led to the abolition of the Greater London and Metropolitan Councils as well as various legislative measures aimed at controlling local government spending. Local government proved unable to defend itself against these attacks, because it is traditionally subordinate to the central government, and perhaps, too, because it lacks political representation at national level. But as central government has become increasingly drawn in to deal with local problems itself, the bases for bargaining between centre and local political élites may have been established, demonstrating the interdependence of central and local élites to which Maass drew attention. Yet it is also the case that the Conservative administration has shown a tendency to bypass local authorities in its desire to cope with Britain's acute inner-city problems, establishing urban development corporations based on private business interests to regenerate run-down inner-city areas. The nature of the future relationship between central and local government is uncertain, and the tensions between 'local freedom' and criteria of 'efficiency' remain unresolved.

The British case shows how the balance between different levels of authority can be upset. But other examples of changing relationships between centre and local governments have maintained the overall balance at the same time as taking account of new demands and functions. Whilst it is difficult to graft single features from one system to another, the upheavals affecting British local government present the opportunity of 'borrowing' features from other systems. One of those features is higher level decentralisation.

European federalism and regionalism

There is no one West European pattern of regionalism or federalism, although, with the increasing emphasis on seeking a fundamental reconstruction of the territorial identity of the state, interest has grown in how European federalism operates and how constitutional provision can be made for workable regional government. How far should a unitary state go in deliberately fragmenting its authority?

To answer that question we should examine first some of the theoretical perspectives involved in the idea of federalism and then examine the specific case of European federalism as well as examples of regional decentralisation which are probably just as relevant to contemporary concerns. The distinguishing feature of a federal system is that the barriers which are erected against the intrusions of central government or national assembly are independent of their continued goodwill; neither the whims of the government of the day nor particular party constellations, nor even the continuing hold of local traditions are crucial factors for the survival of a federal state. Whilst it is true that their mainstay, the constitution, can be amended, the majorities needed may be very difficult to secure, and, as in the Federal German Republic, the constitution may stipulate that the federal system itself is beyond the reach of amendment. Yet there can be no absolute guarantees of original federal powers, since in the final analysis the territorial distribution of power runs up against the will and power of the national political authority, and the powers of constituent states are continually subject to pressure either by consent or by the tacit acceptance that the central government must assume certain responsibilities.

The conventional model of a 'pure' federal system requires three features to be present:

1. a clear specification of the powers of the states and of the federation, and also that the powers of the states should be significant ones;
2. supportive institutions (such as a constitutional court) in order to preserve the demarcation between the federation and the states;
3. a distribution and division of powers within the federal state so that, according to Wheare, '... the general and regional governments are each, within a sphere, co-ordinate and independent.'[11]

On such criteria, a 'strong' federal system will be seen as one in which the states exercise a wide range of powers quite independently of the federation with a whole gamut of institutional checks serving to keep the balance between the two – preventing the system flying apart or keeping the central government in its place. 'Weak' systems will be seen as those where the powers of either the federation or the states are excessively modest, where the supportive institutions lack an effective jurisdiction, and where the failure to secure powers for each level within a 'closed sphere' results in a lack of clear definition of responsibilities.

Insistence on the presence of all three features leads to the conclusion that if they are not, then the system is not only 'weak' but also that it is not 'genuine'. We shall be able to judge the suitability of one appellation or another to European systems in the course of relating the details of their arrangements, but we should appreciate first the defect of setting up one 'pure' federal model as the single standard of judgement. It may be that a variety of 'federal-type' solutions are of relevance to present-day problems of power distribution, rather than an archetype of mainly historical significance. It can be conceded directly that the European systems fail on the third requirement, since there is a considerable intermeshing of state and federal activity. In this respect they contrast considerably with the federal concept of the United States whose constitution was conceived in quite different circumstances.

Sawer, in dealing with the distinctive stages through which federalism can pass, used the terms 'co-ordinate', 'co-operative', and 'organic'.[12] The first of these conforms to the conditions we have already set out; the second, co-operative federalism, requires the states to have some 'bargaining capacity' in order that the joint authority exercised by the centre and the states should not hide a simple domination by the federation; in the third case, the organic type, the capacity to bargain is substantially lost, and, in effect, the states will become the administrative agents of the central government. At that point, one has to consider whether the guarantees of the federal structure and the extent of original powers are insufficient to warrant the federal label. An alternative description of the third stage is that of 'administrative federalism', since it draws attention to the essential nature of centre-state relationship, with total initiative really left to the federation, but the federal structure still preserved.

The three European federal systems are probably to be allocated nearer to the third stage. Their main strength is in the character of the supportive institutions, and the states may be losing, or have lost, their bargaining capacity. This is undoubtedly true for Austria, possibly for Switzerland, less certainly for West Germany. In all three, the powers of the national governments are very wide, leaving the component states only small areas of autonomy. But both the enforced co-operation and centralisation are modified by the presence of supportive institutions, guarantees which make it difficult for the national governments to do as they please with the states.

Historically, the association of the Swiss cantons since 1291 is of importance, but for most of the time the links were external and confederal only. In its modern form the confederation draws directly on the experience of the United States, and the powers of the national government were fully determined as recently as 1874. The parallels with the United States are in the legislative institutions: there is the same form of territorial representation – the upper house, the Council of States, represents the interests of the cantons and has coequal powers with the National Council which is elected on the basis of population. Express powers are granted to the federation (Switzerland remains a confederation in name only) and residual powers to the cantons. The Swiss federal government has a very long list of enumerated powers, and these have been supplemented by convention and constitutional amendment to give a strong centralist drift.

A major difference lies in the area of constitutional jurisdiction. We have seen earlier that the Federal Tribunal has no power to invalidate legislation, and that instead the referendum is used for this purpose. It is a moot point whether this is an effective check.

Obviously, where there are fundamental issues at stake, the referendum will provide a potent counter-balance, but on lesser issues the challenge may not be made, and the sum total of these encroachments over the years gives a centralist impulse. The impetus can be maintained by the ploys open to the federal government to avoid challenge by referendum – notably in the use of decrees (*arrêtés*) in place of 'laws' as the former escape by being declared 'urgent' or 'not universally binding'. This subterfuge has often been necessary in the field of finance, since although actual functions are weighted heavily in favour of the federation, the constitution divided the powers of taxation between the federation and cantons, and the financial powers of the federation have not been commensurate with its responsibilities. As a consequence, the federal government for long had to rely on makeshifts of 'once-for-all' and 'crisis' taxes, avoiding challenge on the grounds of urgency; only in recent years has the position been regularised by formal amendment to the constitution. As the national government has taken on greater responsibilities in economic policy and social welfare, so have the cantons looked to the centre for positive initiatives, while their own powers showed a relative decline.

The federal structure has worked well as a containing force because the federation has always avoided becoming a power set up against the interests of the cantons. If, as has been alleged, a Swiss national is proud *not* to know the name of the president of the Confederation in the current year (the office is a rotating one from members of the Federal Council), this pretended ignorance at least underlines the passive nature of federal government in popular thinking, even if this view does not accord with reality. The terms on which the federal power can act 'nationally yet neutrally' have to be appreciated in historical, political, and constitutional senses. We have already referred to the consensual framework within which the social cleavages are contained – the religious and linguistic differences, and in the past the potential, and sometimes actual, conflicts among the cantons and between the classes. It is now true to say that these conflict sources have reached a minimal point. It has helped that the lines of cleavage have overlapped, rarely giving a clear-cut division and a simple polarisation. To this cross-cutting one has to add the determined lack of external involvement, a united front of non-entanglement. Swiss parochialism has helped to maintain her stability.

The political basis for the neutralisation of the federal government stems from the permanent government coalition; this never-ending collegial caucus is made possible by the lack of full government responsibility to the Federal Assembly – an arrangement which serves to take much of the heat out of national politics; local issues tend to loom large and the voters (and parties) find much political stimulation within the cantons. The powers of the upper house, directly representing the cantons, and the use of the referendum also act to neutralise the centripetal tendencies of federation, and even if national government emerges as the prime force, all the factors we have mentioned help to ensure that it is never a sudden shift.

The actual powers of the cantons are relatively modest; any well-developed local government administration would be capable of handling the reserved powers, chiefly education, cultural affairs, and police. But that would considerably underestimate the true position. To the considerable financial powers of the individual cantons, one also has to add their wide *administrative* powers and responsibilities. The bureaucracy which serves the federal government is relatively small; by the nature of a federal system, it is not possible to proceed by a simple deconcentration of central government services. Instead, the services must be decentralised, and the bureaucracy thus becomes an integral part of each canton, with central control through powers of inspection. The cantons have a wide administrative competence, and it is this responsibility which continues to give the cantons a real base, with localist sentiments and constitutional guarantees acting as supports.

The idea of 'administrative' federalism is one that can usefully be applied to the Swiss system to distinguish it from strong 'co-ordinate' types. This may also be true for West Germany, but there are several differences in other respects from Switzerland. The most important contrast is the lack of strong localist loyalties in present-day Germany. The federal system which was resurrected in 1949 owed as much to the influence of the United States, in her role as an occupying power, as to the precedents of the weak federalism of the Weimar Republic or that of Imperial Germany. The argument favoured by the United States was that since Nazi Germany had imposed a strictly unitary system, a federal form of democracy would be the best protection against an undesirable centralism. The Weimar system had been deliberately devised as a weak federal form – in order to escape the predominance that Prussia had enjoyed in the Bismarck period and later, a hegemony rather than federalism. One of the few, easy agreements reached by the wartime allies was that the Prussian state should not be recreated after 1945. The component parts of the Federal German Republic were put together from the three zones of occupation of the western allies, with the later addition of the Saar. Some of the states, such as Bavaria and the Hanseatic cities of Hamburg and

Bremen, had historical sanction, others were virtually new creations. It was rather a hotch-potch with great variation in size from the small city-states to the mammoth North-Rhine Westphalia having some 30 per cent of the total population. Nor did the states have any option but to join - Bavarian separatist inclinations were ignored.

The sharing of powers between federation and states is complex. The Basic Law gives specified powers to the federation and the residue to the states (Länder). The residual powers are mainly concerned with cultural affairs – religion, education, and the mass media. But there is a further category of concurrent powers (including: nationalisation, transport, nuclear energy, civil and criminal law) on which both the federation and the states are free to legislate, with the important qualification of Article 31 that, 'Federal law overrides Land law'. The Basic Law also gives another category of federal legislation, so-called 'framework laws', by which the general principles are laid down by the federal government and each Land is then free to fill in according to its own wishes by state legislation.

The idea of the framework law gives the keynote to German federalism, and there are other provisions which empower the federal government to delegate functions to the Länder, even where the powers belong exclusively to the federation. And the constitution explicitly makes the states the responsible agents for the execution of federal law. As in Switzerland, this provision gives them a strong administrative base and a wide executive competence. Similarly, the Länder have their own constitutionally-guaranteed sources of revenue (a range of indirect taxes plus inheritance taxes and an entrenched proportion of the income tax yield); however the federal government is better provided for than in Switzerland, and the federation has the power to equalise financial burdens between the richer and poorer Länder. A picture emerges of each Land with its own large civil service administering the bulk of the nation's internal affairs; each one with its own responsible government headed by a minister-president, its own court system and police force, considerable revenue, along with the full guarantees of a federal state.

These guarantees are provided by the presence of a constitutional court and the second chamber of the federal parliament, the Bundesrat. We have already seen that the Federal Constitutional Court, although a new creation, has wide powers of judicial review which also preserve the central-local balance. The Bundesrat provides a political balance, and it does this in a novel way by giving a direct representation to the *governments* of the states with some weighting according to their size. The Bundesrat has been described by Heidenheimer as, 'The only chamber in the world which is in effect a continuous congress of state (Land) ministers who vote in accordance with the instructions of their governments.'[13] This arrangement gives the state governments a powerful federal platform, a direct link to the federal authorities, and an opportunity to form a common front against incursions from the centre. And the governmental flavour of the Bundesrat is further underlined by the stipulation that all the members of a state delegation must vote the same way – of particular importance as Land governments are usually based on coalitions.

The powers of the West German Bundesrat are fewer than those of the Swiss Council of States. But it does have equal powers in some matters, over constitutional amendments, the federal budget, legislation affecting the competences of the Länder, and over proposals affecting the apportionment of tax revenues. In all other questions it has a qualified veto, which, depending on the size of the negative vote in the upper house, will require the Bundestag to override it with a simple or a two-thirds majority. A crisis over this blocking-power of the Bundesrat almost came to a head in the course of the legislation on the ratification of the treaties consequent upon Brandt's Ostpolitik in 1972. The potential power of the Bundesrat to obstruct the policies of the federal government is undoubtedly great. In recent years the CDU-CSU when in opposition had a majority in the Bundesrat, and this situation often led to confrontation. The party line-up was the operative factor rather than any real threat to the interests of the Länder governments. However, the usual emphasis is more on co-operation with the federal government. Moreover, the Länder also seek to protect their position, so that irrespective of their political colouring they will work to amend government legislation to their own advantage. A large part of the work of the Bundesrat takes place in committee and in liaison with central government officials; in addition, civil servants from the Länder can deputise for their ministers in Bundesrat committees. Administrative solutions will be sought, not political confrontation, and the Bundesrat acts as a useful clearing-house.

Austrian federalism has superficial similarities with the West German, but in almost every respect it is weaker – in relation to the powers of the states and the supporting institutions. The present system is a revival of the one in operation during the inter-war years, and as in Germany there is little historical sanction for the constituent Länder. The nine states are on average far smaller than the corresponding ones in West Germany, and to a large extent they depend on financial aid from the federal government to perform their functions. Their original powers are few; only minor cultural and planning matters are reserved to the states, whilst the federation has all major police powers and control of the educational system, and the judicial system is completely federal.

Central controls are more powerful too: the federal government has a direct veto over many Land activities, including a financial veto, and the Länder are subject to central inspection and control in most of their activities as well as to the audit of the Central Accounting Office (*Oberster Rechnungshof*), though this body is itself independent of the federal government. As in West Germany, the position of the states is guarded by a constitutional court, but there is less to protect, and historically the court has favoured the claims of the centre. The other supportive institution is the Bundesrat, but this body is very weak in comparison with its West German counterpart, a suspensory veto which can be overcome by a simple majority in the lower house, and its members are elected from the provincial assemblies on a party-proportional basis, so it is a party line-up in the Bundesrat, not the voice of the state governments.

At this modest level, one is entitled to ask whether a federal system is really in operation at all, to say that the trappings are there without the content. One might go even further and be tempted to regard all three European federal states as 'weak' forms, perhaps with the additional comment that *all* forms of territorial pluralism represent a phase in a country's development, that in the long run the centripetal, national forces are too strong to be denied. Indeed, even where the powers of the states are firmly entrenched, the effect may be just to create an obstacle to a more rational re-allocation of powers and functions which is always possible in a unitary state. And with a continually changing socio-economic balance, it is desirable that a re-definition should occasionally take place. Even where federalism has historical justification, the criterion of the success of the federal form may be the extent to which it acts as a solvent on local loyalties; the erosion is resisted only by backward-looking localist parties, out of touch with the problems of a modern state.

Forceful as these arguments are, they probably rely too much on the 'co-ordinate' view, that it is pseudo-federalism unless the states have strong original powers, distinctive functions, and powerful supports. But the alternative model of 'administrative' federalism may be more relevant to developed societies, where the need to secure a decentralisation of central government power is admitted on grounds of 'efficiency' as well as to secure economic and social development. The merit of administrative federalism is that it ensures a complete decentralisation of the bureaucracy, not just its deconcentration, and usually in units large enough to be viable. Whilst it is possible to stop short of providing guarantees of this decentralisation, the benefit of a strong backing is that (whether by second house, constitutional court, or referendum) the federal units are encouraged to preserve their identity. The effects of a wide measure of administrative decentralisation are also apparent in the calibre of those who actively participate at the state level; recruitment from the ranks of those who have served in state assemblies and governments offer a broader base than is available in a unitary system, whilst service in local government only exceptionally provides this opportunity – Belgium is a good example. In spite of the national supremacy of two major parties in West Germany, experience in Land assemblies provides an alternative channel of recruitment for national political figures – a number of post-war chancellors first rose to power at the Land level.

Yet it is this aspect of political recruitment and the linkages of national political figures with sub-national government which indicates that administrative federalism is not the only significant aspect of federal government. Sub-national government is, as we have seen, reinforced when major national political figures need a local power base in order to become national actors, and beyond this the existence of federal – or regional – institutions provides a valuable framework within which party political struggle can be played out. Austria and Germany provide important examples of parties in opposition at the national level supporting federal forms of decentralised government, wherein power considerations have prevailed over inherited ideological inclinations,[14] and the balance of power in these countries has been significantly promoted in the process. The same is true of local/regional government in France and Italy.

It follows from this that although federal systems are the exception in Western Europe, once one discards federalism as a 'type' and concentrates instead on the idea of a federal *situation*, then regionalism can provide an approximate equivalent, as is evident for Belgium, Italy, France and Spain. Once the 'regions' have been satisfactorily defined, sometimes no mean problem in itself, then the advantages of a regional solution are apparent: in the first place it does not require a basic restructuring of the state. Secondly, regionalism can best take into account relevant socio-economic factors, rather than – as with federalism – making the units an accident of original demarcation. Finally, given the strong unitary traditions in Western Europe, it is simply easier to make progress in this way.

As we use the term here, 'regionalism' is not put forward as a doctrine along with other 'isms', but an expression of two quite different sets of forces which meet at a regional level; one is an argument for greater decentralisation of government involving an extension of local autonomy upwards; the other is an attempt to decentralise the machinery of central government, not only for the day-to-day running of services – although there are proven advantages in having large, standard areas to ensure inter-departmental co-ordination – but also in order to formulate and implement some form of national economic planning. These two separate forces, democracy and administration, are not entirely divorced from one another: the need for a regional component in national administration, once pressing because serious regional imbalances seemed to demand it, later became urgent as hard-pressed national governments faced 'resource squeeze', and needed to control expenditure.

Regional decentralisation requires that a number of important decisions should be taken by a representative body with a constituency based on the whole region. We have already outlined the requirements for strong decentralisation, and it will be apparent that these are rarely fulfilled in European forms of decentralisation. The former structure of government for Northern Ireland is the best example – with some of the most deplorable results. In miniature, the government of Northern Ireland reproduced most of the functions of central government, except those which by definition fall outside the province of homerule: defence and foreign affairs. The powers of the Stormont government were further limited in respect of control over foreign trade and exchange. Unlike the position in a federal state, all the enabling powers of the government of Northern Ireland stem from a statute of the British Parliament: the Government of Ireland Act of 1920 and subsequent British legislation. These powers can be amended or rescinded without the express consent of the Northern Ireland Stormont or government: 'direct rule' from Westminster could be imposed at any time, as in fact occurred in March 1972. In all matters, save the essential constitutional position of Northern Ireland, there is only the right to be consulted. Under Section 1 of the Ireland Act of 1949, however, the British government is committed to obtain the consent of the Northern Ireland Parliament in any matter affecting Northern Ireland's status as an integral part of 'His Majesty's dominions and of the United

Kingdom', thus precluding the unification of Ireland except on terms acceptable to the Protestant majority in Northern Ireland. Her economic weakness, plus the fact that the power of the British government is needed to guarantee a continued existence, always forces the authorities in Northern Ireland to lean heavily on the British government for support.

In many ways the Northern Ireland government until 1972 acted as an administrative agent for the national government, routinely providing services similar to those for the rest of the United Kingdom, even if the authority for these required separate legislative treatment. The resulting freedom of action may appear somewhat limited, but it is as well to bear in mind that the European federal systems do not amount to much more in practice – a great deal of the activity of the German Länder is concerned with administering federal laws, and the exercise of concurrent powers under the constitution, as well as the device of the 'framework' law, acts as a disguised form of devolution. Indeed, the government in Northern Ireland was in some ways stronger: its ability to use the Special Powers Act to restrict civil liberties went beyond what the government of a German Land could accomplish, and unlike the position in West Germany there is no protection of a constitutional court. In this respect, such an advanced form of government decentralisation may result in greater 'freedom' (for the Protestant majority) but not a democratic consensus for all sections of the population – short of the imposition of direct rule, the minority in Northern Ireland might feel that it is the direct representation in the British Parliament which serves their interests better.

Besides the strong form of regional decentralisation evident in Northern Ireland's home-rule system, Britain also provides examples of the weak forms – those which fail to meet any of the five conditions we have set out for effective decentralisation. In this latter category fall the proposals for English local government envisaged by the Redcliffe-Maud Commission; these would have meant setting up eight English provinces above the highest level of local government. However, they would have been indirectly-elected from lower-level units, provided no services themselves, and would have chiefly acted as planning and consultative bodies. Even these modest moves to decentralisation were shelved indefinitely. The case against an extended regional decentralisation of British government was succinctly put by Sir Richard Clark. Firstly, he argued that there is little popular demand for this; secondly, at least for England, it would be impossible to have units small enough for local identification, and yet sufficiently large for law-making and administration. His third argument concerns the provision of social services; these are geared naturally to the central government: 'Indeed, a change of system towards regional government would almost certainly be resisted by the poorer regions which would then have less scope for bringing pressure on central government to provide ad hoc support. There is no middle course in this area: either there is responsible regional government in the social services or there is not.'[15]

A natural response of the central government to regional problems is to seek a measure of deconcentration of government services. Thus Scotland, in spite of its distinctive character and problems, has never been given a decentralised government form; instead, there has been a sporadic process of purely administrative devolution dating from the middle of the nineteenth century, and this dispersal has built up to the extent that, besides the Secretary of State for Scotland, there are a number of junior ministers concerned solely with Scottish affairs. They and the civil servants concerned administer certain services direct or with the appropriate local authorities. Since much of this activity takes place in Scotland, the extent of deconcentration is high. Yet the ministers are firmly part of the central government and the civil servants, although preponderantly Scottish, are members of a unified service. Similarly, British governments long held out against popular pressure for directly-elected assemblies for Scotland and Wales, but as one result of the report of the Royal Commission on the Constitution made in 1973, assemblies for both were planned as part of a programme of devolution.[16] A more pressing reason for action was the large increase in support for the Scottish and Welsh national parties. But the failure of the 1979 referenda on the issue to gain sufficient support effectively buried even those modest plans to increase decentralisation.

Although there are similarities between British and French unitary traditions in the sense that neither has favoured strong decentralisation, it is important to bear in mind the earlier distinction made between 'fused' and 'dual' hierarchies of administration. The fused system combines elements of deconcentration and decentralisation in the same office or area; the formula for building up a system of regions by grouping together a number of second-tier units, as has been the case in France, works well since the machinery of government administration is already articulated along these lines. Dual systems do not easily adapt to this type of regional deconcentration, and local government bodies will prefer to deal with the ministry direct rather than with an intervening layer of regional administrators.

For fused systems, with or without regional level of administration, co-ordination is partly ensured by the existence of a government representative standing in a direct and general relationship to local government. In dual systems, policy implementation requires either the creation of ad hoc agencies, or else each ministry separately carrying out its share of an agreed plan and dealing individually with the local authorities. The danger of a powerful regional administration is that it may lack flexibility – as could be seen from the problems of co-ordination within the French department – and much will depend on the discretionary power the central government ministries are prepared to give the regional offices. Where they are considerable, a regional hierarchy makes sense, but if it just becomes a cumbersome intermediate apparatus, then the fragmentation associated with dual systems is likely to work better.

The essence of French regionalism is that it was conceived as an integral part of national planning and administration, a deconcentration rather than decentralisation. Although French national planning got under way soon after the war, the early versions, such as the Monnet plan (1946–1953), were concerned with the modernisation of industry rather than with social and regional development. Regional planning was only later integrated with national planning. Basic to the regional contribution was the creation of planning units larger than the existing departments, and what finally resulted was a structure of twenty-one regions. What is questionable is whether such a planning apparatus can alone ever lead to a decentralisation of government. The careful hierarchy of the planning process makes for equitable treatment; it may do little to increase local competence whilst its 'vertical' ethos is likely to provoke resistance at the lower levels.

As we have seen, French national politicians, with their powerful local roots, prevented the fragmented system of local government being regrouped at a higher level, whilst the larger urban communes and departments achieved de facto independence from the central government control exercised by the prefect. Attempts from the late 1960s onwards to increase the content of French decentralisation at the regional level thus consistently failed, though even the weak forms of regions that were established proved to be significant in the long run. What the Socialist government's regional reforms of Gaston Deferre did was to recognise the de facto independence of the larger communes and departments, but also reintegrate them within a regional framework where the power of the prefect over the smaller units reappears. However the reforms went beyond mere legal and administrative reorganisation, since the regional councils were turned into directly-elected bodies, and the first regional elections were held in 1986. This reform reinforces the trend towards an increased party political influence in local government, leading to alternation of local élites in place of the system of 'entrenched notables': but the tradition, and many of the structures, of state-rule through a combination of notables and technocrats remains strong.

There is an understandable hesitancy on the part of central governments to engage in regional experiments of decentralisation; only in circumstances of peculiar difficulty are they likely to concede very much in their direction. The Belgian example is a case in point; only when the rise of the linguistic parties had begun to threaten the cohesion of the party and political systems, did the major parties, themselves subject to internal pressures, make radical constitutional reforms to meet the demands of the two language communities, providing for regional culture autonomy and economic decision-making. The difficulty of effecting the constitutional changes, requiring a two-thirds majority in the Belgian Parliament, is counter-balanced by the fact that, now once secured, they are even more difficult to upset. The clear language frontier in Belgium makes the regions linguistically homogeneous, and that factor, together with the linguistic division of the parties, has made nonsense of the old Belgian unitary state form. In Belgium we can see regional decentralisation merging with federalism, reinforcing the idea of a 'federal situation' as a fitting description of a large part of the territorial axis.

Spain, too, has moved far away from unitary state tradition perpetuated by Franco's dictatorship. Partly as a reaction against fascist centralisation and partly to meet the demands of the Basques and Catalans, the 1979 constitutional reforms incorporated the principle of regional autonomy, and there are now seventeen so-called 'autonomous regions', each with its elected assembly and regional government. These regions inherited local governments which were totally unable to cope with the demands of the modern urban and industrial state, and so they have had to build whole new systems of administration in a situation of financial weakness and political delicacy; thus they need to maintain opposition consensus while a tradition of democracy is built up. The decentralisation measures fell far short of meeting the claims of the Basque separatists, but it has also been clear that most of the other regions do not have a strong territorial identity, with the exception of Catalonia, Galicia and Andalusia. The result is peculiar: the patchy nature of regional consciousness has made local autonomy appear irrelevant in some areas and inadequate in others, an effect that would be apparent if regional government were to be applied in Britain, and yet the very difficulties inherited by the regions, and the long and still continuing process of legislation, organisation and experimentation may create the bases of local self-consciousness which the 'creation of tradition' requires.

Italian regional government also belongs to the strong form of decentralisation. It can also be seen as a reaction against the centralisation imposed by fascist rule. Regional governments were provided for in the 1948 constitution, and they were given a democratic basis in establishing them by direct election. Although the constitution provided all the necessary sanctions, only five regions came into being without delay and the full complement of twenty was not reached until 1970. Part of the reason for the long postponement was the unwillingness of the Christian Democratic government to have a number of left-wing regional governments sniping at its authority. The regions first set up all showed some cultural distinctiveness, besides being on the periphery: Val d'Aosta, Trentino-Alto Adige, Friuli-Venezia Giulia in the north, and the islands of Sardinia and Sicily. All had particular localist features, some were very small – one with a population of around 100,000. A reading of the constitutional provisions (Articles 114–133) gives an indication of their character. The regional assembly elects an executive junta, headed by a president; there is also a regional commissioner representing the central government, a figure armed with powers similar to those of the prefect in respect of local government, especially over legislative activity. Although the constitution gives the regions power to levy taxes, they remain financially dependent on state grants. The regions do not have a permanent territorial status; new ones can be created by mergers proposed by local initiative and confirmed by referendum. The most important protection the regions have is the constitutional court; this helps to guarantee their existence (to this extent the Italian regions come close to enjoying the guarantees of federalism); and the court also acts as arbiter when the central government has disallowed regional legislation or administrative actions. Powers given to the regions by the constitution are not very great, but the political and redistributive significance of the regions, as mediated by the parties, has come to be important. More significant have proved to be the planning powers as they first developed in Sardinia and Sicily, and their originating statutes gave them wider powers in this respect than were listed in the constitution. But the impetus has come just as much from the central government's own commitment to regional development and from its own resources and machinery set up to cope with the economic problems of the *Mezzogiorno*, all of Italy south of Rome together with the islands of Sicily and Sardinia.

The principal agent of government policy has been the *Cassa per il Mezzogiorno*; this is a semi-autonomous public body charged with developing the public utilities and agriculture. Picturesquely described as a 'giant watering-can' the *Cassa*, by means of government funds and the raising of large loans, first injected money to build up the primary economy and later moved on to projects of direct industrialisation. A curious relationship has developed between the regional (as well as the local) governments and the regional arm of the central government development agencies, for it is one which tends to bypass the normal administrative hierarchy, and it has led to a partnership in which the relatively weak local and regional government can benefit from the competent supervision of the *Cassa*, as well as from the free flow of funds. Such a body may be government deconcentration in disguise, but its operational freedom may show a greater compatibility with regional self-government. These remarks apply with particular force to the *Mezzogiorno* as an area which is quite unable to lift itself by its own bootstraps.

The rather different versions of 'regionalism' which have come about in various countries make it evident that the term is likely to continue to span a variety of structures, an awkward half-way house below national government which has yet to find any definitive solutions. It is in the large, unitary states that the strongest case can be made for regional government, but, as the experience of Britain shows, the traditions of centralised administration run counter to a significant devolution of power. The advantage of the unitary system is that areas of devolution are in principle quite flexible, whilst federal states face the problem that state boundaries are virtually immutable and can become an increasing hindrance to rational planning and cooperation. The most glaring example of this inadequacy is metropolitan New York. The fact that this conglomeration bestrides three separate states points to the need for a drastic solution, and a solution, extremely difficult to implement, would be to create a fifty-first state of the union. In Europe, such problems may in the future cut across existing national boundaries; a current example is the Aachen-Liège-Maastricht triangle which involves three countries, but, with growing economic interdependence, the European states will find that the spatial problems of government are closely linked to others. Here we are approaching the supranational aspects of the subject of government power; it is in the concept of supranationality that ideas of 'deconcentration' and 'decentralisation' have, so to speak, to be tilted on their heads, to give levels of concentration and centralisation above the level of national government; to this question of political integration we can now turn.

Notes and references

1. C. Wilson (ed.), *National Separatism*, Cardiff: University of Wales Press, 1982, p. 1.
2. On this whole subject, see S. Rokkan and D. Urwin (eds.), *The Politics of Territorial Identity*, Sage Publications, 1982.
3. A. Maass (ed.), *Area and Power: A Theory of Local Government*, Collier-Macmillan, 1959.
4. J. Fesler, 'Centralization and Decentralization', in *The International Encyclopedia of the Social Sciences*, Collier-Macmillan, 1968, vol. 2, p. 371.
5. G. L. Weil, *The Benelux Nations: The Politics of Small-Country Democracies*, New York: Holt, Rinehart and Winston, 1970, p. 77.
6. A recommendation of the *Royal Commission on Local Government*, (Redcliffe-Maud), HMSO, Command 4040, June 1969, vol. 1, para 5.
7. *Royal Commission on Local Government*, op. cit., vol. 2, para 268.
8. F. Ridley and J. Blondel, *Public Administration in France*, Routledge and Kegan Paul, 1964, p. 93.
9. Y. Meny, 'France', in E. C. Page and M. J. Goldsmith (eds.), *Central and Local Government Relations: A Comparative Analysis of West European Unitary States*, Sage, 1987.
10. R. A. W. Rhodes, 'Territorial Politics in the United Kingdom: The Politics of Change, Conflict and Contradiction', in *West European Politics*, October 1987 – a special edition on 'Tensions in the Territorial Politics of Western Europe'.
11. K. C. Wheare, *Federal Government*, Oxford University Press, 1953, p. 11.
12. G. F. Sawer, *Modern Federalism*, C. A. Watts, 1969, pp. 117–30.
13. A. J. Heidenheimer, *The Governments of Germany*, New York: Thomas Crowell, 1961, pp. 119. The Bundesrat, as Heidenheimer points out, is a 'throwback' to an earlier form of princely representation.
14. C. C. Hodge, 'The Supremacy of Parties: Federation and Parties in Western Europe,' *West European Politics*, April 1987.
15. Sir R. Clarke, *New Trends in Government*, HMSO, 1971.
16. The Kilbrandon Report of 1973 (the Royal Commission on the Constitution) formed the basis for the specific government proposals made in November 1975: *Our Changing Democracy: Devolution to Scotland and Wales* (Command 6348). The proposals envisaged a degree of devolution for domestic affairs and an elected assembly each for Scotland and for Wales.

Additional references

M. Anderson (ed.), *The Frontier Regions of Western Europe*, Frank Cass, 1983.

D. Ashford, 'Reconstructing the French "Etat": Progress of the *Loi Defferre*', *West European Politics*, July 1983.

P. Blair, *Federalism and the Judicial Process in West Germany*, Oxford University Press, 1981.

V. Bogdanor, *Devolution*, Oxford University Press, 1979.

M. Burgess (ed.), *Federalism and Federation in Western Europe*, Croom Helm, 1986.

B. Burrows and G. Denton, *Devolution or Federalism?*, Macmillan, 1980.

J. Cornford (ed.), *The Failure of the State: On the Distribution of Political and Economic Power in Europe*, Croom Helm, 1975.

H. Drucker and G. Brown, *The Politics of Nationalism and Devolution*, Longman, 1980.

A. Gunlicks (ed.), *Local Government Reform and Reorganisation: An International Perspective*, New York: Kennikat Press, 1981.

A. Gunlicks, *Local Government in the German Federal System*, Durham. Duke University Press, 1986.

G. Gustafsson, 'Modes and Effects of Local Government Mergers in the Scandinavian Countries', *West European Politics*, October 1980.

T. O. Hueglin, 'Regionalism in Western Europe: Conceptual Problems of a New Political Perspective', *Comparative Politics*, July 1986.

G. Ionescu, *Centripetal Politics*, Hart-Davis, MacGibbon, 1975.

P. King, *Federalism and Federation*, Croom Helm, 1982.

M. Kolinsky (ed.), *Divided Loyalties: British Regional Assertion and European Integration*, Manchester University Press, 1978.

P. Madgwick, and R. Rose (eds.), *The Territorial Dimension in United Kingdom Politics*, Macmillan, 1982.

Y. Meny and V. Wright (eds.), *Centre-Periphery Relations in Western Europe*, Allen and Unwin, 1985.

R. Morgan (ed.), *Regionalism in European Politics*, Policy Studies Institute, 1986.

R. Nanetti, *Growth and Territorial Policies: The Italian Model of Social Capitalism*, Pinter, 1988.

E. Page and M. Goldsmith (eds.), *Central and Local Government Relations: A Comparative Analysis of West European Unitary States*, Sage, 1987.

R. Rhodes and V. Wright (eds.), *Tensions in the Territorial Politics of Western Europe*, Cass, 1987.

F. Ridley, 'Integrated Decentralization: Models of the Prefectoral System', *Political Studies*, March 1973.

W. Riker, *Federalism: Origin, Operation, Significance*, Boston: Little, Brown, 1964.

S. Rokkan and D. Urwin (eds.), *The Politics of Territorial Identity: Studies in European Regionalism*, Sage Publications, 1983.

G. Sawer, *Modern Federalism*, C. A. Watts, 1969.

L. Sharpe (ed.), *Decentralist Trends in Western Democracies*, Sage Publications, 1979.

E. Tiryatian and R. Rogowski (eds.), *New Nationalism of the Developed West*, Allen and Unwin, 1985.

L. Tivey (ed.), *The Nation-State: The Formation of Modern Politics*, Oxford: Martin Robertson, 1981.

C. Williams (ed.), *National Separatism*, University of Wales Press, 1982.

The Reforms of Local and Regional Authorities in Europe: Theory, Practice and Critical Appraisal. Strasbourg: Council of Europe, 1983.

Models of integration

The spatial aspects of politics we considered in the preceding chapter in relation to national politics apply equally to political integration which cuts across existing national boundaries. From this point of view, the political development of Europe is of particular relevance. Ortega y Gasset argued that the feeling for and the idea of 'nationality' was Europe's 'most characteristic' discovery. Yet now a reverse process is under way – a movement beyond the nation-state as one of the most significant forms of political innovation.

The broad sweep of European history from the Romans, through the eras of Charlemagne and Napoleon, to the twentieth century shows the continual potency of a European-wide concept. Yet at the same time Europe also has to be regarded as the home of the nation-state, each country jealous of its sovereignty, and unlikely to accept for long a unity imposed by force. The effect of these two opposed ideas has been to set up lasting tensions which the two 'world' wars of this century, equally to be thought of as European civil wars, only partially dispelled. Neither armed force nor national expansionism has brought about a unified Europe. The use of force to forge one Europe came to its ultimate expression in Hitler's attempt to impose his 'new order' on the European states.

The experience of peace since 1945 does not mean that the attempt to secure a unified Europe by coercion will never be made again, but that the present era is well-suited to negotiation and the use of reason. At least for Western Europe there have been various pressures at work in recent years acting towards a growing unity. Of these, the economic considerations have probably been uppermost: the need for the wider markets, the harnessing of investment potential, the desirable mobility of labour and capital – all of these made the boundaries and restrictions of the nation-state an increasing hindrance to the fulfilment of economic possibilities. Alternatively, the economic pressures can be viewed as a continuing crisis to which the process of 'capitalist internationalisation' is a response, as Miliband saw it: 'The European Economic Community is one institutional expression of this phenomenon and represents an attempt to overcome within the context of capitalism one of its major 'contradictions', namely the constantly more marked obsolescence of the nation-state as the basic unit of international life.'[1]

Seen only in this light, the success of economic partnership, technical co-operation, and political ventures is altogether unremarkable. And it can be further argued that remoteness of the new organisations established makes them far less amenable to popular pressures then are the individual governments of the countries concerned. Nevertheless, this defect may be offset by the heightened expectations which economic advance brings in its train. Popular demand to share in the benefits of growing material abundance could make the 'distributive state', and its supra-national counterpart, a live object of political pressure. To achieve this, new political structures will have to come into being at the same time as old concepts of national sovereignty are abandoned and the apparatus of the nation-state is dismantled.

Considered from two aspects, the 'undoing' of the nation-state is particularly relevant to Western Europe. Here are concentrated a great proportion of the world's most advanced nations, but at the same time it is largely an assemblage of small and medium-sized states; the chequer-board of their boundaries is an impediment to economic rationalisation. If for no other reason, the economic influences are likely to modify the national political structures, although, as we shall see in the following section, there have been other influences at work in Western Europe as well.

We should start by examining the meanings that can be attached to the term 'integration' and the alternative processes by which it can be achieved. Ultimately, full political integration involves the adoption of a common political authority, with similar structures and processes for all the previously independent states. Once achieved, there is a considerable political simplification, but whilst the development is still under way, the coexistence of authorities and of more or less competitive structures, will lead to a more complex situation. This complexity is especially true of Western Europe, since the form of integration which has emerged so far is still open-ended. At the other extreme, in the crude sense of 'primitive' integration – by conquest or imposed hegemony – the simplification can take place without any intermediate stages; integration is direct, structures and processes are laid down centrally, and the only delay is in securing a common loyalty to the new state form.

Any other mode of integration has to allow for an intermediate coexistence of authority. This duality raises a number of questions: How is the coexistence to be effected? Is the coexistence of authority to be based on a static or a changing balance? How far are the political authorities in a position to regulate the balance? What final political forms are likely to emerge?

To attempt an answer to these questions, we can first refer to the classic solution of securing integration by political means – the federal blueprint. Federalism is one example, and in some ways the most practicable, of securing full political union outright. It involves the immediate creation of a central political authority, a territorial dispersion of power, and a binding commitment to irrevocable union. The initial conception is necessarily static: on the one hand the right to secede must be denied, and on the other, the founding members cannot countenance an erosion of their stated powers from the word 'go'. Just the same, this territorial pluralism, even if conceived as a genuine balance, appears as a period of extended transition, within which supranational loyalties become paramount and the powers of the central authorities become decisive. At some point, the instruments used to maintain a territorial power dispersion, although *formally* operating as was originally conceived, at length assume a secondary importance. Distinctions between such 'advanced' federal states and unitary ones can still be made, but the territorial aspects of the federal state lose out in the end to the national division of powers.

The leading future of federalism, besides its detailed power arrangements, is the emphasis on a final idea of the political system. The alternative to this finality is not really a 'confederation' of states, because this arrangement requires the member states to be distinct entities, without any loss of sovereignty; it amounts to a series of treaty relationships amongst fully responsible states, and a purely instrumental, or even non-existent, authority at the centre. As with federalism, a confederation lays down a final political form.

The real alternative is a form of integration which does not detail the extent of integration nor carry a conception of the end-product – what are usually labelled 'functional' or neo-functional solutions. As this description implies, integration proceeds by the harmonising of *particular* governmental structures and policies. In principle, it is never final, never total, but a steady aggregation; nor is the process of necessity overtly political. The harmonisation can take place in a variety of social and economic sectors, and to a large extent leave the political structure of the nation states apparently unaffected. At the minimal level, the functional form of integration can be defined as, 'a union with joint, but limited liability for a particular activity'.[2] But it is clear that this version given by Mitrany represents only a point of departure. One cannot remain long with the fiction that membership from one activity to another will vary at random: the nature of one partnership will affect later ones both with regard to membership and content. It is also more than probable that there will be preconditions at the outset, making some types of partnership desirable and some potential members unacceptable. And although the unions are 'limited', they do represent common goals – ones which at least must be consonant with the goals in the non-integrated sectors.

A new element is brought into play when political integration is defined as, '. . . the process by which member states give up making key public policies independently and instead make them jointly within a supranational cadre or pass them on to a new supranational administration.'[3] Here one has the germ of a *general* political authority, extremely limited if the 'public policies' in question relate only to one sector, but with great potential if the supranational authority becomes multifunctional. Even here, however, the emphasis is on the coexistence of this new authority with the pre-existing ones of the nation-states. What is quite different from the federal version of coexistence is that the functional form avoids any head-on confrontation with the national political authorities; instead there will be a whole series of minor conflicts and compromises. And the 'confrontation' need never occur if the *final* political form is never given a specific rendering. Because the functional system of integration at no stage seeks a solution embracing, '. . . the totality of political responsibilities in the field of foreign policy or defence, nor looking to a federal super-state as its ultimate objective', the form of the system may remain open indefinitely.[4] An approximation to federalism might only emerge when political integration had become an established fact in many other ways; full political union could then more resemble a topping-out ceremony.

A third rendering of political integration gives an indication of what these 'other ways' might be. Ernst Haas defined it as, '. . . the process whereby political actors in several distinct national settings are persuaded to shift their loyalties, expectations and political activities towards a new centre, whose institutions possess or demand jurisdiction over pre-existing national states.'[5] This version of integration extends the meaning considerably away from an exclusive focus on institutions to the people involved, and it underlines what is particularly true for functional integration that the required change in behaviour and attitudes will be gradual, an assimilation to the new centre. In sum, there is a dual development which is interconnected: the modification of behaviour goes together with the building-up of new, supranational institutions.

The questions we posed originally about the coexistence of authority in the intermediate stages of integration appear to be partly answered. Functional integration allows for coexistence, since it does not set up new, general political authorities, but allows for a gradual redistribution of authority, in effect, a sector-by-sector approach. There is a continually changing balance, and the 'final' political form, although for long kept nominally open, is related to how this balance evolves.

The question that remains to be answered is: How far are the political authorities in the member states in a position to regulate the balance? This question can be put in other ways: Does functional integration have a dynamic of its own, or can a limit to further integration be imposed? Is the undermining of national sovereignty inevitable? Functional integration is certainly not irreversible, even if it does generate its own dynamic. To use the analogy made by Walter Hallstein, at one time the leading exponent of the Community viewpoint within the Commission, integration is like riding a bicycle: the choice is simply between going forward or falling off. One can accept that at any point an individual government can cry 'halt', and only if coercive pressure exists at the centre can a member state be forced to remain within the fold; yet the nature of functional integration precludes the setting-up of a general coercive power so that basic freedom of action is preserved right up to the point of declared political union.

Less radically, a government may attempt to put a stop to further integration – by veto, non-co-operation, the 'empty chair'. Such possibilities are not eliminated by the majority voting, since the attempt to apply a majority verdict to disputed policies can prove too costly; the consensual element is vital as long as governments cannot be coerced. Thus a cut-off point can be dictated by individual governments, and this resistance can hold up the *formal* process of integration indefinitely. But at a more fundamental level the development may continue unchecked; in particular, as we have just seen, progress depends on the attitudes and behaviour of *all* political participants, not only those operating at the top level of decision-making, and at the informal, social levels they may not be readily amenable to government influence.

There are two other factors which serve to make functional integration progressive. The first of these has been termed the 'spillover' effect; that is, integration in one sector encourages a like process in similar or related sectors. For example, the implementation of common economic and trade policies may lead to a demand for definite social safeguards; social provisions will be made, and it will be desirable to have a common policy in all member states. The second factor is the 'enmeshing' of the activities of *parallel* institutions in the participating states. Such institutions may be private agencies or ones of government; there will be increasingly close relations between opposite numbers in particular integrated fields, and as new developments take place these relations will be strengthened. Patterns of initiation and response are formed which go beyond a simple co-operation towards a permanent relationship.

These two effects are supplemented by a third – the creation of supranational cadres; no significant degree of integration could take place without the provision for personnel to administer the integrated sectors. And once these officials are appointed they will tend to acquire a loyalty to the organisation rather than to the states of their origin, at least with regard to their own area of work. This development is a first sign of a political will emerging within the supranational organisation.

We can conclude that there is an independent dynamic of integration; with the cumulative effect of this movement, it is realistic to admit that at some stage a point of no-return will be reached. When and how this critical stage would be determined is problematic. One view is that it would be unlikely to occur through the mere accumulation of institutions, but the resolution of the issue would depend on a combination of institutional development, plus the onset of a particular economic or political crisis which would either cement or fragment the system. In this crisis there would be a test of the most fundamental index of integration, of loyalties.

This view, that 'crisis-cum-institution' will in the end mark the transference from sovereign nation state to a new super-state, is only one possibility. Thus it can be argued that the widespread 'need' to have a recognisable national sovereignty – typical of the era of the nation state – may lead to fallacious ideas of sovereignty when it is placed in the context of functional integration: the vision of Western Europe one day emerging as a kind of super-state can be regarded as a simple extension of the nation-state syndrome. Both nationalism and the nation state were functional to the growth of industrial society, but is it necessary to look for an equivalent in 'post-industrial' society? It could equally be the case that the transition to advanced capitalism enquires the muting of strong national attachments; if this were so, then the final unit of integration could emerge quite unlike existing state forms, neither explicitly claiming sovereignty, nor requiring strong political attachments.

Even if it is maintained that the final unit would have to acquire state-like qualities if it were to survive in a world of other states, there is still an alternative argument that the co-existence of two types of authority, national and supranational, need not reach a crisis-point. It is simply that member governments find it increasingly difficult to act independently – even in those areas which are wholly within their own province. The power of these implied limitations, a form of 'seepage' which runs from the integrated to the non-integrated areas, is that governments see that it is in their own interests to act in common. Earlier commitments are likely to induce common attitudes and interests *in advance* of the question of the non-integrated areas being raised, the more so if this process operates over an extended period of time. Thus the assertion of sovereignty, though always feasible, need never become a live issue.

This general discussion of political integration can now be related to the actual developments that have taken place within Western Europe. Before we look at the practical implications of the functional model, as seen in the European Community, it is helpful to look at the background to European integration – in the eyes of the idealists and the realists.

European perspectives
That Western Europe does form a recognisable entity has been an assumption underlying all the comparisons we have so far made in this book, and it is further shown by the increasing cohesion shown by many of the states since 1945; the central question concerning us here is the political form which is likely to result. A number of alternative models is available, all with a relevance for the not-too-distant future. Is a new Europe to be basically a 'Europe of States', conveniently sheltering behind an umbrella of association? Or is it to emerge as a tightly-knit federal union? Again, is the political basis likely to be a direct expression of democratic will, or rather the apparatus of a remote and manipulative bureaucracy? And whatever form it takes, is a new Europe to be identified as a world force or one preoccupied with its own backyard? Answers to these questions lead to radically different views as to what integration could mean in practice. But important as the questions are, they do not admit of simple and direct answers. And assessment has to take into account a range of factors: the general drift of West European development in recent years, the weight of formal integration so far achieved, the basic compatibility of the nation states, and the degree to which a common political culture is a necessary ingredient.

The outcome of the Second World War was important in two

respects. It was a turning-point for Western Europe, now relegated to a secondary place in world affairs; the new global balance between the Soviet Union and the United States made the one concerned with Western Europe as extended frontier to be sealed off, and the other interested to secure Western Europe as a political and military ally. A second, and related effect was to bring about an equality of power *within* the area; there was no West European 'victor' able to impose its hegemony or willing to give decisive leadership to the other states. Both developments made European statesmen aware of their subordinate position in world politics; some saw that their main hope of self-assertion, even survival, lay in making collective approaches.

This is one strand in the reorientation; there are two others which serve to give a more rounded picture. At one extreme there was the vision of a united Europe on the part of idealists. From their point of view the new equality after 1945 presented an unrivalled opportunity to achieve full political union, a federal system of government. This union would at last give expression to the 'European Idea', the institutional realisation of a common European culture. For the idealists political integration was the culminating step in an age-old mission, but for realists at the other extreme it was the third strand in the reorientation which was conclusive: that the needs of advanced capitalism made the old political boundaries outmoded; the real advances towards integration would only be secured by economic imperatives. We do not necessarily have to choose between these competing versions. None of the three favours the nation state as a suitable vehicle for future development, and the strength of the movement towards European integration lies in the fact that at different times each of these diverse motives has preserved the initial momentum.

This momentum can be traced ultimately to the critical rapprochement between France and Germany; without this reconciliation scarcely any permanent advance could have been made, and from it has resulted the most tangible set of integrated institutions. It is worth reviewing the terms on which reconciliation came about. The lever was undoubtedly the shift in allied, chiefly American, policy towards the western zones of occupied Germany from 1946 onwards – a shift occasioned by the complete rupture of the western allies from the Soviet Union. Later than her allies, who early on began to appreciate the cost to themselves of a permanently weakened Germany, the French government slowly began a reversal of the historic policy of reparation and annexation: the economic fusion of the Saar with France soon after the war was still in the classic mould of Franco-German relations. Given the history of these relations between the two countries, this policy was understandable. Its reversal was dramatic, but it did not mean an abandonment of French aims. The point of the new strategy of reconciliation which French governments began to pursue was made crystal-clear by the Socialist, André Philip; 'The only way to ensure that a new Germany shall not dominate Europe is to see that Europe dominates the Ruhr' – a Europeanisation of the 'German Problem'.[6]

The efforts made by the United States to secure a rehabilitation of Germany were at first economic, but the political and military implications soon become apparent; full statehood for West Germany meant that her willing participation could only be achieved if she were an equal partner. But this change would only be accomplished if it were on terms with both French and German thinking. To successive French governments the post-war instability of France and weakness of her economy appeared to be more immediate dangers than those from a weakened and truncated Germany. A planned reconciliation could give economic and political benefits outweighing transient gains of a continued and solitary reprisal.

At first sight, West Germany might appear as simply the passive object of policies laid down by the western allies – forced willy-nilly to accept their definition of European realities. But from 1949 onwards an increasingly independent German voice had to be taken into account; the German electorate had a choice between two leaders whose policies were opposed, Kurt Schumacher and Konrad Adenauer. For Schumacher, the Social Democrat leader – never able to achieve power – a West German government should *prove* itself to be independent of the occupiers, and follow a policy directly aimed at German reunification. For Adenauer, in power for the whole of the critical period, the considerations were different. As he was a Rhinelander and a Catholic, one can possibly doubt the strength of his commitment to a reunified Germany. It can be said that, in effect, he practised a separatism for the whole of West Germany in a fashion parallel to the separatism he had briefly supported for the Rhineland after the First World War. His decision to side unequivocally with the western powers brought the taunt from Schumacher that he was 'the chancellor of the allies'; on this view he forfeited the remote possibility of reunification which a neutralist policy would have offered.

One of the first fruits of the Franco-German accord was the Schuman Plan put forward by the French government in May 1950 to pool European coal and steel production under the control of a supranational authority. In the words of its sponsor, it was designed 'to end Franco-German hostility once and for all'. The 1951 treaty setting up the European Coal and Steel Community (ECSC) was specifically designed, according to Schuman, '. . . to enable Germany to accept restrictions on her own sovereignty which is gradually being restored to her.'[7] Thus the High Authority of the ECSC served to replace the more direct supervision exercised by the Allied High Commission in Germany. It would be a mistake to see the ECSC in these instrumental terms alone, as only concerned with the regulation of basic production and representing a disguised 'occupation' of Germany. With its nucleus of six states, it was to be a model for later integration, and was then the first step of an open-ended 'jump into Europe'.

The ECSC was a strange amalgam of idealism, hard-headed calculation of economic benefit, and an attempt to gain strategic security – precisely the three strands of reorientation we noted earlier. But it was hardly a manifestation of a popular mandate, rather an attempt to forge European unity 'by stealth' – especially on the part of the idealists who saw that their first attempts to secure outright political unity were unlikely to get off the ground. Later developments were to show that supranational devices could be advocated too far in advance of national acceptability. The Pleven Plan, put forward in October 1950, aimed to create a European Army, with an eventual extension to a 'Political Community' as well, and it foundered on just those national susceptibilities. The main proposal in the Pleven Plan for a European Defence Community – a military equivalent of the ECSC – would have solved the dilemma of securing German military participation without the embarrassment of a German national army, but it was eventually rejected by the French National Assembly in 1954.

This failure apart, the ECSC proved to be the successful prototype for the technical co-operation of 'Euratom' (1956), and in the multi-functional European Economic Community (1957). There was a threefold link between the Communities: a common membership, the structural solutions arrived at, and the underlying purpose of securing ever-wider integration. But the smooth evolution in organisation and areas of competence was matched by the continuing problem of creating a purposive *political* instrument from this supranationalism; the 'community approach' which was successful in functional terms was not the means to secure a rapid political unity. It was a disillusion for the idealists, but not for the governments or the economic interests concerned.

If the original six EEC countries represented an 'inner ring' of successful functional integration, the larger number outside this ring was made up of states for which these tight commitments were for long unacceptable, and those countries preferred looser alliances such as the European Free Trade Association and the Nordic Council, with strictly limited aims and no supranational authority. Even in a modified way such organisations, together with military treaties and the setting-up of various inter-governmental bodies, also have some passive integrative effect; attitudes and behaviour are affected by this limited co-operation, and the co-operation is often seen as a prelude to a later, and more explicit, integration of countries in the 'outer ring', as has proved to be the case. The reasons for many countries being unwilling or unable to take on additional commitments were various: traditional policies of 'neutrality' in the case of Sweden and Switzerland, the delicate international position of Austria and Finland, the political unacceptability of Greece, Portugal, and Spain. For the United Kingdom it was the strength of her other commitments which made for hesitation. Denmark and Ireland were contingently affected by British reluctance because of their dependence on trade with Britain.

Institutional features of the European Community

On one level, the institutional structure of the Community is relatively straightforward, on another, in terms of its future evolution, it represents a complex of possibilities. We can first set out the basic institutional arrangements and then take account of some of the imponderables. The keynote principle is that of supranationalism, by which a permanent executive body exists, independent of the member states, and able to take a range of decisions on its own account. This feature is integral to the 'Community Method' which David Coombes defined as: 'A process of unification by which "supranational" institutions, acting initially within limited sectors, are expected to have wide-ranging effects on political behaviour and by this means to provide an impetus for growing political union.'[8] It entails, 'progress towards political unity by integrating one sector at a time'; the Community Method is an extremely subtle instrument because it combines a pragmatism in determining the nature and the timing of the sectors to be integrated with an overall strategy contained in the cumulative effect of sector integration.

The institutional framework of the Community consists of four major organs: the European Parliament, the permanent executive Commission, the Council of Ministers, and the Court of Justice. Of these institutions, the European Parliament started out as the weakest body, since in effect it was mainly a consultative assembly.

Its one sanction, by a two-thirds majority, was to enforce the resignation of the Commission en bloc, a nuclear weapon too powerful to be of practical importance, and an unreal one as the Parliament was given no complementary power over the appointment of members of the Commission. Its actual powers were limited to debating the annual report of the Commission, suggesting amendments to the Community budget, though these were not mandatory, making detailed studies of particular topics, and questioning individual members of the Commission in the areas of their responsibility. As a consultative body, the European Parliament did not carry much more weight than the numerous specialised committees, nominated by the member governments, advising the Commission on various aspects of policy. Amongst these are the Economic and Social Committee, flanked by those concerned with monetary policy, economic policy, budgetary matters, transport, scientific and technical questions, and agriculture. At the outset, their expert nature perhaps carried more weight than did the Parliament which inevitably had something of the character of a supranational debating society. Until the direct elections of 1979 the members of the European Parliament were seconded from their national assemblies, and its proceedings attracted little interest or comment – besides having no impact on Community policy. Inevitably, if the idea of 'political union' were to be advanced, it meant grasping the nettles of direct election *and* the powers of the European Parliament. In fact, they work in tandem: direct election gave the Parliament an injection of much-needed legitimacy, and since 1979 it has visibly increased its authority, especially on budgetary issues but also in attracting wider attention as a political forum.

The permanent Commission is a hybrid of administration and political competences. Coombes summarised its main functions as three-fold:[9]

1. Initiation of Community legislation. The Commission makes policy proposals to the Council of Ministers. The Council can only make amendments by unanimous vote; otherwise the Commission proposal has to be accepted or rejected. This procedure ensures that thorough negotiation takes place before proposals are laid on the table.
2. A 'mediating' function. This aspect follows directly from the first: the need to negotiate at a sub-ministerial level to iron out the differences of interest amongst the member states.
3. Implementation of Community legislation. Once policy has been agreed, the Commission can take consequent 'Decisions'

and make 'Regulations' – both important forms of delegated legislation. In cases of breach of Community law, the Commission can intervene and if necessary refer the case to the Court of Justice.

To these can be added the technical and advisory functions of the Commission, generally that it acts to co-ordinate the actions of member states in particular fields, and the Commission's status as the diplomatic representative of the Community.

Behind all these functions lies the theme that the Commission represents the 'conscience' of the Community, serving its interests rather than those of any member states. This infusion, quite apart from the political powers, distinguishes the Commission from a normal bureaucracy. The 17 members of the Commission are appointed for a four-year, renewable term by agreement amongst the member governments, and with a strict regard for national balance. But they are in no way subordinate to the governments – Commission members are explicitly barred from taking outside instructions. Nor do they seek anonymity; on the contrary, they are expected to emerge as figures in their own right, and in this respect the calibre of Commission personnel has been noteworthy, not only because it has included a proportion of committed 'Europeans', but individual members are frequently important political or administrative figures in their home country. Beneath this collegiate body is the administrative and research staff of the various Community projects, some ten thousand in all, seven thousand of these forming the central bureaucracy.

The Council of Ministers (usually composed of the foreign ministers of the member states) remains the basic decision-making body of the community. It provides the focus of sovereignty, since the Council is not responsible to any Community institution; its members are only answerable to their own governments. Whilst majority voting is the rule, weighted according to the size of the state, in practice unanimity has to be secured on any matter which a single country defines as fundamental to its interests. The working relationship between the Commission and the Council of Ministers is maintained by the Council's subordinate offshoot, 'Coreper', the Committee of Permanent Representatives. Formally, this is not a decision-making organ, but because the Council only meets infrequently, and anyway changes composition according to the subject under consideration, the Committee will make a number of recommendations many of which the Council will later approve 'on the nod'. The importance of these government nominees (civil servants, diplomats, and 'experts') on Coreper derives from their key linking position as national representatives in Brussels and the channel of information to their own governments. As almost all committee business passes through Coreper, it is strategically placed to influence governments and the Commission. The Committee of Permanent Representatives thus makes for a continuity and homogeneity which the Council of Ministers by itself could not impart. Coreper represents a real centre of power, and with some justice it can be regarded as a true location of the 'technocrats' just as much as the Commission.

Unlike the other three institutions, the Court of Justice, located in Luxembourg, has a passive rather than an active role. Its functions are related to the implementation of the original Treaty provisions and subsequent Community legislation, such as directives issued by the Commission. In this context it should be noted that it is an entirely different body, the European Court of Human Rights at Strasbourg, which hears cases involving alleged breaches of the European Convention on Human Rights. The powers of the Court of Justice may be used in respect of national governments and individual firms and enterprises, usually on the basis of complaints brought to it by the Commission. The Commission may enforce the Court's rulings by imposing sanctions – exacting fines or withholding subsidies. It may be argued that Community law unequivocally represents a form of supranational law, binding alike on member states and their citizens. But the reality is somewhat different, for supranational law ultimately has to rely on a political authority for its enforcement, and the Community does not have that authority. In the final analysis it must rely on the cooperation of national governments and national courts, and governments are still free to define 'national sovereignty' in their own way: there is nothing to prevent a government from flouting a Court ruling, and for practical purposes the Commission is powerless. As Paul Taylor concluded: 'The Communities' ability to execute its laws within states is inevitably limited by the absence of any Community agency for this purpose ... and no Communities presence within the states ... In the complex and original legal procedures developed in the European Communities, the states have carefully preserved their traditional values.'[10] That is not to say that a tight system of enforceable supranational law will not emerge, but it is mistaken to think that a legal integration can be a substitute for *political* integration – the former depends on the latter.

This general outline of Community institutions is sufficient as a basis for comparison with national institutions, and it is apparent that none of the three main organs has an exact equivalent at national level. Popular representation was for long absent, the Commission is more than a civil service but less than a government, the Council of Ministers is neither a government nor really a legislature. Above all, there is the almost complete lack of *reciprocal controls*, and this deficiency is aggravated by the blurred division of legislative responsibility between Council and Commission. Finally, Coreper occupies a shadowy, if strategic, halfway house between the two, exercising functions which nominally belong to the others.

Some institutional parallels can be drawn, most obviously with the two federal states, West Germany and Switzerland. Thus the German Bundesrat can be likened to the Council of Ministers: both consist of essentially governmental delegations, acting in a legislative capacity and with a power of veto (individual ministers in the case of the Council, but the body as a whole in the case of the Bundesrat). But there the similarity ends, for the Bundesrat faces a federal government with considerable powers of its own, which the Bundesrat can only marginally affect, and the federal government is also politically responsible to an elected body, the Bundestag. The European Commission, if for the moment it is likened to the federal government, lacks this connection with the European Parliament, and the latter, in turn has lacked it with the electorate.

Another parallel can be drawn with the Swiss Federal Council; in some ways it shows a resemblance to the Commission: this parallel is seen in the collegial nature of both and the guaranteed terms of office, as well as in the fact that the Federal Council, like the Commission, lacks the normal attributes of a parliamentary executive – this is shown by the 'qualified' responsibility which governs its existence. In its permanence, the Swiss system of federal government comes nearest to what one might term an administrative form of democracy, and thus has some likeness to the Commission. The missing requirement here is that the personnel of the Commission do not emanate from the European Parliament, either as a source of recruitment or in the actual mode of appointment.

Problems of development
The conclusion must be that the institutions of the Community, compared with what has evolved on a national level, are still inadequate to bear the weight of extended *political* integration. That judgement does not imply any breakdown: a tailing-off in the rate of sector integration and a fall in demand for new political

institutions could well leave the system functioning for an indefinite period. That is also true if economic integration gathers pace. Thus even if the creation of a single market by 1992 is realised, the institutional structure need not change in any significant way. The increase in the number of Community members from the original six to nine in 1973 with the accession of Britain, Denmark and Ireland, ten with Greece in 1981, and twelve from 1986 with the entry of Portugal and Spain, with others such as Turkey knocking at the door, creates continuous and long-term problems of adjustment so that radical changes of institutional structure may be shelved – especially since the unanimous agreement of member governments is required. However, we can examine some of the issues raised by 'development'.

The specific demand for the direct election of the European Parliament, as provided for in the original Treaty of Rome, was eventually met in 1979. Obviously the Parliament is no longer content with a consultative role. But what direction should it take? The assembly may strengthen its control powers at the same time as 'legitimising' the Community as a whole. In Hallstein's view the Parliament should 'dramatize and popularize the great decisions' – with the implications that this function was the prime one. But such a dramatisation would work only if the assembly were really *linked* to the decision-making process. Any parallel with the *actual* weakness of national parliaments is misleading, for they have a historical legitimacy, a live relationship to their executives, informal controls, party discipline, a common legislative-executive recruitment. In future the European Parliament will necessarily seek real powers in two areas: political responsibility and financial controls.

The vexed question of political responsibility can be shunted around in various ways. The obvious solution of having the European Commission solely responsible to Parliament would have an immediate impact on the power of the Council of Ministers. This implication is quite unacceptable to most governments on the argument that that executive power should rest with state-appointed European ministers rather than with an 'independent' Commission. Only in the 'final' phase might such ministers have nothing but strictly European duties and no longer be a part of a national government, and only *then* would it be necessary to have a strong European Parliament. Explicit here is the mistrust of both a strong Commission and a popular assembly – not surprisingly the Commission and the European Parliament are often regarded as in alliance for a more 'European' solution than governments – and possibly their electorates – will countenance.

However the question of political responsibility is solved or just left unanswered, the role of the Commission remains ambiguous. At first the 'dialogue' between the Commission and Council appeared to be formally on the basis of equality, but the reality was soon different: for several years the Council eroded the Commission's powers, reducing its proposals to preliminary drafts which the Permanent Representatives re-examine and re-shape before passing them to the Council for final approval. The strategic power of Coreper is well in evidence, and it led to a political downgrading of the Commission. The problem for the Commission is how to rescue its power of initiative: consulting with Coreper and other bodies before submitting its proposals, withdrawing them for modification if they are rejected by the Council of Ministers, but trying to ensure that ultimately it is the Commission's proposals that are voted on, not those of the Council or Coreper.

The troubles of the Commission can be traced to the fact that it exists in a political vacuum, a result of the 'failure' to settle the question of securing political responsibility. The other matter, that of securing financial controls is just as intractable, but concerns the Assembly not the Commission. Historically, the power of financial control has been central to the evolution of parliamentary institutions, but the scope for this in the Community arrangements is limited.

It is difficult to see how the European Parliament could indefinitely extend its financial authority without upsetting the whole Community system. The vast sums collected by the member states and paid into Community funds are largely earmarked in advance for established support schemes – chiefly farming subsidies which still account for some two-thirds of the Community's budget – and those schemes can only be altered by inter-government agreement. With important national interests at stake – as with the Common Agricultural Policy – it is hard to visualise member governments willingly conceding authority to the European Parliament. Even though the aim of the present arrangement was partly to make the Community financially independent – giving permanent sources of revenue rather than contributions from the member states – the result has been to impart an inertia to the system. The Community budget has to be agreed by the Council of Ministers and the scope for intervention by the European Parliament is still limited. It does have the power, by a two-thirds vote, to reject the entire draft of an annual budget and request a re-submission, but that right is mainly of symbolic value. Parliament also has direct control of a part of the

Community's budget (relating mainly to administration, research, foreign aid and information services) and use of the European Court of Auditors to scrutinise Community revenues and expenditure. But since the question of political responsibility remains unresolved, the slices of financial power given to the European Parliament are lacking in vital substance: a ritual dance of 'blustering confrontation' results which ultimately does not affect the necessity for and the substance of inter-governmental agreement.

Yet the position is far from static. Increasingly, the European Parliament has flexed its muscles, a spectacular occasion was in December 1982 when it rejected the terms of a budget rebate for Britain and West Germany agreed by the Council and Commission. Behind that episode lurked the whole question of the reform of the Common Agricultural Policy which has proved to be inequitable and inefficient. If an 'insoluble' crisis on financing the CAP arises, then the Parliament will use the opportunity to demand more power. That will also become increasingly apparent as the objectives of Community expenditure become more differentiated – for instance in the financing of the Regional and Social Funds. But in the end the question involves the problem of power *and* responsibility. Can Parliament hope to extract greater power whilst the Council of Ministers has to shoulder the real responsibility for decisions taken?

Much depends on whether we can really speak of an evolving *European* party system – on whether the idea of 'transnational' parties has substantial meaning.[11] Any assessment will have to depend on the experience of several directly-elected European Parliaments, but it is clear that even a transnational party is affected by its double basis of loyalty: national interest and party interest. Those two interests do not necessarily coincide, and resort to majoritarian decision-making and discipline within a party group would be an invitation to fragmentation. Yet unless the transnational parties can develop supranational qualities, the ability of the European Parliament to assert its authority over the other Community institutions will always founder on the assertion of national interest. Paradoxically, however, if any one 'European' party – conservative or socialist, say – did emerge as dominant in the Parliament, then *national* governments of a different political persuasion would be all the more concerned to resist parliamentary encroachments on their authority. The potential of the various cross-currents makes it evident that precise parallels with existing party systems, and the terms of their evolution, are not to be drawn.

There are other problems of Community development. One source of unease is associated with the bureaucratic and possibly 'illiberal' tendencies of the Community which may in part result from the political weakness of the Commission and Parliament. An expression of the bureaucratisation process is seen in panacea of creating a 'harmony' of regulation throughout the Community – a 'harmonisation madness'. In this context a distinction should be made between *negative* integration, the removal of barriers, and *positive* integration, requiring conformity in standards. Left to itself, the negative form results in lop-sided development; harmonisation seeks to prevent the distortion.

Over the past two decades there has been a growing emphasis on 'international' rather than supranational integration. This shift was made evident in the Davignon 'formula' of 1970 which proposed more effective cooperation between the *member governments* especially in the important non-integrated sectors of foreign relations and defence. Moreover, the successive enlargements of the Community have made it even more important to coordinate the policies of governments and to carry all members along in the establishment of clear priorities for the Community. One indication of the preference for inter-governmental initiative is the procedure that has been adopted for regular summit meetings of the heads of governments which take place twice a year in the various capital cities. These European Council meetings (in addition to the frequent meetings of foreign ministers and others of a more specialised competence) are significant in giving the Community a political profile besides acting as a springboard for new approaches to integration.

There is a fundamental conflict between the supranational approach and the inter-governmental alternative, for inevitably the Council of Ministers is strengthened by the latter and the Commission is relegated to an instrumental role. Nevertheless, the success of a more 'logical' process of integration brings with it the need for permanent implementation, and some of the objectives, for instance the commitment to 'political and monetary union' as first set out by the Werner Committee in 1970, would only in the initial stages be entrusted to intergovernmental agreement. Yet the actual machinery set up to implement new policies need 'not enhance the Commission's role; it is conceivable that various ad hoc arrangements will be devised, such as has been the case with the European Monetary System established in 1979, to avoid a concentration of authority within the permanent Commission which otherwise might become a monstrously blown-up 'substitute' government.

One indication of an alternative – and radical – route was given in a special report presented by the Commission in June 1975; in essence the Commission proposed the creation of an 'independent' European government – that is, independent of the governments of the member states. In effect such a body would amount to a fusion of the Commission and the Council of Ministers since it would combine the policy and executive functions of both. A parallel report adopted by the European Parliament called for 'a single decision-making centre which has the character of a real European government'. Any substantial development, however, would have to take the commitment to political and monetary union as only the *beginning* of an extended stage of transition.[12]

It is with this background that we can evaluate the developments that have taken place in the 1980s – and most particularly the terms and the thrust of the Single European Act which, after an extended period of ratification by the member states, came into force in July 1987. Its genesis can be traced in the momentum provided by the Draft Treaty of European Union approved by the European Parliament in 1984, although its provisions, unlike the Draft Treaty, are best seen as milestones along the way to an as yet unspecified form of 'union', and missing from the Single European Act is any attempt at institutional innovation: the existing actors are kept in their present roles.

By far the most important provision is the commitment to create a single, free internal market for the Community by 1992. The agreement is to remove all the existing barriers to trade, movement of workers and members of professions, freeing capital movements and the liberalisation of the financial services market chiefly affecting banking and insurance. Some idea of the complexity of the programme is made apparent from the fact that no fewer than three hundred separate measures have to be agreed.

The second important provision direction relates to the realisation of the tight timetable of 1992: decisions will be binding on all member states provided that they are passed by a qualified majority vote in the Council of Ministers of just over two-thirds (54 of the total 76 votes).[13] Even though there are several reserved areas where the unanimity rule will still apply – especially in the sensitive matters of VAT harmonisation and public procurement policies – the principle of majority voting supplies a vital element of supranationalism to the Council and thus to the member-states.

A third feature of the Single European Act is the expressed determination to implement reforms in three fields: agricultural policy, the 'structural' funds (regional development fund, social fund, and the agricultural fund), and the reform of the

Community's system of finance. Yet the proposals put forward by the Commission and in non-specific terms set out in the Single European Act imply a considerable transfer of resources and a shift in the relative size of contributions from individual countries, and in these respects national interests – and expressions of national sovereignty – are likely to prove paramount, since in most questions of reform the unanimity rule prevails. In other words, inter-governmental bargaining and the 'package-deal' technique still represent the core of the integrative dynamic.

It can persuasively be argued that – far from 'overcoming' the nation state – the essential directing impulse of European integration has been to emphasise the key role of national governments, albeit on the basis of their interaction rather than preserving their sovereign and unilateral authority. If that is the case, then it may continue to be more rewarding to look to the 'European dynamic' as a product of domestic political processes rather than seeing the European dimension as a force in its own right.

A European political culture?

At the present time the whole political structure of the Community still resembles an artificial construction rather than the product of important social forces. Although we should expect the arrival of powerful political forces on the European stage, so far they have been remarkably absent. It is the hiatus between the facts of integration and the orientation of social forces which provides the main imponderable for the future. If these were to be marshalled, a new dynamic would be at work; they remain the missing parts of the jigsaw.

Yet one could hardly expect to see the pressing of popular demands and expressions of solidarity to come about before there were adequate means for them to be articulated and aggregated; and they require a definite focus for activity. So far, the Community has attracted interest group attention on a consultative basis – over three hundred such organisations operate in Brussels. This is the reality of 'popular' pressure on the European Community, not the sporadic demonstrations by 'angry farmers' protesting at agricultural pricing policies.

Apart from such outbursts, a necessary step towards a new era of 'European' politics would be the reorientation of national institutions. A natural shift in interest representation is to be expected; without further ado these will gravitate to new decision-making centres, although their favoured approach is still to lobby the member governments. Other institutions are less mobile: the parties are geared to certain channels of action, the national decision-making process, and bound by their own national traditions and concerns. Only direct elections from a *single* European-wide constituency would ever really throw the parties in the European Parliament into a melting-pot. They have developed a number of loose transnational federations: the Confederation of Socialist Parties, the Federation of Liberal and Democratic Parties (ELD), the Christian Democratic European People's Party (EPP) – together with the wider European Democratic Union (EDU) which in addition to the Christian Democrats brings in the British Conservatives. The Communists on the other hand rejected any such formal ties on the grounds that they are artificial and have purely an electioneering value. It remains to be seen how far commitments to common policies and European election programmes develop beyond a loose cooperative intent. It is interesting that those parties espousing 'working-class solidarity' have been the least inclined to subordinate themselves to a federal party.

Even if this transfer to a European scene of operations were to be a prolonged process, the underlying compatibility of the institutions is not really in question. It applies to the political parties, for their history is one of commitment to the institutions of liberal democracy and to the parliamentary system. Alongside these major uniformities, individual variations appear insignificant. Differences are real in such aspects as the form of legal system, the role of a civil servant, the detailed means of controlling executive power, but these are particular flavours, political styles, not evidence of different political values.

Institutional modification is only one aspect of the refashioning of political cultures which 'integration' implies. In the definition we took earlier from Haas, its full expression requires that 'expectations and political activities' would shift to a new centre, and the same applies to the other ingredient he includes, namely the 'loyalties'. As the centres of power change, we can expect that the direction of political activities and expectations will shift along with the modification of institutions, but the question of 'loyalties' is more difficult to evaluate. There are two related problems: Are the new loyalties a necessary constituent of the type of integration which is now taking place in Europe? Is there a likelihood of a loyalty emerging with a distinctive European colouring?

We have already seen that the nation state can be viewed as a product of various forces, and this applies to the concomitant of 'nationalism', the apex of domestic allegiance; the European context of the form of the nation state is a product of changes in economy and society over several hundred years. Yet the development of advanced, international capitalism points to a weakening of the loyalty demanded by the nation state; the growing inability of the West European countries to wage war on their own account at least points to the redundancy of chauvinism. But it does not follow that a reduction in these national loyalties must have an equal compensation – a simultaneous heightening of 'European' awareness. The requirements of a diffuse and functional system of integration do not pose sharp questions of commitment.

Strong pressures to full political union, to be successful, would need to build on this wider identity. The relatively modest integration that has already taken place did need a certain commitment on the part of some politically-relevant people. The point is: who, at different times, are these people likely to be? At successive stages in the course of integration different sets will be involved. An illustrative scheme applying to European integration involves three distinct stages. The initial steps were the concern of several élite groups. Some of these had a purely propaganda value out of all proportion to their numbers, and advocated outright federal union. Other groups, more concerned with concrete benefits, operated within the national governments as politicians or top administrators. Together these groups secured the initial, formal advances. Once these had been made, wider circles were involved in the maintenance and extension of the institutions.

This first stage of development involved the minimum number of people to set the process of functional integration under way. The two other stages involve a much wider public. The second required the acceptance, even a desire for integration by 'informed' public opinion; and the third stage needs the extension of these attitudes to the broad mass of people: in the end that integration – a 'European identity' – becomes a part of ordinary thinking. The initial phase of élite commitment and mass passivity is quite in line with the functioning of liberal democratic politics. From the three-stage model we should expect the impetus to further change to come from within 'informed' public opinion. Survey findings have consistently shown that the young, the more-informed and the better educated sections of a community have tended to favour European integration.[14] This category is necessarily diffuse in character and cuts across established party lines, but its lack of specific relationship is probably advantageous in bringing about fundamental changes of attitude in the population as a whole.

This leaves the third stage, mass acceptance, as a remaining doubtful quantity. We originally introduced this discussion in terms of 'loyalty', but it is apparent that this term can have different connotations. At the minimum there can be the readiness to co-operate with the political authorities, providing support in the willingness to pay taxes. At the other extreme, political support implies 'loyalty' in a strong sense of active commitment. What has yet to be decided is whether European integration is ever likely to need this powerful sense of identity, the characteristics of the nation state, and further whether new European political authorities could ever successfully promote it. It is not too much to say that the definition of Europe's world role in the future depends on the precise nature of her new political culture.

Notes and references

1. R. Miliband, *The State in Capitalist Society*, Weidenfeld and Nicolson, 1969, p. 14
2. D. Mitrany, quoted in A. Buchan (ed.), *Europe's Future, Europe's Choices*, Chatto and Windus/The Institute for Strategic Studies, 1969, p. 164.
3. D. P. Calleo, *Europe's Future: The Grand Alternatives*, Hodder and Stoughton, 1967, p. 56.
4. A. Buchan, op. cit., p. 162.
5. E. B. Haas, *The Uniting of Europe*, Oxford University Press, 1958, p. 16.
6. Quoted by F. R. Willis, *France, Germany and the New Europe, 1945–1967*, Oxford University Press, 1968, p. 58.
7. ibid., p. 104.
8. D. Coombes, *Politics and Bureaucracy in the European Community*, George Allen and Unwin/PEP, 1970, p. 26.
9. D. Coombes, op. cit., pp. 78–82.
10. P. Taylor, *The Limits of European Integration*, Croom Helm, 1983, pp. 290/2. The fundamental weakness of the legal system was made apparent in 1979–80 in the course of the 'lamb war' with Britain: France continued to ban imports from Britain, even though she had on two occasions been found guilty by the Court of contravening Community rules.
11. See G. Pridham and P. Pridham, *Transnational Party Cooperation and European Integration*, Longman, 1981.
12. The Tindemans Report (January 1976) on 'European Union' shows one approach to the 'stage of transition', proposing that the 'European Council' (the heads of government at their regular summit meetings) should be integrated with Community institutions, so that the distinction between 'political' matters and formal treaty obligations would disappear. Once the European Council had reached *broad* agreement, the Council of Ministers (foreign ministers) would proceed, as necessary, to majority voting on *specific* matters, and hence would become the single decision-making centre.
13. The 76 votes in the Council of Ministers are distributed as follows: 10 each (France, Germany, Italy, UK); 8 (Spain); 5 each (Belgium, Greece, Netherlands, Portugal); 3 each (Denmark, Ireland); 2 (Luxembourg). The size of the qualified majority – 54 out of 76 – ensures that the five largest states cannot dominate, since for measures to be carried they would need the support of at least two of the smaller states.
14. See R. Inglehart, 'Long-Term Trends in Mass Support for European Integration', *Government and Opposition*, Summer 1977, also 'Political Generations in Europe', *European Journal of Political Research*, June 1977 (whole issue). More generally, see R. Inglehart, *The Silent Revolution: Changing*

Values and Political Styles Among Western Publics, Princeton University Press, 1977.

Additional references

S. Bulmer and W. Wessels, *The European Council: Decision-Making in European Politics*, Macmillan, 1987.

S. George, *Politics and Policy in the European Community*, Oxford University Press, 1985.

Lord Gladwyn, *The European Idea*, Weidenfeld and Nicolson, 1966.

W. Hallstein, *Europe in the Making*, Allen and Unwin, 1972.

A. Kerr, *The Common Market and How it Works*, Oxford: Pergamon, 1980.

E. Kirchner and K. Schwaiger, *The Role of Interest Groups in the European Community*, Aldershot: Gower, 1981.

D. Lasok and J. Bridge, *Law and Institutions of the European Communities*, 4th ed., Butterworth, 1987.

J. Lodge (ed.), *European Union: The European Community in Search of a Future*, Macmillan, 1986.

M. Palmer, *The European Parliament*, Oxford: Pergamon, 1981.

R. Pryce (ed.), *The Dynamics of European Union*, Croom Helm, 1987.

H. Simonian, *Privileged Partnership: Franco-German Relations in the European Community*, Clarendon Press, 1985.

P. Taylor, *The Limits of European Integration*, Croom Helm, 1983.

L. Tsoukalis (ed.) *The European Community: Past, Present and Future*, Oxford: Blackwell, 1983.

C. Tugendhat, *Making Sense of Europe*, Viking Press, 1986.

C. and K. Twitchett, *Building Europe: Britain's Partners in the EEC*, Europa Publications, 1981.

D. Urwin, *Western Europe Since 1945: A Short Political History*, Longman, rev. ed. 1989.

The material in this section gives a range of background information about the individual West European countries: major socio-economic and constitutional comparisons as well as specific political information. The table of socio-economic comparisons generally provides data for a particular recent year, and where possible the data should be supplemented to show comparative rates of change. Besides the sources mentioned, an amount of statistical and comparative information is contained in:

C. Cook and J. Paxton (eds.), *European Political Facts, 1918–1973*, Macmillan, 1975.
A. Day and H. Degenhardt, *Political Parties of the World*, Longman, 1980
Europa Yearbook (vol. I), Europa Publications.
G. Hand, J. Georgel, C. Sasse, *European Electoral Handbook*, Butterworth, 1979.
OECD, *Main Economic Indicators*.
J. Sallnow and A. John, *An Electoral Atlas of Europe, 1968–1981*, Butterworth, 1982.

The table of constitutional comparisons is necessarily couched in general terms as all countries show particular variations under a given head. The 'national profiles' are designed to give a brief historical and political outline of each of the states, and the main developments have been taken into account until June 1983. The summaries of election results are based on information given in *Keesing's Contemporary Archives* and the election reports appearing in *West European Politics* and *Electoral Studies*. The short reading list for each country can be supplemented by the various chapter references.

1. European Socio-Economic Comparisons

	1 Population (millions)	2 Population Density (per sq. km)	3 Percentage of Population in Cities over 100,000	4 Percentage of total pop. under 15 years	5 Employment in Agriculture etc. % of Labour Force	6 Trade Union Membership % of Economically Active	7 Gross Domestic Product (per capita, rank order)	8 Consumer Prices 1987 (1980=100)	9 Nuclear Energy Production (million tons oil equivalent)	10 Students in Higher Educ. (per 1000 of population)	11 Infant Mortality (% live births)	12 Health Expenditure (as % of GDP)	13 Telephones per 1000 people	14 Predominant Religion
Austria	7.6	90	31	17.9	7.8	50	15	131	0.0	23	1.03	8.2	492	1
Belgium	9.9	323	30	18.5	2.8	64	14	145	8.8	25	0.97	7.1	440	1
Denmark	5.1	119	38	18.1	5.9	65	7	158	0.0	23	0.82	6.1	783	2
Finland	4.9	15	22	19.4	11.0	66	10	161	4.3	26	0.58	7.2	617	2
France	55.4	101	33	20.9	7.3	17	9	167	56.8	23	0.77	8.4	608	1
Germany	61.0	246	34	20.0	5.3	34	8	121	26.7	25	0.86	8.2	621	3
Greece	10.0	76	29	21.0	28.5	19	18	366	0.0	17	1.22	4.2	355	4
Iceland	0.2	2	48	25.9	10.3	76	4	1.052	0.0	–	0.54	7.8	525	2
Ireland	3.5	50	26	28.9	15.7	35	17	191	0.0	19	0.87	8.0	265	1
Italy	57.2	190	27	16.8	10.9	29	13	211	2.0	21	1.01	6.7	448	1
Luxembourg	0.4	142	30	16.9	3.7	55	5	140	0.0	2	0.79	–	548	1
Netherlands	14.6	391	31	19.0	4.9	22	11	122	0.9	27	0.64	8.3	609	3
Norway	4.2	13	19	19.6	7.2	37	3	180	0.0	21	0.78	6.4	622	2
Portugal	10.2	111	12	22.5	21.7	29	19	347	0.0	10	1.59	5.7	180	1
Spain	38.7	77	31	22.6	16.1	25	16	204	8.4	24	0.94	6.0	363	1
Sweden	8.4	19	28	18.0	4.2	61	6	167	15.7	–	0.59	9.4	890	2
Switzerland	6.6	159	18	17.2	6.5	23	2	126	5.0	17	0.68	7.9	832	3
United Kingdom	57.8	232	58	19.0	2.5	38	12	153	13.2	18	0.95	6.1	524	3
Turkey	50.9	65	31	36.2	55.7	–	20	841	0.0	9	6.50	–	67	5

European Socio-Economic Comparisons

Notes and Sources for table on p. 310
The figures are for 1986 unless otherwise indicated.
1. Supplement to the OECD *Observer*, No. 152, June/July 1988.
2. OECD *Observer*, No. 152.
3. Based on information in the *UN Demographic Yearbook*.
4. OECD *Observer*, No. 152; figures for Germany and Greece estimated.
5. OECD *Observer*, No. 152.
6. F. J. Harper (ed.), *Trade Unions of the World*, Longman, 1987 and other sources. Data is mainly from the period 1982–1985.
7. Rank order derived from Purchasing Power Parity figures, OECD *Observer*, No. 152.
8. OECD *Observer*, No. 152.
9. OECD *Observer*, No. 152.
10. OECD *Observer*, No. 152.
11. OECD *Observer*, No. 152; 1985 figures.
12. OECD *Observer*, No. 145, April/May 1987; 1985 figures.
13. 1 = Predominantly Roman Catholic
    2 = Predominantly Protestant
    3 = Approximate Roman Catholic and Protestant parity.
    4 = Greek Orthodox
    5 = Muslim (Turkey).

2. European Constitutional Comparisons

	State Form	State Structure	Head of State	Effective Executive Head	Leg.-Executive Relationship	Second Chamber Composition	Second Chamber Powers	Constitutional Jurisdiction	Constitutional Change	Direct Methods	Voting Systems
Austria	1	7	9	13	16	21	30	31	39	50	57
Belgium	2	6	8	13	16	22	28	33	40	49	59
Denmark	2	5	8	13	16	26	26	34	43	47	59
Finland	1	5	9	14	17	25	30	34	40	52	60
France	1	5	9	14	17	21	27	32	39	51	54
Germany	1	7	10	13	16	23	29	31	42	52	56
Greece	1	5	10	13	16	26	26	35	40	51	61
Iceland	1	5	9	13	16	25	30	34	41	49	59
Ireland	1	5	9	13	16	21	30	35	38	48	55
Italy	1	6	10	13	16	22	28	31	42	46	59
Luxembourg	2	5	8	13	16	26	26	33	40	52	60
Malta	1	5	10	12	16	26	26	35	42	52	55
Netherlands	2	5	8	13	16	21	28	34	40	52	58
Norway	2	5	8	13	18	25	30	34	40	49	60
Portugal	1	5	9	12	17	26	26	32	42	52	57
Spain	2	6	8	13	16	20	30	32	42	51	60
Sweden	2	5	8	13	16	26	26	34	41	49	59
Switzerland	1	7	11	15	18	20	27	31	38	45	60
United Kingdom	2	5	8	13	16	24	30	35	37	52	53

Key
1. Republic. 2. Monarchy. 3. (not presently operative)*. 4. (not presently operative). 5. Unitary state. 6. Unitary state, with constitutionally entrenched regions. 7. Federal system. 8. Hereditary monarchy (Luxembourg, a grand duchy). 9. President, by popular vote. 10. President, by legislature (and other representatives). 11. Rotating presidency, from Federal Council. 12. Prime minister (president with reserve powers). 13. Prime minister or equivalent. 14. Hybrid or mixed: president and prime minister. 15. Collegial executive. 16. Unified system. 17. Partial unification, no assembly powers over executive actions of president. 18. Partial unification; in Switzerland fixed life for Federal Council, in Norway fixed life for Storting. 19. (not presently operative). 20. Directly-elected second chamber. 21. Indirectly-elected, usually from local government (Ireland, functional). 22. Mixed: direct, indirect, appointed. 23. Appointed by state governments as their representatives. 24. Hereditary and/or government appointed 25. By and from assembly (quasi 'second chamber'). 26. No second chamber. 27. Co-equal with lower house (in France, this depends on government). 28. Nominally co-equal, in practice subordinate. 29. Co-equal for certain matters, otherwise qualified veto. 30. Suspensory powers only. 31. Full constitutional court (in Switzerland, no power over federal legislation). 32. Constitutional Council (legislation) and Council of State (administration). 33. Council of State (administration), courts (basic rights); Luxembourg Council of State has suspensory powers over legislation. 34. Advisory bodies on legislation

and courts. 35. Courts only; no power to query legislation. 36. (not presently operative). 37. No special procedure, as for ordinary legislation. 38. Legislative process plus referendum (in Switzerland, a majority of voters in a majority of cantons). 39. Special majority in legislature, or an ordinary one with referendum. 40. Intervening election and special legislative majorities. 41. Intervening election, no special majorities. 42. Special majority in legislature. 43. Intervening election and referendum. 44. By referendum used at government discretion. 45. Full rights of challenge, but only constitutional initiative at federal level. 46. Rights of challenge to legislation and initiative. 47. Challenge to legislation, on initiative of minority in assembly. 48. Referendum on constitutional changes and on other basic issues. 49. On initiative of assembly, consultative (on basic constitutional issues). 50. Popular initiative. 51. On government initiative. 52. No use made of direct methods (or no recent use). 53. Relative majority in single-member constituencies. 54. Second ballot in single-member constituencies. 55. Proportional Representation by system of Single Transferable Vote in multi-member constituencies. 56. Effectively proportional, combining relative majority in single – member constituencies with straight party list; the latter is used to secure overall proportionality. 57. Proportional Representation with straight party list. 58. PR, with one national constituency, 59. PR, with sub-national constituencies; overall proportionality by allocation of remainders. 60. PR, sub-national constituencies, no overall proportionality ensured. 58–60 all provide freedom (to varying degrees) for voters to express individual preferences or vote the straight party list. 61. PR, but with second distribution of seats to leading parties; effectively non-proportional.

---

* 'not presently operative': constitutional developments in certain countries (e.g. the revision of the Portuguese Constitution in 1982) mean that some constitutional arrangements are no longer applicable in Western Europe.

3. Political profiles

AUSTRIA

The first Austrian Republic came into being in November 1918 on the collapse of the Austro-Hungarian Empire; the parliamentary system of government which resulted from the constitution of 1920 proved to be unstable and constitutional amendments in 1925 and 1929 sought to rectify this – the 1929 amendment by providing for a directly-elected president with reserve powers. However, the causes of instability were more deep-rooted. The truncated state had Vienna as its capital city, with about one-third of the country's total population; it was the contrast between this large metropolitan centre – 'Red Vienna' – and the largely rural and clerically-dominated remainder of Austria which set the pattern to politics in the inter-war years. On an extra-parliamentary level the conflict was seen in the clashes between the two paramilitary formations, the anti-Socialist *Heimwehr* and the Socialist *Schutzbund*. The uneasy balance between the two major parties, the Christian-Socials and the Socialists, was broken in 1933 when Chancellor Dollfuss (Christian-Social) suppressed the constitution, replacing it in 1934 with an authoritarian system. But at the last election to be held, in 1930, neither the Austrian Nazis nor the *Heimwehr* made any impact, and the ruling Christian-Socials were clerical-conservative rather than fascist. On the left, the Socialists united the working class, with the tiny Communist Party of no importance.

In March 1938 Austria was incorporated into the Third Reich, and with its collapse the country was immediately occupied by the wartime allies. The Second Austrian Republic was set up in 1945 and the former constitution reactivated. Nevertheless the occupation continued until 1955, and only with the signing of the Austrian State Treaty in that year was full sovereignty restored; the peace treaty enforced on Austria a 'permanent neutrality' making her ineligible to join any military or political alliance. Whilst the protracted treaty negotiations dragged on, Austrian self-government was early restored and elections were first held in November 1945. It should be noted that, although Austria is formally a federal state with nine constituent Länder, political life is highly centralised and dominated by the national parties. The two contestants of the inter-war years remained: the Socialists and the People's Party (formerly Christian-Socials), but the old bitterness disappeared, and in the special conditions of the post-war period they ruled jointly in 'permanent' coalition from 1945 until 1966, after which the People's Party ruled alone with an absolute majority in the Nationalrat until 1970.

The 1970 election led to the first purely Socialist administration, a minority government dependent on the small, right-wing Freedom Party. Subsequent elections in 1971, 1975 and 1979 all gave the SPÖ an absolute majority in the Nationalrat, and socialist predominance was confirmed by the party's continuing promotion of successful presidential candidates. The decade was dominated by Dr Bruno Kreisky who as chancellor avoided radical policies and instead presided over the rapidly growing economy. The 1978 referendum on nuclear energy rejected government policy and was a blow both to Kreisky's prestige and that of the traditional élites. By 1983 the Green/Alternative vote eroded the SPÖ vote sufficiently to put an end to its majority, and in 1986 the Green/Alternative alliance gained entry to the Nationalrat.

Without a majority in 1983, the SPÖ turned to the FPÖ for support, and the latter's slow transformation into a governmental liberal party briefly met with success. This development was, however, reversed in 1986, with the nationalist wing of the leadership, capturing the party-secretaryship and dramatically recasting the party's image. Unable to continue in government with the new-look FPÖ, the SPÖ called for an early election.

Political tension was already high following the storm of controversy which had followed the nomination and election in 1986 of Kurt Waldheim, the ÖVP-sponsored presidential candidate. Waldheim's presidential candidature sparked fierce controversy in Austria and abroad because of allegations that he had been involved with Nazi war-crimes during the 1939–45 war. Although, as a result of the 1986 assembly election the ÖVP and FPÖ had won a majority, the ÖVP was unwilling to form a coalition with the now right-wing FPÖ. The major parties had fought the election campaign in a conciliatory mood, so that, with the SPÖ's adoption of a more pragmatic approach to the crisis of Austria's public industries, the SPÖ and ÖVP reverted to the 'grand coalition' in January 1987. The governmental consensus was uneasy however, since both coalition parties were faced by the gradual break-up of their electoral blocs, and a rising protest vote on their flanks.

The Waldheim crisis still remained unresolved early in 1988 and added considerably to tensions within the government coalition and within the ÖVP. Thus the liberal wing of the ÖVP supported the SPÖ's call for Waldheim's resignation, against vice-Chancellor Mock's staunch defence, and the ÖVP'S 'industrial' wing favoured major SPÖ tax-reform proposals against the opposition of the rest of the party. Whilst those favouring Waldheim's resignation hoped to reduce political tensions in the country by nominating a joint

SPÖ/ÖVP presidential candidate, many believed that an early Nationalrat election was unavoidable. However, President Waldheim resisted calls for his resignation, and the parties were forced to come to terms with the unsatisfactory situation, especially with regard to Austria's relationships with other countries.

Elections to the Nationalrat, November 1986

	1986 seats	1986 %	1983 %	1979 %	1975 %
Socialist Party (SPÖ)	80	43.1	47.7	51.0	50.4
People's Party (ÖVP)	77	41.3	43.2	41.9	43.0
Freedom Party (FPÖ)	18	9.7	5.0	6.1	5.4
Green/Alternative	8	4.8	3.2	–	–
Communist Party	–	0.7	0.7	1.0	1.1
Others	–	0.4	0.2	–	0.1

Reading

W. T. Bluhm, *Building an Austrian Nation*, Yale University Press, 1973.
F. L. Carsten, *Fascist Movements in Austria: From Schönerer to Hitler*, Sage Publications, 1977.
P. Gerlich, 'Consociationalism to Competition: The Austrian Party System since 1945', in H. Daalder (ed.), *Party Systems in Denmark, Austria, Switzerland, the Netherlands and Belgium*, Pinter, 1987.
B. Jelavich. *Modern Austria, 1800–1986*, Cambridge University Press, 1987.
P. J. Katzenstein, *Corporatism and Change: Austria, Switzerland and Industrial Policy*, New York: Cornell University Press, 1984.
R. Luther 'Austria's Future and Waldheim's Past: The Significance of the 1986 Elections', *West European Politics*, July 1987.
B. Marin, 'From Consociationalism to Technocorporatism: The Austrian Case as a Model-Generator', in L. Scholten (ed.), *Political Stability and Neocorporatism*, Sage, 1987.
A. Pelinka, 'Austrian Social Partnership', *West European Politics*, January 1987.
K. R. Stadler, 'The Kreisky Phenomenon', *West European Politcs*, January 1981.
K. R. Stadler, *Austria*, Ernest Benn, 1971.
K. Steiner [ed.], *Modern Austria*, Palo Alto: Society for the Promotion of Science and Scholarship, 1981.
K. P. Stiefbold, 'Segmented Pluralism and Consociational Democracy in Austria', in M. O. Heisler (ed.), *Politics in Europe*, New York: David McKay, 1974.
M. A. Sully, *Political Parties and Elections in Austria*, C. Hurst, 1981.
M. A. Sully, *Continuity and Change in Austrian Socialism. The Eternal Quest for the Third Way*, New York: Columbia University Press, 1982.

BELGIUM

Belgian independence resulted from the successful revolution in 1830 against William I of the Netherlands. Since 1831 Belgium has been a constitutional monarchy and the relatively liberal form of that constitution has been maintained ever since. The monarchy was only once seriously in question in the dispute subsequent to Leopold III's war-time behaviour, and this crisis was only finally resolved by his abdication in 1951. The predominantly Roman Catholic allegiance of the population has given the progressive Social-Christian Party a leading place in Belgian politics for much of the past century, and it has been almost always the dominant governing party, in coalition with the Liberals (Party for Liberty and Progress) or the Socialists. The strict unitary form of the Belgian state and the power of these three parties only masked the underlying social tensions resulting from the language question. The linguistic frontier is clearly marked: Flemish is the language of the majority of the population (about 55 per cent) in the north of the country, and French in most of the remainder; Brussels is a predominantly French-speaking enclave within Flanders. Over the years numerous reforms have been made to meet the demands of the two language communities, particularly those of the underprivileged Flemish. A measure of the growth of discontent is provided by the rise of the linguistic parties, the Flemish *Volksunie* and the *Rassemblement Wallon* of the French-speakers. They received only 2.2 per cent of the vote in 1954 but reached a high-point of 22.4 per cent in 1971.

Their subsequent decline has been entirely offset by the divisions affecting the major parties (Social-Christians, Socialists, and Liberals) – all three have developed autonomous linguistic wings. The linguistic issue is therefore the main cause of contention both within and between parties and a factor which has been a cause of governmental instability. Composition of governments has had to reflect a linguistic balance; strict parity in cabinets, separate ministers for education and culture, as well as for the relations between the two communities.

Major constitutional reforms were agreed in 1971 which, although falling short of a federal solution, gave a large degree of devolved power to the linguistic areas – guaranteed regional autonomy for cultural, educational, and regional economic affairs, and the establishment of elected councils for the regions; responsibility to main parliament being restricted to budgetary matters. Guarantees also had to be worked out for the French-speaking minority, for their deputies would inevitably be in a minority in parliament. The regulation of Brussels was central to the new constitutional formula: the city was designated as a third region and given an official bilingual status, but the city's limits were permanently fixed to prevent further Francophone encroachment into surrounding Flemish areas.

The constitutional compromise settled the principles of reform, but agreement on the detailed legislation required proved just as difficult to reach. In particular, the position accorded to Brussels satisfied neither side: the French-speaking population regarded the permanent restriction on Brussels as artificial, whilst Flemish-speakers continued to regard Brussels as an integral part of Flanders and saw the creation of Brussels as a third region to be a denial of the Flemish majority position in the country as a whole. Since 1971 successive governments have stumbled on the problem of passing detailed implementing laws relating to the constitutional changes.

However, substantial progress was made in the 1970s towards agreement on linguistic decentralisation. Subsequent to the 1977 election a broad-based government was formed, including the major linguistic parties and controlling four-fifths of assembly seats. One result was the *Pacte Communautaire*. It provided for a second-chamber Senate to represent the communities, with voting requirements to protect the French-speaking minority. It also agreed the election of regional assemblies and the strengthening of the previously established cultural councils. In addition, an arbitration court was to be set up to adjudicate between the various representative organs. Full implementation of the so-called Egmont Pact foundered on the Brussels issue, since the Flemish-speakers were unwilling to see it become a full 'region' under Francophone control. Constitutional recognition of Flanders, Wallonia and Brussels as regions was subsequently achieved, but devolution plans for the Brussels region could not be implemented, and in the 1980s the Brussels problem was effectively handled by ignoring it.

The process of constitutional reform proved difficult to expedite and the language issue has continued to be a major cause of governmental instability, but by the late 1970s the mounting economic crisis was at least equally as threatening, and following the 1981 election, a centre-right coalition of Social-Christians and Liberals, excluding the Socialists was formed, the language issue being relegated in importance, as far as possible, by the party élites. This approach was successfully promoted in particular by the Fleming Christian Democrat, Dr Wilfred Martens, prime minister of successive coalitions from 1979. Nevertheless, in October 1987 internal coalition tensions caused the government to fall over a minor and local language-issue, and another early election was held.

One outcome was that the linguistic-territorial divide became more marked in the tendency (noticeable since 1968) for the Flemish and Wallonian regions to move respectively towards the right and the left. Wallonia produced a major Socialist advance which resulted in the francophone Socialist Party becoming the country's largest party, whilst the north of the country swung towards the right-wing Liberals.

In these circumstances, the Christian Democrats found that their pivotal centrist position was under severe strain, with their trade-union wing in particular unwilling to continue the coalition with the Liberals. The inability of the Christian Democrats to resolve this problem led to a hiatus of several months before a new government could be formed. Eventually, in May 1988, Dr Martens formed a five-party coalition involving the Flemish and Wallonian Socialists and Social-Christian/Christian Peoples' Parties, with Volksunie making the fifth member. This wide coalition, it was hoped, would command a two-thirds majority and be able to enact constitutional reforms to resolve the specific problem of the Brussels region.

Elections to the Chamber of Representatives, December 1987

	1987 seats	1987 %	1985 %	1981 %	1978 %
Christian People's (CVP)	43	19.5	21.3	19.3	26.1
Social-Christian (PSC)	19	8.0	8.0	7.1	10.1
Socialist Party (BSP)	32	14.9	14.5	12.7	13.0
Socialist Party (PSB)	40	15.7	13.8	12.4	12.4
Freedom & Progress (PVV)	25	11.5	10.7	12.9	10.4
Liberal Reform (PRL)	23	9.4	10.2	8.6	6.0
Volksunie	16	8.0	8.0	9.8	7.0
Rassemblement/FDF	3	1.4	1.2	4.2	7.1
Communist Party	0	0.9	1.2	2.3	3.3
Ecolo	3	2.6	2.5	–	–
Agalev	6	4.5	3.7	4.8	–
Vlaamsche Blok	2	1.9	1.4	1.1	1.4
UDRT	0	0.1	1.1	2.7	0.9
Others	0	1.6	2.4	2.1	2.5

Notes: The Ecologist/Alternative party followed the pattern set by splitting into linguistic wings in 1985. Rassemblement Wallon and Front des Francophones are the Francophone parties in Wallonia and Brussels – their votes and seats are shown together. The vote shown for the Communist Party includes that for various splinter groups. UDRT is a right-wing liberal party. Voting is compulsory and results in a turnout of about 95%.

Reading
R. Anstey, *King Leopold's Legacy*, Oxford University Press, 1966.
M. Covell, 'Ethnic Conflict and Elite Bargaining: The Case of Belgium', *West European Politics*, October 1981.
M. De Ridder and L.-R. Fraga. 'The Brussels Issue in Belgian Politics', *West European Politics*, July 1986.
K. Deschouwer, 'The 1987 Belgian Election: The Voter did not Decide.' *West European Politics*, July 1988.

W. Dewachter, 'Changes in a Particratie: The Belgian Party System from 1944 to 1986', in H. Daalder (ed.), *Party Systems*, op. cit., 1987.

J. Fitzmaurice, *The Politics of Belgium*, Hurst, 1988 (rev. ed.)

M. O. Heisler, 'Institutionalising Societal Cleavages in a Cooptive polity', in Heisler (ed.), *Politics in Europe*, op. cit.

X. Mabille and V. R. Lorwin, 'The Belgian Socialist Party', in Paterson and Thomas (eds.), *Social Democratic Parties in Western Europe*, Croom Helm, 1977.

X. Mabille and V. R. Lorwin, 'Belgium', in S. Henig (ed.), *Political Parties in the European Community*, Allen and Unwin, 1979.

J. de Meyer, 'Coalition Government in Belgium', in V. Bogdanor (ed.), *Coalition Government in Western Europe*, Heinemann, 1983.

A. Mughan, 'Modernization and Ethnic Conflict in Belgium', *Political Studies*, March 1979.

C. Rudd, 'The Aftermath of Heysel: The Belgian Election of 1985', *West European Politics*, April 1986

J. Rudolf, 'Belgium: Controlling Separatist Tendencies in a Multinational State', in C. Williams (ed.), *National Separatism*, Cardiff: University of Wales Press, 1982.

DENMARK

Denmark is one of the oldest European states in having a continuous national sovereignty for several hundred years; from the fourteenth century until early in the nineteenth she was a major European power with considerable possessions in Scandinavia and northern Germany. Already in the twelfth century a unified royal power had emerged, one which for a time coexisted with the provincial assemblies, or Landstings. Early evolution was marked by full government participation for the nobility and the decline of the popular assemblies. Government by king and council of the nobility resulted; moreover, the monarchy was an elective position. In 1660 there was a shift to royal absolutism and the Act of Royalty which resulted transformed the Danish monarchy from a constitutional force to a completely autocratic one, a situation which continued until well into the nineteenth century; it was an enlightened despotism – compulsory elementary education was introduced in 1814. Just as suddenly, in 1849, there was a reversion to full constitutional rule, with elections to parliament on a democratic franchise. However, the principle of government responsibility to the lower house, the Folketing, was not established until 1901. The main political cleavage was initially between the conservative Right and the Left (the Venstre) supporting progressive and agrarian interests. The Venstre split in 1905 to give a Radical Left which voiced the interest of small farmers and urban liberals. The fourth historical party, the Social Democrats, quickly rose to prominence and formed its first government in 1924. With its rise, both the Venstre and the Radical Left became gradually more bourgeois in orientation, but for long the Social Democrats were able to rule with the support of the Radical Left.

In the earlier years of the post-war period the Social Democrats were in a dominant position, but gradually the system developed the form of a balanced cluster: the Conservative, Venstre, and Radical Left parties represented the bourgeois interests, whilst on the left the Social Democrats were flanked by the Socialist People's Party, the Left Socialists, and the Communists. The new constitution of 1953 reduced parliament to one house only, the Folketing, and at the same time provided for the use of the referendum as a popular check on the legislature; constitutional changes were also made subject to approval by referendum. Danish accession to the European Community was decided by a constitutional referendum held in October 1972 and resulted in a large vote in favour, 63.7 per cent. However, this decisive result was actually accompanied by a growing diffusion of the party system, as was clearly demonstrated in the subsequent elections. Only five parties were represented in the 1971 Folketing but eleven in 1977. The situation of 'electoral chaos' showed an extent of disaffection from the traditional parties without giving any pronounced polarisation. The sudden rise of the maverick Progress Party (anti-tax, anti-government) to be the second largest in the Folketing was indicative of the fragmentation.

Subsequently, the electoral situation stabilised, and briefly, in 1981, the pattern of Social Democratic minority government reasserted itself. In 1982, however, the severity of Denmark's inflationary problem led to the establishment of a minority centre-right, four-party coalition made up of the Conservative People's Party, Liberal Democrats, Centre Democrats and Christian People's Party, led by a Conservative Prime Minister, Poul Schlüter. This coalition broke the recently established cycle of biennial elections and the 1984 election confirmed its position. Subsequently, in 1986, an advisory referendum on the Single European Act was successfully used to bolster the government's standing. However, the coalition's dependence on votes from the Radical Liberal party meant that its environmental, defence and security policies were subjected to repeated veto in the Folketing, a situation unresolved by the 1987 election. The breadth of the alliance in the Folketing, ranging from the Progress Party to the radical Liberal party was a source of severe strain, and in April 1988 Schlüter called for an early election when a Folketing majority based on the left-wing parties reaffirmed Denmark's unwillingness to permit nuclear-armed ships in its waters. The election left the coalition with the same number of seats, but shifted its centre of gravity, and that of the Folketing, to the right, since the Progress Party significantly improved its position. The new coalition, a three-party one (Conservatives, Venstre and Radical Liberals), was a minority government, with only 67 of the 179 seats. In the Danish context, however, this minority position did not necessarily imply an unstable government, since with the diffused character of party positions the government could count on support from other parties for particular measures and rely on a strategy of winning a 'majority for the occasion'.

Elections to the Folketing, May 1988

	1988 seats	1988 %	1987 %	1984 %	1981 %
Socialist's People's	24	13.1	14.6	11.5	11.3
Social Democrats	55	30.0	29.3	31.6	32.9
Radical Liberals	10	5.6	6.2	5.5	5.1
Christian People's	4	2.1	2.4	2.7	2.3
Centre Democrats	9	4.7	4.8	4.6	8.3
Conservative People's	35	19.4	20.8	23.4	14.4
Liberals (Venstre)	22	11.9	10.5	12.1	11.3
Progress	16	9.0	4.8	3.6	8.9
Others	0	4.2	6.6	5.0	5.5

Notes: 'Others' includes the Left Socialists and the Justice Party which lost their parliamentary representation by falling under the 2% barrier in 1986 and 1981 respectively. In 1987 Common Course, a leftist nationalist party secured 2.2% of the vote.

Reading

N. Andrén, *Government and Politics in the Nordic Countries*, Stockholm: Almqvist and Wiksell, 1964.

J. Fitzmaurice, *Politics in Denmark*, C. Hurst, 1981.

J. Fitzmaurice, 'Denmark', in S. Henig, *Political Parties in the European Community*, op. cit.

S. Hurwitz, *The Ombudsman*, Copenhagen: Det Danske Selskab, 1968.

W. Jones, *Denmark: A Modern History*, Croom Helm, 1986.

K. E. Miller, 'Policy Making by Referendum: The Danish Experience', *West European Politics*, January 1982.

M. N. Pederson, 'The Danish 'Working Multiparty System': Breakdown or Adaption', in H. Daalder (ed.), *Party Systems*, op. cit., 1987.

A. H. Thomas, 'Social Democracy in Denmark' in Paterson and Thomas (eds.), *Social Democratic Parties in Western Europe*, op. cit.

A. H. Thomas, 'The Danish Folketing Election of 1984', ·*West European Politics*, January 1985.

See also, *Scandinavian Political Studies*.

FINLAND

Until 1809 Finland was a province of the Swedish monarchy, and from then until an independent public was declared in December

1917, she was an autonomous Grand Duchy of Imperial Russia. For the several hundred years during which Finland was a part of Sweden, a strong representative system was maintained, although a more authoritarian form of government resulted from the constitution acts of 1772/89. These acts remained the basis of later tzarist rule which was exercised by a governor-general with an estate system of representation and this form persisted until 1906. The 1906 Parliament Act effected a sudden transformation – proportional voting and a single-chamber assembly – a modern political form which gave full expression to national aspirations. At the same time there was a rapid political mobilisation and the Social Democrats quickly became the largest political party. Following independence, and under the influence of the Russian Revolution, a bitter civil war ensued between the right-wing monarchist and nationalist forces, the 'Whites', and the 'Reds' who wished to follow the Soviet example. A new Constitution Act of 1919 gave the basic form of mixed parliamentary and presidential government which has remained unaltered. Party politics in the inter-war period were dominated by the cleavages of the civil war, and although the republic did not quite succumb to these pressures, there was a marked shift to the right, especially seen in the Lapua Movement, the paramilitary Civil Guards, and support for these from the regular army. There was considerable harassment of the left, with the Communist Party banned from 1930 onwards. Since 1945, some of the deep divisions in Finnish society have been healed, but in spite of the multi-party system a moderate social polarisation remains apparent. Unstable left-of-centre coalitions have been the rule; however, the 1919 innovation of a strong president (popularly-elected, actually via an electoral college) existing alongside parliamentary government has mitigated the effects of government instability. The president is an integral part of the Finnish system, particularly as he can represent the national viewpoint in relations with the Soviet Union. The latter is an active factor in Finnish politics and is naturally hostile to Finland becoming involved in western treaty organisations.

The looming presence of the Soviet Union enforces cohesion on the fragmented party system. Coalitions are always very broadly based, and there is a desire to avoid polarisation, but governments have been short-lived, reflecting the difficulty of harmonising different views, especially on economic matters.

The unity and continuity provided by President Uhro Kekonnen between 1956 and 1981 was impressive, and he imparted a particular style to Finnish politics. He was replaced by the Social Democrat, Mauno Koivisto, in 1982, just as the position of the

Social Democrat Party was being increasingly challenged. Kekkonen himself had come from the Centre Party, and the Centre Party provided the pivot of most coalition possibilities until changes in the 1980s led to its unexpected exclusion from government in 1987. Until then, the composition of coalitions depended on electoral performance, but the Communist-orientated SKDL participated frequently in government – the desirability of placating the Soviet Union has to be remembered. However, the League was a wide alliance of semi-autonomous groupings and was afflicted by internal factionalism. In 1982 it brought down the centre-left coalition by voting against the defence budget. Consequently, following the 1983 election, the League was excluded from government, and in 1985 a Stalinist wing broke away from the Communist Party component of the League, to fight the 1987 election independently.

This election confirmed the shift away from the left, which had been signalled by the Conservative gains in 1979. In 1983 the Rural Party, somewhat surprisingly given its Poujadist character, had become coalitionable and the four-party coalition of Social Democrats, Centre, rural and Swedish Peoples' parties successfully survived the full four-year assembly term. In the 1987 election, thanks to a change in the electoral system, the Conservatives gained nine additional seats despite only marginally increasing their percentage of the vote, and the party became too important to be excluded any longer from government. The new four-party coalition, changed only by replacing the Centre party with the Conservatives, was, moreover, led by Finland's first Conservative prime minister since World War II. Unlike the Swedish Conservatives, however, the Finnish Conservatives adhered firmly to the pattern of established consensus politics and made no demands for privatisation or other system change. The Social Democrats remained in government, as President Koivisto wished to avoid a government/opposition style of polarisation, but this achievement was at the expense of the excluded Centre party. President Koivisto was himself given a further term in office by the popularly-elected electoral college in February 1988, having failed to obtain an absolute majority by direct election. In the popular vote he secured 43 per cent of the total, whilst his nearest rival, in a field of five, the Conservative prime minister, recorded 23 per cent.

Elections to the Eduskunta, March 1987

	1987 seats	1987 %	1983 %	1979 %	1975 %
Social Democrats	57	24.1	26.7	23.9	24.9
SKDL	16	9.4	14.0	17.9	18.9
Conservatives (KK)	53	23.1	22.2	21.7	18.4
Centre Party	40	17.6	17.7	17.4	17.5
Liberal People's Party	0	1.0	–	3.7	4.4
Rural Party (SMP)	9	6.3	9.7	4.0	3.2
Swedish People's	12	5.3	4.6	4.5	5.0
Christian Union (SKL)	5	2.6	3.0	4.6	4.5
Ecologists	4	4.0	1.5	–	–
Constitutional People's	0	0.1	0.4	1.2	1.7
Others	5	7.4	0.2	1.1	1.6

Notes: The Liberals merged with the Centre Party to contest the 1983 election, but fought alone again in 1987. The Rural Party is not an agrarian party but more a popular protest movement. The Constitutional People's Party is a break-away from the Swedish People's Party which represents the Swedish linguistic minority. Others in 1987 includes the Aaland Islands (1.9%, 1 seat), Deva, a Stalinist break-away from the SKDL (4.3%, 4 seats), and a Pensioners' Party (1.2%).

Reading

R. Alapuro et al. (eds.), *Small States in Comparative Perspective*, Norwegian University Press, 1985

D. Arter, 'Kekkonen's Finland: Enlightened Despotism or Consensual Democracy?' *West European Politics*, October 1981.

D. Arter, 'The 1983 Finnish Election: Protestor Consensus?', *West European Politics*, October 1983.

D. Arter, *Politics and Policy-making in Finland*, Wheatsheaf, 1987.

D. Arter, 'The 1987 Finnish Election: The Conservatives out of the Wilderness' *West European Politics*, October 1987.

N. Elder, A. Thomas and D. Arter, *The Consensual Democracies? The Government and Politics of the Scandinavian States*, Oxford: Blackwell, 1988 (rev. ed.)

R. Helenius, 'The Finnish Social Democratic Party', in Paterson and Thomas (eds.), *Social Democratic Parties in Western Europe*, op. cit.

P. Kastari, *Constitution Act and Parliament Act of Finland*, Helsinki: Ministry for Foreign Affairs, 1967.

D. G. Kirby, *Finland in the Twentieth Century*, C. Hurst, 1979.

J. Nousiainen, *The Finnish Political System*, Harvard University Press, 1971.

P. Pesonen, 'Party Support in a Fragmented System', in R. Rose (ed.), *Electoral Behavior*, op. cit.

A. F. Upton (ed.), *The Communist Parties of Scandinavia and Finland*, Weidenfeld and Nicolson, 1973.

See also, *Scandinavian Political Studies*.

FRANCE

When it was first approved by popular vote in September 1958, the constitution of the Fifth French Republic was regarded by most observers as a stop-gap contrivance, a form of legitimation for the exercise of personal power by de Gaulle, the 'lesser evil' in view of the threat from the Army in revolt in Algeria. The apparently cyclical pattern of French politics since the Revolution of 1789 by which: 'Constitutional Monarchy gives way to Republic and the Republic in turn is replaced by some form of dictatorial government' (D. Pickles, *The Fifth French Republic*, Methuen, 1962, p. 10) appeared to show the decline of parliamentarianism of the Fourth Republic (1946–1958) and its replacement by a non-democratic form. The new constitution made certain institutional innovations, the total effect of which was to create a new balance of power and a form of presidentialism in which all other institutions were aligned against the party system in the Chamber of Deputies; it was these parties which were held responsible for the troubles of the Third Republic (1871–1940) and the Fourth. Whilst all previous attempts to create a strong executive power had resulted in dictatorship, the Fifth Republic showed the possibility of integrating the party system with a strong, directly-elected president. Once de Gaulle was firmly in power, he deliberately avoided making the army the basis of his support, and this showed in his determination to liquidate the Algerian problem; he instead relied on popular approval for his actions, by the use of the referendum, and extended its use to a form of general policy approval.

1958 (September)	The new constitution	79.25% in favour
1961 (January)	Algerian policy	75.00% in favour
1962 (April)	Algerian settlement	90.70% in favour
1962 (October)	Method of presidential election	62.00% in favour
1969 (April)	Reorganisation of Senate etc.	53.15% against

To these results should be added that of the presidential election of December 1965 when de Gaulle won 55.2 per cent of the vote at the second ballot. The turning-point in securing the fortunes of the Fifth Republic came with the 'events' of May 1968, starting with student unrest, pitched battles with the riot-police, and escalating into a general strike. Although the government made some concessions, the sweeping nature of the Gaullist election victory in June 1968 showed the underlying strength of the regime. Paradoxically, the electoral success was accompanied by a weakening hold of de Gaulle over the electorate – as was shown by the defeat of his reform proposals in the 1969 referendum, a reverse which led directly to de Gaulle's resignation. His successor, Georges Pompidou, previously prime minister, was elected with an impressive majority in June 1969 (58.2 per cent at the second ballot, but on a low poll). The result indicated that the presidential system was taking root, since Pompidou managed to hold the Gaullist electorate together even though he lacked de Gaulle's personal appeal.

Gradually, the parties re-asserted their position. For the 1973 assembly election the Socialists and Communists fought on a joint election programme, and in the event the Gaullists lost their overall majority but had the support of the Independent Republicans and the Democratic Centre. The death of President Pompidou in April 1974 soon reopened the contest for power, but with a new twist: the Gaullist image had become somewhat tarnished, and in the May 1974 presidential election, the leader of the Independent Republicans, Valéry Giscard d'Estaing, proved to be the stronger representative of 'the parties of the majority', and he went forward to the second ballot. For their part, the Socialists and Communists united behind François Mitterrand, the leader of the Socialist Party. At the second ballot Giscard d'Estaing was successful, but it was a close contest with Mitterrand securing 49.2 per cent of the vote against 50.8 for Giscard d'Estaing.

When Giscard d'Estaing first decided to run again for the presidency, and another seven-year term, it appeared obvious that he would win, but by 1981 the left was seen as a legitimate vehicle for social and economic reform, and Mitterrands's victory at the second ballot by a margin of 3.5 per cent was decisive.

Once elected, Mitterrand proceeded to dissolve the National Assembly seeking to align it politically with the Presidency, and the June 1981 election, in giving the Socialists an outright majority, enabled the French 'mixed' governmental system to continue as before. The sweeping Socialist victory and continued decline of the Communist Party did not prevent the participation of the latter in government from 1981 to 1984 in the interests of left unity. Although a series of successful social reforms was enacted, the impossibility of reflation in one country in the face of world-wide recession, and the unpopularity of Pierre Mauroy's government following attempts at education reform, forced Mitterrand to engineer a change in government leadership which led to the formation of the Fabius government in July 1984.

The 1981–86 period of Socialist Government was the first extended period of government by the left in modern French history, and, although its more ambitious policies had to be modified, or were later overturned by the succeeding administration, a series of significant institutional, judicial and social reforms were implemented. The transformation of the French left into a force for government, in contrast to its tradition of opposition, was perhaps the most significant development.

In line with its programme, and to save the Socialists from a massive defeat in the impending National Assembly election, the government introduced a system of proportional representation based on the 96 departments, each with a five per cent barrier. As a consequence, the left was only narrowly defeated, helped by the fact that the economy had recovered significantly since 1984. The pattern of voting showed a consolidation of the centre, with a much weakened Communist Party on the left, and the anchoring of the National Front on the right. The success of Le Pen's National Front at the national level was a serious shock to the dominant right-wing parties, and with the presidential election due in 1988 the right's vote was threatened by a serious split. This incipient fragmentation was of fundamental importance given the principal outcome of the 1986 election – a right-wing assembly majority supplying the governments, but the latter in turn forced to co-exist or 'cohabit' with a Socialist President.

Mitterrand recognised the democratic legitimacy of Jacques Chirac's claim to the premiership and Chirac – unlike Raymond Barre – accepted the feasibility of 'cohabitation'; as a result, the French political system surmounted its second major 'crisis of change' within five years. Previous evaluations of the presidential nature of the Fifth Republic's constitution had to be reappraised, and in particular recognition of the supra-constitutional nature of the original Gaullist conception of presidentialism came back into favour. Nevertheless, the Presidency was still seen as a key to political power, and complex manoeuvres in advance of the 1988 presidential election dominated the French political scene in the period after the 1986 election.

Mitterrand's convincing victory in 1988 against a divided right led to the appointment of a Socialist prime minister and an attempt to form a centre-left, liberal–socialist coalition with elements of the UDF. The difficulties surrounding this strategy which became evident immediately following the appointment of the new prime minister led to the dissolution of the National Assembly and an early election was held in June 1988.

Elections to the National Assembly, March 1986

	%	Seats	Seats 1981	Seats 1978
PS and Left Radicals (MRG)	31.4	209	283	117
Communist Party	9.8	35	44	86
Other Left	2.7	7	6	1
Total Left	43.9	251	333	204
RPR (separate lists)	11.2	148	83	153
UDF (separate lists)	8.3	129	66	125
RPR + UDF (joint lists)	21.5	[147]	–	–
Other moderate Right	3.9	14	6	9
Total moderate Right	44.9	291	155	287
National Front	9.7	35	–	–
Ecologists	1.2	–	–	–

Notes: Election by proportional representation replaced the dual ballot system for the 1986 election, but the double ballot system was subsequently restored by the incoming administration. The 147 seats of the RPR/UDF joint lists were distributed as follows: 71 seats to the RPR, 76 seats to the UDF.

Presidential Election, April/May 1988

Candidates	Main Support	Ballots I %	Ballots II %
F. Mitterrand	PS	34.1	54.0
A. Lajoinie	PCF	6.8	
Other Left	Various	4.5	
A. Waechter	Ecologists	3.8	
R. Barre	UDF	16.5	
J. Chirac	RPR	20.0	46.0
J.-M. Le Pen	PNF	14.4	

Elections to the National Assembly, June 1988

	% First Ballot	Seats 1st + 2nd Ballots
Extreme Left	0.4	–
Communist Party	11.3	27
Socialist Party and Left Radicals	36.0	277
Other pro-Mitterrand	1.7	
Ecologists + Regionalists	0.4	–
RPR ⎱ UDF ⎰	37.6	129 130
Other Right	2.8	13
National Front	9.7	1

Notes: At the first ballot there was a poll of 65.7 per cent. Candidates scoring less than 12.5 per cent were eliminated; those securing 50.0 per cent were elected at the first ballot, but in the great majority of constituencies a second ballot was necessary. Inter-party pacts (RPR with UDF, PS with PCF) meant that the candidate with the larger vote went forward to the second ballot and the other stood down. The RPR and UDF also had electoral pacts for the first ballot. The nature of the electoral system means that there is no close correspondence between votes at the first ballot and the total number of seats a party wins.

Reading

M. Anderson, *Conservative Politics in France*, Allen and Unwin, 1975.
W. G. Andrews, *Presidential Government in Gaullist France, 1958–74*, New York: Albany, 1982.
J. Ardagh, *France in the 1980s*, Penguin Books, 1982.
D. Bell and B. Criddle, *The French Socialist Party: The Emergence of a Party of Government*, Oxford University Press, 1988.
P. Cerny (ed.), *Social Movements and Protest in France*, Frances Pinter, 1982.
P. Cerny and M. Schain (eds.), *French Politics and Public Policy*, Frances Pinter, 1980
J. Charlot, *The Gaullist Phenomenon*, Allen and Unwin, 1971.
J. Frears, *France in the Giscard Presidency*, Allen and Unwin, 1981.
J. Hayward, *Governing France: The One and Indivisible Republic*, Weidenfeld and Nicolson, 1983 (2nd edn.)
J. Howorth and G. Ross (eds.), *Contemporary France: A Review of Interdisciplinary Studies*, Frances Pinter, 1987.
H. Machin and V. Wright, 'Why Mitterrand Won: The Presidential Election of 1981', *West European Politics*, January 1982.
P. Naville, 'France', in *Contemporary Europe: Class, Status and Power*, op. cit.
K. Reif, 'Party Government in the Fifth Republic', in R. S. Katz (ed.), *The Future of Party Government*, vol. 2, Berlin: De Gruyter, 1987.
F. Ridley and J. Blondel, *Public Administration in France*, Routledge, 1979.
G. Ross, S. Hoffmann and S. Malzacher (eds.), *The Mitterrand Experiment: Continuity and Change in Modern France*, Oxford University Press, 1987.
D. Thomson, *Democracy in France since 1870*, Oxford University Press, 1969.
P. M. Williams, *Crisis and Compromise: Politics in the Fourth Republic*, Longman, 1964.
V. Wright, *The Government and Politics of France*, Hutchinson, 1987.
V. Wright (ed.), *Continuity and Change in France*, Allen and Unwin, 1984.

THE FEDERAL GERMAN REPUBLIC

The Federal German Republic came into existence in 1949 with the promulgation of an Occupation Statute by the three western occupying powers, the United States, Britain, and France. Its area was therefore defined by their zones of occupation, with the later addition of the Saarland. Complete sovereignty did not come to the new state until 1955 when the Occupation Statute was withdrawn and West Germany became a full member of NATO. The period 1945 to 1949 was marked by the slow reactivation of political life, 'democracy under licence', beginning with the licensing of acceptable political parties (including the Communist Party) and proceeding to the establishment of Länder governments. As western relations with the Soviet Union worsened, so there was increasing pressure to set up a West German state. A decisive step was the creation of a German 'Bizonal Economic Council' in 1947 as a rudimentary government form for the British and American zones. West German delegates drafted a Basic Law, approved by the western powers, which was intended as a temporary constitution pending peace settlement and the reunification of east and West Germany; this came into force in 1949. In many ways the new constitution was in marked contrast with that of the Weimar Republic (November 1918–March 1933). For a strong president with wide reserve powers, it substituted a weak figurehead; this change was deliberate, since the aim was to create a strong government leader, a chancellor, who although responsible to the lower house, the Bundestag, would have a decisive say in government policy. Unlike most other states, there is no provision for popular initiative or referendum, since they were felt to undermine the representative institutions. Like the Weimar Republic, West Germany is a federal state, but the system is securely based on a constitutional court and a powerful upper house, the Bundesrat. An apparent consequence of these innovations has been stable government; although social and economic factors are equally relevant in accounting for stable political life.

German economic recovery in the 1950s and 1960s was reflected politically in the assimilative power of the two major parties, the Christian Democrats and the Social Democrats, and a rapid run-down in the number of parties. Extremist parties of left and right were uniformly unsuccessful, and just as significant was the failure of the so-called 'Refugee Party' appealing to those uprooted either from East Germany or from the lost territories. This assimilation was at its height in the Adenauer era (1949–1963); thereafter the hold of Christian Democracy weakened under Chancellors Erhard and Kiesinger, and subsequent to the 1965 elections (in 1966) the Social Democrats entered into a 'Grand Coalition' with the CDU. In 1969 the Christian Democrats were finally ousted by a new 'social-liberal' coalition (SPD and Free Democrats) under Willy Brandt who sought a reconciliation with Germany's eastern neighbours. Brandt's Ostpolitik resulted in treaties with the Soviet Union and Poland, ratified in 1973, confirming the territorial status quo east of the Oder-Neisse line. A Basic Treaty was also concluded with the German Democratic Republic which effectively gave official recognition to the existence of two German states, although the Federal Republic still maintains its commitment to eventual reunification. In addition, a four-power pact guaranteeing and regularising the special position of West Berlin, reached in 1971, can be seen as integral to the overall settlement.

The SPD-FDP coalition at first only had a narrow majority, and a parliamentary stalemate forced an early election in 1972, but the popularity of Brandt and his Ostpolitik resulted in a comfortable majority. However, Brandt resigned in May 1974 after the discovery of an East German spy on his personal staff (although remaining leader of the SPD), and was replaced by Helmut Schmidt as chancellor. The SPD-FDP coalition won both the 1976 and 1980 elections, but in 1980 it was aided by the reaction against the 'chancellor candidate' adopted by the CDU-CSU, Franz-Josef Strauss, since Strauss, leader of the right-wing Bavarian CSU, alienated many CDU supporters in other parts of the country.

By 1982, the coalition which had held together since 1969 showed various signs of strain. Schmidt faced discontents in his own party, dissatisfaction with his style of leadership and with his commitment to nuclear defence policy, and the SPD was losing the support of young voters to the new pacifist/ecological party, the Greens, who gained representation in several Länder assemblies. At the same time, the FDP suffered serious losses in the Länder and began to question the wisdom of continuing the federal coalition. Furthermore, the two parties substantially disagreed on the fiscal and economic policies to be used in the face of the deepening recession. In October 1982 the coalition collapsed and the Free Democrats sided with the CDU-CSU in passing a vote of 'constructive no-confidence' against Schmidt, that is, in electing the CDU leader, Helmut Kohl, as chancellor. The switch, although fully constitutional, was widely felt to require the sanction of the electorate, and in consequence a new election was held in March 1983. The result of the election was a confirmation of the change, since the new coalition (CDU-CSU with FDP) was returned with a decisive majority. Besides the sharp fall in support for the SPD, the other feature of the 1983 election was the rise of the Greens as representative of the 'new politics'. Much of that party's support was gained at the expense of the SPD.

The rise of the Greens put the SPD in an awkward dilemma. On the one hand, the more radical elements in the party played with the possibility of a red–green alliance. But if the SPD took this course it would jeopardise much of its traditional support, and there were serious doubts, too, as to the reliability of the Greens as potential coalition partners. On the other hand, if the SPD took a completely hostile attitude towards the new party it might experience a continuing seepage of younger voters to the more radical party and thus experience a secular decline. One commentary on the debate in the SPD was the experience of the red–green coalition in Land Hesse which was formed in December 1985 but broke down over the nuclear-energy issue; at the subsequent Land election in April 1987 the CDU and FDP emerged with a governing majority.

Although Kohl's CDU-CSU/FDP coalition suffered severe internal tensions over foreign policy and civil liberties, the chief effect was to strengthen the position of the FDP, especially in several Land elections, and – with the SPD in disarray – there was little chance of the coalition not surviving the 1987 federal election. In the event, both smaller parties, the FDP and Greens, made gains, whilst the CDU and SPD became more vulnerable. In particular, the FDP strengthened its pivotal position in the party system – thus preserving the possibility of a future opening to the SPD, and the SPD for its part preferred this option to moving towards the Greens – a party which anyway was torn by bitter factional disputes between its 'realist' and 'fundamentalist' wings.

Elections to the Bundestag, January 1987

	1987 Seats	1987 %	1983 %	1980 %	1976 %	1972 %
CDU-CSU	223	44.3	48.8	44.5	48.6	44.9
SPD	186	37.0	38.2	42.9	42.6	44.9
Free Democrats	49	9.1	6.9	10.6	7.9	8.4
Greens	42	8.3	5.6	1.5	–	–
Others	–	1.3	0.4	0.5	0.6	0.4

Notes: The CSU is the Bavarian partner of the CDU and won 9.8 per cent of the total vote in 1987. West Berlin does not participate in federal elections, but sends 22 representatives (in 1983: CDU 11; SPD 7; FDP 2; Alternatives 2) to the Bundestag, where they do not vote in plenary sessions. The neo-fascist NPD gained 0.6% of the vote in 1987, just sufficient to entitle it to a state subsidy.

Reading

K. Baker, R. Dalton, K. Hildebrandt, *Germany Transformed: Political Culture and the New Politics*, Cambridge, Mass: Harvard University Press, 1981.

M. Balfour, *West Germany: A Contemporary History*, Croom Helm, 1982.

V. Berghahn, *Modern Germany*, Cambridge University Press, 2nd ed., 1988.

A. Boenau, 'Changing Chancellors in West Germany', *West European Politics*, July 1988.

T. Burkett and S. Padgett, *Parties and Elections in West Germany*, C. Hurst, 1987.

R. Burns and W. van der Will, *Protest and Democracy in West Germany*, Macmillan, 1988.

D. P. Conradt, *The German Polity*, New York: David McKay, 1981.

G. Craig, *Germany, 1866–1945*, Oxford University Press, 1981.

H. Döring and G. Smith (eds.), *Party Government and Political Culture in Western Germany*, Macmillan, 1982.

W. Hanrieder (ed.), *West German Foreign Policy, 1949–1979*, Westview Press, 1979.

N. Johnson, *Government in the Federal Republic of Germany: The Executive at Work*, Pergamon, 1973.

W. Kohl and G. Basevi, *West Germany: A European and Global Power*, Lexington Books, 1981.

E. Kolinsky, *Parties, Opposition and Society in West Germany*, Croom Helm, 1984.

E. Krippendorff and V. Rittberger (eds.), *The Foreign Policy of West Germany*, Sage Publications, 1980.

A. Markovits, *The West German Left: Red, Green and Beyond*, Polity Press, 1988.

A. Markovits (ed.), *Modell Deutschland*, New York: Praeger Books, 1982.

E. Moreton (ed.), *Germany Between East and West*, Cambridge University Press, 1987.

S. Padgett, 'The West German Social Democrats in Opposition 1982–86'. *West European Politics*, July 1987.

W. Paterson and G. Smith (eds.), *The West German Model*, Frank Cass, 1981.

G. Smith, *Democracy in Western Germany: Parties and Politics in the Federal Republic*, Gower, 1986 (3rd edn.).

G. Smith, 'Consequences of the West German Election', *Government and Opposition*, vol. 22/2, Spring 1987.

GREECE

Greece achieved her independence from the Ottoman Empire in 1827, and after a short period as a republic, became a monarchy in 1831. Since 1862, with sharp discontinuities, the line was that of the House of Gluckbörg, and styled the 'King of the Hellenes'. This idea of greater Greece did not accord with the boundaries of the original small state, so much of Greek political development until the 1920s was related to the problems of realising the 'Great Idea' and resulted in foreign entanglement and dissension at home when the ambitions were unsatisfied. This nationalism has particularly affected the armed forces which became involved in politics at an early date. Disaffection in the army and navy over the failure to secure Crete led to a revolt against the parliamentary system and the monarchy (1909–1911); the effect of this however was to lead to a more democratic constitution in 1911, replacing that of 1864. As a result of the war with Turkey, beginning in

1912, Greece expanded her national territory considerably with the addition of Crete and Macedonia. With the accession of King Constantine I (1913–1922) there began a pattern of constitutional government, coup, and military dictatorship, which has repeated itself ever since. The whole period from 1917 until 1935 was marked by active military intervention, especially after the defeat of the Greek army in Asia Minor in 1922. A new (Second) republic was declared in 1924; this persisted until 1935, punctuated by attempted military coups. The elections of 1935 gave the pro-monarchist parties a majority and led to the return of King George II who had ruled previously from 1922 to 1924. The constitutional system was then undermined from within: rising to power by constitutional means as prime minister, General Metaxas became the strong man of Greek politics from 1936 until 1941. He assumed dictatorial powers, using the pretext of the growing internal threat of the Communist Party.

In the war years, the common struggle against the Italian and German occupiers did not obscure the cleavage between left and right; from 1943 onwards the resistance groups were often locked in their own battles. The return of the government in exile and its attempts to disarm the resistance groups and reimpose national order were hardly effective. Following a referendum King George II once more returned to the throne. It was a signal for open warfare between the Communist 'Free Democratic Government' against the British-backed Greek National Army, and from 1947 the Americans began their permanent involvement in Greek politics.

By 1949, the Communist challenge had been defeated, and from 1950 until 1967 a stable parliamentary system was maintained under a new, and liberal constitution, though the Communist Party continued to be outlawed. Fairly moderate conservative governments were the rule, but the stability was superficial; the monarchy had lost none of its ability for becoming involved in politics, and this led to the resignation of Constantine Karamanlis, prime minister from 1955 until 1963. Social discontents were also growing; in 1964 the new, radical Centre Union under Giorgios Papendreou obtained an absolute majority. On dubious constitutional grounds, King Constantine forced Papendreou out of office. For fear that the Centre Union and the left (EDA) would be returned with greater strength in the elections announced for April 1967, the military took power. The leader of the military junta, George Papadopoulos, exercised increasing personal power. A republic was declared in June 1973, and Papadopoulos became president. However, he was in turn deposed by an army coup in

November 1973 following a savage repression of student disorders. The new leaders of the regime, proved to have few ideas and little popular backing, and the dictatorship ignominiously collapsed in the course of the confrontation in 1974 between Turkey and Greece over Cyprus; Greece was simply not in a position to defend her interests on the island. Power was handed back to the civilians in July 1974, Karamanlis returning from exile to become prime minister. The relief at the end of the military dictatorship brought a refreshing moderation to Greek politics.

Political life was soon fully restored: the Communist Party was able to operate freely for the first time since 1947. Elections to a constituent assembly were held in November 1974 and the moderate parties were overwhelmingly successful. A referendum on the form of state followed in December and by a large majority (69.2 per cent) the electorate opted for a republic rather than a restoration of the monarchy.

In the 1974 election the victorious party was the New Democracy movement which had rapidly built up around the person of Karamanlis. New Democracy was also helped by the provisions of the electoral system – a 'reinforced proportional' type by which the largest parties (those receiving more than 17 per cent of the vote) qualified for an additional share of seats. Of the remaining parties the one formed by Andreas Papendreou was the most significant: his Pan-Hellenic Socialist Movement (Pasok) promised an alternative of democratic socialism to the broadly conservative outlook of New Democracy and the revamped Centre Union.

A new constitution was approved by the Constituent Assembly in July 1975, but there was bitter opposition in the assembly to the introduction of specifically presidential elements. The president is elected by the assembly (for a five-year term and by a two-thirds majority) but he can only be removed by impeachment. The president can dissolve the assembly, without requiring the assent of the prime minister, and he is able to initiate a referendum on any fundamental national issue. The president may also proclaim martial law – and he has final control over the armed forces. This presidential injection has potential similarities with the Fifth French Republic. A further election was held in November 1977. Even though New Democracy retained its overall majority in the assembly, Pasok made a spectacular advance, and the left-wing vote as a whole rose to 37.4 per cent. The way was thus open for a simple bi-polarity in Greek politics, a conclusion evidenced by the decline of the Centre Union and the subsequent fragmentation of its parliamentary group.

The overwhelming victory of Pasok in the November 1981 election confirmed the move to bi-polarity – besides promising an era of radical change. Pasok was hostile to NATO and had pledged to withdraw Greece from the European Community of which she had become a full member in 1981. Initially the restraining influence of President Karamanlis seemed fundamental to the preservation of Greece's still fragile democracy, but in practice the actual moderation of Pasok in office was a more significant factor. Thus whilst a whole range of progressive social legislation was enacted, Greece remained in the EC and made considerable use of EC funds to promote restructuring of the economy, particularly aiming to overcome the urban/rural divide. Although Pasok was hostile to NATO the position of US bases were guaranteed until 1989. The proposed withdrawal from the military structure of NATO was coupled with a continuity of political cooperation, however, tension over Greek–Turkish border disputes continued to place strain on Greece's membership of the alliance. The pragmatic nature of Pasok's socialism was also shown by the range of austerity measures the government imposed in late 1985 to combat the serious economic problems.

The 1985 election which preceded these measures was won by Pasok with an absolute majority in parliament. The election followed the replacement of Karamanlis by Christos Sartzetakis as President in a parliamentary manoeuvre which outraged the right,

Elections to the Parliament of the Republic, June 1985

	1985 Seats	1985 %	1981 %	1977 %	1974 %
New Democracy	126	40.8	35.8	42.8	54.3
Centre Union	–	–	0.4	11.9	20.5
Pasok	161	45.8	48.0	25.3	13.6
Communist Party (Interior)	1	1.8	1.3	2.7	
Communist Party (KKE)	12	9.9	10.9	9.3	9.4
Others	–	1.6	3.6	8.0	2.2

Notes: 'Others', besides miscellaneous left-wing groupings, includes the Progressive Party (1.7%) in 1981 and the National Rally (6.8%) in 1977, which merged with New Democracy in 1981. The KKE is the Moscow-oriented Communist Party whilst the 'Interior' one is Eurocommunist. In 1974 they fought as a common United Left. The electoral system is one of 'reinforced' proportional representation: the largest parties (effectively only Pasok and New Democracy) are entitled to a bonus of parliamentary seats. This form of adjustment promotes the formation of single-party governments.

but helped consolidate the left-wing vote. In this connection, it should be noted that the presence of a large Communist Party on Pasok's flank acts as an incentive to the governing party at least to maintain its radical image. Subsequent to 1985, severe losses by Pasok at local elections raised doubts as to whether it would long be able to hold its place as the dominant party at national level.

Reading

J. P. C. Carey and A. G. Carey, *The Web of Modern Greek Politics*, New York: Columbia University Press, 1968.

R. Clogg (ed.), *Greece in the 1980s*, Macmillan, 1983.

R. Clogg, *Parties and Elections in Greece*, C. Hurst, 1988.

K. Featherstone and K. Katsoudas (eds.), *Political Change in Greece: Before and After the Colonels*, Croom Helm, 1987.

Y. A. Kourvetaris and B. A. Dobratz, *A Profile of Modern Greece in Search of Identity*, Clarendon, 1987.

N. M. Limberes, 'The Greek Election of June 1985: A Socialist Entrenchment,' *West European Politics*, January 1986.

C. Lyrintzis, 'The Rise of Pasok' *West European Politics*, July 1982.

G. Th. Mavrogordatos, 'The Greek Party System: A Case of "Limited but polarised pluralism"?' *West European Politics*, October 1984.

N. Mouzelis, *Modern Greece: Facets of Underdevelopment*, Macmillan, 1977.

N. Mouzelis and M. Attalides, 'Greece', in *Contemporary Europe: Class, Status and Power*, op. cit.

E. O'Ballance, *The Greek Civil War, 1944–1949*, Faber and Faber, 1964.

A. Papendreou, *Democracy at Gunpoint: The Greek Front*, André Deutsch, 1971.

H. R. Penniman (ed.), *Greece at the Polls*, American Enterprise Institute, 1981.

ICELAND

After many centuries of Danish rule (since 1381), Iceland became substantially independent in 1918, still sharing the Danish king as a common sovereign. In 1944, the country became an independent republic, and although the present constitution dates from that year, the roots of her parliamentary institutions go back to the tenth century, especially the popular assembly, the Althingi. The government is responsible to the assembly, but a popularly-elected president has reserve powers.

The major and traditional parties of government since 1918 have been the Independence Party and the Progressives, broadly corresponding to conservative and centre-agrarian outlooks respectively. However, the Icelandic party system is particularly hard to categorise, and domestic political issues are dictated by special concerns. With only one per cent of the total land area under cultivation, and the great bulk of the population concentrated in Reykjavik, fishing is the basis of the Icelandic economy – a factor which explains the intensity of the 'cod wars' with Britain in the 1960s and 1970s. The presence of a large American NATO base on the island also acts as a continual political irritant for the left-wing parties. Although Iceland has full employment, she is dogged by the most severe rate of inflation in Western Europe (around 130 per cent in 1983), so that the economic performance of government has been a major factor in explaining party and coalition fortunes. A centre-left coalition of Progressives, Social Democrats and Peoples' Alliance, formed after the 1978 election, lasted only until 1979, and the subsequent coalition of Progressives, Peoples' Alliance and a small breakaway group from the Independence Party, although it survived for four years, proved highly unpopular.

The 1983 election led to a stable Independence/Progressives coalition, which reduced inflation to some 20 per cent over the following four years, and the coalition presided over a period of labour relations which was remarkably peaceful by Icelandic standards. The coalition expected to be confirmed in government by the 1987 election, but a serious split occurred in the Independence Party, and following the election the coalition had to be widened to include the Social Democrats.

Developments in the party system rather than in the government formula, however, were the more dramatic. Although electoral volatility had become marked in Iceland as elsewhere, new parties are usually ephemeral, and the Independence Party had more or less maintained its dominant position. As a result of the 1987 election, however, the Feminist Alliance which first entered parliament in 1983 doubled its representation, mainly at the expense of the Peoples' Alliance. Such success of a new party is unusual, but the survival of the Feminists is not guaranteed, since the problem of moving beyond a single group of issues may prove difficult, as other parties take up the core feminist demands. The split in the once-dominant Independence Party was the result of personal factionalism coupled with tensions over the development of a 'neo-liberal' ideology in the party. The breakaway of the Citizens' Party was provoked by a tax scandal concerning a charismatic IP parliamentarian, Albert Gusmundsson, and were he to retire, the Independence Party would re-establish itself, as the Peoples' Alliance and Social Democrats have already done in roughly similar circumstances. The effects of electoral volatility were reinforced in the 1987 election by the lowering of the voting age from 20 to 18, the redistribution of seats from the rural to the more volatile urban areas, and by the increase in the number of Althing seats from 60 to 63. In any case, the four 'old' parties still attracted 75 per cent of the vote in 1987, and the 11 per cent of the vote captured by the Citizens' Party could prove to be a temporary loss.

Elections to the Althing, April 1987

		1987		1983	1979	1978
	Seats	%		%	%	%
Independence Party	18	27.2		38.7	35.4	32.7
Citizens' Party	7	10.9		–	–	–
Progressive Party	13	18.9		18.5	24.9	16.9
Social Democrats	10	15.2		11.7	17.4	22.0
New Social Dem.	0	0.2		7.3	–	–
People's Alliance	8	13.3		17.3	19.7	22.9
Feminists	6	10.1		5.5	–	–
Others	1	4.2		1.0	2.6	5.5

Note: Others includes a splinter group from the Progressive Party in 1987 (1.2%, 1 seat).

Reading

N. Andrén, *Government and Politics in the Nordic Countries*, Stockholm: Almsqvist and Wiksell, 1964.

G. Arnason, 'Fluidity in Icelandic Politics – The Election of April 1987', in *West European Politics*, January 1988.

N. Elder, A. Thomas and D. Arter, *The Consensual Democracies? The Government and Politics of the Scandinavian States*, op. cit.

G. Gislason, *Iceland, 1918–1968*, London: University College, 1968.

O. Th. Hardarson and G. H. Kristinsson, 'The Icelandic Parliamentary Election of 1987', *Electoral Studies*, December 1987.

J. Madeley, 'European Elections – Iceland', *West European Politics*, October 1980.

J. Madeley, 'The 1983 Iceland Election', *West European Politics*, January 1984.

S. A. Magnusson, *Northern Sphinx. Iceland and the Icelanders*, C. Hurst, 1977.

J. Nordan and V. Kristinsson (eds.), *To Mark the Eleventh Centenary of the Settlement of Iceland*, Reykjavik: Central Bank of Iceland, 1975.

The Constitution of the Republic of Iceland, Reykjavik: Information Office of the Ministry for Foreign Affairs, 1948.

THE REPUBLIC OF IRELAND

After many centuries of English domination, a measure of Home Rule was eventually granted to Ireland in 1914, suspended until after the war, with civil war in Ireland intervening in the meanwhile. The civil war underlined the differences between the loyalist Irish, mainly Protestant and concentrated in Ulster, and the nationalist-dominated south who were Roman Catholic. The Government of Ireland Act of 1920 took account of this division and set up a parliament for Northern Ireland in Belfast as well as one in Dublin. The fighting which followed led to the repeal of the 1920 Act and the granting of virtual autonomy to Southern Ireland by the passing of the Irish Free State Act of 1922. At the same time, Northern Ireland was granted Home Rule, still sending representatives to the British Parliament. Effective independence had thus been gained for 26 of the 32 Irish counties. In the remaining six counties, the majority favoured continued allegiance to Britain, but this part of Ulster also contained a large minority of Roman Catholics, who if not necessarily republican or nationalist in sympathy, represented a sharp and permanent basis of cleavage in Northern Irish society. A new constitution for Southern Ireland was approved by referendum in 1937, becoming Eire, that is, the Irish Republic, and the constitution affirmed that the national territory included Northern Ireland as well (Article 2). Until 1949 the Irish Republic was still regarded as a part of the Commonwealth. The Ireland Act, passed in Britain in 1949, confirmed the status of the Republic of Ireland, although she was not to be treated as a foreign country, nor her citizens as aliens. Additionally, the Ireland Act reiterated the position of Northern Ireland as an integral complement of the United Kingdom, and her constitutional position could not be altered without the consent of the Northern Irish parliament.

The political scene in the Irish Republic has for long been dominated by the two republican parties, Fine Gael (United Ireland) and Fianna Fail (Soldiers of Ireland); their different viewpoints are largely historical in origin: Fine Gael supported the Treaty with Britain to set up the Irish Free State, whilst Fianna Fail rejected its terms for the partition of Ireland. Both parties have lost any radical image they once had, and their domination has produced a party system unlike any other in Western Europe, since a class basis of politics is scarcely apparent, and any traditional 'left–right' scaling is difficult to apply. There are also strong localist and personal elements which are strengthened by the voting system, a single transferable vote in multi-member constituencies; this system enables supporters to place the candidates of their party in order of preference.

In 1972 two important referenda were held. The first, in June, resulted in an overwhelming vote in favour (80 per cent) of membership of the European Community, and in December an amendment of Article 44 of the constitution was approved deleting reference to the 'special position' accorded to the Roman Catholic Church (84 per cent in favour). Although this result was interpreted as a gesture of reconciliation to the Protestant community of the North, successive Irish governments have not felt otherwise able to take much positive action to further Irish unity, wishing neither to risk an open breach with Britain nor to countenance the risk of violence spreading across the border to the Republic. The imposition of direct rule over Northern Ireland in

1972 was generally welcomed, and initiatives favouring all-Irish participation in matters affecting Northern Ireland have emanated from Britain.

Although both Fianna Fail and Fine Gael are constitutionally and historically committed to a united Ireland, it was Fianna Fail which took the stronger line in calling for an eventual British withdrawal from Northern Ireland. The Anglo–Irish Agreement of 1985 represents a major step towards normalising Irish politics, with Fine Gael signing the Agreement as part of its radical programme of modernising Irish political life, whilst the Progressive Democrats split from a Fianna Fail over its hesitation in accepting the Agreement. Subsequently, the election of February 1987 and the formation of Fianna Fail minority government led to Fianna Fail also endorsing the Agreement. Sinn Fein, a political fringe group in Eire which has been of some importance through its exclusive aim of reuniting Ireland, broke its 60-year abstentionist policy to compete in the 1987 election but polled a derisory 1.9 per cent of the vote.

For much of the post-war period – and indeed since the early 1930s – Fianna Fail was in a dominant position, with a Fine Gael/Labour coalition not appearing to be a credible alternative, because of Fine Gael's more 'middle class' electorate. Nevertheless from the early 1970s a balanced party system with alternating government emerged, with a Fine Gael/Labour coalition ruling for the first time in 1973–77; as Fine Gael shifted towards being a progressive liberal party its affinity with Labour as coalition partner became apparent. But the development of moderate bipolarism was accompanied by governmental instability, as the Fine Gael/Labour coalition of 1981 was in a minority in the Dail; it was not destined to last for long, and the same was true of the brief Fianna Fail government which followed the February 1982 election.

Three elections in eighteen months led to a further Fine Gael/Labour coalition which lasted for five years until broken, and apparently irrevocably, by disagreement over how to handle Ireland's formidable economic problems. These are most apparent in the size of Ireland's national debt, which is one-and-a-half times the GNP, as well as in the reappearance of large scale emigration due to the pressure of unemployment.

The 1980s also saw the referendum used in relation to moral issues. The Catholic Church apparently consolidated its position in the amendment to the constitution of 1983 guaranteeing the right to life of the 'unborn child' (66.9 per cent of voters supported this amendment), as well as through the subsequent referendum establishing the constitutional inadmissibility of any divorce legislation. The 1986 divorce referendum was a response to proposed Fine Gael legislation, and the result showed a remarkable reversal of public opinion during the course of the campaign. Nevertheless, many observers regarded the referendum result (63.5 per cent against divorce legislation) as representing the Pyrrhic victory of a disappearing Ireland; they saw, too, the defeat of Sinn Fein and the rise of the Progressive Democrats as striking indicators of Ireland's changing politics, and – with the declining strength of the two largest parties – the party system appeared to be entering a stage of flux.

Elections to the Dail, February 1987

	1987 seats	1987 %	1982 (Nov) %	1982 (Feb) %	1981 %	1977 %
Fianna Fail	81	44.1	45.2	47.3	45.3	50.6
Fine Gael	51	27.1	39.2	37.3	36.5	30.5
Progressive Democrats	14	11.8	–	–	–	–
Labour	12	6.4	9.4	9.1	9.9	12.6
Workers' Party	4	3.8	3.3	2.3	1.7	1.6
Others	4	6.7	3.0	4.0	6.7	5.7

Notes: Percentage figures refer to 'first preferences' which under the Single Transferable Vote system tallies only approximately with the final number of seats won, the larger parties benefiting from the system.

Reading

R. K. Carty, *Party and Parish Pump: Electoral Politics in Ireland*, Ontario: W. Laurier University Press, 1981.

B. Chubb, *The Government and Politics of Ireland*, Oxford University Press, rev. ed., 1982.

J. Coakley, 'Moral Consensus in a Secularising Society: The Irish Divorce Referendum of 1986', *West European Politics*, April 1987.

D. Boyce, 'Separatism and the Irish Nationalist Tradition', in C. Williams (ed.), *National Separatism*, University of Wales Press, 1982.

M. Gallagher, *Political Parties in the Republic of Ireland*, Manchester University Press, 1985.

P. Mair, *The Changing Irish Party System: Organisation, Ideology and Electoral Competition*, Pinter, 1987.

J. A. Murphy, *Ireland in the Twentieth Century*, Dublin: Gill and Macmillan, 1975.

E. Norman, *A History of Modern Ireland*, Penguin Books, 1973.

B. D. O'Leary, 'The Anglo-Irish Agreement: Folly or Statecraft?', *West European Politics*, January 1987.

B. D. O'Leary, 'Towards Europeanisation and Realignment? The Irish General Election', *West European Politics*, July 1987.

A. Orridge, 'The Irish Labour Party', in Paterson and Thomas (eds.), *Social Democratic Parties in Western Europe*, op. cit.

R. Sinnott, 'Interpretations of the Irish Party System', *European Journal of Political Research*, 12:3, 1984.
J. Whyte, 'Ireland: Politics Without Social Bases', in R. Rose, *Electoral Behaviour*, op. cit.
See also, Northern Ireland (United Kingdom).

ITALY

The unification of Italy was finally achieved in 1870 as a monarchy under the House of Savoy until 1946 when she became a republic. The period until the First World War was one of domination by the anticlerical Liberals, the popular force of national unification; modern mass parties scarcely existed, parliamentary majorities were 'managed', the electorate was restricted, and there was a Papal prohibition on Catholics participating in all political life. By 1919 this had all changed and the sharp political cleavages were given full expression; the transition to a stable parliamentary system based on mass parties faced severe problems. The contending forces of the Nationalists, Fascists, Catholic Populists, Socialists (and, from 1921, the Communists) shared nothing of the government experience of the rapidly declining Liberals. The political and industrial turmoil of the post-war years soon led to a radicalisation of Italian politics. The inability of the moderate left and moderate right to work together, Socialists and Catholics, even though these were the two largest parties, gave the lever to the small Fascist movement, which through its militia succeeded in imposing its own version of order on large parts of the country, often with the connivance of local prefects. In October 1922 the King offered the premiership to Mussolini, and the March on Rome which followed was a display of Fascist power. The government remained nominally parliamentary until 1924. Elections were held in April, but these took place in an atmosphere of Fascist terror, and under a law made for the benefit of the Fascists which stipulated that the party winning 25 per cent of the votes would be allotted two-thirds of the seats in the Chamber of Deputies. From January 1925, the system of Fascism and personal dictatorship under Mussolini was instituted, whilst still preserving the symbols of the monarchy and the Pope. The Vatican indeed, welcomed Mussolini, for the Lateran Treaties of 1929 restored all the privileges of the Church that had been swept away in 1870 – the Vatican had been the enemy of a united Italy.

In the period of reconstruction after 1945, a popular plebiscite voted for a republic in 1946, and a new constitution came into effect in 1948. This provided for full parliamentary government, extensive democratic rights, a constitutional court, and far-reaching provisions for regional government. From the beginning, political life has been focused on the powerful Christian Democratic Party which has been in power since the first elections in 1946, though almost always in coalition; for a brief spell (1948 until 1953) it actually had a majority of seats. This stability has to be matched against the deep political cleavage between Christian Democracy and the powerful Communist Party, the strongest in Western Europe. However, the polarisation has never come to full effect, since the Christian Democrats avoided becoming a clerical-conservative party. This was shown clearly from 1962 onwards when it initiated a policy of seeking an opening to the left, that is, left-of-centre coalitions which stopped short of the extreme left. It was the question of co-operation with the Christian Democrats which in turn divided the left, essentially into three groupings: the excluded Communists, Socialists willing to join a Christian Democratic coalition, and Socialists who regarded such coalitions as divisive of working-class unity.

At the other end of the political scale, the left-inclination of the Christian Democrats gave some encouragement to the extreme right, especially the MSI (*Movimento Sociale Italiano*) which arose as a splinter party but which harbours a considerable neo-fascist potential. Various combinations of the centre-left formula have been applied in recent years – the Christian Democrats with one or more other parties: the Social Democrats, the Socialists, the Republicans, though not all the minor parties have been represented in every coalition.

The extreme difficulty of fashioning a majority can be illustrated by the presidential election which took place in December 1971. The Italian president is elected for a seven-year term by an electoral college consisting of the two houses of the Italian Parliament with representatives from the regions, over a thousand electors in all. The 1971 election resulted in twenty-two inconclusive ballots before a Christian Democrat was elected at the twenty-third attempt. Although the formal powers of the president are not great his importance lies in his ability to help build coalitions, and the stability of his office can help offset the instability of government which has become an endemic feature of post-war politics. Italian presidents have not always been important figures, but Alessandro Pertini, a life-long Socialist, commanded widespread respect as president from 1978 to 1985, and helped smooth the path for the first non-Christian Democrat prime minister of the early 1980s.

Whilst in the early post-war years and even up to the late 1960s, the Christian Democrats had a firm hold on national government and, indeed, on all aspects of political life, their paramount position was gradually eroded, although they remain the most important political force. The most significant indicator of this change was the referendum held on the Divorce Law in May 1974, when the Vatican hierarchy and the DC supported the call for the repeal of the liberal divorce law of 1970 and were dramatically defeated. On an 88 per cent turn-out, 59.1 per cent (19 million against 13 million) voted in favour of retaining the law, and the DC lost the support of traditional voters and key 'flanking' organisations such as Catholic Action. This major defeat was confirmed by the municipal and regional elections of 1975 when the Communists recorded massive gains, becoming the largest party in seven of the fifteen regions contested, and subsequently dominating the governments of most large cities and several regions.

The decline of the DC was matched by the rise of the Communist Party which had embarked on a new strategy before the electoral tide had turned. The leader of the PCI, Enrico Berlinguer, enunciated the terms of an 'historic compromise' in 1973: the compromise aimed at promoting alliances with *all* progressive forces in Italian society, a form of pluralism was implied, rather than the hegemony of a class organised through a political party. Under certain circumstances, therefore, collaboration with the DC would become part of PCI strategy, rather than an insistence that Christian Democracy would have to be supplanted. This move was not a tactical concession, but a recognition that a bare electoral majority in favour of the left was inadequate to ensure peaceful progress, and that the political power of the right represented more than the presence of the DC in government.

Electoral support for the PCI and its new course was confirmed in the June 1976 election which saw the PCI vote jump from 27.3 to 34.4 per cent. But the advance was insufficient to gain access to government, and in the economic and terrorist crises which wracked Italy in the later 1970s the PCI was drawn in to collaboration with the DC in the call for the 'defence of the state' despite its inability to gain ministerial representation.

In the face of negative electoral reaction, the incomprehension of party activists, and the objections of intellectual élites, the PCI withdrew its support from the DC minority government, and in the June 1979 election, after decades of almost uninterrupted growth, the PCI's share of the vote fell. The discrediting of the main opposition party was counterbalanced by the disfavour affecting the ruling DC, which reached a peak in 1981 in the scandal over 'P–2', a secret masonic lodge which appeared to act as the real ruling force in Italy. As a consequence, coalition formation became even more difficult, and to break the deadlock the premiership fell to the respected leader of the small Republican Party, Giovanni Spadolini.

The leader of the Socialist Party, Bettino Craxi was able to profit from the unpopularity of the two major mass parties, and subsequent to the 1983 elections and with the heavy fall of the DC vote he formed a government based on the same five-party basis which had supported Spadolini – DC, PSI, PRI, PSDI and PLI. The new challenge to the major parties was the socialist-lay area posing as a 'third force'.

The 1987 election showed that Craxi's long campaign to strengthen the 'third force' had brought some success for his own party, but the DC also recovered somewhat and its credibility has been restored by the election in June 1985 of its presidential candidate, Franco Cossiga, on the first ballot – the previous DC President, Giovanni Leone, had required 23 ballots before being elected and had been forced to resign amid allegations of financial scandal. With the ratio of Communist voters to Socialist voters lower than 2:1, instead of over 3:1, the system looked far less polarised, and the outlines of a less 'imperfect bipartism' – based on the PSI and DC rather than the PCI and DC – was discernible. This situation made internal coalition politics turbulent, but the electorate was also willing to punish those parties responsible for causing government crisis. This electoral sanction in large measure explains the longevity of Craxi's governments (formally two, but in composition and popular perception a single period) from August 1983 to April 1987. However, his modest success in 1987 was gained largely at the expense of his potential 'lay' allies, and the DC was able to regain the premiership.

Italian politics has changed significantly since the period of 'democratic solidarity', or PCI support for the government in the later 1970s. It is no longer true that Italian society is ruptured by deep-seated cleavages, and the 'structural immobilism' of the party system which for long obscured the considerable changes in Italian society is gradually disappearing. The terroristic right-wing 'strategy of tension', and the revolutionary activity of the 'Red Brigades' largely belong to the past. They are not a true reflection of the political system, which is considerably more stable than its record of unstable government and political violence might indicate.

Elections to the Chamber of Deputies, June 1987

	1987 Seats	1987 %	1983 %	1979 %	1976 %
Christian Democrats (DC)	234	34.3	32.9	38.3	38.7
Communists (PCI)	177	26.6	29.9	30.4	34.3
Socialists (PSI)	94	14.3	11.4	9.8	9.6
Social Democrats (PSDI)	17	3.0	4.1	3.8	3.4
MSI	35	5.9	6.8	5.8	6.1
Republicans (PRI)	21	3.7	5.1	3.0	3.1
Liberals (PLI)	11	2.1	2.9	1.9	1.3
Radicals	13	2.6	2.2	3.4	1.1
Democratic Proletarians	8	1.7	1.5	1.4	1.5
Greens	13	2.5	–	–	–
S. Tyrol People's	3	0.5	0.5	0.6	0.5
Others	4	1.8	2.7	1.6	0.3

Notes: 'Others' represents mainly regional parties/lists

Reading

P. A. Allum, 'Italy', in S. Henig (ed.), *Political Parties in the European Community*, op. cit.

S. H. Barnes, 'Italy: Religion and Class in Electoral Behavior', in R. Rose (ed.), *Electoral Behavior*, op. cit.

S. Bartolini, 'The Politics of Institutional Reform in Italy', *West European Politics*, July 1982.

M. Donovan, 'The 1987 Election in Italy: Prelude to Reform?' *West European Politics*, January 1988.

P. Farneti, *The Italian Party System, 1945–80*, Pinter, 1985.

G. Galli and A. Prandi, *Patterns of Political Participation in Italy*, New Haven, 1970.

D. Hine, 'Social Democracy in Italy', in Paterson and Thomas (eds.), *Social Democratic Parties in Western Europe*, op. cit.

D. Hine, 'Thirty Years of the Italian Republic', *Parliamentary Affairs*, Winter 1981.

P. Lange and S. Tarrow (eds.), *Italy in Transition: Conflict and Consensus*, Frank Cass, 1979.

J. LaPalombara, *Democracy Italian Style*, Yale University Press, 1987.

R. Leonardi and R. Nanetti (eds.), *Italian Politics: A Review Vol. 1*, Frances Pinter, 1987.

P. Nichols, *The Politics of the Vatican*, Pall Mall Press, 1968.

G. Pasquino, 'Sources of Stability and Instability in the Italian Party System', *West European Politics*, January 1983.

G. Pridham, 'The Italian Christian Democrats after Moro', *West European Politics*, January 1979.

G. Pridham, *The Nature of the Italian Party System: A Regional Case Study*, Croom Helm, 1981.

A. Ranney and G. Sartori (eds.), *Eurocommunism: The Italian Case*, Washington: American Enterprise Institute, 1978.

M. Santuccio and S. Acquaviva, *Social Structure in Italy*, Martin Robertson, 1975.

D. Sassoon, *The Strategy of the Italian Communist Party: From the Resistance to the Historic Compromise*, Frances Pinter, 1981.

D. Sassoon, *Contemporary Italy: Politics, Economy and Society Since 1945*, Longmann, 1986.

F. Spotts and T. Wieser, *Italy: A Difficult Democracy*, Cambridge University Press, 1986.

G. R. Urban (ed.), *Eurocommunism: Its Roots and Future in Italy*, Maurice Temple Smith, 1978.

S. J. Woolf (ed.), *The Rebirth of Italy, 1943–1950*, Longman, 1972.

R. Zariski, *Italy: The Politics of Uneven Development*, Hinsdale, Illinois: Dryden Press, 1972.

LUXEMBOURG

From the fifteenth century onwards Luxembourg was controlled by a succession of foreign powers. In 1815 it was created a Grand Duchy with the Dutch king as the first Grand Duke. Following the Belgian secession from the Netherlands, Luxembourg became independent as well. The country's independent existence dates from 1839, but as a much smaller entity than was the case in previous centuries. The main spoken language is German and the Letzeburgesch dialect, but there are strong cultural ties with France and strong economic ones with Belgium – a customs union has been in force since 1921. Luxembourg shed the neutral status it had tried to maintain since 1867 after the Second World War and joined the Benelux union in 1947. The country was also a founder member of the European Coal and Steel Community and of the EEC. As she has entered these external commitments, so has her international position increased in importance. The Grand Duke is a purely representative monarch and the government is responsible to the Chamber of Deputies. The assembly is unicameral and there is an unusual legislative checking device whereby the legislation has to be passed by the assembly a second time, with a three-month interval. If this procedure is not adopted, then the administrative body, the Council of State, has a suspensory veto.

The party system follows a typical European pattern: Christian-Socials, Socialists, Liberals, and Communists. The Christian-Socials are the largest party and until 1974 had participated in every government since 1919, and since 1945 had supplied every prime minister. The normal pattern was a coalition with either the Liberals or the Socialists, a formula which first broke down in 1974 with a sharp fall in the Christian-Social vote and the formation of a liberal–socialist coalition which forced the Christian-Socials into opposition. The Christian-Social/Liberal coalition was again formed after the 1979 election, but was again replaced by a liberal-socialist coalition following the 1984 election, which showed a marked recovery in the fortunes of the Socialist Party.

Elections to the Chamber of Deputies, June 1984

	1984 seats	1984 %	1979 %	1974 %	1968 %
Christian-Socials	25	34.9	34.5	28.0	35.3
Socialists	21	33.6	24.3	29.0	32.3
Liberals (Democrats)	14	18.7	21.3	22.1	16.6
Social Democrats	–	–	6.0	9.1	–
Communists	2	5.0	5.8	10.4	15.5
Independent Soc.	1	2.5	2.2	–	–
Green/Alternatives	2	5.2	1.0	–	–
Others	0	0.6	4.9	1.4	0.3

Notes: Others in 1979 includes 'enrôles de force' with 4.4% of the vote and 1 seat. This movement sought compensation from Germany for those forcibly recruited into the German armed forces in World War II. In 1984 it dissolved and its Deputy joined the Christian-Socials. The Social Democrats were formed in 1971 and dissolved in 1983. Two of its Deputies joined the Christian Socials, the third remained as an Independent.

Reading

A. Herchen, *History of the Grand-Duchy of Luxembourg*, Luxembourg: Linden, 1950.

M. Hirsch, 'Luxembourg', in S. Henig (ed.), *Political Parties in the European Community*, op. cit.

M. Hirsch, 'The 1984 Luxembourg Election', *West European Politics*, January 1985.

M. Hirsch, 'Tripartism in Luxembourg: The Limits of Social Concentration', *West European Politics*, January 1986.

C. Hury and J. Christophory, *Luxembourg*, Oxford: Clio Press, 1981.

P. King (ed.), *Benelux*, Hull University Press, 1977.

G. L. Weil, *The Benelux Nations: The Politics of Small Country Democracies*, New York: Holt, Rinehart and Winston, 1970.

MALTA

Malta became a British colony in 1814 after the island had been taken from the French. In 1947 she was granted self-government with a British-appointed governor who had powers in foreign affairs, defence, and currency. In 1955 the Maltese Labour Party came to office and made a radical proposal for the full integration of Malta with the United Kingdom and this proposal received the support of three-quarters of the voters at a referendum in 1956. The constitution was suspended in 1958 following the breakdown of negotiations towards integration, and by the 1960s there was a general desire for independence. The opposing Nationalist Party came to power in 1962 and full independence was gained in 1964 with a new constitution making the government responsible to the single-chamber House of Representatives. The Nationalist government negotiated a defence agreement with Britain, the main importance of which for the Maltese was a financial contribution to the underdeveloped economy of Malta. She suffers from a relative overpopulation – a third of a million people and little more than 100 square miles, few natural resources and a chronic shortage of water.

From 1971 until 1987 Malta was dominated by the Labour Party, and for most of that period by its leader, Dom Mintoff. This ascendancy produced radical changes in Malta's foreign and domestic policies, so that the polarisation between the two parties and their followers increasingly became a source of social and political disturbance. Mintoff pursued a strongly independent line which came to veer towards 'neutro-nationalism'. Initially he demanded a revision of the defence agreement with Britain, threatening to close the NATO defence establishment on the island, and eventually in March 1972 a new agreement was reached with Britain (and interested NATO partners) to last for seven years. Britain finally withdrew her forces in 1979, and Mintoff sought close links with China and the Arab states, particularly Libya, provoking a sharp and hostile reaction from the Nationalist Party which accused the Labour Government of fostering unduly close relations with Communist states, these links apparently being a further indication of Labour's intention to stay in power at any cost.

In December 1974, Malta had become a republic, thus severing her connection with Britain. The president of the republic, elected for a five-year term by the House of Representatives, had powers substantially the same as those of the former governor-general, and was not a politically significant figure. Mintoff's power seemed absolute, and the Labour Party's economic policies, which included 'radical' policies, such as import substitution, designed to increase Malta's industrial base, and a form of 'neo-corporatism' which saw two representatives of the main General Workers' Union sitting in on cabinet meetings, were bitterly resented by business interests close to the Nationalist Party. Complaints of intimidation and election irregularities were made frequently, and the 1981 election confirmed Labour Party domination of Parliament based on a minority of votes using the Single Transferable Vote System. The outcome was allegedly also influenced by the gerrymandering of the constituencies, and such action seemed to substantiate the Nationalists' fears of Labour holding permanently on to power.

Maltese politics polarised sharply in the early 1980s. The Nationalist Party boycotted parliament for 18 months following the 1981 election, and this action eventually led to a limited resolution of government and opposition hostility in March 1983.

In 1984 Mifsud Bonnici replaced Mintoff as leader of the Labour Party and Prime Minister, and a more conciliatory period began although strong tensions remained by the time of the 1987 election.

In January 1987, in return for the Nationalists agreeing to a constitutional guarantee of Malta's non-aligned status, Labour agreed to a constitutional amendment giving the party with a majority of votes a one-seat majority in parliament. This enabled the Nationalists to claim a bonus of four seats following the 1987 election, and thus to form the government. Although the new government seeks membership of the European Community, Malta's constitutionally non-aligned status may increase the difficulties involved in realising this aim. Further amendments to the constitution (requiring a two-thirds majority) would need the agreement of the Labour Party. Malta's Mediterranean position could prove of importance to the development of a Mediterranean policy on the part of the EC. The transition to Nationalist rule resulted in an interim agreement leading to the appointment of a Labour Party nominee as acting president of the republic as a balancing compensation for a period of Nationalist rule.

Elections to the House of Representatives, May 1987

	1987	%	1981 %	1976 %	1971 %
Nationalist Party	31 + 4*	50.9	50.9	48.8	48.1
Labour Party	34	48.9	49.1	51.2	50.8
Others	–	–	–	–	1.1

Notes: 96.1% of the electorate voted. The asterisk indicates that the bonus system is operative to give the Nationalists the requisite one seat majority. The electoral system is that of the Single Transferable Vote in multi-member constituencies. The voting age was reduced to 20 in 1976.

Reading

D. Austin, *Malta and the End of Empire*, Frank Cass, 1971.
J. Craig, 'Malta: Mintoff's Election Victory', *West European Politics*, July 1982.
E. Dobie, *Malta's Road to Independence*, University of Oklahoma, 1967.
D. Fenech, 'The 1987 Maltese Election: Between Europe and the Mediterranean', *West European Politics*, January 1988.
S. Howe, 'The Maltese General Election of 1987', *Electoral Studies*, December 1987.

THE NETHERLANDS

Although the modern state of the Netherlands dates from 1815, when the existing Stadtholder, William of Orange-Nassau, was created monarch of the north and south Netherlands, her period of greatness was in the seventeenth century as a leader in trade and science. From the late sixteenth century onwards the Dutch Republic, composed of the seven United Provinces, was more of a confederacy than a unified state. A parliamentary system was only established in 1814, and this was not substantially democratised until 1848. The fragile union of the north and south Netherlands was broken when the south revolted in 1830, and became the independent state of Belgium in 1831. The bicameral system of the States-General was reformed in 1848; the estate system of representation was abolished in favour of direct suffrage, whilst the upper house was elected by members of the provincial councils as it continues to be at present. At the same time, the principle of ministerial responsibility to the States-General was established. As the franchise was extended between 1887 and 1919, so the modern parties took shape, but the party system which resulted was based on the peculiarities of the cleavages in Dutch society, especially those of religion. In this, a fundamental feature was that the political élites, Calvinist or Catholic, have not been identified with a single state church. Thus religious pluralism has made for a political pluralism; both Protestants and Catholics had to face powerful secular influences, and these three together compose the three 'pillars' of Dutch society – any one of them is a minority so there is a natural tendency to compromise.

Thus despite the apparently introverted nature of the various religious parties, this isolation is modified by the necessity to work in harmony with others or to risk political exclusion. Initially, and until the First World War, the alliance was between Catholics and Calvinists against the Liberals, fought over the question of education, with both groups alternating in office. Fear of the Socialists drove the religious parties together with the Liberals, and for the most of the inter-war period it was the Socialists who were excluded, and the wide class appeal of the religious parties prevented the Dutch Labour Party from obtaining more than a quarter of the vote.

In the post-war period coalitions became more broadly based, frequently with the inclusion of the Labour Party. A prominent feature was the long-term decline of the three major religious parties: in the 1950s they accounted for about half the vote compared with only a third in the early 1970s. The three parties (one Catholic, two Protestant) amalgamated to form the Christian

Democratic Appeal, first as an alliance and then as a unified party in 1980. However, the fusion stabilised rather than improved their position. The resulting simplification of the party system is rather obscured by the multiplicity of very small parties encouraged by the generous system of proportional representation: no fewer than twelve parties were successful in the 1982 election, but most of them are quite marginal to coalition formation. The core of the system consists of Labour, Christian Democrats and Liberals – accounting for about 85 per cent of the vote in 1986.

The centrist Christian Democrats occupy an ambiguous position. As a centrist pivot they were in alliance with the Liberals from 1977 until 1981 and also led a coalition with Labour and D'66 in 1981–82. The CDA was strengthened by the 1986 election, and a tendency towards a two-bloc system was confirmed: the 1986 election resulted in renewed strength of the centre-left vote, as represented by D'66 and the Labour Party, whilst the aggregate vote of CDA and the right-wing Liberals, in coalition together since 1982, has remained constant, despite a sharp fall in support for the VVD in 1986. The coalition had a common basis on the need for financial retrenchment, and it managed to weather the intense storm of opposition aroused by the decision to site intermediate-range nuclear missiles in the Netherlands which united the parties in the radical bloc.

Elections to the Lower Chamber of the States-General, May 1986

	1986 seats	1986 %	1982 %	1981 %
Labour Party (PvdA)	52	33.3	30.4	28.2
Christian Democrats (CDA)	54	34.6	29.3	30.8
Liberals (VVD)	27	17.4	23.1	17.3
Democrats '66	9	6.1	4.3	11.0
State Reform Party (Calvinist)	3	1.8	1.9	2.0
Radical Political Party (Catholic)	2	1.3	1.6	2.0
Communist Party	0	0.6	1.8	2.1
Reformed Political Assoc. (Calvinist)	1	1.0	0.8	0.8
Pacifist Socialist Party	1	1.2	2.2	2.1
Reformist Political Fed. (Calvinist)	1	0.9	1.5	1.2
Evangelical People's	0	0.2	0.7	0.5
Centre Party	0	0.4	0.8	0.1
Others	1	1.2	1.6	1.0

Notes: The CDA first came into being to contest the 1977 election. 'Others' in different years include the Farmers' Party, Democratic Socialists '70, Party of the Middle Classes and Roman Catholic Party. The representation of very small parties is possible because the whole country is a single constituency and the effective electoral quota is considerably less than 1 per cent of votes cast.

Reading

H. Daalder and G. Irwin (eds), 'Politics in the Netherlands: How Much Change?', *West European Politics*, special issue, January 1989.

H. Daalder, 'The Dutch Party System: From Segmentation to Polarisation – And Then?', H. Daalder (ed.), *Party Systems*, op. cit., 1987.

K. Gladdish, 'The Centre Holds: The 1986 Netherlands Election', *West European Politics*, January 1987.

K. Gladdish, 'Opposition in the Netherlands', E. Kolinsky (ed.), *Opposition in Western Europe*, Croom Helm, 1987.

R. Griffiths (ed.), *The Economy and Politics of the Netherlands since 1945*, The Hague: Martinus Nijhoff, 1980.

F. E. Huggett, *The Modern Netherlands*, Pall Mall Press, 1971.

P. King (ed.), *Benelux*, Hull University Press, 1977.

A. Lijphart, *The Politics of Accommodation: Pluralism and Democracy in the Netherlands*, Berkeley and Los Angeles: University of California Press, 1968.

A. Lijphart, 'The Netherlands: Continuity and Change in Voting Behavior', in R. Rose (ed.), *Electoral Behavior*, op. cit.

A. McMullen, 'The Netherlands', in F. Ridley (ed.), *Government and Administration in Western Europe*, Oxford: Martin Robertson, 1979.

H. van Mierlo, 'Depillarisaton and the Decline of Consociationalism in the Netherlands 1970–85', *West European Politics*, January 1986.

Z. Scholten, 'Corporatism and the Neo-Liberal Backlash in the Netherlands', in I. Scholten (ed.), *Political Stability*, op. cit.

M. P. C. M. van Schendelen (ed.), *Consociationalism, Pillarisation and Conflict Management in the Low Countries*, Rotterdam: Erasmus Universitaet, 1984.

S. B. Wolinetz, 'The Dutch Labour Party: A Social Democratic Party in Transition', in Paterson and Thomas (eds.), *Social Democratic Parties in Western Europe*, op. cit.

NORWAY

Although Norway has one of the oldest and least-amended constitutions of Western Europe, dating from 1814, in fact her history until recent times has been one of foreign domination. Prior to 1814, Norway had been under Danish rule for several centuries, and from then until 1905 in union with Sweden. The periods of Danish and Swedish influence left their mark on Norwegian culture and politics; the strong oppositional elements showed in the reaction to the Danish-dominated city-life, bureaucracy, and language in counter-movements of cultural defence and language outside the main cities. There were also the struggles between the assembly, the Storting, and the Swedish monarchy, with the assembly a focus for national demands. This role it could take because the 1814 constitution gave a system of representation which was the most democratic in Europe, almost all men over the age of twenty-five had the vote. Both the cultural and national issues came to the fore in the nineteenth century. By 1884, the principle of government responsibility to the Storting was recognised, and in 1905, using a consultative referendum, the country opted to become an independent monarchy (of Danish origin). The Norwegian party system has been heavily influenced by historical factors, and cultural and constitutional issues were supplemented by class ones.

The first party divisions were represented by the Right (Höyre) against the Left (Venstre), the one conservative and pro-union with Sweden, the other liberal and agrarian. These were joined by the Norwegian Labour Party which first won representation to the Storting in 1903; it soon showed its strength in making an appeal to fishermen, small farmers, as well as the urban worker. In 1927 it became the largest party, and dominated Norwegian politics from 1933 to 1965; apart from the war period it was in office for all but four weeks. Until 1961, the Labour Party had an absolute majority in the Storting, but in 1965 it was replaced by a coalition of the bourgeois parties: Right-Conservative, Venstre-Liberal, Centre-Agrarian, and the Christian People's Party. That these non-socialist parties had never been able to form a united and single opposition party to Labour underlines the various bases of cleavage in Norwegian politics, not least territorially and culturally.

The new coalition represented the actualisation of the 'two bloc' system in Norwegian politics. However, the alliance broke up early in 1971, caught up in the turmoil over the question of membership of the European Community. Deep divisions were evident within the parties, and the result of the referendum held in September 1972 (53.5 per cent against joining) indicated a sharp territorial cleavage: northern and rural areas were most deeply opposed. Although a clear majority in the Storting favoured membership, the referendum result was treated as binding.

There then followed the 'electoral earthquake' of the 1973 election in which the Labour Party received its lowest vote in forty years and the Liberal Party split, only to disappear from parliament in 1985. The Labour Party formed a minority administration, and since there is no provision for early dissolution of the Storting, its position was fairly secure: with the help of the Socialist Left, Labour remained in office until 1981.

The rehabilitation of conservatism general to Scandinavia in the 1980s was shown by the 1981 election which led to the formation of a minority conservative government, with a Conservative prime minister for the first time in 50 years. In 1983 the Conservatives were able to form a 'bourgeois' coalition with the Centre and Christian People's parties, and this alliance continued in office after the 1985 election. This election was interpreted as a 'pro-welfare state backlash', and the new Storting had the highest proportion of women MPs of any liberal democracy – 35 per cent. The rejection of the government's policies resulted from the doubtful effects of its alternative 'neo-liberal' strategy. With the two blocs finely balanced (77 seats to 78), the Progress Party's two votes became critical for the government, and its vote against the government in May 1986 led directly to the formation of Mrs Brundtland's minority Social Democratic government. In the early 1980s the Progress party, under the leadership of Carl Hagen, sought to transform itself from being a protest party into a credible neo-liberal party of government. Operating on the Conservative party's flank it seriously undermined the cohesion of the 'bourgeois' bloc.

The 'protest' Progress Party began to become particularly important when the established parties came to agree on the need for public spending cuts for the mid-1980s. The Progress Party's strategy of protest against the effects of the cuts was amply rewarded in local elections after 1985, and in early 1988 its continuing success, recorded by opinion polls placing it second in popularity only to a much weakened Labour Party, was a cause of concern for the established parties.

Elections to the Storting, September 1985

	1985 seats	1985 %	1981 %	1977 %	1973 %
Labour Party	71	40.8	34.3	42.4	35.3
Conservatives (Höyre)	50	30.4	31.6	24.7	17.5
Christian People's	16	8.3	9.3	12.1	12.2
Centre (Agrarian)	12	6.6	6.7	8.6	11.0
Socialist Left	6	5.5	4.9	4.1	11.2*
Progress Party	2	3.7	4.5	1.9	5.0
Liberal (Venstre)	0	3.1	3.9	3.2	3.5
Liberal People's	0	0.5	0.6	1.7	3.4
Others	0	0.6	0.8	0.9	0.8

Notes: The asterisk indicates that in 1973 a joint Socialist Electoral Alliance, including the Communist Party, competed.

Reading

T. Andenaes (ed.), *The Constitution of Norway*, Oslo: Norwegian Universities Press, 1962.

T. K. Derry, *A History of Modern Norway*, Oxford University Press, 1973.

H. Eckstein, *Division and Cohesion in Democracy: A Study of Norway*, New Jersey: Princeton University Press, 1966.

N. Elder, A. Thomas and D. Arter, *The Consensual Democracies? The Government and Politics of the Scandinavian States*, op. cit.

K. Heidar, 'The Norwegian Labour Party: Social Democracy in a Periphery of Europe', in Paterson and Thomas (eds.), *Social Democratic Parties in Western Europe*, op. cit.

S. Kuhnle, K. Strøm and L. Svåsand, 'The Norwegian Conservative Party: Setback in an Era of Strength', *West European Politics*, July 1986.

R. B. Kvavik, 'Interest Groups in a "Cooptive" Political System: The Case of Norway', in M. O. Heisler, *Politics in Europe*, op. cit.

J. Madeley, 'The 1981 Norwegian Election and the Resurgence of Scandinavian Conservatism', *West European Politics*, July 1982.

J. P. Olsen, *Organised Democracy: Political Institution in a Welfare State: The Case of Norway*, Bergen: Universitaetsforlaget, 1983.

A. Os and A. Rudd, 'Norway's Ombudsman', in D. C. Rowat, op. cit.

N. R. Ramsøy, *Norwegian Society*, C. Hurst, 1974.

S. Rokkan, 'Geography, Religion and Social Class: Crosscutting Cleavages in Norwegian Politics', in *Party Systems and Voter Alignments*, op. cit.

S. Rokkan, 'Norway: Numerical Democracy and Corporate Pluralism', in *Political Oppositions in Western Democracies*, op. cit.

D. Urwin, 'Do Resources Decide, but Votes Count – In the End? (Review Article) *West European Politics*, April 1987.

H. Valen and S. Rokkan, 'Norway: Conflict Structure and Mass Politics in a European Periphery', in R. Rose (ed.), *Electoral Behaviour*, op. cit.

See also, *Scandinavian Political Studies*.

PORTUGAL

Portugal has had a cohesive national existence since the eleventh century and was a monarchy until 1910. The overthrow of the monarchy led to one of the most unstable parliamentary systems in European experience. From 1910 to 1926, 'There were six presidents, forty prime ministers and two hundred cabinet ministers. In all political changes the action of the military was critical.'* In this period there were also twenty-four revolutions and coups d'état. The army finally put paid to the republic in 1926, and this soon resulted in the rise to power of Dr Antonio de Oliveira Salazar, first as finance minister and finally as dictator from 1932 onwards. The form of the new state (*Estado Novo*) was given expression in the constitution of 1933. The legislature consisted of a corporate (functional) upper house and a lower one elected on a limited franchise. Power rested with the prime minister and the sole legal political organisation, the *Uniao Nacional*. All the elections (and all the seats) were always won by the ruling party by use of the 'block vote' (a relative majority in multi-member constituencies), and opposition groups were only allowed to form for the period of the election campaign. The post

* G. L. Field, *Comparative Political Development: The Precedent of the West*, Routledge and Kegan Paul, 1968, p. 141.

of president was reserved for a leading member of the armed forces. Salazar stayed in power as prime minister until 1968 when he was succeeded by Dr Marcello Caetano. In 1971 Caetano attempted various measures of cautious liberalisation, including a greater freedom to the press and religious tolerance. The most intractable problem was that of the Portuguese African empire which was officially regarded as an integral part of Portugal. Although the overseas possessions were of great economic value, their continued subjugation was extremely costly and required a large army to keep the various nationalist movements in check. The post-Salazar era of moderate dictatorship succeeded mainly in fomenting the frustrations felt throughout Portuguese society, and Caetano was overthrown by a military coup in April 1974. The coup was engineered by some 400 officers, largely junior in rank, and they led the revolutionary Armed Forces Movement (MFA). The MFA was determined to take a lead in shaping the new republic, but the armed forces were not united politically: a right-wing coup was thwarted in September 1974, and for the following year the left-wing of the MFA held sway. Thus although elections to a national assembly were held in 1975, the MFA and its Supreme Revolutionary Council regarded them only as a 'pedagogic exercise', refusing to cede power to the parties, and committing the country to socialism. However by the end of 1975 the revolutionary mood of the Portuguese people had subsided, and there was a general reaction against the wholesale nationalisation and sweeping land expropriations which had taken place. In its turn a left-wing military coup was scotched in November 1975, and from then on the moderate military leaders appear to have taken the decision to hand back full power to the parties as soon as possible, whilst still preserving a political role for the armed forces.

There were two immediate consequences. One was the calling of fresh elections to determine the composition of a normal party government. The other result was a 'constitutional agreement' made between the parties and the armed forces, taking the form of a provisional constitution to be in force for five years before it could be subjected to revision. The leading features of the constitution were: the direct election of a president (assumed to be a member of the armed forces); the establishment of a civilian government responsible to the elected assembly *and* to the president; the formation of a 'Council of the Revolution' composed of the president, service chiefs and representatives from the MFA. The functions of the Council were shadowy: to guarantee democratic institutions and to preserve 'the spirit of the

Revolution' of April 1974.

Assembly elections were held in April 1976 and the presidential one the following June. Both showed the supremacy of the moderate political forces. The Socialists became the largest single party, and the new President, General Ramalho Eanes, was supported by the three large moderate parties and won 61 per cent of the popular vote. However, the 1976 assembly election did not produce a cohesive governing majority, and no combination appeared adequate to meet the deepening economic crisis, so that eventually, in 1978, a period of technocratic non-party government was instituted. That indeterminacy was ended by the December 1979 election which showed a significant swing to the right benefiting a three-party grouping, the Democratic Alliance (AD), consisting of Social Democrats (PSD) actually right-wing liberals, Christian Democrats (CDS), and the small Monarchist Party (PPM). The Democratic Alliance confirmed its position in a further election held in October 1980. That election, held so soon after the 1979 contest, was necessary prior to making change to the 1976 constitutional agreement. Clearly, the left-wing influence on that agreement made it unsuitable with a conservative government in power – some changes were approved in 1982, in particular the abolition of the Council of the Revolution – thus removing the direct political influence of the military.

The shift to the moderate right in Portuguese politics was temporarily checked after the 1983 election, by the election to the Presidency in 1986 of the Socialist candidate, Mario Soares. This campaign had seen a strong injection of left-right polarisation, with the PSD and CDS confronting the left, as it had in 1980 when General Eanes had won his second victory. Nevertheless, the 'austerity government' of Social Democrats led by Socialists, ruling from 1983 to 1985 resulted in heavy socialist losses, whilst left-wing fragmentation was exacerbated by the formation of the Democratic Renewal Party by former President Eanes.

These developments led to the formation of a PSD minority government led by Cavaco Silva. Silva presented an image of strength and efficiency; the economic upturn of 1985–87 and the entry of Portugal into the EC together with the stability provided by single-party government, led to the party's success in the 1987 election. The PSD won an overwhelming majority in parliament and an absolute majority of the votes cast. For an extended period Portugal has been practising a version of 'cohabitation' – a right-wing government co-existing with a Socialist President, the latter still having significant power.

Elections to the Assembly of the Republic, July 1987

	1987 seats	1987 %	1985 %	1983 %	1980 %
Communists	31	12.2	15.5	18.1	17.9
Democratic Renewal (PRD)	7	4.7	17.9	–	–
Socialists	60	22.2	20.8	36.1	30.0
Social Democrats (PSD)	148	50.2	29.9	27.2	50.6
Christian/(CDS)	4	4.4	10.0	12.6	50.6
Others	0	6.1	5.9	6.0	1.5

Notes: Prior to 1983 the CDS and PSD formed the 'Democratic Alliance'. Joint Lists are common and the figures for the Communists and Socialists include those for smaller allied parties.

Reading

J. Braga de Macedo and S. Sergaty, *Portugal since the Revolution: Economic and Political Perspectives*. Westview Press, 1981.

T. C. Bruneau, *Politics and Nationhood: Post Revolutionary Portugal*; Praegar, 1984.

A. de Figueiredo, *Portugal: Fifty Years of Dictatorship*, Penguin Books, 1975.

T. Gallagher, 'Goodbye to Revolution: The Portuguese Election of July 1987', *West European Politics*, January 1988.

L. Graham and D. Wheeler (eds.), *In Search of Modern Portugal: The Revolution and Its Consequences*, University of Wisconsin Press, 1983.

R. Harvey, *Portugal: Birth of a Democracy*, Macmillan, 1978.

M. Kay, *Salazar and Modern Portugal*, Eyre and Spottiswoode, 1970.

W. Opello, *Portugal's Political Development*, Westview Press, 1985.

B. Pimlott, 'Portugal – Two Battles in the War of the Constitution', *West European Politics*, October 1981.

G. Pridham (ed.) *The New Mediterranean Democracies*, Frank Cass, 1984.

R. Robinson, *Contemporary Portugal: A History*, Allen and Unwin, 1979.

M. Soares, *Portugal's Struggle for Liberty*, Allen and Unwin, 1975.

SPAIN

Spain ceased to be the leading European power in the seventeenth century and gradually lost her European possessions. In the nineteenth century there was considerable internal strife, revolution and civil war with the main protagonists the monarchists and the liberals. These conflicts were not resolved and after 1900 there was the additional cleavage of socialism, represented by a parliamentary wing and by a powerful anarchist movement. After the First World War, a succession of corrupt and incompetent governments led to a coup by General Primo de Rivera in 1923 which was accepted by the monarch, King Alfonso XIII. A period of fairly mild dictatorship then followed until 1930 when de Rivera was forced from office, and a year later the Second Republic was declared (the First Republic was a short-lived one from 1873 to 1874).

Although the change was mainly a result of growing left-wing support and militancy, the republican government that followed was primarily liberal-republican and anti-clerical, rather than socialist, and in its attempt to deal with numerous strikes and uprisings it became reactionary. Its success in dealing with disorder was nullified by the growing social discontent. Elections were held in 1936, but the results did nothing to resolve the basic social tensions. The party system was extremely fragmented, with no less than twenty identifiable party groupings represented as a result of the election. However, there were two major alignments: the Catholic and conservative National Front against the left-wing Popular Front. The government which resulted represented a victory for the republican forces, with increasing left-wing influence; both Communists and Anarchists appeared to wield greater influence in the post-election period, and there was a marked increase in civil strife, centring on the question of the agrarian reform.

This conflict, together with the lack of cohesion of the party system, indicates that even without Franco's intervention, the prospects for parliamentary government were dim. The undoubted shift to the left in Spanish politics between 1931 and 1936 was regarded with foreboding by the Church hierarchy, the army, and by landed interests – about 1 per cent of the population owned half the land in Spain. The army revolt against the Republic began in July 1936 in Spanish Morocco and was led by General Franco; civil war began in earnest and continued until March 1939. Franco's dictatorship was initially influenced by the examples of German and Italian fascism and by the help he had received from these countries in winning the war.

Francoism implanted an essentially conservative, military dictatorship which left Spanish society substantially unchanged. Towards the end of his long rule Franco attempted cautious reforms, and he settled the problem of succession by providing for the eventual restoration of the monarchy, and when Franco died in November 1975 King Juan Carlos initiated a period of controlled but intensive liberalisation which the Falange traditionalists and the military diehards were powerless to resist. Political parties were allowed free expression, and a constituent assembly was elected in June 1977. The parties were in broad agreement in establishing parliamentary government and on the desirability of retaining a constitutional monarchy – Juan Carlos himself had largely contributed to the fashioning of the democratic consensus. The constitutional proposals, which also incorporated extensive measures of regional government, were approved by referendum in December 1978 (87 per cent in favour, in a poll of 68 per cent of the electorate). The subsequent election confirmed the overwhelming support of the electorate for parties with a modernising and centrist image. Initially, a disparate collection of former Francoists, conservative democrats and Social-Christians made up the Democratic Centre Union (UCD) which was able to dominate the centre ground and won the 1977 and 1979 elections. The Spanish right was reduced to a marginal force. Both the Communist (PCE) and Socialist (PSOE) parties vied for the same centre-left ground in the later 1970s, and in 1979 the PSOE abandoned its marxist heritage and moved to directly challenge the UCD in the centre. The UCD collapsed in 1982 as a result of internal problems of leadership and weak organisational structure, and its place was taken by the conservative Popular Alliance. The Socialists won an absolute majority in both 1982 and 1986.

A clear demonstration of the moderation of the PSOE was its decision to enter NATO, a reversal of policy endorsed by referendum in 1986 and by the subsequent June election. This strategy was successful because the Communists, although committed to a pluralist democracy, were still strongly handicapped by their past reputation; the PCE has now been reduced to a marginal element. A variety of regional challenges to the new state had already been partially defused by significant concessions in the direction of regional devolution.

The ability of the PSOE to establish itself as a dominant centre party depends on its ability to maintain its core support and its new, loosely attached electorate. Following the 1986 election (the

Elections to the Cortes, June 1986

	1986 seats	1986 %	1982 %	1979 %
Communists/IU	7	4.6	4.1	10.8
Social & Democratic Centre	19	9.2	2.8	–
Socialists (PSOE)	184	44.4	48.2	30.5
Dem. Centre Union	–	–	6.8	35.0
Popular Alliance (Cons.)	105	26.0	26.0	6.0
Catalan Cons. (CU)	18	5.0	3.9	2.7
Basque Nationalists (PNV)	6	1.5	1.9	1.7
Basque Extremists (HB)	5	1.1	1.0	1.0
Others	6	8.2	5.3	12.3

Notes: 'Others' include various regional and left-wing groupings.

same year as Spain entered the EC), the high unemployment rate of over 20 per cent (50 per cent among 16–24 year olds) began to weaken its attraction, and the PSOE faced increasing difficulty in maintaining trade-union loyalty. Yet its waning support was not matched by the strength of its opponents: the Communists were stronger industrially than electorally, and the right was divided internally. Hence continuing PSOE dominance appeared to be ensured by the lack of a viable alternative.

Reading
J. Amodia, *Franco's Political Legacy from Fascism to Democracy*, Allen Lane, 1977.
D. Bell (ed.), *Democratic Politics in Spain*, Frances Pinter, 1983.
R. Carr and J. Fusi, *Spain: Dictatorship to Democracy*, Allen and Unwin, 1981.
R. Carr (ed.), *The Republic and the Civil War in Spain*, Macmillan, 1971.
J. Fusi, 'Spain: The Fragile Democracy', *West European Politics*, July 1982.
M. Gallo, *Spain under Franco*, Allen and Unwin, 1973.
J. Maravall, '*Spain: Eurocommunism and Socialism*', *Political Studies*, June 1979.
J. Marcus, 'Triumph of the Spanish Socialists: the 1982 Election', *West European Politics*, July 1983.
K. Medhurst, 'Spain's Evolutionary Pathway from Dictatorship to Democracy', in G. Pridham (ed.), *The New Mediterranean Democracies*, Frank Cass, 1984.
B. Pollack and G. Hunter, 'Spanish Democracy after Four General Elections', *Parliamentary Affairs*, July 1987.
P. Preston, *The Triumph of Democracy in Spain*, 1986.
R. Robinson, 'From Change to Continuity: The 1986 Spanish Election', *West European Politics*, January 1987.
H. Thomas, *The Spanish Civil War*, Penguin Books, 1965.
N. Torrents and C. Abel (eds.), *Spain: Conditional Democracy*, Croom Helm, 1983.

SWEDEN

Sweden provides an example of relatively smooth political development over a long period of time. A national monarchy was established in 1523 in winning independence from the Danes, and since that time Sweden has been free from foreign domination. Apart from her one excursion as a great power in the seventeenth century, Sweden has avoided external entanglement, pursuing a policy of neutrality since 1814. The main representative institution, the Riksdag, dates from the fifteenth century, and for a period in the eighteenth century there was a strong, though not democratic, system of parliamentary government. Modern political development dates from the constitution of 1809, itself a reaction against a spell of royal absolutism. Whilst the king was given full executive power, the constitution provided a system of checks and balances; especially important were the financial powers of the Riksdag, the institution of the Ombudsman, and the open publication of public documents. However, the Riksdag itself was based on an estate system of representation with four chambers: nobility, clergy, burghers, and farmers; the first two of these were based on privilege and the whole system was quite unsuited to the development of parliamentary government. The reform of 1866 created a bicameral system, but until 1921 the upper house was based on a limited franchise of wealth and it shared full powers with the lower one. Thus in spite of the power balance given by the constitution, Swedish government was oligarchical throughout the nineteenth century. Moreover, the principle of government responsibility to a parliamentary majority was not finally established until 1917. Modern parties date from the reforms of 1866. At first the conflict was between the conservative groups of privilege and the liberals who sought a democratisation of the Riksdag and parliamentary government. The Swedish Social Democrats (founded in 1889) made common cause with the Liberals, but once the franchise had been widened the Social Democrats quickly became the largest party in the lower house of the Riksdag (from 1914) and the Liberal Party declined in importance. The fourth strand in the party system was added in 1913 with the formation of the Agrarian Party (later Centre) which saw itself as a parallel to Social Democracy in protecting the interests of the farming community and for this reason often joined forces with the Social Democrats.

The Social Democratic Party was almost continuously in power from 1932 until the mid-1970s. Early on, the party became reformist, and the class-compromise has been a feature of Swedish politics in this century. From being economically one of the most backward European states in the last century, on most counts Sweden is now the most advanced. The long period of office enjoyed by the Social Democrats has led to the development of a high 'distributive capability', in social welfare and insurance, not seriously question by the other parties. Fundamental constitutional reforms have taken place in recent years: a unicameral Riksdag with three instead of four-year terms, and provision to remove governments by simple majority no-confidence votes which was previously impossible. Other constitutional changes came into force in 1975 which had the effect of making the Swedish monarchy purely representative in character, and in case of government crisis the power of initiative is given to the Speaker of the Riksdag.

The 1976 election brought about a dramatic change in the political balance. After ruling for 44 years, the Social Democrats were forced out of office by an alliance of 'bourgeois' parties (Centre, Liberals, and Conservatives). Although the coalition broke up in 1978 over the nuclear energy issue, which had allowed it to break the Social

Democrats' hold on government, the bloc held its own in 1979, with the Conservative Party asserting its bloc dominance, in line with the Scandinavian trend. In 1980, in an advisory referendum, the vote went against the use of nuclear energy, and the issue is now closed. Some disarray within the bourgeois bloc enabled the Social Democrats to form a minority government in 1982, relying on 'shifting majorities' in the Riksdag and the support of the Communists. The apparently indecisive situation continued after both the 1985 and 1988 elections. The Social Democrats remained in government and worked hard to restore the Swedish 'social democratic concensus' which entailed moderating the scope of the controversial 'wage-earner investment funds' – seen by opponents as a 'backdoor nationalisation' of Swedish industry. The Social Democrats also overcame the loss of prime minister Olof Palme (assassinated in 1986) who had the status of an international statesman. However, the 1988 election saw the entry of the Greens into the Riksdag (the first new party for many years) and they posed a future threat to the Social Democrats and to the established party system.

Elections to the Riksdag, September 1988

	1988 seats	1988 %	1985 %	1982 %	1979 %	1976 %
Social Democrats	156	43.6	44.7	45.6	43.2	43.4
Conservatives	66	18.2	21.3	23.6	20.3	15.6
Centre Party	42	11.4	12.5	15.5	18.1	24.1
Liberals	44	12.2	14.2	5.9	10.6	11.1
Communists	21	5.9	5.4	5.6	5.6	4.8
Christian Dem.	0	3.0	–	1.9	1.4	1.4
Environmentalists	20	5.5	1.5	1.7	–	–
Others	0	0.2	0.4	0.2	0.8	0.3

Notes: In 1985 the Christian Democrats won a single seat on the Centre Party list. Turnout in 1988 was 83% (usually around 90%).

Reading

P. Aimie, 'The Strategy of Gradualism and the Swedish Wage-Earner Funds', *West European Politics*, July 1985.

N. Andrén, *Modern Swedish Government*, Stockholm: Almqvist and Wiksell, 1968.

J. B. Board, *The Government and Politics of Sweden*, Boston: Houghton Mifflin, 1970.

F. G. Castles, 'The Political Functions of Organised Groups: The Swedish Case', *Political Studies*, March 1973.

N. Elder, A. Thomas and D. Arter, *The Consensual Democracies? The Government and Politics of the Scandinavian States*, op. cit.

N. Elder, *Government in Sweden: The Executive at Work*, Pergamon Press, 1970.

H. Hancock, *Sweden: The Politics of Post Industrial Change*, Holt, Rinehart and Winston, 1973.

R. Huntford, *Brave New Sweden*, Penguin Books, 1974.

W. Korpi, *The Working Class in Welfare Capitalism*, Routledge, 1978.

G. Petri and P. Vinde, *Swedish Government Administration*, Stockholm: SI-Prisma, 1978.

D. C. Rowat, op. cit., various contributors, 'Sweden's Guardians of the Law'.

B. Ryden and V. Bergström, (eds.), *Sweden: Choices for Economic and Social Policy in the 1980s*, Allen and Unwin, 1982.

B. Särlvik, 'Sweden: The Social Bases of the Parties in a Developmental Perspective', in R. Rose (ed.), *Electoral Behaviour*, op. cit.

D. Sainsbury, 'The 1985 Election: The Conservative Upsurge is Checked', *West European Politics*, April 1986.

R. Scase, 'Social Democracy in Sweden', in Paterson and Thomas (eds.), *Social Democratic Parties in Western Europe*, op. cit.

See also, *Scandinavian Political Studies*.

SWITZERLAND

The Swiss confederation originated in the thirteenth century as a treaty of alliance between three independent cantons. By the sixteenth century there were sixteen members, and twenty-two in 1815. For a short time after 1798, Napoleon imposed a centralised government, but the peace settlement of 1815 reintroduced the confederal form. The modern state form dates from 1848; this constitution created a federation, and a revision in 1874 further increased the powers of the federation at the expense of the cantons. In principle, the cantons are self-governing, but their area of autonomy is very limited. However, the constitutional structure is such that minority influences are given full weight. The Federal Assembly is composed of two houses with coequal powers, the National Council and the Council of States. In the latter, the twenty full cantons have two seats each and the six so-called 'half-cantons' one seat apiece;* this gives the smaller cantons, and in effect the language and religious minorities, a majority in the upper house. A second feature is that the federal government, the Federal Council, has emerged as a form of permanent collegial government, the membership so devised that its members come from different cantons, besides preserving a linguistic and religious balance. Its seven members represent a coalition of the four major parties in approximate relation to their strength in the National

---

* The total of twenty-six includes the new full Canton of the Jura created in 1978, meeting demands for autonomy of the Francophone minority in the Canton of Bern.

Council. The built-in stability is further enhanced by the fact that, although the Federal Council is 'responsible' to the Federal Assembly, it is not dismissable within its four-year term. The national referendum was introduced in 1874, and although this gives the possibility of popular challenge to federal legislation and of proposing constitutional changes, measures will only be carried if they receive a majority of votes in a majority of the cantons.

These various constitutional provisions and conventions, when added to the extreme localism of Swiss political life, help explain the coexistence of potentially divisive factors. Of approximately 5.5 million inhabitants, over 3 million are German-speaking, over 1 million French-speaking, with small minorities of Italian and Romansch. The other line of division is religious, with approximately 55 per cent Protestants and most of the remainder Roman Catholics. The intense conservatism of Swiss political life is shown by the fact that female suffrage was only finally approved by popular referendum in February 1971 by a two-to-one majority (in 1959 it had been rejected by a similar proportion); on a cantonal level the preponderantly Italian and French-speaking cantons had already given women the vote. A recent stress in Swiss political and social life has been the heavy reliance on a foreign labour force (mainly Italian) accounting for a third of the whole. A referendum aimed at sharply restricting immigrant labour failed in June 1970, but the result was close: 655,000 against and 558,000 in favour, with a high referendum poll of 74 per cent. But a further referendum held on this issue in 1974 was decisively rejected by a 66 per cent vote against. Nevertheless, the federal government felt obliged to bring in several measures of its own aimed at 'stabilising' the immigrant population.

Elections in recent years have confirmed the position of the four leading parties, and parties active in the campaign to curb immigration have been notably unsuccessful. Whilst the extension of the vote to women in 1971 appears to have made little difference to the balance of party fortunes, voting turn-out has fallen significantly: it has been under 50 per cent since 1979, falling to 46.5 per cent in 1987. The female vote represents a potential for electoral mobilisation, and although the dominant position of the four leading parties has been maintained and the composition of the permanent coalition of the Federal Council remains unaltered, the volatility of the electorate has increased. One result has been the rise of the ecology parties, and the programmes of the main parties have been significantly affected, with stronger competition for electoral support.

Elections to the National Council, October 1987

	1987 Seats	1987 %	1983 %	1979 %	1975 %
Radical Democrats	51	22.9	23.4	24.0	22.2
Social Democrats	41	18.4	22.8	24.9	25.4
Christian Democrats	42	20.0	20.6	21.1	20.6
Swiss Peoples' Party ('Peasants')	25	11.0	11.1	11.5	10.1
Independents' Party	9	4.2	4.0	4.2	6.2
Liberals	9	2.7	2.8	2.8	2.3
Greens	9	4.8	2.9	–	–
Progressives/ Alternative Greens	4	3.5	3.5	2.1	1.3
Evangelical People's Party	3	1.9	2.1	2.3	2.0
National Campaign/ Republican	3	2.9	3.5	0.6	3.0
Communists	1	0.8	0.9	2.1	2.2
Others	3	6.8	2.5	4.4	4.7

Notes: The first four parties listed form a permanent coalition with seats on the Federal Council in the ratio of 2:2:2:1, a proportion which has remained constant since 1959. The National Action Party is a xenophobic party, as was the Republican Movement. Others in 1987 includes 2 seats for 'The Motorists', an anti-ecology backlash party.

Reading

B. Barber, *Freedom in the Alps*, Princeton University Press, 1974.

C. Church, 'Consociationalism under Pressure? The Swiss Case', *West European Politics*, January 1989.

H. E. Glass, 'Consensus and Opposition in Switzerland', *Comparative Politics*, April 1978.

H. P. Hertig, 'Party Cohesion in the Swiss Parliament', *Legislative Studies Quarterly*, February 1978.

C. Hughes, *The Federal Constitution of Switzerland*, Oxford University Press, 1954.

C. Hughes, *The Parliament of Switzerland*, Cassell/The Hansard Society, 1962.

C. Hughes, *Switzerland*, Benn, 1975.

G. Ionescu et al. 'Can the Confederatio Helvetica be Imitated?', *Government and Opposition*, Vol. 23/1, Winter 1988.

P. J. Katzenstein, *Corporatism and Change: Austria, Switzerland and Industrial Policy*, op. cit.

H. Kerr, *Switzerland: Social Cleavages and Partisan Conflict*, Sage Publications, 1974.

H. Kerr, 'The Structure of Opposition in the Swiss Parliament', *Legislative Studies Quarterly*, February 1978.

H. Kerr, 'The Swiss Party System: Steadfast and Changing', in H. Daalder (ed.), *Party Systems*, op. cit.

K. D. McRae, *Conflict and Compromise in Multi-lingual Societies: Switzerland*, Waterloo: W. Laurier University Press, 1983.

M. Mowlam, 'Popular Access to the Decision-making Process in Switzerland', *Government and Opposition*, Spring 1979.

L. Papadopoulos, 'The Swiss Election of 1987: A Silent Revolution Behind Stability?', *West European Politics*, April 1988.

H. Pannimon (ed.), *Switzerland at the Polls*, American Institute for Public Policy Research, 1983.

J. B. Rees, *Government by Community*, Charles Knight, 1971.

D. Sidjanski, 'The Swiss and Their Politics', *Government and Opposition*, Summer 1976.

J. Steinberg, *Why Switzerland?*, Cambridge University Press, 1976.

J. Steiner, *Amicable Agreement versus Majority Rule*, Oxford University Press, 1973.

THE UNITED KINGDOM

Unlike the great majority of European states, British constitutional and political development has shown a relatively peaceful evolution over several centuries, and in this respect most nearly resembles the Scandinavian countries, notably Denmark and Sweden – in all three political advance was unhindered by foreign intrusion. Unlike the other two countries, however, the British constitutional system does not stem from a particular date, has not been codified, and has the peculiarity of being quite flexible. For this reason it is necessary to refer to a number of constitutional landmarks such as: the Magna Carta of 1215, the Petition of Right (1628), the Bill of Rights (1689), the Act of Settlement (1701), and the Parliament Acts of 1911 and 1949. The net effect of these was first to create a constitutional monarchy, and later a parliamentary system of government (which by the terms of the 1911 and 1949 Acts gave legislative supremacy to the House of Commons). But much of the constitutional system has developed by means of convention rather than by statute, in particular the idea of a cabinet system of government responsible to the party with a majority in the House of Commons. Although the roots of the party system are to be found in the eighteenth century, the full acceptance of responsible and majority party government dates from the 1830s and was a natural consequence of the 1832 Reform Act; modern party politics can be said to date from that time. In spite of her early constitutional development, political democracy was a later addition; various reform acts (1867 to 1928) progressively extended the franchise, but complete adult suffrage was achieved no earlier than for many other countries.

The importance of the British pattern of development lay in the fact that (over a long period of time) basic social and political crises were resolved singly, each one dealt with before the next arose. Significantly, the shifts in power took place without the *status* of the former power-holders being undermined; the 'ascriptive' nature of British political culture aided stable evolution. In other European countries the non-resolution and accumulation of basic problems helped to multiply the points of social cleavage, and this was often accompanied by a failure to create mass parties of a non-extremist kind. The absence of multiple cleavage is shown by the nature of the British party system: for long periods only two major parties have been involved: the Conservative and Liberal parties until the First World War, Conservative and Labour thereafter. The decline of the Liberal Party from 1916 onwards was due in part to internal dissension, and probably related to this, in its failure to appeal to a sufficiently large social grouping. The Labour Party, founded in 1900, formed its first minority administration in 1924, and again from 1929 until 1931; it was able to rule for the first time as a majority party from 1945 until 1951. As a corollary to the long-term effects of Liberal decline, the Conservative Party has been in power for much of the last fifty years. It owed its strength to its pragmatic nature, its close association with the leading values of British society, and its ability to win support from a large minority of the working class. Its position was further enhanced by the unwillingness of the Labour Party to question the fundamental values with which the Conservative Party was identified; unlike most left-wing parties in Europe, Labour never went through a Marxist or anti-clerical phase. The result was an underlying consensus in British politics, epitomised in the concept of the 'loyal opposition'. Although the institutionalisation of opposition on two-party lines makes political cleavage more durable, it works on the assumption that the two parties are geared to the smooth alternation of government, and that implies a high continuity of policy from one government to another, a willingness to absorb rather than reverse changes.

The alternation in government between Labour and Conservatives has been most evident since 1945: Labour, 1945–1951; Conservatives, 1951–1964; Labour, 1964–1970; Conservatives, 1970–1974; Labour, 1974–1979, and Conservatives since 1979. In the earlier period there was a degree of continuity, especially in the acceptance of the fundamental changes implemented by the Labour Government after 1945 – widespread nationalisation, the creation of the 'welfare state', extensive decolonisation. But increasingly the basis of the party consensus was eroded, and that became especially evident by the 1970s as the extent of Britain's economic malaise began to become apparent.

The two-party format was sharply disturbed in the course of two elections held in 1974. The February 1974 election was called in response to the growing trade-union challenge to the

Conservative Government's economic and wages policies, and was fought in terms of the issue 'Who governs Britain?', polarising the two major parties. But the electorate failed to respond in those terms, and almost a quarter of the vote went to the minor parties. The Labour Party won that election as well as the contest in October 1974 – yet at the second election it had the support of only 28.6 per cent of the *electorate*, whilst the Conservatives had their lowest share in recent history. There was a large Liberal 'protest' vote, and the nationalist parties were highly successful: the SNP took 30 per cent of the Scottish vote and the Ulster Unionists, formerly allied to the Conservatives, won 58 per cent in Northern Ireland. Electoral dissatisfaction with the party system was high, and the referendum on British membership of the European Community held in June 1975 (62.5 per cent in favour) also showed that party lines gave a misleading picture.

As a result of by-election losses, the Labour Government was forced into a minority position from April 1976 onwards, and it had to rely on support from the minor parties, especially the so-called 'Lib-Lab Pact' (in force from March 1977 until July 1978). Support from the nationalist parties was conditional upon the holding of referenda on the proposed Scottish and Welsh assemblies, but that alliance ended when the results were negative. In Scotland 32.5 per cent of the electorate was in favour and only 11.8 per cent in Wales, whereas the stipulation was for at least 40 per cent of the electorate to be in favour of the devolution proposals. Eventually, the Labour Government was defeated in March 1979 on a no-confidence motion (lost by a single vote) which made a general election inevitable.

The May 1979 election gave the Conservatives under Margaret Thatcher (party leader since 1975) a comfortable majority, and the Labour Party suffered from the widespread strikes of the previous winter. The party system reverted to its bi-polar form, but with a sharper polarisation: the Conservatives moved to the right and Labour continued its leftwards drift – this led a score of moderate Labour MPs to break away to form a new Social Democratic Party (SDP) in 1981. As economic conditions worsened in the early 1980s – with unemployment eventually rising to over 3 million – the gap between the two major parties widened, whilst the Liberals and SDP sought to build up a consensual middle ground and hoped to 'break the mould' of the two-party system. As a consequence of the weakness of the Labour Party and victory in the conflict with Argentina over the Falkland Islands, the Conservatives won a massive majority in the early election of June 1983. Labour support collapsed, but the Liberal-SDP Alliance secured only 23 seats (3.5 per cent) despite receiving a quarter of the vote.

The reputation enjoyed by Margaret Thatcher as a purposeful leader, her deliberate shunning of compromise and consensus, her insistence on the virtues of market forces, sound money and individual responsibility all served to intensify political division. The various measures designed to weaken the power of trade unions and to privatise large areas of the state-run economy also underlined the gap between Government and Opposition. Conservative policies were in addition widely perceived as undermining the welfare state. For its part, Labour attempted to modify its radical image under its new leader, Neil Kinnock, from 1983 onwards. Yet in the election of June 1987, although it restored its position somewhat, the Labour Party failed to convince the electorate that its alternative policies would work, and the Conservatives still had a comfortable majority. The challenge of the Alliance began to peter out, and disarray followed: a majority of the SDP opted to form a new party with the Liberals in 1988, but a significant minority rejected the merger. The two-party system appeared to be as entrenched as ever, but it is geographically highly distorted: the Conservatives became absolutely dominant in the more prosperous southern part of Britain, whilst the Labour Party was in a similar position in the depressed northern parts of England and in Scotland.

Elections to the House of Commons, June 1987

| | 1987 | | 1983 | 1979 | 1974 Oct. | 1974 Feb. |
	Seats	%	%	%	%	%
Conservatives	376	42.3	42.4	43.9	35.8	38.1
Labour	229	30.8	27.6	36.9	39.3	37.2
Liberals	} 22	} 22.6	} 25.4	13.8	18.3	19.3
SDP				–	–	–
SNP	3	1.3	1.1	1.6	2.7	2.0
Plaid Cymru	3	0.3	0.4	0.4	0.6	0.6
Others/Ulster	17	2.3	3.1	3.4	2.9	2.8

Notes: From 1983 onwards the number of seats was increased to 650 (previously 635) and there were extensive boundary changes. The Liberals and the SDP formed an 'Alliance', sharing the constituencies between them. 'Others/Ulster' comprises: Official Unionists (9 seats), Democratic Unionists (3), DPUP (1), Sinn Fein (1) and SDLP (3). There was a poll of 75.3 per cent.

Northern Ireland

The failure of the system of 'Home Rule' (introduced to Northern Ireland in 1922) to provide the means for a democratic integration for the Roman Catholic minority led to an escalation of political violence from 1968 onwards and finally to the imposition of direct rule by Britain in March 1972. A plebiscite held in March 1973 showed a high proportion of the voters (57.4 per cent) in favour of the continuing attachment to the United Kingdom. In the same month the British government put forward a number of constitutional proposals designed to overcome the bitterness between the two communities; a 'bill of rights' (itself a basic innovation) and a novel 'power-sharing' executive. The new assembly was to be elected by proportional representation for a fixed four-year term and work through committees in parallel with government departments. The committee chairmen were together to form a collegial executive; the whole proposed structure was an amalgam of existing local government practice and the leading characteristics of the Swiss constitutional system.

However, the 1973 election to the new assembly gave one third of the seats to diehard 'Loyalists' bent on wrecking any parliamentary consensus. The old Ulster Unionist party fell completely under their influence and in consequence the majority Protestants effectively became identified with the loyalist intransigence. The constitutional proposals were incorporated into the Northern Ireland Constitution Act of 1973, and came into force in January 1974. Provision was also made for a 'Council of Ireland' which would bring representatives of the Republic and of Northern Ireland together to cooperate on matters of mutual concern. A meeting between representatives from the Irish Republic, Northern Ireland, and the British Government resulted in the 'Sunningdale Agreement' (December 1973) and a positive vote on the terms of this agreement by the Northern Ireland assembly in May 1974 led to direct action by the Protestants, and culminated in a general strike called by the Ulster Workers' Council. The renewed breakdown of civilian government led to the resignation of the Chief Minister (Brian Faulkner, Ulster Unionist) who anyway no longer represented the wishes of the loyalist Protestant majority. In consequence, the British Government had no alternative but once more to impose direct rule (May 1974). Previously when direct rule had been established, in 1972, political violence and terrorism emanated from the IRA (Irish Republican Army) as a means of enforcing British withdrawal and securing Irish unity, but armed Protestant groups ultimately redressed the balance of violence.

Later in 1974, a new Northern Ireland Act was passed which provided for the election of a Constitutional Convention (not a legislative body or an assembly proper) which was supposed to work out the basis for a constitutional agreement between the various parties involved. However, the result of the election predictably gave the Loyalists a majority in the new Convention and their ingrained outlook was against *any* power-sharing solution. Indeed, the Loyalists simply wished to restore the *status quo ante*, a reversion to Protestant dominance as in the old Stormont up to 1972. A major difference in the Northern Irish situation was that sectarian murder had meanwhile become the normal pattern of political life. A further important difference was that people and parties in Britain were increasingly concerned at the cost of maintaining this social catastrophe in being: yet they could see no acceptable basis on which they could shed their responsibility for the future of the province.

From 1982 onwards the British government sought to foster cross-community cooperation, initially through the creation of an elected assembly (without any real powers) as a prelude to measures of devolution. But widespread mistrust of the assembly led to an extensive boycott, and it became merely a forum for hard-line Unionists, eventually being disbanded in 1986. Much more significant was the signing of the Anglo-Irish Agreement in November 1985 between the Irish and British governments, since it effectively brought the former into a direct involvement with the Northern Irish problem, and the Agreement cleverly side-stepped the quest for a non-existent basis of consensus in Northern Ireland that had baffled successive British governments. Although formally the Agreement did not derogate British sovereignty, in fact the inter-governmental cooperation envisaged spanned not only cross-border security matters, but also various specific aspects of government agencies with Northern Ireland (including policing, basic rights and fair employment). Despite the mutual suspicions of the two governments, the Agreement succeeded in moving the focus away from the warring factions in Northern Ireland, and the fact that the British government was able to ignore the bitter opposition of the Unionists to the Agreement was a major development. Inter-governmentalism could ultimately be a way of forcing the sectarian élites grudgingly to accept a political accommodation.

Reading

A. Ball, *British Political Parties*, Macmillan, 1987.

H. Berrington (ed.), *Political Change in Britain*, Frank Cass, 1983.

A. H. Birch, *The British System of Government*, Allen & Unwin, 1986.

I. Bradley, *Breaking the Mould? The Birth and Prospects of the Social Democratic Party*, Oxford: Martin Robertson, 1981.

M. Burch and M. Moran (eds.), *British Politics: A Reader*, Manchester University Press, 1986.

D. Butler and D. Kavanagh (eds.), *The British General Election of 1987*, Macmillan, 1988.

D. Coates, *Labour in Power? A Study of the Labour Government, 1974–1979*, Longman, 1981.

H. Drucker et al., *Developments in British Politics 2*, Macmillan, 1986.

H. Drucker (ed.), *Multi-Party Britain*, Macmillan, 1983 (2nd edn.)

P. Dunleavy and C. T. Husbands, *British Democracy at the Crossroads*, George Allen and Unwin, 1985.

M. Franklin, *The Decline of Class Voting in Britain*, Oxford University Press, 1987.

J. Hayward and P. Norton, *The Political Science of British Politics*, Wheatsheaf, 1986.

D. Howell, *British Social Democracy: A Study of Development and Decay*, Croom Helm, 1977.

J. Jowell and D. Oliver (eds.), *The Changing Constitution*, Clarendon Press, 1985.

D. Kavanagh, *Thatcherism and British Politics: The End of Consensus?*, Oxford University Press, 1987.

J. Mackintosh, *The British Cabinet*, Stevens (3rd ed.), 1977.

G. McLennan, D. Held, S. Hall (eds.), *State and Society in Contemporary Britain*, Polity Press, 1984.

R. Miliband, *Capitalist Democracy in Britain*, Oxford University Press, 1982.

P. Norton, *The British Polity*, Longman, 1984.

G. Peele, *British Party Politics: Competing for Power in the 1980s*, Oxford: Philip Allan, 1989.

R. M. Punnett, *British Government and Politics*, Gower (5th ed.), 1987 (bibliography).

P. Riddell, *The Conservative Government, 1979–1983*, Oxford: Martin Robertson, 1983.

R. Rose, *Politics in England*, Faber, 1985.

A. Sked and C. Cook, *Post-War Britain: A Political History*, Penguin Books (2nd ed.), 1984.

NORTHERN IRELAND

Y. Alexander and A. O'Day (eds.), *Terrorism in Ireland*, Croom Helm, 1983.

P. Arthur, *Government and Politics of Northern Ireland*, Longman, 1980.

K. Boyle, T. Hadden and P. Hillgard, *Law and State: The Case of Northern Ireland*, Martin Robertson, 1975.

W. Cox, The Anglo-Irish Agreement, *Parliamentary Affairs*, January 1987.

R. Harris, *Prejudice and Tolerance in Ulster*, Manchester University Press, 1972.

I. McAllister, *The Northern Ireland Social Democratic and Labour Party*, Macmillan, 1977.

B. O'Leary, 'The Anglo-Irish Agreement: Folly or Statecraft?', *West European Politics*, January 1987.

B. O'Leary, 'Explaining Northern Ireland: A Brief Study Guide', *Politics*, 5:1, April 1985.

R. Rose, *Governing without Consensus: An Irish Perspective*, Faber and Faber, 1971.

R. Rose, *Northern Ireland: A Time of Choice*, Macmillan, 1976.

P. Teague (ed.), *Beyond the Rhetoric: Politics, the Economy and Social Policy in Northern Ireland*, Lawrence and Wishart, 1987.

C. Townshend, *Consensus in Ireland: Approaches and Recessions*, Oxford University Press, 1988.

D. Watt (ed.), *The Constitution of Northern Ireland: Problems and Prospects*, Heinemann, 1981.

F. Wright, *Northern Ireland: A Comparative Analysis*, Dublin: Gill and Macmillan, 1987.

Party Representation in West European Parliaments since 1946
A Research Note by Michael Smart

The gradual movement towards closer European integration since the Second World War has made the comparison of political trends between one country and another a subject of growing interest. For example, it is sometimes claimed that 'Europe' is moving to the left or right, or that a particular group of parties is getting stronger or weaker. The fact that such statements often contradict each other suggests a need for a measure which can show broad political movements over Europe as a whole and can also serve as a yardstick against which changes in individual countries can be assessed. This involves two main questions. Firstly, it is necessary to establish some classification of parties, however imprecise this may be because of the diversity of national conditions. Secondly, since the ratio of population to each parliamentary representative varies extremely widely between countries (from 4,000 in Iceland to over 120,000 in Western Germany), the strengths of parties represented in different national parliaments need to be weighted by population. The table below (p. 383) has been compiled on this basis so as to show the balance of political forces in Western European parliaments at a series of dates since 1946, making it possible to deduce broad trends of movement. The graph on pp. 384-5 represents the data shown by the table in a somewhat simplified form.

Definition of the area covered
'Western Europe' comprises fifteen countries, namely, the original six EEC and the five Nordic countries together with the UK, Ireland, Austria and Switzerland. The choice is justified by the geographical coherence of the resulting unit, and by the close political and economic relationships between most of the countries, which formed the main core of the OEEC and of the Council of Europe when these bodies were founded in the immediate post-war period. In addition, they all share competitive parliamentary systems in which two or more parties have always been strongly represented since the end of the war. There are also close family

relationships between many of their parties, particularly on the left, facilitating a regular scheme of party classification. These relationships have been to some extent strengthened and made more visible by the association of parties (for the nine countries in the area which belong to the European Community) in the European Parliament.

Party classification

This is based on eleven streams shown below. The streams have been defined empirically by grouping those parties which seem to have the closest resemblances. In the main, the streams represent the parties' self-images or overt historical traditions rather than any ostensibly objective criterion of support. The usefulness of such criteria in this particular context is limited both by their heterogeneity (for example, covering class, religion, economic interest and nationality) and by the difficulty of applying them to such cases as multi-class parties.[1] Apart from party traditions (which are largely recognised and confirmed in the composition of the groups in the European Parliament),[2] attention is also given to the character of the alliances contracted with other parties. This is particularly important in relation to parties in the liberal and radical tradition, between which the contrasts are especially wide.

On this basis, the following streams have been identified. The streams, which are virtually the same as those shown in Gordon Smith's classification on pp. 122-3, are set out in an order moving very broadly from conventional left to right, apart from the last two. There are however wide areas of uncertainty or overlap between parties in different countries, especially on the right or centre, and the order should therefore not be regarded as more than a very approximate indication of polictical position.

Party streams

(1) *Communist*: including such close allies as the French *progressistes*.

(2) *Independent Socialist*: including the French PSU, the Italian Socialist Party during the period of collaboration with the Communists up to 1956 (and the Proletarian Democrats subsequently), the Dutch Pacifist Socialists, and various Scandinavian groups. The stream includes 'ultra left' elements, notably in the Italian Proletarian Democrats, which contrast with other parties within it or their policies but are in general too diffuse and changeable to constitute a separate stream.

(3) *Social Democratic*: in general, identical with parties affiliated to the Socialist International. For this reason, both the Italian

parties (Socialist and Social Democratic) are included in spite of their frequently divergent political attitudes.

(4) *Liberal Radical*: together with the Liberal Conservative stream, this includes a wide range of parties affiliated to the Liberal International and concurrently the majority of those belonging to the Liberal Group in the European Parliament (with the exception of the French UDF). However, this tradition covers a particularly wide spread of political positions, distinguished largely by the character of the alliance or coalitions into which individual parties enter. The Liberal Radical stream is thus defined as comprising parties which may find their allies either on the left or the right and which for this reason can often occupy a pivotal position in their countries stronger than their numbers might suggest. Another feature found in some of the longer established parties, though probably of declining significance, is a tradition of anticlericalism or (in Britain) of association with religious dissent.

This stream includes the French radicals (MRG only since 1978), British Liberals, German FDP, Italian Radicals and Republicans, Dutch Democrats 66 and Danish Radical Left. The SDP has also been included, although its origins give it certain affinities with the Social Democratic stream.

(5) *Liberal Conservative*: although within the liberal tradition, these parties have since the war found their allies almost invariably on the right or centre. Moreover, their attachment to traditional economic liberalism sometimes causes them to be regarded as to the right of Central or Christian parties (as in the Netherlands). The stream includes the Italian, Belgian, Dutch and Scandinavian Liberals and the Swiss Radical Democrats, together with the Austrian Freedom Party and the Irish Progressive Democrats.

(6) *Centre-Christian Democratic*: this predominantly includes most parties within the European Community with an explicitly Christian orientation. Although these are often allied with parties to the right, or effectively represent the bulk of right-wing opinion in their countries (notably in Germany, Belgium and Austria), they also often include significant left-centre elements (sometimes related to associated trade union movements), justifying a 'centre' classification separate from the Conservative stream. The French CDS (largely descending via the reformists from the MRP) are included in this stream.

The stream also includes two other groups of broadly centrist outlook: the Centre parties of Norway, Sweden and Finland, which have developed from a traditional agrarian base; and the Christian parties of these three countries, which are concerned largely with issues bearing on personal morality. Finally, the stream includes the Irish Fine Gael and the Danish Centre Democrats.

(7) *Conservative*: including the French Independents, the former Deutsche Partei, the Swiss People's Party and Republican Movement, and the British and Scandinavian Conservatives. The stream also includes the Republican component of the UDF which although linked with the Liberal group in the European Parliament has largely continued French conservative traditions and also had certain links with British and Scandinavian Conservatives.

(8) *Nationalist*: this includes only two parties, of strong nationalist character, which are linked in the European Parliament. These are the RPR and its successive Gaullist predecessors (accounting for the bulk of the stream's coverage) and the Irish Fianna Fail. Neither party can easily be located on a left-right axis or be satisfactorily identified with any of the other streams. In this respect, they bear a certain resemblence to the ethnic and regional parties, which similarly cut across conventional categories.

(9) *Extreme Right*: a variegated group of parties sharing a strong hostility to parties of the left and moderate right and a general refusal to co-operate with them. This stream includes the Italian Monarchists and MSI, the former Deutsche Reichspartei, and also certain parties of a 'poujadist' or right-wing populist character (in addition to the original Poujadists, the Dutch Farmers, the Finnish Rural Party and the Danish Progress Party).

(10) *Ethnic and Regional*: including the various French and Flemish parties in Belgium, the Südtiroler Volkspartei in Italy, the former Bavarian Party, the Swedish Party in Finland, and Nationalists of various types (Irish, Scottish and Welsh) in the UK Parliament, together with Ulster Unionists since 1974.

(11) *Ecologist*: including the groups which have secured representation at different elections since 1979 in the Swiss, Belgian, German, Luxembourg, Italian, Austrian and Finnish Parliaments. Like the ethnic and regional parties, these seem to lie outside the conventional left-right spectrum, although they may in time take up a more definite place, or perhaps become assimilated to other groups.

There remain a few parties which do not clearly belong to any of the above streams, and which are put in a residual miscellaneous group together with independent members of national parliaments without any party affiliation. The most notable of these are the former German BHE (Refugee Party), the Danish Justice Party and the Swiss Landesring.

Calculation of party strengths
This is based on a system of points which are awarded to each

country according to its end-decade (i.e. 1950, 1960, 1970 and 1980) population as shown in the UN Demographic Yearbook. Metropolitan France has a constant weight of 200 points to which the weights of the other countries are related, subject to a minimum of three per country. For example, the faster population growth of the Netherlands compared with France has raised its weight by successive stages from 48 points in 1950 to 53 in 1980.

The points are distributed among the party streams represented in each country's lower house according to the number of members returned at the last general election, using the D'Hondt system (highest average). The main source of election returns is *Keesing's Archives*, except for France, where special calculations have been made of the members returned for Metropolitan France only.

Each point represents a notional unit of political strength. A party failing to win any points at all would be regarded as insignificant on the European political scene, while a party with 3 or 4 members in one of the major countries' parliaments (such as the Scottish National Party in 1987) would win a single point and so be considered marginally significant. The minimum of three points for the smallest countries assures marginal significance in this sense for a party winning over a quarter of the seats in Luxembourg or Iceland parliaments, and seems justified by common sense even if it slightly modifies the strict application of the population criterion.

The aggregation of the points shows the relative strength of the streams at any time throughout Western Europe. The relativity normally changes with each national election, indicating trends both in the distribution of political strength as a whole and in the relationships between particular streams. (For example, the relative strengths of Communist and Social Democratic parties may be of special interest). In the table the strengths of each party are shown as percentages of the total for Western Europe at the end of the year since 1985 and at certain other dates since 1946. It should be noted that the series is broken by the first post-war German elections in August 1949, the figures for 1946 representing the other fourteen countries.[3]

Party groupings

For a broad analysis of trends, it is convenient to group some of the streams together, as shown below. The most appropriate groupings for this purpose seem to be: Socialist (2–3) and a very broad Right and Centre group (5–8). The remaining streams are left ungrouped, except that the small Ethnic and Regional and Ecologist streams (10–11) are included in the miscellaneous group.

Parliamentary Representation in Western Europe since 1946
Percentages of total in each party stream

Date	Com.	Ind. Soc.	Soc. Dem.	Lib. Rad.	Lib. Con.	Centre Chr. Dem.	Cons.	Nat.	Ext. Right	Eth. Reg.	Ec.	Misc.
June 1946	12.8	5.2	31.1	3.3	4.2	25.7	13.5	0.9	2.0	0.5	—	0.9
July 1949	13.9	2.3	31.3	3.2	4.2	29.1	13.3	1.1	0.8	0.3	—	0.5
August 1949	11.9	1.8	31.7	5.1	3.4	30.8	11.5	0.9	0.8	1.0	—	1.1
December 1950	11.6	1.7	29.2	5.0	3.1	30.8	14.8	0.9	1.0	1.0	—	0.9
1955	8.7	2.4	27.6	4.8	3.1	28.9	16.6	4.0	2.5	0.2	—	1.1
1960	5.5	0.1	28.8	3.6	3.0	29.9	19.3	7.7	1.6	0.2	—	0.2
1965	7.5	0.1	32.6	4.2	4.2	26.9	13.3	9.5	1.1	0.4	—	0.1
1970	7.1	0.8	30.3	3.0	3.8	26.3	14.9	11.6	1.2	0.7	—	0.2
1975	9.0	0.2	33.4	3.7	3.1	26.6	12.8	7.4	2.1	1.6	—	0.1
1980	10.1	0.4	32.1	4.5	3.2	25.5	15.8	6.2	1.1	1.2	—	0.1
1985	8.2	0.5	35.6	4.2	3.7	24.3	16.0	3.7	1.4	1.1	1.2	0.1
1986	7.5	0.5	32.0	4.0	3.6	24.8	17.6	5.1	2.5	1.1	1.3	0.1
1987	6.9	0.5	32.9	4.5	3.6	24.0	16.8	5.1	2.3	1.0	2.4	0.1
June 1988	6.6	0.5	34.8	4.6	3.6	24.3	16.4	4.6	1.3	1.0	2.4	0.1

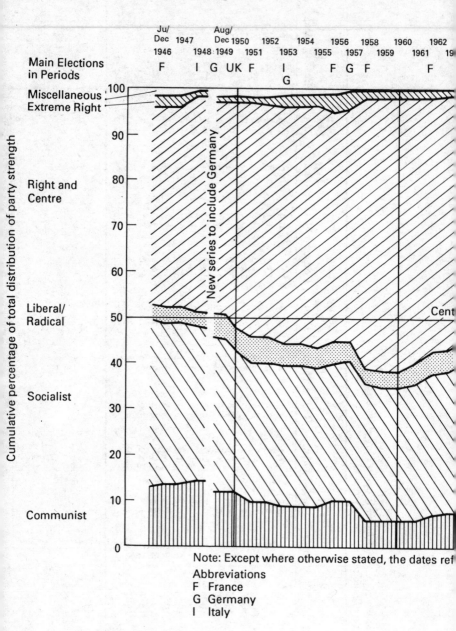

Main Elections in Periods

	Ju/ Dec 1947	Aug/ Dec 1950	1952	1954	1956	1958	1960	1962
1946	1948	1949	1951	1953	1955	1957	1959	1961	19
F	I	G UK F	I G		F G F			F

Cumulative percentage of total distribution of party strength

New series to include Germany

Miscellaneous Extreme Right

Right and Centre

Liberal/ Radical

Cent

Socialist

Communist

Note: Except where otherwise stated, the dates ref

Abbreviations
F France
G Germany
I Italy

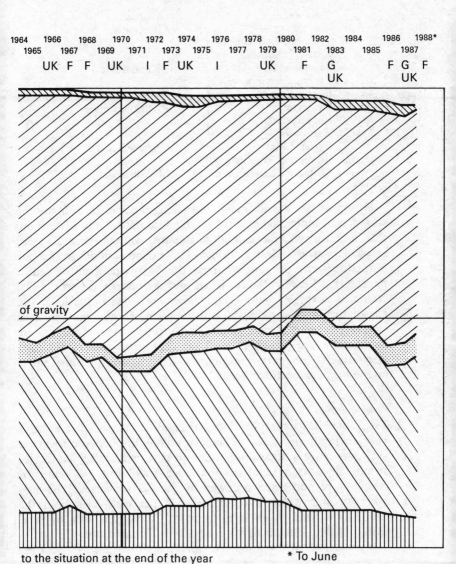

to the situation at the end of the year   * To June

	Stream		Grouping
1	Communist		Communist
2	Independent Socialist	}	
3	Social Democratic		Socialist
4	Liberal Radical		Liberal Radical
5	Liberal Conservative		
6	Centre-Christian Democratic	}	Right and Centre
7	Conservative		
8	Nationalist		
9	Extreme Right		Extreme Right
10	Ethnic and Regional	}	
11	Ecologist Miscellaneous		Miscellaneous

Grouping has the advantage of making it easier to compare the situation in individual countries (which do not usually cover more than a minority of the individual streams) while leaving the main internal contrasts clearly visible. For example, it illustrates the normal pattern of opposition in the Norwegian and Swedish Parliaments between the Socialists and the bourgeois parties. The strengths of these groupings are shown on p. 384 in the form of a cumulative graph, together with a note of the main national elections in each period. (For this purpose, 'main elections' are defined as those changing over 1 per cent of the total distribution of points between party groupings, and so making a strong impact on the European political scene.)[4]

Commentary

The table shows that the Social Democratic and Centre streams have always been by far the largest, accounting between them for well over half the total distribution of party strength. The Centre stream shows a gradual decline since 1960[5] but has remained clearly in second place, followed by the Conservatives. The only other streams which have exceeded 5 per cent have been the Communists and (from 1958 to 1981) the Nationalists, together with the Liberal-Radicals for a short period around 1959.

Fluctuations in the minor streams make it easiest to assess the long-term trends from the graph, where the groupings smooth out swings of support between (for example) the Centre and Conservative streams in France and Germany, or the effects of the changing patterns of the Italian Socialist parties. The graph also provides a more representative overall coverage, at some cost in precision, because of the many cases where an individual stream is not represented in a particular country (e.g. Conservatives in Germany, Italy and Belgium, Centre in the UK or Nationalists outside France and Ireland), whereas grouping permits broad comparability over Europe as a whole.[6] On this basis, the main trends over the period appear to be:

(1) A slight rise in Communist support up to 1948, followed by a declining trend until 1960; then a gradual recovery up to 1978, reversed by the Italian elections of 1979 and the French of 1981 and a continuing subsequent decline.

(2) A fairly steady decline in Socialist strength until 1955, followed by a long period of stability with only minor fluctuations until the French election victory of 1981. This was followed by a sharp decline up to 1987, since when the French elections of 1988 have produced a marked recovery.

(3) The Liberal-Radical stream has varied within a fairly narrow band, mainly reflecting the fortunes of the German Free Democrats.

(4) Right and Centre parties, taken together, showed a strong rising trend of support (accelerated by the French elections of 1958) up to 1960. Their support then declined steadily until 1967, recovering up to 1970, then falling to a level in 1974 which remained stable until it was significantly reduced by the French elections of 1981. It recovered with the next round of main elections but has fallen back since 1987, particularly following the 1988 French elections.

A notional centre of gravity can be traced by following the 50 per cent line along the graph. This shows the centre, initially located in the small but pivotal grouping of Liberal-Radical parties, moving to the Right and Centre with the British elections of 1950, where it remained until the French elections of 1981. These moved it back to the Liberal-Radical grouping until the German and British elections of 1983, which returned it to the Right and Centre.

Conclusion

The analysis supports the empirical observation that political movements in one European country are often mirrored in a number of others. Among the large number of elections during the period covered (averaging 13 per country), very few show a movement strongly against the trend noted over the five-year cycle of elections in which they occur. Where a particular national election appears to be at variance with the preceding trend (e.g., the French elections of 1958 and 1968), it is likely to represent a turning point, and so to be followed by elections in other countries showing the same tendency. Many of the causal factors at work no doubt reflect specific conditions in particular countries, which are not (or only coincidentally) found in others. But some factors may be common to a number of countries, suggesting at least partial explanations of parallel changes. For example, it may be suggested that the electoral fortunes of Communist Parties throughout Western Europe have been strongly affected by the policies of the Soviet Union and Western reactions to them; or that parties of the Extreme Right, and perhaps also ethnic and regional parties, have done best in conditions of political and economic instability; or that the successes and failures at different times of the movement towards European integration have affected support for the parties most committed to it. The analysis can provide a frame of reference within which these and other possible explanations of general political trends can be tested by more detailed research.

At the same time, it is necessary to emphasise the limitations of this, and perhaps of any, method of quantitative comparison between countries.[7] Apart from the approximate nature of the classification of political streams, the fact that many of them are represented in only a few countries precludes any precise comparison of the general movement with that in particular countries such as could normally be made in the regional analysis of a national election. (However, the emergence of the Scottish and Welsh Nationalists has produced similar complications in the analysis of British elections.) Moreover, variations in national electoral systems may give an exaggerated impression of the underlying movements of opinion in countries which do not have proportional representation, notably the UK and France for most of the period since 1958. A complementary analysis based on votes cast in national elections could thus prove instructive, although methodological problems would arise on account of differences in the basis of the franchise and also in turn-out both between countries and within countries over time.[8] However, parliamentary representation has a more obviously direct effect on the composition of governments and the process of political decision making, and can therefore be regarded as a major political indicator deserving study and analysis in its own right.

Finally, the analysis illustrates the general durability of established political traditions, and the consequent pattern of overall stability. For this reason, the short term trends noted on p. 378 may be seen largely as swings of the pendulum over the middle ground, altering the composition of governments to a disproportionate extent, but in large measure reversed on the next cycle of elections. (In any case, the largest shift recorded in any five-year period, between 1956 and 1961, affected only 8 per cent of the total distribution between groupings). The relatively small amount of long term movement may be shown by comparing the distribution of strength by main groupings in June 1988 with that which obtained in August 1949, when all the countries had held post-war elections:

	Comm.	Soc.	Lib. Rad.	Right and Centre	Extreme Right	Misc.
			55			
Aug 1949	11.9	33.5	5.1	46.5	0.8	2.1
June 1988	6.6	35.2	4.6	48.8	1.3	3.5
Change 1949–88	− 5.3	+ 1.7	− 0.5	+ 2.3	+ 0.5	+ 1.4

The long term shift (represented by the sum of the positive changes) was 6 per cent, accounted for mainly by a decline in Communist strength offset by gains in the Right and Centre, Socialist, Miscellaneous (in effect Ecologist) and Extreme Right groupings. The comparison of course conceals much larger proportionate changes in a number of individual countries and there are currently questions over the future of the Gaullists and Extreme Right (in France), and Ecologists more generally, which might have a significant impact before long on the overall pattern. Nevertheless, it is remarkable that in June 1988 no main broad political tendency (apart from the important exception of Communist decline) was decisively stronger or weaker in the whole European scene than it had been almost four decades earlier.

Notes

1. This general approach is followed in two fairly recent studies: Jean Vanlaer, *200 Millions de Voix, Une geographie des familles politiques Européenes*, Brussels 1984; and Klaus Von Beyme, *Political Parties in Western Democracies*, Aldershot: Gower 1985. Both authors relate party families to the four dominant conflict lines in modern European political history identified by Stein Rokkan, *Citizens, Elections, Parties*, Oslo: Universitetsforlaget, 1970. These conflict lines are religious, ethnic, city/rural and workers v. bourgeoisie. They all appear to have some continuing relevance, although newer conflict lines, e.g. environmental or public v. private sector, may be becoming increasingly important. Both Vanlaer and Beyme pay particular attention to the contrasts within European liberalism. See also Michael Steed and Derek Hearl, *Party Families*, London: Liberal European Action Group, 1985, which draws a distinction between Liberal–Radical and Liberal–Conservative parties similar to my own.
2. A study by Geoffrey and Pippa Pridham points to a number of similarities between these parties both in their general outlook in their bases of electoral support. See S. Henig (ed.), *Political Parties in the European Community*, London: George Allen and Unwin, 1979, Chapter 11, 'The Party Groups in the European Parliament'.
3. Calculations have also been made for the three new (or revived) democracies of

Southern Europe – Greece, Spain and Portugal. These currently show the Socialist parties as appreciably stronger than in the other European democracies. However, it is difficult to establish comparable classifications for parties on the right and centre and these countries have therefore not been included in the analysis.

4. Of the 195 national elections in the period studied, 28 have ranked as main elections in this sense. These have all been in the four largest countries. It is noteworthy that nearly all the 19 'main elections' since 1958 have taken place in France (8) or the UK (7), reflecting the character of their electoral systems as well as their size. French elections have had a particularly striking impact on the distribution of party strength and accounted for 6 out of the 7 elections in which the shift between groupings exceeded 3.3 per cent, the largest (in 1958) amounting to 8.5 per cent.

5. The decline in part reflects the long term shift in support in Belgium and the Netherlands since the mid 1960s from Christian to lay (Liberal) parties. The gains of Liberal–Conservative parties in these countries have incidentally been offset by substantial losses in Scandinavian countries. In these, both Liberals and Centre (formerly Agrarian) parties have tended to lose ground to Conservative parties, which have assumed a more leading position in the Right and Centre.

6. The largest two groupings (Socialist and Right with Centre) were represented in June 1988 in all fifteen countries' Parliaments, while Communists and Liberal-Radical parties were both represented in the majority (7 and 8 respectively). In addition, Ecologist parties have since 1979 secured representation in 7 parliaments. The first two groupings have between them accounted for at least 80 per cent of total party strength, reflecting a situation where the main political contenders in each country have normally been one or more parties within each of them. The sole exceptions have been Ireland and Iceland, in which parties outside the Socialist grouping have predominated; and Italy (together with France up to 1958), where the Communists have been the largest group in opposition to the Right and Centre parties.

7. A review of the first edition of this book draws attention to these limititations, but does not in my view disprove the use of the analysis as one indicator, among many others, of the extent of political change (see Derek W. Urwin and Kjell A. Eliassen, 'In search of a continent: the quest of comparative European politics', *European Journal of Political Research*, March 1975).

8. Such an analysis was in fact published in *The Economist* on 29 November, 1975 (pp. 16–19, 'Who will rule Europe in 1995?'). The analysis, which is taken back to 1935, shows a pattern of movement over the post-war period up to 1975 broadly similar to that presented in this note.

Index

Adenauer, K. 64, 199–200, 221, 292
administration *see* executive power
agrarian (Centre) parties 31–2, 43, 53, 99–100, 380–81, 382–5
agricultural-industrial contrasts 28–32, 42–3
Alfonso XIII, King of Spain 362
Allardt, E. 56, 80
Almond, G. 6–7, 11, 62, 80, 232
Andreski, S. 159, 186
armed forces *see* military
Aron, R. 5, 10
assembly-executive relations 129, 134–41
  see also governments and assemblies
associational groups 59–71
Austria
  assembly and government 195, 202–3, 212
  constitutional balance 130, 134, 137, 138, 141–7, 311–12
  executive power 221, 236
  integration, political 294
  non-democratic variants 179
  parties 40, 54, 84, 91, 95–6, 102–3, 108–111 *passim*, 117–18, 122–4, 314–15, 380–81: Christian-Socials 21, 35, 117; Communist 117, 179; People's 54, 196; pluralism and 54, 72–3; Socialist 21, 35, 95, 117–18, 194, 196
  profile, political 312–15
  society and politics 15, 21, 22, 35, 36, 40, 42, 309–10
  territorial axis 268, 272–3, 274
authoritarianism, 'creeping' 182–5

Bagehot, W. 127
balance

party systems 94–104 *passim*
social 3, 6–7
see also constitutional balance
Barry, B. 8, 11
Bauer, O. 118
Belgium
  assembly and government 195, 196, 211
  constitutional balance 131, 137, 147, 311–12
  non-democratic variants 179
  parties 18, 40, 84, 89, 91–6 *passim*, 100–101, 102, 179, 316–18, 380–81: *Front des Franco-phones* 18, 100, 318; Liberty and Progress (Liberal) 18, 51–2, 92, 100–101, 316–18, 380; *Rassemblement Wallon* 18, 100, 316, 318; Social Christian 18, 52, 53, 95, 200, 316–18; *Volksunie* 18, 100, 316, 318
  profile, political 315–19
  society and politics 16–18, 40, 309–10
  territorial axis 252, 259, 263, 274, 279
Bendix, R. 5, 6, 10, 126
Berlin, I. 9, 11
Berlinguer, E. 180, 346
Bill of Rights 130
Birnbaum, N. 34, 45
Blondel, J. 13, 41, 45, 93, 162, 207, 213, 233
Brandt, W. 173, 272, 331
Briggs, A. 231, 248
Britain
  assembly and government 192–4, 198, 202–3, 206–7, 210–14 *passim*
  constitutional balance 127, 131, 132–3, 141–5, 150–52, 311–12

executive power 220–27 *passim*, 237–40, 243–4
integration, political 294, 299, 301
non-democratic variants 160, 162, 175–6, 179, 183
Northern Ireland 18–19, 152, 175, 183, 275–6
parties 87–94, 95–6, 103, 106–7, 110, 118, 122–4, 173–6, 183, 370–77, 380–81; Conservative 26–7, 34–6, 51, 59, 75, 79, 87, 212, 381; Labour 33–4, 58–9, 75, 79, 87, 91–2, 94, 212, 225, 265; Liberal 51, 53, 87, 92, 380; Nationalist (Irish, Scottish, Welsh) 16, 18–19, 87, 93, 150, 152, 277, 381; pluralism and 51, 60–61, 73, 75–6, 79; Social Democratic 87, 380
profile, political 370–77
society and politics 13, 16, 18–19, 26–7, 33–6, 309–10
territorial axis 250, 256, 259–66, 275–8, 280–81
bureaucracy, constitutional 217, 222–6
Butler, D. 56, 80

Caetano, M. 359
central-local relations 256–66
Centre parties *see* agrarian
Chapman, B. 228, 248
Christianity *see* religion
civic culture 6–8, 61–2
civil service 132, 202, 207–12, 218–19, 226–34
Clark, Sir R. 276–7, 282
class
and civil service 230–33
and fascism 155–8
and military 159–62
and party system 50–51, 55–8, 97
and society and politics 13, 25, 32–7
cleavages 37–44
and party system 41–44
coalitions 93–4, 107, 114, 138, 193–5, 198–9, 213, 219

cohesion, party 106, 109
colonialism 167
commune 258–9
communism 23–4, 29–31, 51, 56, 92, 105, 110, 176–82, 202, 218, 379, 382–8
see also under individual countries
competitiveness, party 106, 109
conservatives 305, 380–88
see also under individual countries
Constantine II, King of Greece 136, 334
constitution
comparisons 311–12
elective function 192
constitutional balance 125–53
assembly-executive relations 129, 134–41
democracy, direct 134, 145–50
dynamics 150–52
European 125–8
jurisdiction 131–3, 142–5, 268–9
power, distribution of 128–50
constitutional bureaucracy 217, 222–6
control/s
executive 242–8
of parliament 191–203; elective 191–8; personnel 198–203; rule 203–12
totalitarian 154–55
convention government 135
Coombes, D. 226, 240, 294, 295–6
Cornforth, M. 9, 11
corporatism, age of 60, 71–9
Craxi, B. 346–7
Crozier, M. 226
Cunhal, A. 178

Daalder, H. 226, 248
Dahl, R. A. 2, 10, 106, 109, 213
Dahrendorf, R. 230
de Gaulle, C. 54, 116, 135–49, 165, 198, 201, 211, 325–6
see also France, Gaullists
de Rivera, Gen. P. 362
de Tocqueville, A. 5, 130
decentralization 253–8, 266, 273–82

decisive encounters, sites for 106–9
deconcentration 254–6, 277–8, 282
democracy
　direct 134, 146–50
　liberal 1–11
　local 258–66
Denmark
　assembly and government 197,
　　211
　constitutional balance 130, 136,
　　145, 149–50, 311–12
　executive power 244–6 *passim*
　integration, political 294, 299
　non-democratic variants 175, 179
　parties 49, 59, 90, 91, 95, 100,
　　111, 122–4, 175, 179, 319–
　　21, 380–81
　profile, political 319–22
　society and politics 28, 32, 36,
　　309–10
depersonalization of state 222
development problems and
　political integration 298–308
devolution 254–5
Dicey, A. V. 143
dictatorship 130, 154
　executive power 217, 223
　military power 168–72, 184
　transition from 165–72
diffusion in party systems 94–104
　passim
dissolution of parliament 193
Dogan, M. 29–30, 45
Dollfuss, E. 118, 313
dominance in party systems 94–104
　passim, 119
dual government systems 260–66
Duverger, M. 44, 90, 119
dynamics, constitutional 150–52
Dyson, K. 235–6, 248

Eanes, Gen. R. 360–61
Eckstein, H. 4–6, 10, 60
ecological parties *see* agrarian
economic liberalism 1, 4
Edinger, L. J. 64–5, 80
education of civil servants 227–32
elections 106, 299, 381–6
elective functions of parliament
　191–8

electoral systems 86–94, 382, 386
élites 5, 9, 220–35
employers' associations 63, 65, 70,
　71–9
Epstein, L. D. 51, 79
equality 51–8
ethnic parties 381–5 *passim*
　see also nationalist
Eurocommunism 56
　see also communism
European Economic Community
　145, 149–50, 153, 284, 290,
　293–308
executive-assembly relations 129,
　134–41
executive power 217–49
　bureaucracy, constitutional 222–
　　6
　controlling 242–8
　élites, administrative 226–34
　leadership 217–22
　policy styles 234–42
extremism 172–85
　communism, European 176–82
　of middle 182–5
　right-wing 172–6

fascism 154–8
　neo- 174–6
Faulkner, B. 374
federalism 16, 64–5, 84
　and constitutional balance 133–4,
　　142, 149
　and integration, political 286,
　　290–91, 298
　and territorial axis 254, 256–7,
　　266–82
Fesler, J. 254, 282
Finer, S. 33, 45, 161, 186
Finland
　assembly and government 197,
　　198, 200, 211–12
　constitutional balance 132, 137–
　　8, 143, 145, 311–12
　executive power 246
　integration, political 294
　parties 50, 92, 95, 101, 102, 107,
　　118, 122–4, 200, 321–4,
　　380–81; Communist
　　(Democratic League) 101,

178, 202; Swedish People's
15, 92, 381
profile, political 322–5
society and politics 15, 309–10
Fogarty, M. P. 54, 80
France
Action Française 21, 166
and Algeria 144, 148, 164–5
assembly and government 189,
197, 198, 200–2, 204–5,
209–10
constitutional balance 131, 133–
49 *passim*, 204–10 *passim*,
311–12
executive power 220–34 *passim*,
237, 240–41, 244–5, 247
Fifth Republic 54–5, 66–8, 84,
93, 96, 98, 127, 137–39, 144,
189, 193, 204–5, 209–10, 241
Fourth Republic 44, 49, 53, 54,
66, 95, 98, 115–17, 132,
135–39, 164–5, 197, 204, 209
integration, political 291–3
military in 162–5
non-democratic variants 172,
174–5, 177–81
parties 84–5, 87–8, 91–8 *passim*,
115–17, 122–4, 325–9, 379–
86; Communist 30, 44, 66,
85, 88, 92, 98, 165, 181, 202;
Gaullist (RPR, UDR, UNR)
35, 44, 54–5, 66, 84–5, 88,
95, 98, 103, 115–16, 141,
210, 381; *Movement
Républicain Populaire* 22, 44,
53–4, 66, 115–16, 380;
pluralism and 45, 49, 54–5,
59, 66–8; Poujadist 44, 66,
115–16, 381; Republicans
(UDF) 44, 98, 380; Socialist
44, 55, 58, 66, 68, 85, 88, 98,
107, 115–16, 140, 142, 175,
181, 197, 202, 241, 278, 386
profile, political 325–30
society and politics 16, 21–2, 30–
31, 35, 44, 309–10
territorial axis 256, 262–5, 274,
277–9
Third Republic 66–7, 117–18,
138, 148, 164

Vichy 21
Franco, F. 157, 168–70, 217, 279,
362
fused government systems 260–65

German Democratic Republic 129,
173
Germany, pre-1945 and Federal
Republic 127–8, 298
assembly and government 195,
199, 200, 202–3, 208–9, 211
constitutional balance 130–45
passim, 311–12
executive power 221–32 *passim*,
235–8; 246
integration, political 291–3, 301
military in 160–65
non-democratic variants 154–8,
173–4, 179, 183
Ostpolitik 173
parties 52, 84–92 *passim*, 95–8,
103, 112–15, 122–4, 173,
330–33, 380–81, 385–6;
Catholic Centre 25, 52, 115;
Christian Democrats 26, 31,
53, 56, 64, 75, 95, 97–8,
103, 173, 195, 199, 272,
331–2; Christian-Social
Union 27, 31, 195, 272, 331;
Communist 36, 85, 114, 179,
202; Free Democrats 98,
195, 200, 331–2 380; Greens
39–40, 98, 102, 110, 332–3;
National Socialist (Nazi) 7,
25–6, 35, 91–2, 113–14, 117,
154–5, 173, 185, 202;
pluralism and 49–53, 55–6,
59, 63–4, 74–5; Social
Democrats 26, 37, 56, 74,
97–8, 102, 111, 114, 136, 195,
331–3
profile, political 330–33
society and politics 24–6, 31, 34–
9, 309–10
territorial axis 256, 259, 262–3,
266–76 *passim*
Giscard d'Estaing, V. 55, 84, 327
goals, party 106–11
government
group interests and 60–62, 73

party systems and 83–94
governments and assemblies 189–216
  communications 212–15
  elective functions 191–8
  parliamentary decline 189–92
  personnel functions 198–203
  rule functions 203–12
  see also parliamentary system
Gramsci, A. 179
Greece
  constitutional balance 136, 311–12
  integration, political 294, 299
  non-democratic variants 159, 165, 170–72
  parties 103, 122–4, 171, 334–7; New Democracy 103, 172; pluralism and 58–9; Socialist 58, 103, 172
  profile, political 333–7
  society and politics 28, 36, 309–10

Haas, E. B. 287, 305
Hallstein, W. 288, 299
Harrison, M. 66, 80
Heady, F. 225–6, 248
Heidenheimer, A. J. 272, 282
Heisler, M. O. 237, 248
Hitler, A. 158, 165, 284
homogenous society 13–14, 41–2

Iceland
  assembly and government 202, 212
  constitutional balance 137, 145, 311–12
  non-democratic variants 178
  parties 103, 122–4, 178, 202, 337–9, 382
  profile, political 337–9
  society and politics 15, 309–10
identity, territorial 250–73
ideology of fascism 154–8
imbalance in party systems 94–104 *passim*, 119
independent parties 381
industry
  contrasts with agriculture 29–32, 42–43

fascism and 156, 157
  politics and 63–79
inertia, party traditions 48–55
instability, parliament 196–7
integration, political 284–308
  European Community 294–8
  European perspectives 290–94
  development problems 298–308
  models of 284–90
interest groups 59–71
Ireland, Republic of
  assembly and government 194
  constitutional balance 130–1, 137, 145, 311–12
  executive power 245
  integration, political 294, 299
  parties 88–9, 93, 95, 102–3, 341–2, 380–81; Fianna Fail 95, 102, 103, 381; Fine Gael 103, 381; Labour 20, 103; Progressive Democrats 21–2, 103, 342, 380; Sinn Fein 342
  profile, political 339–43
  society and politics 15, 20–21, 309–10
  identity, territorial 262
Italy
  assembly and government 197, 199, 202, 211
  constitutional balance 130–1, 132, 136–7, 142–8 *passim*, 311–12
  executive power 219–20, 227, 228, 232, 245
  non-democratic variants 154–5, 157, 172–4, 179–81
  parties 15, 68–71, 88, 89, 93–5 *passim*, 107, 122–4, 343–7, 379–81, 385; Catholic 52; Christian Democrats 22–4, 29–30, 53, 68–71, 95, 98–9, 103, 147–8, 174, 180, 193, 199, 219–20, 265, 280; Communist 23–24, 29–30, 69, 71, 78, 98, 147, 174, 179–81, 197, 199–202, 265; Liberal 51–2, 92, 380; *Movimento Sociale Italiano* 174; pluralism and 49, 52–4, 68–71, 77–9; Radical 102,

147; Republican 92, 380;
Socialist 148
profile, political 343–8
society and politics 12–13, 21–4,
29–30, 309–10
territorial axis 265, 274, 280–81

Janowitz, M. 159, 186
Jordan, G. 237
Juan Carlos, King of Spain 136,
169, 363
jurisdiction, constitutional 131–3,
142–5, 240, 263–9

Karamanlis, C. 335–7
Kekkonen, U. 323
Kinnock, N. 59, 373
Kirchheimer, O. 35, 55, 80, 110–11
Kohl, H. 75, 332
Koivisto, M. 323–4
Kreisky, B. 221, 314
Kvaavik, R. 237, 248

Labour parties *see* socialism
language and national minorities
15–19
LaPalombara, J. 69, 80
Lassalle, F. 50
Lavau, G. 91–2, 119
lae *see* jurisdiction; legislation
leaders 155, 199–200, 217–22
left, perpetuation of 55–9, 96
see also communism; socialism
legislation 191, 203–12, 295–6
Lehmbruch, G. 72, 80
Leo XII, Pope 52
Leopold III, King of Belgium 147,
315
Leys, C. 90
liberal democracy, politics of 1–11
liberal parties 43, 52–3, 305, 380,
382–6
see also under individual
countries
liberalisation after dictatorships
169
Lijphart, A. 5, 10–11
Lipset, S. M. 4, 10, 27, 44–5, 83,
101, 119
local democracy 258–66

Luxembourg 179, 297, 309–10
constitutional balance 136, 311–
12
parties 89, 95, 102, 122–4, 179,
381–2
profile, political 348–9

Maass, A. 254, 266, 282
Macpherson, C. B. 1–2, 10, 11, 125,
152
Mair, P. 105, 119
majority
absolute 95, 97–100, 119
electoral system 86–8
Malta 15, 21, 89, 91, 350–52
Mannheim, K. 232, 248
Martins, W. 318
mass
appeal of fascism 154–5
society 5
Merkl, P. 64, 80
Miliband, R. 182, 186, 284
military power 159–72, 184
and dictatorships 168–72
ministers 217–21, 225, 242–3
minorities, national 2, 15–19, 250–
51
Mintoff, Dom 351–2
Mitchell, J. 247, 249
Mitrany, D. 286–7, 307
Mitterrand, F. 85, 141, 175, 181,
205, 221, 241, 327–8
modernisation and fascism 157,
165, 169, 171
Moore, B. 154, 186
Mosca, G. 159–60
Mussolini, B. 52, 154, 157, 174,
186, 344

Napoleon III 148–9
nationalism 250–53, 305, 381–4
see also under individual countries
nations of Western Europe 309–77
constitutional comparisons 311–
12
parliamentary representation
since 1946 378–89
political profiles 312–77
socio-economic comparisons
309–10

Netherlands
  assembly and government 195–6,
    197, 198, 211
  constitutional balance 130, 136,
    311–12
  executive power 236, 245–6
  military and 160
  non-democratic variants 179
  parties 24–5, 53; Catholic
    People's 14, 24; Christian
    Democratic Appeal 100, 196,
    200; Democrats ('66) 100,
    195, 380; Labour 25, 100,
    196; Liberal 53, 100, 196,
    380; pluralism and 53, 59,
    73; Radical Catholic 24, 100
  profile political 352–5
  society and politics 13, 14, 24–5,
    36, 42, 309–10
  territorial axis 263
'new' politics 39–41, 381–3
nominal quality of constitutions
    130–1
non-democratic variants 154–88
  communism, decline of 176–82
  dictatorships, transitions from
    165–72
  extremism today 172–85
  fascism 133–7
  'middle' extremism 182–5
  military and 159–65
  right-wing extremism 172–6
normative quality of constitution
    126, 129–30, 133
Northern Ireland *see* Britain
Norway
  assembly and government 193,
    199, 212
  constitutional balance 131, 144,
    146, 311–12
  executive power 240, 244, 245
  parties 27, 95, 99, 111, 122–4,
    356–7, 380–81; Centre
    (agrarian) 31–2, 59, 380;
    Conservative 240; Labour
    95, 99; pluralism and 59
  profile, political 355–8
  society and politics 15, 27, 31–2,
    36, 43, 309–10

Ombudsman 243–4
opposition 2, 106–12, 191
Organski, A. F. K. 156, 158, 165
Otley, C. B. 160, 162, 186

Papadopoulos, G. 335
Papandreou, A. 336
Papandreou, G. 335
'parallel hierarchies' 218
parliamentary system 5–6, 9, 84,
    217, 242
  controls 191–203
  decline 112–19, 189–92
  European Community 294–301
  and party systems 112–18, 198–9,
    208–9
  since 1946 378–86
  see also government
Parris, H. 224, 248
Parry, G. 232, 248
party systems 83–124, 379
  characteristics of 94–104
  constitution and 135, 151
  determining features 83–94
  European Comunity 301, 305
  inertia 48–55
  opposition 2, 106–12, 158–60,
    189–191, 242
  parliament and 112–19, 193–7,
    199–200, 208–9
  pluralism and 48–82
  social cleavages 41–44
  streams 379–81
  trends 104–6
  see also under individual
    countries
personnel functions of
    parliament 198–203
Pertini, A. 345
Philip, A. 292
pluralism: parties and interests 3,
    48–82
  corporatism, age of 71–9
  group interests 59–71
  inertia of party traditions 48–55
  left and right perpetuation 55–59
policy style 234–42
politics of liberal democracy 1–11
  assemblies and governments
    189–216

constitutional balance 125-32
executive power 217-49
integration, political 284-308
nations of Western Europe 309-77
non-democratic variants 154-88
party system 83-124
pluralism 48-82
society and 12-47
territorial axis 250-83
Pompidou, G. 326-7
popular control of government 125, 128, 189-90
Portugal
constitutional balance 130-1, 311-12
integration, political 294, 299
non-democratic variants 152, 159, 165-8, 178-9
parties 54, 103, 122-4, 166, 167-8, 178-9, 358-9
profile, political 358-61
post-industrial society 38-41
power, decentralisation of 253-8, 266, 273-80, 282
power distribution and constitutional balance 128-50
assembly-executive relations 129, 134-41
democracy direct 134, 145-50
jurisdiction, constitutional 131-3, 141-4
power, executive *see* executive power
power, limitation of 125-8
presidency 84, 135-40, 217
see also leaders
proportional representation 86-92, 382
Pulzer, P. G. 33, 45

red-green parties 31-2, 53
referenda 145-50, 169, 171, 214, 219
regionalism 252-3
religion and politics 13-14, 19-28, 31, 42-4, 52-5, 66, 68-9
Richardson, J. 237, 248
right-wing parties 55-9, 172-6, 381-6

see also under individual countries
Rokkan, S. 32, 45, 101, 119
role theory approach 127
Rose, R. 45, 49, 79, 152-3
rule function of parliament 203-12
rural-urban contrasts 28-32, 42-3, 259

Salazar, A. de O. 131, 166-7, 358
Sartori, G. 30, 127, 152
Sawer, G. F. 267-8, 282
Schmidt, H. 136, 200, 332
Schmitter, P. 76, 80
Schumacher, K. 7, 292
second chambers in parliament 211-12
sectionalism in society 13-14, 40-44
semantic quality of constitutions 130
Senior, D. 261
size of parties 94
Smart, M. 48, 378
Smith, G. 379
Soares, M. 361
social balance 3, 5-6
socialisation in parliament 201
socialism, social democracy and labour parties 33-4, 36-7, 42-4, 49-51, 53, 58-9, 110-11, 305, 379-86
see also under individual countries
society and politics 12-47
class 13, 25, 32-7
cleavages, new 37-41
cleavages and party systems 41-44
languages and national minorities 15-19
religion 13-14, 19-28, 31, 42-3
rural-urban contrasts 28-32, 42-4
social bases 12-15
socio-economic
comparisons 309-10
reasons for fascism 155-8, 168-9, 182
Sombart, W. 50-51
Sorel, G. 110
Soviet Union 217, 291, 323

Spain
  assembly and government 202
  constitutional balance 136–7,
    311–12
  integration, political 294, 299
  non-democratic variants 152,
    159, 165–6, 168–70, 178
  parties 103, 122–4, 362–4;
    Communist 92, 169, 178–9,
    202; Socialist 103, 170;
    nationalist (Basque, Catalan)
    169–70; pluralism and 59
  profile, political 361–4
  society and politics 16, 20, 28, 36,
    309–10
  territorial axis 250, 252, 274,
    279–80
stability 92–3, 139, 196–8
Stokes, D. 56, 80
Strauss, F. – J. 331
Sturzo, Dom L. 52
Subramaniam, V. 223, 248
supranationalism 256, 287, 289,
  294, 303–4
Sweden
  assembly and government 202,
    206–7, 209, 211
  constitutional balance 136, 144,
    146, 311–12
  executive power 220, 227, 230–
    31, 235, 238–40, 243–4, 246
  integration, political 294
  non-democratic variants 178
  parties 89–90, 99–100, 108, 122–4,
    365–6, 380–81; Centre
    (agrarian) 31–2, 53, 76, 99,
    100; Communist 99, 178, 202;
    pluralism and 59, 62–3, 73,
    76–7; Social Democrats 53,
    76–7, 95, 99–100, 108, 128,
    239
  profile, political 364–7
  society and politics 31–2, 36,
    309–10
  territorial axis 263
Switzerland
  assembly and government 192
  constitutional balance 130, 133–
    4, 136, 138, 143–4, 148–9,
    311–12

  executive power 246
  integration, political 294
  parties 40, 84, 89, 92–4, 95, 101–
    2, 108, 110, 122–4, 369,
    380–81; Christian Democrat
    101; Liberal 52–3, 92, 380;
    People;s 101, 381; Radicals
    52–3, 101, 380
  profile, political 367–70
  society and politics 16, 19, 24, 40,
    309–10
  territorial axis 251, 256, 259, 260,
    268–71
symbolic capability of constitution
  127

Taylor, P. 297, 307
territorial axis 250–83
  decentralisation modes 253–8,
    273–82
  federalism and regionalism 266–
    82
  identity, resurgence of 250–53
  local democracy patterns 258–66
Thatcher, M. 75, 87, 183, 221, 233,
  238, 265, 373
Togliatti, P. 178
totalitarianism 154–5
trade unions 63–7, 70–79, 168–9, 178
Turkey 299, 309–10

unified system 134–8, 189–92
United Kingdom *see* Britain
United States
  assembly and government 208
  constitutional balance 129, 140–
    41, 142, 144, 311–12
  executive power 217, 224–5
  integration and 291
  parties 50–51, 61–2, 83–4, 89
  society and politics 309–10
  territorial axis 267–71, 281
urban-rural differences *see* rural-
  urban

Verba, S. 6–7, 11, 232
Vile, M. J. C. 2, 10, 133, 152
vom Stein, F. 223
vulnerability of liberal democracies
  182–5

Waldheim, K. 314–15
weakness of unified systems 189–
    192
Weber, M. 126, 222, 226, 232, 248

Wheare, K. C. 267, 282
Williams, P. H. 66, 80
Williams, P. M. 204, 215
Woolf, S. J. 157, 186